MEALS MATTER

ARTS AND TRADITIONS OF THE TABLE

ARTS AND TRADITIONS OF THE TABLE
PERSPECTIVES ON CULINARY HISTORY

Albert Sonnenfeld, Series Editor

For a complete list of titles, see page 353.

MEALS MATTER

A Radical Economics Through
Gastronomy

Michael Symons

Columbia University Press *New York*

Columbia University Press
Publishers Since 1893
New York   Chichester, West Sussex
cup.columbia.edu
Copyright © 2020 Columbia University Press

Library of Congress Cataloging-in-Publication Data
Names: Symons, Michael, 1945– author.
Title: Meals matter : a radical economics through gastronomy / Michael Symons.
Description: New York : Columbia University Press, [2020] | Series: Arts and
    traditions of the table: perspectives on culinary history | Includes bibliographical
    references and index.
Identifiers: LCCN 2019040719 (print) | LCCN 2019040720 (ebook) |
    ISBN 9780231196024 (cloth) | ISBN 9780231551601 (ebook)
Subjects: LCSH: Food habits—Economic aspects. | Food habits—Social aspects.
Classification: LCC GT2850 .S96 2020 (print) | LCC GT2850 (ebook) |
    DDC 394.1/25—dc23
LC record available at https://lccn.loc.gov/2019040719
LC ebook record available at https://lccn.loc.gov/2019040720

Printed in the United States of America

Cover image: Diego Rivera, *Wall Street Banquet* (1928). The diners are served ticker
tape, which for a century transmitted the latest stock market prices. © 2019 Banco de
México Diego Rivera Frida Kahlo Museums Trust, Mexico, D.F./Artists Rights Society
(ARS), New York, De Agostini Picture Library/M. Seemuller/Bridgeman Images.

Cover design: Lisa Hamm

CONTENTS

Contents

PROLOGUE

Meals Before Money

Restaurant in a Garden

This was the place for a lazy Sunday lunch . . . once you had wound up from the city into the hills, found the garden path to an old, two-story stone home, and entered a dining room sheltering beside a venerable pear tree. The summer menu included zucchini flowers picked by the restaurateur that morning, globe artichokes cut by a cook out the window, and more than abundant raspberries from down steps for one month every year. The prosciutto and mortadella were cured by a local family, and the small growers' wines would never be mass advertised. Rather than mood music, the room relied on the occasionally raucous, sometimes silent, but often sublime hum and clink of dining.

I have eaten at some great restaurants. They have taught me much, and I thank them—a few appear in this book. But I learned most from this small and not especially famous restaurant, the Uraidla Aristologist, where, in the Adelaide Hills, South Australia, I was coproprietor with Jennifer Hillier through the 1980s and into the 1990s.

Our fascination with meals (and my exhaustion from Sydney environmental journalism) led, in 1977, to the Tuscan region of Italy, where we had opened a restaurant, the Cantina di Toia, still thriving when visited three decades later.[1] Galvanized by vegetable gardens, town markets, old stone hearths, and seemingly universal food enthusiasm, I researched the history of worsening industrial eating back home in Australia for my first book, *One Continuous Picnic*, which was published in 1982, during the early months of the Aristologist.

With that "gastronomic history of a nation" attracting some interest, I instigated the Australian gastronomic symposiums in 1984; undertook a Ph.D. degree in sociology on the intellectual denial of meals; and launched into further books. Such activities contributed to, and flowed from, running a household business approximating the good life, and not just for us.

Many customers of the Uraidla Aristologist appreciated cooking that respected traditions and seasons, and person-to-person service. Some were put off, however. The whimsical name, which meant that small town's "student of dining," probably announced a sometimes disconcertingly intellectual, even political, earnestness. Our slogan, "Tuscany up Greenhill Road," might have been too obscure. Seemingly more unnerving than any inconsistency in our standards, and long before health regulations, we expected smokers to repair to an adjacent room, or outdoors.

I was particularly struck by a young couple who, after reading our menu, begged forgiveness for leaving for a nearby establishment, because our dishes would be "too spicy." The puzzle was that our cooking was based on Italian and French standards and so gentler than the East-West "fusion" where the diners were headed. The other proprietor would have been first to admit, nonetheless, to seeking approachability.

A popular-sounding name might have signaled a more safely commercial venture. A more predictable menu and on-tap Coca-Cola, or overdecorated dishes and mock servility, would have communicated: the customer is always right. The Aristologist was not going to stop putting meals first, as best we could, but around that time, the ruling ethos moved explicitly behind financial profit. *Neoliberalism* took hold. Governments acceded to the dictatorship of money. We were meant to obey the Market.

Neoliberalism had taken the stage when the so-called Chicago Boys— economists mainly trained at the University of Chicago—brought their ideology to Chile, following the coup in 1973. Thatcherism swept into the

FIGURE 0.1 Author with zucchini flowers, Uraidla Aristologist Restaurant, South Australia, 1982. Photo by author.

United Kingdom from 1975, Reaganomics into the United States in 1981, and Rogernomics into New Zealand from 1984. Australia called it "economic rationalism." The old social contract of equal individuals with rights in democratic republics, and later the welfare state, lost out to privatization, outsourcing, corporate-friendly legislation, high-end tax cuts, and so-called growth. Trade unions were an antiquated impediment. MBAs became glamour degrees. Tearing down the Berlin Wall on November 9, 1989, seemed to confirm the triumph of free enterprise, globalization, and restructuring—with no purpose higher than profit.

In Oliver Stone's bitter movie *Wall Street* (1987), tycoon Gordon Gekko proclaimed, "Greed . . . is good." While economists typically spoke of the "rational pursuit of gain," "maximization of net advantages," or "self-interest," the most influential economist of the second half of the twentieth century, Milton Friedman of the University of Chicago, campaigned publicly for "greed," claiming that a corporation's entire social responsibility was "to use its resources and engage in activities designed to increase its profits" (1970, 134).

For a while I felt silly. Here we were taking appetites seriously, when, according to economists, think-tanks, and now politicians, only greed counted. Discomfort soon turned to curiosity, however. Why did mainstream economists belittle life-giving systems and support a Midas fantasy? Why ignore the sounds, sights, and smells of actual markets in favor of a mere system of prices? Why this perversion of potentially the most caring of all disciplines—studying the ancient Greek *oikos* (*ecos*) or "household"? The new *oikonomia* or "household management" neglected more than just the domestic but discarded a whole nest of households, still known to seventeenth- and eighteenth-century thinkers.

Over further years of dining and working, I borrowed from intellectual history, social theory, and economics itself to investigate mathematical mystification's tilt at world domination. Eventually, I found *neo*liberalism had systematically corrupted liberalism, which had a gastronomic basis. Epicurean-influenced philosophers—among the most notable being Thomas Hobbes and John Locke—had understood that self-interested individuals, following their appetites, combined with one another for sustenance. Through the nineteenth century, however, economists transmuted healthy appetites into holy greed. That insanity could best be understood as capitalist logic. Business corporations, programmed for profit, systematically exploited life-giving economies, and economists twisted their theoretical model to suit.

If the upending of liberalism can be demonstrated in a single piece of evidence, it is Adam Smith's often-quoted statement of 1776 about the individual "interest" of the butcher, brewer, and baker. Economics textbooks have routinely misread "interest" as financial. In context, Smith clearly referred to the mutual benefits for the butcher, brewer, and baker of sharing food. Through the "co-operation and assistance of great multitudes . . . the butcher, the brewer, or the baker," he wrote, "we expect our dinner." Similarly, in making the market sacred, economics texts employ Smith's "propensity to truck, barter, and exchange." But they lift the market into such a mathematical abstraction, so far above physical sharing, that I capitalize theirs as the Market.

Again, rather than equality being a policy commitment, economics kept it as a merely formal attribute of market players. The laws of mainstream economics apply to all—whether female, straight, white, gay, or a food delivery cyclist. That might sound progressive, except that the most impoverished person is also treated as identical to a global corporation, which might be Nestlé, McDonald's, Privat Group, TripAdvisor, or Saudi Aramco. According to such equality, every individual is charged exactly the same at a luxury resort, although one person might scarcely notice, and another end up in debtors' prison.

Public debt, the finance industry, and the Washington consensus might sound more important than a slice of bread and glass of beer. Yet modern economic thought took off from the exchange between a baker and a brewer, and needs to again. In this book, I restore economics through gastronomic liberalism, reinvigorated.

The Gastronomic Turn

This radical alternative to neoliberal economics relies on a gastronomic outlook on life. In the years of the Italian sojourn, meals were dismissed in my country as, variously, privileged leisure, self-indulgence, refueling, women's work, or fattening. When *One Continuous Picnic* (1982) praised fresh foods, I was warned frequently that freshness was a "lost cause." But my book had done something even more outrageous, using meals to explain Australian history, and so convincingly that I both opened and closed with Jean Anthelme Brillat-Savarin's "Tell me what you eat, and I shall tell you what you are." That is the fourth of his twenty aphorisms, designed to get gastronomy underway, and opening his *Physiology of Taste* that appeared in 1825.

My preoccupation became Brillat-Savarin's *gastronomy*. This is the *nomos* (ancient Greek, law or managing) of the *gastēr* (stomach, belly, or gut), and an appreciation not only of fine foods but of our whole stomach-structured lives, with the aim of doing better. Ancient Greek philosopher

Epicurus had said that knowledge and wisdom were ultimately based on the "pleasure of the stomach." Likewise, for Karl Marx, history's "first premise" was "eating and drinking, housing, clothing and various other things." We follow our individual stomachs, and yet, crucially, we are what we eat, *together*. Rather than compete, diners come together *convivially*—from the Latin for living together. We seek *company*—from the Latin for bread-sharing. We want *collaboration, community, conversation* . . . to begin a list of numerous *com-* or *col-*, "with" words.

So modernity's puzzling neglect of meals led to doctoral studies into the intellectual disdain for any science of gastronomy (Symons 1992). My undergraduate degree had been in mathematics with its seductive, philosophical idealism. Now I found Epicurean materialism (e.g., Symons 2007a), while sociology taught me that two centuries of *rationalization*—to borrow sociologist Max Weber's term—had both suppressed gastronomic sensibilities and made them all the more urgent. Fortunately, good gardening, cooking, and dining were soon attracting "foodies." Those paying attention to meals gained that jaunty label in 1982 (the same year as "yuppies"). Foodies are the prospective revolutionaries in this book (that's the "*delicious* revolution").

One of my dissertation's examiners, a sociologist, required that I remove any reference to a "so-called" new science of gastronomy.[2] Scholars, however, were generally softening their disapproval and soon added to an existing anthropology of food with food history, food in literature, and the sociology of food, and, from the late 1990s, multidisciplinary "food studies." When twenty-six "sociologists, artists, geographers, and cultural, American, and literary studies people" blogged together, they confirmed food studies' complexity, diversity, fluidity—in a word, "mess" (Cook et al. 2011, 105). The bloggers referred to John Law's *After Method: Mess in Social Science Research* (2004). Not unusually, Law's book made no mention of meals, despite "mess" originally meaning a meal (as in "mess of pottage" and "officers' mess").

In France, Italy, and elsewhere, "gastronomy" usually has come to concern specialist food. But gastronomy can bring together not merely exceptional ingredients but *everything*. Grandly, in 1825, Brillat-Savarin (1826, §18) had envisaged "the systematic knowledge of everything that relates to human-beings insofar as they nourish each other." He specified gastrono-my's intersections with natural history, physics, chemistry, cookery, and, significantly here, commerce and political economy, and he indeed wrote about "everything"—chocolate, frying, obesity, dreams, death, the end of the world, the artificial life of social influencers, and much more.

Studying "everything" could be messy, especially now that the general store of knowledge has exploded even beyond Google's digital farms. For-tunately, while ambitious, gastronomy is also disciplined, literally adopt-ing a focus (*focus*, Latin, hearth), which, for me, is meals. Rather than *food* studies, and *food* this and that, gastronomy begins more profoundly with *meals*. Meals plainly involve food *and more*, and that *more* brings in soci-ety, culture, art, religion, science, technology.... The gastronomic or *stomach-centered* author takes on (and takes in) the world. Gastronomy provides *the diner's sense of the world*.

Speaking of the "diner's sense" implies not only a primary focus—meals—but also investigative methods: learning from the senses, and so through empiricism and hedonism. In exemplary manner, Brillat-Savarin made detailed observations and from intimates, for example, discovered that the "truffle is not a positive aphrodisiac; but it can, in certain situa-tions, make women tenderer and men more agreeable" (§44). As this quo-tation suggests, conversation is intrinsic to meals, and so to gastronomi-cal method. The second of *Physiology of Taste*'s twenty aphorisms was "Animals feed; people share meals; and only those with wit know how to dine."[3]

Gastronomy provides unparalleled insights into our lives, and that includes into spheres that might appear to have lifted off, such as religion, art, and economics.

Slow-Cooked

Such was money's rule that, for too long, economics became something *they* did. With a question, and a general approach to answering it, I even-tually realized I had already taken steps toward a more grounded, gastronomic economics—gastronomics. A concluding speculation in my sociological dissertation in 1991 suggested using "cuisine" for "the entire ensemble of natural and social bodies and forces associated with human sustenance"—close to what I now call an "economy." Next, I protested in *The Shared Table* (1993) the relegation of the original economics as "mere" home economics. The biggest leap came with my book inquiring into why humans cook (Symons 1998). As Scottish literary biographer James Boswell (1924, 179 n.1) recorded in his journal on August 15, 1773, human beings are the "Cooking Animal." Toolmaking did not separate us from the rest of nature, he wrote. Neither did memory, judgment, nor the faculties and passions. But "no beast is a cook."

When considered at all, the most common theories of cooking are *transformational*. Like the dictionary meaning, "cook—to prepare (food) by heating," they take their cue from fire, which makes raw ingredients more digestible, tasty, or expressive. For anthropologist Claude Lévi-Strauss (1978, 495), turning the *raw* into the *cooked* was a "language." The energy advantages of cooking as predigestion lay behind Richard Wrangham's evolutionary hypothesis in *Catching Fire: How Cooking Made Us Human* (2009), an idea enshrined in the subtitle of Michael Pollan's *Cooked: A Natural History of Transformation* (2013).

In 1998, in my history of cooks and cooking, I published another theory. The primary tool was not fire but the much older, Stone Age flints, which evolved into cook's knives, and into such associated implements as hoes, scythes, axes, and cleavers. Cutting up enables sharing of both food and tasks (through exchange and other methods). This *distributional* theory puts cooking at the center of the division of labor and its products. Sharing food and sharing jobs go together; one demands the other, including not only through families but also, as that book showed, distribution through market exchange, and through government redistribution.

Food redistribution has always been the key responsibility of central administrations. Early in what has been termed "civilization," the first ancient temple-states arose with public kitchens, vast stores of staples, along with great sacrifices to divide up beasts—and these banquets sustained administrators, soldiers, infrastructure workers, and the indigent. Replacing high priests, armed monarchs turned religious feasts into courtly banquets, still in beautifully decorated halls with music. Over time, the state's redistribution shifted from contributed foodstuffs to their more flexible substitute, money; but the pooling and disbursement of taxes still served essentially the same function. "Cooks made us," I concluded.

Applying this appreciation of cooking to modern economics, I soon found its gastronomic roots. Rather than the later financially calculative (especially capitalist) direction, eighteenth-century political economists started with the distribution of food and labor, even if they did not always call that a "meal" nor give cooks much credit. As James Steuart put it in *An Inquiry Into the Principles of Political Œconomy* in London in 1767, the "principal object of this science is to secure a certain fund of subsistence for all the inhabitants," each person meeting the other's "reciprocal wants" (2–3). How obvious, that economics concerned eating and drinking, rather than profit! Unhappily, economists devised ways to relegate nourishment to mere "utility," "preference," "subjectivity," "externality," or "inefficiency," and to press the abstract Market as *the* economy. Economists no longer did economics (household management), so much as Aristotle's *chrematistics* (the science of financial gain). Seeking also to make a distinction, Richard Whately (1832, 6) derived *catallactics*—the "Science of Exchanges." Nevertheless, early in the nineteenth century, practitioners crowded out material concerns by claiming the title "economists" for themselves.

Investigating economists' narrow advocacy of just one social organizing tool—prices—included following up the "Austrian school," who insisted that individuals should strive freely for financial gain, nations should run along business lines, and nature should adjust. Between them, Austrian and Chicago leaders have reset government aims and policies and collected swags of Nobel Prizes, though economics is not an original Nobel category—instead, the Swedish National Bank began sponsoring a special "Sveriges Riksbank Prize in Economic Sciences in Memory of Alfred Nobel" in 1969.

Before the nineteenth century was half done, corporate logic had unleashed "more massive and more colossal productive forces" than previously known, observed Karl Marx and Friedrich Engels in the *Manifesto* of 1848 (chap. 1). Profit's insistence on cost-benefit calculation worked wonders of Weberian rationalization, in which traditional authority gave way to bureaucratic. Many consumers benefited, unquestionably, but it was also obvious that the "single, unconscionable freedom"—the liberty of money—has "torn away from the family its sentimental veil," compelled all nations, "on pain of extinction . . . to introduce what it calls civilisation," and subjected "Nature's forces to man." Elevating profits above provisions, and money above other forms of social order . . . here was the Market as a demanding God, "rising or falling, plunging or recovering; the subject of emotions—jittery, nervous, buoyant or confident" (Maddox 1998, 106). With money triumphant, liberty no longer meant "down with the king" but "minimal" democracy, leaving real government to industry lobbyists and committees in a toppling, financialized world.

Many progressive economists, such as Nobel-winner Joseph E. Stiglitz (2013), acknowledge that through such nostrums as financial deregulation, tax cuts for the wealthy, and underinvestment in infrastructure, education, health care, and welfare, the wealthy have been "manipulating the system to seize a larger slice." That broadly accords with the Marxist declaration that economic players are divided between owners and nonowners of the means of production.

However, mainstream economists made more sense once I realized, digging further, that their ascetic, moneymaking "individuals" were not people at all. In league with that, the legal system granted corporations a fictitious "personhood" and therefore selected human rights, notably to property and market freedom. This book brings people together against corporations, so alien as to lack the basic economic need to eat and drink. Instead, corporate logic had made money into the supreme rationalizing, antigastronomic force.

A "Total Reconsideration"

Traversing the modern history of political philosophy and economic theory using gastronomic assumptions, this book charts the appropriation and corruption of liberal ideas by corporation-aligned jurisdictions and mainstream economists, until Market rule unleashed the mocking of liberals, along with their learning, sophistication, and civility. This requires a reexamination of the writings of, among others, Hobbes, Locke, Quesnay, Rousseau, and Brillat-Savarin, on one side, and Smith as a bridge to Say, Ricardo, Jevons, Menger, Mises, Robbins, Hayek, Friedman, and Becker, on the other. Other social theorists, including Marx, Weber, Simmel, and Polanyi, are called on, along with more recent investigators. My hope is that this book will encourage scholars across a sweep of disciplines to incorporate further gastronomic interpretations of not merely economics but Epicureanism, liberalism, politics, and society more generally.

To summarize the narrative, Brillat-Savarin's gastronomy, developed here as the diner's sense of the world, emerged from the Enlightenment thought of Hobbes, Locke, Rousseau, and others, who started with the appetite driving individuals to self-preservation in cooperation with others. A presumption of natural equality supported rights to the free pursuit of well-being and its necessary property, under a social contract that supported a democratic commonwealth.

This remained a left-liberalism, inasmuch as equality is both the assumed starting point ("formal equality") and desirable ("substantive equality"). By contrast, nineteenth-century or "classical" liberals and their twentieth-century "neoliberal" successors wanted competition to generate aspirational inequality. (Certain brands of right-wing politics deny both formal and substantive equality.) Formal equality also lay behind the often unjust "equality before the law" and "legal personhood" of corporations, whose purpose had been sharpened to profit. But how can we grant corporations human rights when they do not even eat?

Supporting the transcendence of fundamental human needs, including within scholarship, nineteenth-century or "neoclassical" economists rationalized interpersonal interactions, so that equal individuals bought and sold in no physical market but in a formal Market—a system of prices. The rational, gain-seeking player is an artificial person acting like a corporation, summed up as *Homo economicus*.

In response, gastronomic economics emphasizes that we rely on multiple levels of households. We in no way live in a single, "*the* economy," especially not as a mere system of debits and credits. Enlightenment intellectuals were familiar with the original or "domestic" economy and extended that by speaking, by analogy, of the "political economy." This was also known as the "body politic" because the human body circulated nourishment internally as an "animal economy" within the overall "natural economy."

In recent times, numerous small food producers, artisans, homemakers, waiters, baristas, and eaters have rejected the economics of greed in favor of an economics of appetite. Such meal-lovers get back to basics with fresh, local, and "slow" foods, street markets, school gardens, urban farms, and action on sustainability. They base domestic life on meal sharing and call for food justice in a new, global banquet. In knowing that we are what we eat, together, the left-liberal enthusiasms of foodies might yet rescue us. That includes the social sciences, which for too long joined philosophy in dismissing eating and drinking as unworthy.

While many readers will be familiar with aspects, they might still be surprised how far, from a gastronomic starting point, "classical" liberal lawmakers and "neoclassical" and "neoliberal" economists have twisted our world. The high theology of the Market is so pervasive that it can affect even stern critics. In *The Livelihood of Man*, economic historian Karl Polanyi (1977, xliii, xlvi) recognized decades ago that to improve civilization's "chances of survival, the problem of man's material livelihood should be subjected to total reconsideration." The "chief impediment," he said, was the absolute priority given to the "motive of economic gain." Gastronomy must undertake Polanyi's rethink by avoiding his narrow understanding of "economic" in that quotation. Likewise, politicians swallowed "It's the economy, stupid," also as if it means money. The answer, involving several economies, lies in front of our noses.

More recently, in *Undoing the Demos*, political theorist Wendy Brown (2015, 31, 35, 41, 221–22) vividly portrayed neoliberalism's "relentless and ubiquitous economization of all features of life." In disseminating "the model of the market to all domains and activities," neoliberal rationality hollowed out people as *Homo economicus* and recast the "state as the manager of a firm." Since markets now "know best," everyone was caught on the "perpetual treadmill of a capitalist economy that cannot cease without collapsing." Even the Left suffered ubiquitous "civilizational despair," she wrote. Brown's pessimism flowed from her acceptance that "economization" is total, rather than just a forceful ideology that mistakes money for meals, corporations for diners, and prices for economies. While there's life, there's hope. By the epilogue, I recommend the ancient expression of tangible togetherness, "eat, drink, and be merry."

English columnist George Monbiot (2016) observed that neoliberal thinkers and activists were ready with a clear alternative when the inadequacies of Keynesian economics became apparent in the 1970s, just as Keynes had been prepared when laissez-faire economics led to catastrophe in 1929. Monbiot did not want a reprise of Keynes's stimulation of consumer demand to promote economic growth—these were the "the motors of environmental destruction." But he had no response, given that the "left and centre have produced no new general framework of economic thought for 80 years." Designing a replacement system to prevailing neoliberalism would require a left-leaning "Apollo programme."

Having taken an embarrassing number of years, this research has felt like an Apollo program. Not that I have invented much; instead, I have brought together established elements of economic theory, social and cultural theory, political philosophy, and intellectual history. The result might not look like conventional economics, but that's the book's strength: it reestablishes the basics. The neglected discipline of gastronomy regrounds theory, making it literally radical. The answer to the Market is not better metaphysics but knowing that meals matter. Meals are complex and many-faceted but also recurring, so they offer repeated opportunities to get them right—yet again within hours. Recent micro- and macroeconomics are useful but, like even the most wonderful kitchen scales, minor contributors to the merriment. Restraining recent mathematics to a technical subbranch, gastronomic economics—gastronomics—makes the "dismal science" smile again. Our world, afresh.

Academically, my immediate intention with this book is to investigate the exceedingly inflated claims of mainstream economics. From the associated necessity of outlining an alternative, I recover the Enlightenment version, based in more authentically economic concerns. Along with that, my hope is to persuade scholars in more established disciplines to further resist money's rationalization of the world, and to help restore a diner's sense of things. If that happens also to further gastronomy, so be it.

Methodologically, this book is unapologetically gastronomic. Brillat-Savarin's foundational text, *Physiology of Taste*, might appear disorganized, but, given its topic and transdisciplinary requirements, a gastronomic work must be forgiven for erring on the side of the conversational, mixing wit with gravity.[4] Given the gastronomic regrounding, some words might have unexpected uses, hence the glossary at the end of the book. If a description of a meal happens to set the table for each of the following chapters, then that is because talking about meals talks about the world.

MEALS MATTER

1

IT'S NOT "*THE* ECONOMY, STUPID," BUT MORE THAN FIVE OF THEM

Trattoria Above the Vucciria Market

The letters *S-H-A-N-G-A-I* swung at sunset on a string of Chinese lanterns on a balcony in the center of Palermo, Sicily. A returned seafarer had named his simple trattoria Shangai, after 上海市 (Shanghai), because that city's crowded market alleyways reminded him of home, as would have the souks of North Africa. From a balcony table beneath the lanterns, we looked down past the glowing canvas awnings on the swordfish butchers leaning at great knives, as if guarding not merely their glistening prizes but the whole Vucciria market, radiating from their small, central square.

From this vantage point, we could see the narrow, pedestrian streets, densely packed with foods, disappearing in four directions. Local painter Renato Guttuso captured the scene in *La Vucciria* (1974). His chunky black-and-white linocuts had illustrated Elizabeth David's groundbreaking cookery book *Italian Food* in 1954. In this case, he jammed a huge and brilliantly colored canvas with swordfish and other silvery creatures, along with a side of a beast, eggs, olives, bocconcini, hard cheeses, small goods, lemons, pears, and boxes on boxes of vegetables. Five or six men in caps and white aprons attend their wares so closely that they are scarcely noticed.

More obviously, the artist walks toward the trattoria, followed by his wife, dressed in black, with the other shoppers probably being himself again and three versions of his mistress (Pergament 2007).

Our scene was even busier, because, seemingly, the entire town promenaded before their evening meal and admired the makings, as sellers sliced off, weighed out, and counted helpings. Some items could be consumed in the streets, such as the arancini ("oranges"), deep-fried rice balls containing meat sauce. Other stallholders polished plates for stand-up consumption of more mysterious delicacies. Most purchases were taken to nearby houses. Seen from above, everyone came and went from one gently lit, crowded refectory.

The trattoria was scarcely more than a few tables on a balcony and an interior room, with a cook, young assistant, and waiter, and stocked almost no food. Instead, the waiter took an order, descended to collect the fish from a stall below, and baked it in a small oven on the balcony. With simple antipasti, house wine, spaghetti, and a rough salad, the trattoria exploited fresh convenience. The market has since declined, and the Shangai shut its doors for several years, but it had offered a transporting lesson.

As with all great meals, this brought not just the food but the world together, literally. At a single feast, we were connected through market benches with Palermo's citizens. The table for just two people belonged to not only the small household of the restaurant but the wider household of the market, within, crucially, the city as a household, and then the natural household, including crops and catch of nearby gardens and waters. The meal required not just the oven and market stalls but gardens, boatyards, fishing fleets, and roads, and many people laboring to sustain Palermo's place on earth. Rarely have I felt at home with so many people, none of whom I actually knew. Cooks share in widening circles, I later wrote, including through markets. "This makes the market a public table" (Symons 2000, 123).

Although the market is not commonly interpreted as a great meal, perhaps an exception can be found from 1887, when, concerned at the loss of close-knit traditional communities, German sociologist Ferdinand Tönnies (1974, 60, 62) reflected on the peaceful and just exchange within a town, that is, "within a community of houses which is itself like a more

FIGURE 1.1 At the Shangai trattoria, overlooking the Vucciria market, Palermo, Sicily, 1978. Photos by author.

comprehensive house." This made for a great "participation in the feast at the table."

The domestic table, with food in front of everyone, holds the familiar meal, literally (Latin *familiaris*, "family"). But it is only one way to divide food and associated labor. The trattoria offered an open version of the domestic meal, connecting its guests with the market as another. The town and city hall hosted a further meal, providing transport links and running water, and cleaning up afterward. I refer to this meal as the political banquet. Some of this is already glimpsed in those words—"hall" having often been a large dining place, and "political" from the organized Greek *polis*, city. Individuals dine together in houses, connected through government and market, and all within nature, which is an intricate, metabolic ensemble.

In this chapter I introduce the gastronomic approach by locating it among so-called foodies. Before that, I make an absolutely fundamental point about the plurality of distributional modes or meals, and the economies of which they are at the heart. Their depth and complexity make a mockery of speaking of only one, "*the* economy." To redeploy future president Bill Clinton's notorious reminder to election staff: it's at least five economies, stupid! In fact, this is a major example of modern economists' imperialism, subsuming complexity under the mere money economy, and, further, under the competitive Market. The banquet had already lost some visibility, historically, when food was substituted by more efficient money distribution, but then post-Enlightenment economists danced on its grave.

Given that eighteenth-century economic thinkers were fully aware of multiple economies, today's textbook titles, such as *Economics*, *Principles of Economics*, *Foundations of Economics*, and *Introducing Economics*, stand as monuments to hubris. Restoring economics means acknowledging, from the start, that money is far from all that counts. Human decision-making is immensely more complex.

Homes Within Homes

Each level of meal is associated with a different type of economy, each with its distinctive membership, history, and issues. In Enlightenment thought, an economy gained qualities above those of the individual parts. The frequent illustration was individual bees combining in a hive. Different participants collected nectar and pollen and processed them into honey, or did the housekeeping, or reproduced, so giving life to a higher organism, with its own behaviors. Putting that generally, in an *economy*, functionally separate parts share the work in sharing sustenance. The components *work together*, and *comprehensively*, on *obtaining* and *distributing* nutrients throughout.

The word "economy" derives from the management of the ancient Greek *oikos*, "household." To quote German economic sociologist Max Weber (1968, 357, 359, 363), the members of that original *oikos* or "unit of economic maintenance" typically had a common residence, and "solidarity in dealing with the outside and communism of property and consumption of everyday goods within (household communism)." The abiding principle was everybody contributing what they could and taking what they needed. The size of communal economies has ranged from solitary persons through couples and clusters, along with help and apprentices, to aristocratic establishments, incorporating staffs. In the real world, rather than theory, the communism of the *oikos* has been distorted by patriarchy, and larger communes have tended to prove utopian. Over time, the family lost self-sufficiency or, looked at another way, gained openness, both receiving from and sending out to other families through the greater economic modes.

The *oikos* idea was soon borrowed for other self-sustaining systems. In the *New Testament*, for example, variants of *oikos* suggested care by a city manager, or by God. Early Christian theologians conceived God's reign over the created order. Among others, Irenaeus, Tertullian, Hippolytus of Rome, Origen, and Gregory of Nazianzus understood the triune God or "Trinity" as an economy comprising three mutually supporting parts, and political scientist Dotan Leshem (2016) recently drew a link between the domain of the infinite "head of household" and the overarching Market.

Intellectuals in eighteenth-century Europe took seriously another economy—the *animal economy*, or human person acknowledged as a physical being. Medical scientists studied an orderly, living household of organs with blood, nerves, mind, and so forth. As described by young physician Jean-Joseph Menuret de Chambaud in the *Encyclopédie* in 1765 (11:360), the *œconomie animale* was the "order, mechanism, ensemble of functions and movements that sustain the life of animals, when working perfectly, meaning constantly, quickly and easily, which constitutes the utmost flourishing state of health, and the least disturbance of which is disease, and the cessation of the whole thing is the diametric opposite to life, namely, death."

As a writer on the animal economy or physiology, Anthelme Richerand (who reappears in chapter 3 as Brillat-Savarin's close friend), explained in 1801: "Every thing maintains itself, every thing is connected and mutually agreeable in the animal economy; the functions are reciprocally connected, they act together: the whole represents a circle, of which it is impossible to find the beginning or end" (1803, 38). Thinking organically of a human animal became a way to comprehend not only its life but also mind and spirit as emergent properties.

An animal economy depends on the twists and turns of the gut. Pleasing the stomach has been known as a core task for millennia, not least because supporting tens of trillions of bacteria—fellow diners or "commensals"—is so integral to healthy lives that scientists have also dubbed the microbiota the "forgotten organ" and "second brain." Perhaps this economy is even the "first brain," assisted by the one at the top in moving to food, because, as neuroscientist and engineer Daniel Wolpert (2011) has argued, "We have a brain for one reason and one reason only, and that is to produce adaptable and complex movements." Playing around with the gut microbiota through antibiotics and other lifestyle changes would appear to have been reckless, and behind allergies, including eczema and asthma (Willyard 2011). Other microorganisms work together in the fermentation of vinegar, yoghurt, kombucha, and the like. In turn, each living cell is a nano-economy, with its parts working together to make a tiny world, but that probably shrinks the household idea too microscopically.

Enlightenment thinkers knew the *natural economy*. When setting agriculture within the larger "œconomy of nature," Swedish taxonomer Carolus Linnaeus [Carl von Linné] (1707–1778) and his students found that natural things on "this terraqueous globe" were "fitted to produce general ends, and reciprocal uses" and "so connected, so chained together, that they all aim at the same end" (Stillingfleet 1775, 39–40). In *Origin of Species* in 1859, Charles Darwin spoke of the "natural economy" or "economy of nature"—his successors would introduce "ecology" and "ecosystem," which are further *oeco-/eco* words from *oikos*.

Nature relies on complex distribution, in which people participate in the circulation of matter and energy among photoautotrophs, herbivores, carnivores, and bottom feeders. These distributions or *meals* are given such names as web of life, food cycles, food chains, metabolic interchange, feeding, and "eat and be eaten." Naturalists have long recognized, as Jonathan Swift rhymed in "On Poetry: A Rhapsody" of 1733, that big fleas are preyed on by smaller, and "these have smaller still to bite 'em, / And so proceed ad infinitum."

The animal economy has not lacked investigation (physiology, psychology, nutrition, etc.) and advice, being assailed by pages, screens, and menus about eating this and that, counting calories, and "good" and "bad" fats, etc. While self-help books and blogs put responsibility on the individual, the basic gastronomic truth is that experiences are shared. Eating together multiplies pleasure, care, and health. Accordingly, while not ignoring physiologies and the natural world, and certainly not the original economy, I focus in this book on a further two, intertwined economies: the *political* and *market*.

The redistribution of actual food visibly sustained the earliest Mesopotamian temple-states, so that a ziggurat was a temple-kitchen atop grain stores. The ritual centerpiece was the distribution or "sacrifice" of beasts (Symons 2000, 240–62). With the centuries, the earliest banquets forsook religious patronage in favor of armed royals, who extracted support for daily feasts of the court, along with rations for infrastructure workers, armies, and the needy. As well, the community contribution of staples and livestock was substituted, more flexibly, by money taxation and spending.

Such leaders were hailed for military prowess, diplomatic polygamy, and magnificence, so that the Queen of Sheba brought King Solomon gold, precious stones, and spices (1 Kings 10:10). Nonetheless, the highest reputations, attested by ancient praise, rested on building roads with shade trees, maintaining irrigation works, sponsoring agricultural and culinary improvement, patronizing the arts, caring for widows, and, at the heart, making far-reaching daily banquets. At the dedication of his temple three millennia ago, Solomon sacrificed 22,000 oxen and 120,000 sheep, feeding a "great assembly," only sent away on the eighth day (1 Kings 8:62–66).

Banquets remained at the heart of *political economies*, with emperors and monarchs gathering up meats and delicacies, along with cooks, artisans, soldiers, and intellectuals, while feasts persisted more symbolically in temples and cathedrals. To add to the examples, according to Greek compiler Athenaeus (4.145a–146a), one thousand animals were slaughtered daily for the Persian king's breakfast. While this might appear prodigal, the banquet's numerous participants would take leftovers home to feed their own households and guests. The English ruler from 1377 to 1399, Richard II, reputedly served ten thousand guests every day. His two thousand cooks and three hundred servitors handled twenty-eight oxen, three hundred sheep, vast numbers of fowl, and all kinds of game, slaughtered every morning (Warner 1791, xxxii). The mechanism was discernible (and reappears in chapter 6) at Louis XV's public suppers, and involvement as "baker-king" in the grain trade, but the City was already gaining power to the detriment of meals, including lavish courtly banquets.

Numerous versions remain today, perhaps disguised as the Catholic mass or the U.S. Thanksgiving, and, more widely, submerged under systems of money taxation and public service. The banquet appears more obviously in smaller political economies, such as when each local *contrada* (self-governing community) in Siena, Italy, still impressively holds many nightly street dinners at long lines of trestles, anticipating every Palio horserace.

The name *banquet* is worth retaining for political redistribution, even if citizens no longer gather at "small benches" and public finances ease the cooperation on nourishment. Likewise, the leader of the banquet requires a name, possibly "baker-king," "head," "governor," "minister," "administrator," or "chief victualer," although the person sitting before the assembly, taking overall responsibility, and embodying collective hopes might for good reason be called *president*. The banquet government or presidency has taken various forms, including hierocracy (rule by priests), monarchy or autocracy (one person), aristocracy (the best), democracy (the people), and plutocracy (money), each ending with the Greek *kratos* for "strength, power," which has been backed by physical force, charisma, ideology, and projected democratic agreement.

To generalize perilously, while Enlightenment writers in England saw hope in moving power from monarchy to democracy, some in France found an alternative in increasingly powerful money. Their arguments relied on the differentiation of a *market economy* from the political. Rather than any central authority gathering up and dispersing food (or its substitute), it would be exchanged at a distance, one-to-one. The swapping of loaves, beer, meat, and other specialized items without undue royal intervention offered many attractions, but should the market be permitted to push the banquet aside?

One Superintending Economy?

Economic humanist Karl Polanyi (e.g., 1957, 250–56) detected three historical modes of economic distribution: reciprocity, redistribution, and market exchange. I develop these as communal, redistributive, and market *meals*. This first meal, and closest to the common understanding, is reinterpreted here, following Weber, as family communism. Polanyi's second mode of redistribution is viewed as the banquet at the heart of local, regional, national, and global polities. The third is the market, whose prices are modeled by modern economists as the Market.

Through the nineteenth century, Polanyi found, capitalist rationalization created "market society." Reinterpreting that: those assuming the mantle of "economists," pure and simple, floated off in awe only one, "*the* economy," with human exchange abstracted as scarcely more than a system of prices, only distantly reflective of one aspect of economic life. The broad direction can be charted by such shifts as the dropping of the qualifier in "political economy," the fascination with "value" until little more than that deemed by the Market, and the triumphant application of the differential calculus.

In a much-read, late twentieth-century introduction to economics, Robert Heilbroner (1980, 35) relayed the discipline's boast that the problem of human survival was now solved by "the free action of profit-seeking men bound together only by the market itself." Rather than deliberate household management, an economy should be organized by nothing but price signals—that is, the only legitimate power should be money. That left out survival's dependence on collective decision-making, along with bugs, bodies, families, polities, ecologies, and more. The paid pipers of economic science led the disavowal of satisfying food and drink as even the rationale for market exchange.

The social supremacy of money, acting through the Market, took explicit, and potent, policy form as "neoliberalism." Neoliberalism borrowed some features of liberalism; its attachment to formal equality no doubt assisted in the widespread acceptance of gay marriage, to give one example. However, antagonism to other principles, not least egalitarianism, has been deleterious, promoting populist, plutocratic, surveillance capitalism. As frequently noted in recent times, the elevation of prices to superintend all economies has multiplied inequality, pressed for unlimited expansion (with no sense of tragedy, called "growth"), and humiliated democracy, so that much serious discussion has been slighted as the "political correctness," and worse, of "elites."

An economics that displays the living world as formulas and graphs, like PowerPoint projections, demands urgent gastronomic response. Certainly, calculations and equations provide insights, and critics, both internal and around the periphery, recognize the hazards of wide-eyed theory. However, even children embed themselves in more than the Market and might list personal name, family name, house address, region, nation, species, Earth, the Universe. . . . Bringing the science of gastronomy to the party, I will show how and why economics evaporated into rarefied realms and then propose ways back, reinvigorating liberal basics.

Doing economics in some all-embracing sense could become overwhelmingly complicated, but each subspecialty—domestic, political, market, and so forth—has to acknowledge certain basics, most immediately, that the circulation of nutriment lies at the core. Bodies need pleasurable and healthy diets. Domesticity deserves sensitive attention, not video binges with food deliveries. Governments must accept responsibility for wealth as well-being. Consumers might gain greater awareness of literally con-suming ("taking-up," Latin) together. Ecological cycles can again involve eat-and-be-eaten.

If mainstream economists' image of the market is lines and numbers on a screen, then it is answered by painter Renato Guttuso's cornucopia of bananas, fennel, sweet peppers, mortadella, and octopuses. This sensual vision belonged to, and this is not unusual, a social radical. Left-liberalism has had a promising affinity with good food.

Foodies to the Rescue

An overpopulated world depends on some corporate adventurism, perhaps. More securely, it relies on human skill, ingenuity, curiosity, and enthusiasm, in other words, on artisans, artists, managers, and everyone.

Cooking is central and not merely as transformation—turning the "raw" into the "cooked" as predigestion, or eye-catching composition—but, more socially, as distribution—sharing production. Work brings replenishment, and vice versa. Not only domestically: at a higher level, economics means *housekeeping the state*—to borrow an early-twentieth-century feminist message "that women's political participation was both gender-appropriate and indispensable" (Sawer 2003, 98).

The past two centuries of financial ambition, backed by economic science, promoted technological innovation, the division of labor, and the suppression of meal concerns. In the strange dialectical way of history, however, neoliberalism has carried selected liberal concerns, while profit-seeking marketing has come over the past few decades to recommend hedonic, aesthetic, and recreational rewards. Some consumers wanted the flashy snacks, and others "healthy choices," "organic," and "gourmet." Shelves showed off Provençal olives, aioli, tapenade, ratatouille, and nougat, and boasted noodles, dumplings, fish curry, sushi, and egg tarts. The travel and hospitality industries boomed. Profit's asceticism aroused its antithesis.

With renewed openness to sensuality, sociability, and cultural criticism, foodies emerged. Self-proclaimed English foodie Paul Levy and colleagues detected the cult, semisatirically, for *Harper's & Queen* magazine in 1982, expanding that article into the *Official Foodie Handbook: Be Modern— Worship Food* in 1984 (Woods et al. 1982; Barr and Levy 1985). The emergence of modern—really, postmodern—food worship presaged support for gastronomy.

In the nineteenth century bankers and capitalists were caricatured as plump, top-hatted gentlemen, living on champagne and caviar, with their workers' families, in rags, engaged in "productive consumption"—meaning just enough to keep workers alive (more consumption would have been "unproductive"). For much of the last century, fine dining was still reserved for well-to-do white men, quaffing old red wines between cigars, while their political opponents practiced plain living. The left-liberal tendencies of foodies helped reverse the stereotypes. With some accuracy, right-wing commentators slighted the maturing, countercultural generation as "chardonnay socialists" (Australia), "latte-sipping liberals" (United States), "champagne socialists" (United Kingdom), "smoked salmon socialists"

(Ireland), *gauche caviar* ("caviar left," France), "*Toskana-Fraktion*" ("Tuscan fraction," Germany), and so forth.

The founder of the British restaurant "Bible," the *Good Food Guide*, in 1951, had notably been a socialist, Raymond Postgate. Restaurateur Alice Waters brought politics into her restaurant, Chez Panisse, in 1971 and went on to spread such messages as "If we don't care about food, then the environment will always be something outside of ourselves" (2009). The First Symposium of Australian Gastronomy (which the present author instigated) brought together four dozen scholars, scientists, politicians, intellectual chefs, and "passionate amateurs" in Adelaide in March 1984, among them the former democratic socialist premier of South Australia, Don Dunstan. Ahead of his time, Dunstan had extolled a more climatically suitable, and sybaritic "Mediterranean" way of life and published a cookery book while running a government.

Opposing *fast* food explicitly, and Fascist futurism implicitly, Italian communists came together as Arcigola to oppose McDonald's taking a commanding position at the Spanish Steps in Rome and then forged the wider Slow Food movement in 1989. The Slow manifesto announced: "A firm defense of quiet material pleasure is the only way to oppose the universal folly of Fast Life." The signatories agreed to let "sensual pleasure and slow, long-lasting enjoyment preserve us from the contagion. . . . Our defense should begin at the table. . . . Real culture is here to be found" (Portinari 1989). The international grouping of small farmers' organizations, La Via Campesina (The Peasants' Way), founded in 1993, summed up their response to globalization by coining "food sovereignty."

By 2009 the Simmons Market Research Bureau's national consumer survey, "Packaged Facts," claimed that 14 percent of U.S. adults—or thirty-one million—were foodies, a "desirable demographic, as they are avid, tech-savvy consumers who embrace all sorts of trends." They were not gullible consumers: "Their food passion provides a framework through which they can build relationships, forge new friendships, discover the world, and even examine which behaviors are ethical" (http://www.marketresearch .com/Packaged-Facts-v768/Foodies-Restaurant-2088291/).

According to sociologists in Toronto, Canada, those presenting themselves as "uncommonly passionate about food" valued "quality, rarity, locality, organic, hand-made, creativity, and simplicity." They sought authenticity through geographic specificity, tradition, and cultural connection. They talked about the food industry, food regulations, and food politics as well as "the sensory characteristics of food and the sensual pleasures it brings." And they took that into the public square, so that Josée Johnston and Shyon Baumann (2010, 3, 63, 67–68, 132) concluded: "Put simply, many foodies are gourmets with a political bent."

Cultural sociologist Isabelle de Solier (2013, 2, 25, 62, 102, 169) found foodies in Melbourne, Australia, having to create moral selves without much guidance from tradition. Her ethnography confirmed that cultivating "personal well-being and happiness" through quality food and rejecting fast food as having "low use-value, exchange-value, and sign-value" stood as "a critique of, and resistance to, the dominant mode of global industrial food production and distribution." Overall, foodism appeared as a "new secular material morality."

New York Times food writer Mark Bittman (2014) admitted to cringing at the label "foodie" but found no viable alternative, deciding, "let's try to make the word 'foodie' a tad more meaningful." The general direction was food activism, he said. Good food depended on the whole system, leaving foodies with no option but to engage in "questions of justice and equality and rights, of enhancing rather than restricting democracy, of making a more rational, legitimate economy." That was not such a hard task, he advised. "It's rewarding to find the best pork bun; it's even more rewarding to fight for a good food system at the same time. That's what we foodies do."

The diminutive "foodie" might sound frivolous but avoids inappropriate earnestness about pleasure. A bigger quibble might be that the label narrows the focus to food, when the human distinctiveness is *meals*. Dividing up labor and its products at meals makes human beings *economic*. Some might think that farmers produce mere food, but they participate in the market meal. Contributing taxes for water, train tracks, health, and education—that's the redistributive banquet. *Meals* matter, but "mealie" might not sound as felicitous as "foodie."

Foodies have rediscovered community gardens, sourdough bakeries, food carts, recycling, wind power, organic carrots, cowshare schemes,

"Fallen Fruit" maps of fruit growing in public places, and everyone's right to property, by way of livelihood (with an older emphasis on sustenance). U.S. first lady Michelle Obama scored a hit with the White House vegetable garden. Farmers' markets rose in number in the United States by 17 percent in one year, reaching a total of 7,175 in 2011. The numbers increased, although at slower rate, to a total of 8,669 in 2016 (U.S. Department of Agriculture 2016). Food rescue activists cooked supermarket "waste" for their city's hungry. Often with double lives as viticulturists, home sourdough bakers, and restaurant-goers, scholars had become less reticent about studying something as "lowly" as food and drink, and many came together under the label "food studies."

Food writer Michael Pollan distilled a healthy diet into seven wise words: "Eat food. Not too much. Mostly plants." But you cannot keep a good idea down, and he soon elaborated the seven words into an entire book, *Food Rules: An Eater's Manual* (2009), which included the needs for pleasure and joyful company. Sixty-four rules opened in the same way— "1—Eat food"—but with amplifications: "2—Don't eat anything your great-grandmother wouldn't recognize as food"; and additions: "43—Have a glass of wine with dinner"; "48—Consult your gut"; and "49—Eat slowly." Importantly, "58—Do all your eating at a table"; and "59—Try not to eat alone."

Also paying attention to social economies, the ten-step, Brazilian dietary guidelines, *Guia alimentar para a população brasileira*, published in 2006, included shopping for "natural or minimally processed foods" with only small amounts of "oils, fats, salt, and sugar." Making "food and eating important in your life," Brazilians should "enjoy what you are eating. . . . Whenever possible, eat in company." The tenth step cautioned: "Be wary of food advertising and marketing. The purpose of advertising is to increase product sales, and not to inform or educate people" (http://www.fao.org /nutrition/education/food-dietary-guidelines/regions/brazil/en/).

Foodies reconnect with the substantial (from the Latin, "beneath-standing"). With feet firmly planted in the soil, noses toward the kitchen, and plans for the next meal, foodies understand the world the right way up. Far from being unduly self-centered, nationalist, or speciesist, foodies invite others into the garden, market, and political networks. Foodies can restore economies, one farm, shop, household, kitchen, café, landscape, and pork bun at a time. By dining, baking, starting food businesses, foodies lobby their political representatives and, scarcely noticing, philosophize.

Embracing the immediate realities of life moves toward a coherent and historically identifiable set of ideas and activities. Philosophically, seeking sensory gratification in combination with others requires hedonism, empiricism, and the social contract. A life-giving stream wound from before Epicurus through select Renaissance and key Enlightenment thinkers to present-day meal-lovers. Early modern variations on Epicurean philosophy provided liberalism, and then its distorting lift-off into mainstream economics and soaring misrepresentations.

Now Epicurean materialism returns for an economics of togetherness, because, according to the *diner's knot* or *paradox of the table*, the individual pursuit of taste-pleasures beget table-pleasure, which begets all those "together" words—consumption, commensality, companionship, conviviality, community, commonwealth, etc. Humans are at home here, around private tables, in market squares, belonging to political communities and natural economies, all at once, restoring the wealth of liberalism.

Responding to eternal expansion under the title of *Plenitude*, Boston College sociologist Juliet Schor (2010, 4–7) recommended a "new economics of true wealth," in which people "work and spend less, create and connect more." When people edge away from the Market, no longer preoccupied with well-paying jobs, they "enjoy and thrive more" and reclaim the time to do other things, including "self-provision." She associated "plenitude" with another proposal in this present book: "We don't need to be less materialist . . . but more so," living here and now. In a gastronomic regrounding, economics gets radical, deriving (along with "radish") from the Latin *radix*, *radices*, root.

We Are What We Eat, Together

In this book I focus on the social economies that provide the advantages of the division of labor and its products. Competing with and complementing each other, and also family life, the *political* and the *market* economies are based on food allocating and exchanging, respectively. In the former, the *president* (administrator or government) gathers up food (or its substitute, money) for *redistribution* by means of what is generalized here as the *banquet*. Unhappily, economists came to celebrate the market over the political, and over every other economy, including the natural. Economists became key contributors to rationalization's anti-gastronomic push that distorted political understandings, along with scholarship, and ideas generally.

The few sentences in the previous paragraph have raised a multitude of questions, which I answer in four parts, investigating, respectively: 1. money-advocacy vs. meal-advocacy; 2. the gastronomic basis of Enlightenment liberalism; 3. money's appropriation, and corruption, of those ideas; and 4. hopes to be gained from recent food activism. The epilogue finds comfort in some ancient practical wisdom.

PART 1

INSATIABLE GREED VS. SATIABLE APPETITE

2

IN GREED THEY TRUST

A Disastrous Lunch

Table and chairs are set in the warm, dappled sunlight with glimpses of the harbor; the diners bring honest food and drink to share—an egg dish, seafood, salads, fruits, wine, and cake; and we have all afternoon. The guest is worth getting to know, too, the aspirational celebrity of the recent age . . . *Homo economicus*. This is modern economists' textbook individual.

Four million copies of Robert L. Heilbroner's *The Worldly Philosophers* made generations of economics students a tantalizing promise. Setting them apart from other social scientists, they would gain the secret of seeing the human individual as a free agent who used rational methods to maximize advantage. Heilbroner (1980, 35) spoke wryly of "a pale wraith of a creature who follows his adding-machine brain wherever it leads him." This was *Homo economicus*, or "economic man."

Budding economists would become entranced by an "astonishing game," Heilbroner pledged, because the market system's "lure of gain" now ruled the world. The "invisible hand" of the market had replaced "custom and command" and the "pull of tradition or the whip of authority" in ensuring survival. The guiding rule, through which "society assured its own continuance," was "deceptively simple: each should do what was to his best monetary advantage." The market revolution was the "paradoxical, subtle, and difficult solution to the problem of survival that called forth the economists" (18–19).

Unfortunately, a luncheon invitation for *Homo economicus* proves a mistake. Calling up a food delivery but not eating, this weird figure dominates the conversation, simply spouting numbers, rates, and margins, draws a curve marked 0 percent and 100 percent on a napkin, promises prosperity, and urges investment to promote "growth." Paying no attention to the comestibles, birdsong, nor any of us, *Homo economicus* exhibits no appetite. Yet the economists' presentation of the human person might also be called Greedy Monster. This freely roaming, cashed-up creature strives to outsmart everyone, extracting not from the harbor-side potluck but from the virtual pot of gold. Dissatisfied? Make the pot bigger!

Our luncheon guest's Frankensteins are implicated in an inegalitarian, overpopulated, run-away, tasteless, loud culture, belittling democratic participation and battering away its natural supports. Economists have turned tables into charts and spreads into spreadsheets. Having the ear of governments, they have distracted from the great political banquet. Their core insights validated neoliberal rearrangements. Not enjoying meals, their creature will not last. A commanding fiction, a real-world tragedy, an embarrassing lunch.

Unlike the mainly positive meal reports in subsequent chapters, this disconcerting repast deserves little further comment—other than the rest of the book, which both accounts for the monumental misconceptions of mainstream economists and reclaims abandoned realities. It rediscovers liberalism's gastronomic grounding, which economists helped suppress as they promoted the financial rationalization of the world.

During the Enlightenment, economic thinkers assumed that appetite compelled individuals to work and eat together. But nineteenth-century successors inverted that, depicting an idealized "hand" that demanded individuals become competitively grasping. Economists came to assume that Individuals, who are Rational and motivated by Gain, are ideally organized by the Market. This is no physical market of sellers' cries and vegetal smells. When Nobel-winner James M. Buchanan (1964, 214, 219) described economics as "the theory of markets," he imagined mathematical spaces of supply and demand, capitalized Markets. Such assumptions became so entrenched that economists scarcely noticed their detachment from material life.

Economists not only elevated meals into money, they denied the original (domestic) economy, animal economy (human physiology), great political economy, and natural economy. Some simplistic postulates, extended beyond their capacities and decorated with charts, shape our lives. In this chapter I establish some fundamental characteristics of the economists' model. The complaint is not the thinness of world so much as the bloated claims. *Homo economicus* is an occasionally handy caricature, and the vaunted "free Market" sometimes suggestive. Nonetheless, this science of *oikonomia* or "household management" should be the most caring of all, and can be again.

The Emperor's Apologists

The U.S. Bureau of Labor Statistics (2018) counted 18,650 economists at work in that country in 2018—a tiny number, compared to, say, 1,259,930 accountants and auditors, and 684,470 management analysts. The economists studied, in the bureau's description, the "production and distribution of goods and services or monetary and fiscal policy," possibly processing data using sampling techniques and econometric methods. Measuring incomings and outgoings—where's the harm in that? Well, the bureau found economists intensely concentrated in Washington, D.C., the center of government and lobbying. Economists work for global organizations, such as the International Monetary Fund, whose recruitment pages (accessed June 28, 2019) boasted that half the 2,700 staff were economists, working mostly at the IMF's headquarters in Washington, D.C., although their "exciting career" often took them around the world, working on a "wide range of challenging policy issues." (And spreading the party line or "Washington consensus" about the desirability of reducing government deficits, cutting taxes on high incomes, removing trade protections, privatizing state operations, deregulating business, and protecting capital.)

Other economists are scattered among the skyscrapers of corporations, banks, hedge funds, management consultants, industry associations, and think-tanks, their analyses and forecasts aimed at shaping national policies, at which they have proved hugely successful, and no more so than with the neoliberal agenda, economists lending a scientific aura to rule by money. Networking at academic and policy meetings, often sponsored by business, economists across the globe have framed policies according to a disturbingly narrow ideal, in communication with accountants, managers, consultants, lobbyists, bureaucrats, and politicians. They have promulgated a profit-centered ideology, which makes taxes seem punitive and resource depletion a benefit.

As lauded on Sydney University's web pages, economics "addresses a range of 'big' issues in modern life and plays a central role in shaping the broad framework of society at every level" (http://sydney.edu.au/arts /economics/). The University of Chicago has contributed an "astonishing… proportion of new ideas in economics over the last forty years" in the "conviction that economics is an incomparably powerful tool for understanding society" (https://economics.uchicago.edu/about/). Chicago school founder Frank H. Knight (1933, 4) taught students that the topic of "the *social organization* of economic activity" meant studying, in practice, the "the price system, or free enterprise." Stanford, Princeton, and other universities refer potential students to an American Economic Association video, "A Career in Economics… it's much more than you think," in which four economists talk about their careers (https://www.aeaweb .org., accessed June 16, 2019). For a researcher at Google, Randall Lewis, economics "has taught me how the world actually functions… how an incredibly complex system can actually be understandable based on the individual incentives that people have." Economics now had the tools, Lewis said, to analyze enormous amounts of data "to really help companies and organizations improve their decision making."

The London School of Economics is among home pages to quote more socially inclined economist John Maynard Keynes's claim that the world is "ruled by little else" but the ideas of economists and political philosophers, "both when they are right and when they are wrong." In the concluding paragraph of his *General Theory*, Keynes (1936, chap. 24) went on to blame, in semijest, the elite for believing economists. He wrote that ostensibly "practical" business leaders became "slaves of some defunct economist." Government leaders were even more dangerous: "Madmen in authority, who hear voices in the air, are distilling their frenzy from some academic scribbler of a few years back." British prime minister Winston Churchill allegedly once despaired: "If you put two economists in a room, you get two opinions, unless one of them is Lord Keynes, in which case you get three."

Among other economists warning against being taken too seriously, Cambridge University's Joan Robinson (1978, 75) advocated studying economics, which was a mix of propaganda and science, "to avoid being deceived by economists." Yet financial pundits, government leaders, and megachurch pastors have joined with orthodox economists—follow the gold! Politicians promise greed-made jobs, analysts argue stock upgrades, gossip columnists report super-yachts, and preachers promise prosperity.

Economists raise many internal critiques, but decades of debate only seemed to entrench core assumptions, which infect the ways we all view the world. Speaking at a dinner on December 1, 1988, President Ronald Reagan boasted that his successes "helped prove that economic truth is a lever that can move governments, move history, and truly change the world." A slogan displayed in President Bill Clinton's election campaign headquarters in 1992 reminded staff that it's "THE ECONOMY, STUPID," and the ensuing era of "Clintonomics" concerned "growth," "deficit reduction," "tax reform," "fiscal discipline," "interest rate reduction," "deregulation," "private-sector investment," "removal of tariffs," leading to "recovery" and improved "numbers"—strange words for meal sharing.

Economists might be surprised at being accused of neglecting deliciousness, after-dinner wit, and healthy estuaries . . . responding, what do they have to do with us? That's the point. The discipline detached itself from needy bodies and joyful feasts—from economies, in other words—and publicized a faint outline of just one aspect of a living world, stocked with sights and sighs, textures and texts, and scents and cents. Emaciating economic activities in this way has produced useful data but pushed far too far. Economists took on themselves the mantle of scientists and oversold the political program that contributed to technical innovation, and also riches for the few, household deterioration, democratic decline, cultural crassness, and environmental destruction.

Perhaps their success follows from their neat mathematics, or their cynical view of humanity, but their equations also served powerful interests. Macho economists (it has notoriously remained a largely male profession) have played a pivotal role in the capitalist lunge, borrowing liberal politics so far as it was convenient, and promoting economics as a central concern of politics, which it should be, but not in such a delusory, appetite-free form.

From Politics to Economics, and Back

The original Greek texts, such as Xenophon's *Œconomicus* around 360 BCE, addressed the running of what had later to be specified, tautologically, as the domestic economy. Topics included the social structure of the household, indoor and outdoor tasks, proper behaviors, and guidance on agriculture, health, education, and finance. People soon recognized parallels with other "households," so that theologians and philosophers imagined self-sustaining domains from the human body through the *polis* (city) to God's creation.

Modern economists concentrated increasingly on the market economy and then thinned that to squiggles of supply and demand. "Wealth" had connotations of wellness, well-being, and welfare until, around the time of Adam Smith, finance took over. In further work, economists agreed that value was not intrinsic, not reflective of human labor, but dependent on what individuals would pay. Self-assured experts bobbed before an omnipotent and jealous Market that rewarded the suppliers of what was needed. Pity that leaving it to the Market discounted other values, whether democratic or sustainable, companionable or creative, affective or moral, sensual or intellectual.

With the marginal revolution in the late nineteenth century, mathematics taught not only that lower prices might increase demand, but also that the whole system could approach equilibrium, that is, supply could match demand. In the language of W. Stanley Jevons (1871, vii–viii, 4), the "nature of Wealth and Value" could be considered through "indefinitely small" gains and losses, using the "infinitesimal calculus" of what physicists called statics. This "differential calculus" could be applied to all the "quantitative notions belonging to the daily operations of industry."

That the price system seemed mathematical permitted the illusion of a transcendent political theory. With "rational choice" said to triumph in the Cold War, economics would master everything. For example, rather than treat criminals as violating socially useful laws, they could be viewed as having made rational, profit-seeking choices. Modern economists went further—they not only modeled people *as if* they acted like *Homo economicus*, they expected them to.

And so mainstream economists came to insist, and to institute through government, first, that individuals are universally distinguished by greed. Second, self-interested gain-makers inhabit a price system, a mathematical space of supply and demand. Third, this world is rational; in particular, individuals make rational choices in pursuit of gain. Finally, to establish prices, the world must be plagued by scarcity, so that "growth" (money's expansion) is necessary.

In later chapters I will fill in the deposed gastronomic basis of liberalism and demonstrate the twisting of that into neoliberal politics and plutocratic economics. After examining why these scientists denied basic human needs, I set out what might be done about it. For the present, I investigate the standard assumptions of greed, commodification, rationality, and scarcity.

The Greedy Self-Seeker

In the brilliantly angry movie *Wall Street* (Stone 1987), corporate raider Gordon Gekko enthused: "The point is, ladies and gentleman, that greed—for lack of a better word—is good. Greed is right. Greed works. Greed clarifies, cuts through, and captures the essence of the evolutionary spirit." Gekko became notorious for "Greed is . . . good" but merely repeated a widespread motto. Actual Wall Street traders believed writer-director Oliver Stone modeled Gekko on their colleague Ivan Boesky, who reportedly reassured business students at the University of California, Berkeley, on May 18, 1986: "Greed is all right, by the way. I want you to know that. I think greed is healthy. You can be greedy and still feel good about yourself."

Professional references to "greed" abound: Kenneth Arrow and Frank Hahn wrote in *General Competitive Analysis* (1971, vi–vii) about an "economy motivated by individual greed"; Robert L. Heilbroner (1980, 53) wrote the "market system" could harness people's "self-centered nature" or "greed"; and for philosopher Daniel M. Hausman (1992, 95), "economics studies the consequence of rational greed."

Nevertheless, economists have usually preferred such terms as "self-interest" and, as deserves mention more than once, often misinterpret Adam Smith's sentence in *Wealth of Nations*: "It is not from the benevolence of the butcher, the brewer, or the baker, that we expect our dinner, but from their regard to their own interest" (1.2). The lure of gain did not feature in this introductory section. Rather, Smith wrote of the benefits of the "co-operation and assistance of great multitudes" through the distribution of labor and its products. Far from Smith saying that we expect our dinner from financial greed, he extolled physical sharing. Not that the butcher, brewer, or baker "actually puts dinner on the table," thereby "ignoring cooks, maids, wives, and mothers," historian of economic ideas Nancy Folbre (2009, 59) has pointed out.

In glorifying greed, economists lined up humans for the fate of Midas. Granted his wish that everything he touched turned to gold, King Midas ordered a celebratory feast. His food hardened and lost any taste. Drink became metallic ice. Two and half thousand years ago, philosopher Aristotle (*Politics* 1257b) commented: "what a ridiculous kind of wealth is that which even in abundance will not save you from dying with hunger!" Accordingly, when Donald Trump and Robert Kiyosaki entitled their get-rich airport book *The Midas Touch* (2011), they displayed more knowledge of selling than of Greek mythology. At least King Midas repented (Ovid, *Metamorphoses XI*), whereupon his river still carried a little gold in the more fundamentally valuable alluvium.

Rationality Unbound

Vincent van Gogh only ever sold one work, *The Red Vineyard*, painted near Arles in the south of France. His lifetime earnings were therefore recently estimated as $1,600 in current dollars. Judged by the Market, he was a mediocre artist. After his death he became a genius, because at least seven of his paintings have sold for around $100 million each. Try multiplying such a figure over his 2,100 artworks, including 860 oil paintings: Vincent van Gogh is notionally far wealthier than Bill Gates. Shakespeare's sales would make J. K. Rowling appear a poverty-stricken no-hoper. And to think of Mozart's royalties. . . .

Such examples might sound fanciful, but they are rational, and thinking like an economist. Rationality suggests the reliance on logical deduction, or at least consistency with starting assumptions. It implies cold reasoning; that is, lacking in feeling. Which is to say that rationality might be reasonable, but, to choose another word carefully, it's not sensible. Rationality is nonsensical—not using the senses. Rationality cannot match the mass of empirical, affective, hedonistic, and commonsense knowledge, communicated and improved through honest conversation.

The denial of taste and pleasure is contained in the word's origins, given that "rational" relates to "ration," which, from the Latin, is food and drink kept to a calculated *rate*, vanquishing sensuality and congeniality. Is it rational to prefer pears to apples? Is it rational to fall in love? How rational is it to "earn" many times a living wage from returns on shares purchased when mother sold grandfather's factories? The most rational compensation could well be paying every citizen exactly the same.

Money seems rational, being numerical, and so lacking all qualities of actual bread, dough, bacon, gravy, lettuce, or lolly, to borrow some slang. Money being rational, economists use deduction, mathematics, and game theory, as opposed to common experience. Mainstream economists also call behavior rational when highly purposeful, especially profit-oriented. Law-like relationships, geometric curves, and algebraic symbols might look like this:

$$m_{mf} + f_{mf} \equiv Z_{mf} \geq Z_{m0} + Z_{0f}$$

Taken from Gary Becker's Nobel-worthy paper, "A Theory of Marriage" (1976, 210), this shows "a necessary condition for marriage."

In his classic discussion of the *Nature and Significance of Economic Science*, Lionel Robbins (1932, 141) extolled his "branch of knowledge which, above all others, is the symbol and safeguard of rationality in social arrangements." Censuring the old fogies still addressing "the causes of material welfare," he advocated the modern "different ratios of valuation" (4, 15). Writing on the epistemology of economics, Robbins's colleague Ludwig von Mises (1966, 19; 1981, 17, 97) claimed that economic rationality provided a comprehensive science of human action, because it was aprioristic, that is, reasoned from a basic principle. As he put it, the "theorems of economics are derived not from the observation of facts, but through deduction from the fundamental category of action," namely, from the "economic principle (i.e., the necessity to economize)," sometimes also known as the "value principle or as the cost principle." For an "appetite for food and warmth" to be purposive, it required calculations—"rational action and economic action are therefore co-incident." He was definite: "All rational action is economic. All economic activity is rational action."

Rationality demolishes itself, inexorably, because no logical conclusion is better than its premises, as Mises unintentionally just demonstrated. Assuming survival-of-the-fittest opportunism, it becomes rational to create a demand, find a loophole, exploit some weakness, cut corners, build in obsolescence, hide a flaw, gild the truth, find cheaper workers, disrupt politics, and race to oblivion.

The so-called Laffer curve provided rational justification for trickle-down or supply-side Reaganomics, including cutting tax rates for the rich. Its name comes from a meeting at the Two Continents restaurant in the grand old Hotel Washington, around the corner from the White House, in 1974. Memories have been disputed, but the gist is that two presidential aides at the time, Donald Rumsfeld and Dick Cheney, dined with Arthur Laffer, who was a University of Southern California economist. Laffer sketched a bell curve on a napkin showing that, at one end, a tax rate of 100 percent would so discourage taxable income that it yielded zero tax, as would a tax rate of 0 percent. The trick was finding the rate

FIGURE 2.1 The napkin that changed the world (mock-up of Laffer curve). Photo by author.

somewhere on the bulge that maximized revenue, with an asymmetric curve bulging toward the left (cut tax rates) or the right (tax the rich).

Exposing this and other "dead ideas" that refuse to give up, skeptical economist John Quiggin reported in *Zombie Economics* (2010, 142) that the ensuing tax cuts made the rich richer, without significant trickling down. Nevertheless, agreeing that a 100 percent tax would halt "economic activity," the University of Queensland professor still pronounced the Laffer curve "correct." This was only "correct" in some esoteric way. Quiggin assumed that all "economic activity" aimed at piling up ingots. In reality, even with a 100 percent tax rate, people still must eat and will desperately find a way. Marx and others have spoken of the "natural economy"—that not involving money. "A society can no more cease to produce than it can cease to consume," Marx wrote in *Das Kapital* (*Capital*, 1.6.23). Disengaging from taxable income, people might resort to home production, the black economy, barter (as some accounts of the curve accept), hiding income offshore, or communism. Government policy makers should pay more attention to Laffer's napkin than his sketch.

The main alternative to rationality is real-world observation, although, when economists conduct experiments, they might count pigeon pecks. By keeping pigeons' "deprivation level" (body weight) constant, a team found that "nonhuman workers (pigeons) are willing to trade off income for leisure if the price is right." More specifically, the pigeons demonstrated that "the Slutsky-substitution effect is positive for (exactly) compensated wage decreases, and that leisure is a normal good at all points in the choice space" (Battalio, Green, and Kagel 1981). Poor pigeons.

Price signals bringing supply and demand into equilibrium is a reasonable starting point but provokes screeds of qualifications. In imagining functional relationships, economists devise rules "naïvely," as Karl Polanyi put it (1957, 243–44). He warned that the concept of a self-adjusting Market was a "stark utopia," soon "annihilating the human and natural substance of society," physically destroying people and their surroundings (1944, 3). Claims of rational economic science have also been pooh-poohed in-house by Deirdre McCloskey (1983, 483), whose classic paper called out her colleagues' modernism, as she termed their mathematical disputation, and urged more literary methods to improve the "rhetoric," or "exploring thought by conversation." French exponent Thomas Piketty, author of best-selling *Capital in the Twenty-First Century* (2014, 32), admitted his colleagues' "childish passion" for mathematics and theoretical speculation was "an easy way of acquiring the appearance of scientificity" by people who actually "know almost nothing about anything."

"How could we have got things so wrong?" asked historian of double-entry bookkeeping Jane Gleeson-White (2011, 5). She found that "our world is governed by numbers generated by the accounts of nations and corporations. And yet these numbers are arbitrary, illusory. So how did we come to depend on these fallible beacons to direct our policies, institutions, economies, society?" To posit an answer: economic reasoning tied society to money-maxing. Fascinated by how "ideologists turn everything upside-down," Marx and Engels (*German Ideology*, 1.1.C.nn.) observed: "The judge, for example, applies the code, he therefore regards legislation as the real active driving force."

A tailor takes a tape across the shoulders and around the waist, but the suit is more than measurements—the ultrafine merino wool, subtle color, sit of the lapel, neatness of the stiches, the embodiment of ambition, romance, and so on. And that's just to dress for dinner. Knowing how many to expect is helpful. Price can help assemble the makings—things are often cheapest when in season. But the economists' haggling algorithm is not reality, nor are supply curves, bottom lines, spikes in demand, bubbles, charts, incentives, salient metrics, and (turned into a noun) spends, however cleverly manipulated by quants (quantitative analysts). No ecologist would claim that a count of species—or relationships between selected measurements—was actually *the* ecology. Self-proclaimed economists naïvely pushed a utopian template.

"Growth" in the Face of Scarcity

The "insatiability of man and the niggardliness of nature" were identified by a trio of Yale University professors as the foundation stones of economics (Fairchild, Furniss, and Buck 1926, 8). Neatly redirecting the emphasis from human greed to natural *scarcity*, Lionel Robbins (1932, 14–15) issued this often-borrowed definition: "Economics is the science which studies human behaviour as a relationship between ends and scarce means which have alternative uses." In his text of 1932, met earlier in this chapter, he further declared scarcity to be an "almost ubiquitous condition of human behaviour." He contrasted the "air which we breathe," whose "comparative abundance" made it relatively free, with time. "There are only twenty-four hours in the day. We have to choose between the different uses to which they may be put." For Robbins, scarcity gained cosmic significance. "The material means of achieving ends are limited. We have been turned out of Paradise." This scarcity made for "the unity of subject of Economic Science." Rational economics required the so-called economic problem of scarcity because, with everything available in Paradise for no effort, nothing would command a price.

The ideology of competitive scramble upended widespread belief in plenty. Religious teachers have long said we live amid abundance. Do not be anxious, Jesus said, for the birds of the air do not sow and reap, and yet their heavenly father feeds them (Matthew 6:26). Ancient Greek philosopher Aristotle emphasized early in *Politics* (1932, 1256a, 1257a) that the property required "to give self-sufficiency for a good life is not limitless." It could be handled by economics (*oikonomia*). A separate study was required for chrematistics or money-making (*chrematistika*), which did not accept limits. As Aristotle knew, seemingly more clearly back then, the "technique of exchange," and he gave the example of wine for corn, "is not contrary to nature and is not a form of money-making [chrematistics]; for it keeps to its original purpose: to re-establish nature's own equilibrium of self-sufficiency."

Philosopher Thomas Hobbes might notoriously have called life in nature "nasty, brutish, and short," but he found *"Plenty"* in seventeenth-century England, adding that "this Nutriment, consisting in Animals, Vegetals, and Minerals, God hath freely layd them before us, in or near to the face of the Earth; so as there needeth no more but the labour, and industry of receiving them" (*Leviathan* chap. 24). Citing the New Testament (1 Timothy 6:17), John Locke declared: "God has given us all things richly," and as to the reason, "To enjoy" (*Treatises* 2.5.31). Natural resources are unquestionably *limited*, including Robbins's "air which we breathe." But finitude is not necessarily scarcity. Meat is limited, so cooks apportion carefully. Importantly, nature replenishes, so that scarcity might be the last thing on cottagers' minds during a glut of plums.

A finite resource becomes "scarce," nonetheless, through instability— whether seasonal or from overpopulation, incompetence, war, plunder, deliberate policy, monopoly, hoarding, or opportunism. One Nobel-winning economist with a social justice bent, Amartya Sen, studied starvation during market booms, such as the Bengal famine of 1943, which he experienced as a boy, and which killed between 1.5 and 4 million people. Was it scarcity that killed them? During an economic boom? His explanation: "Market demands are not reflections of biological needs or psychological desires, but choices based on exchange entitlement relations. If one doesn't have much to exchange, one can't demand very much" (1981, 161).

The tyranny of "scarcity" might ensure prices, but power adjusts them. The De Beers company restricted the supply of diamonds (abundant in nature) through the twentieth century to maintain high prices. More generally, scarcity comes and goes, depending where profits are to be made. When prices collapsed internationally in 2008, the banks, after lending imprudently, were deemed "too big to fail," so governments propped them up. When governments borrowed, lenders became prudent and demanded higher interest rates. Agencies rejected the "demand-side" solution of helping ordinary families, stimulating demand, in favor of austerity, and the slowdown rocketed youth unemployment, reaching 50 percent in Spain, 60 percent in Greece, and 20 percent in the United States. Reckless bankers had made an example of democratic resistance. Under an ideology of shortages, the struggle for resources appears inevitable, poverty a permanent presence, armaments necessary, and the pursuit of power desperate. In such ways, scarcity stories are self-fulfilling.

Ultimately, the most delusional consequence of ideological scarcity is the perpetual *more*. Greedy players must maximize, so that, even when not studying the "maximization of *money gains*," economics still assumes the "maximization of *net advantages*" (Robbins 1932, 88) or, in a later definition, "maximizing behavior" (Becker 1976, 5). "More" can sound positive, like super-sizing the Whopper, Big Mac, and Family-Size Coke. But markets expand with more people. Difficulties?—growth will solve them. Pollution?—growth to the rescue. "Growth" is one of modern economists' most successfully misused words, suggesting life, while maximizing destruction. Eternal increase slanders real growers in their fields and gardens. An orchard does not "grow" by marching across the countryside. The word "grow" shares linguistic origins with "grass" and "green," but economists helped destroy such characteristics.

Fighting a war can stimulate industrial activity, or, failing that, creating enemies can stimulate an arms race. Selling water in throwaway plastic bottles can appear economically beneficial, as can expanding the range of trashy snacks and replacing breast milk, available in the home, with powdered cow's milk. The common indicator of "economic development," gross domestic product (GDP), estimates how far vital activities have been sucked into the capitalist sphere. Simon Kuznets (1934, 5–6), who would win a Nobel Prize for his "empirically founded interpretation of economic growth," warned the U.S. Congress in 1934 that a "characterization becomes dangerous" when parameters were not clearly stated; and that the "definiteness" of measurements was misleading. Such indicators as GDP, he cautioned, were "subject to this type of illusion and resulting abuse," especially because they dealt with controversial matters. He gave the still highly pertinent example of totaling incomes, which hid maldistribution. Economists have lately been readier to accept indicators of environmental quality and social "well-being" (OECD 2015). A happiness measure can be influential but still treats the world as formulas.

Giving a coal-mining project the go-ahead might be "good for the economy" in some short-sighted, chrematistic way, but cancers maximize, bubbles burst, and reckless expansion in a finite world leads to global warming, acidification of the oceans, overfishing, deforestation, soil degradation, mass extinctions, loss of biodiversity, food insecurity. Weirdly, standard economics assumes both scarcity—so that resources have a price—and infinite abundance—permitting unlimited growth.

Theoretically, without a historical imagination, economists are left advocating disruption, product innovation, efficiency, labor cost-reduction, sharper marketing, and territorial invasion. Writing in 1942, entrepreneurial enthusiast Joseph Schumpeter (1976, 84) popularized "the perennial gale of creative destruction," which kept capitalism toppling forward. Although he feared that disruption would self-destruct, and monopoly would make way for socialism, the more all-purpose cry remained "growth" from more "creativity." In political theorist Wendy Brown's (2015, 44) interpretation: "Neoliberalism is the rationality through which capitalism finally swallows humanity."

The realistic alternative to scarcity is *sufficiency*. Water, love, learning, and other "priceless" things are not so much scarce as to be tended. The requirement is not expansion so much as sustainability. Fortunately, where greed is never-ending, appetite can be satisfied. The real test for a decent economics is whether the provision of comfortable physical settings, satisfying food and drink, caring companionship, and sufficient time is in tune with the world.

"When economists get it right, the world gets better," economist Dani Rodrik (2015, 5, 17) has accepted. "Yet economists often fail." Appreciating almost every point in this chapter, Rodrik also exhibited faith in the discipline's expanding library of "abstract, typically mathematical" frameworks or models, which are "both economics' strength and its Achilles' heel." The mistake was choosing inappropriately, so that the model might assume perfect competition, when another reality prevailed. "The correct answer to almost any question in economics is: It depends. Different models, each equally respectable, provide different answers." Rodrik recognized how both formal contributions and informal conversations produced a "guild mentality"—an "echo chamber easily produces overconfidence—in the received wisdom or the model of the day." Yet I question his further claim that financially-expansive economics has no "particular ideological bent" (171, 6).

We can use accounts. It's hazardous, that's all, when mere price signals play more than a minor part in companionable thriving.

The Price of Everything, and the Value of Nothing

Boxes of knobbly, round, and elongated potatoes, some pale-colored, some patchy, and others red, crowd a long bench. This is a market, to which economists swear devotion. Yet they have oddly little to say, professionally, about waxy or floury eating qualities, or suitability for baking, boiling, mashing, or frying. They do not question the stallholder about soil or season, nor their family's well-being. Not to remain silent, economists might note that the supermarket down the road is more expensive, or wonder about the financial structure of the industry or tax rates. They could predict a price rise, if production were to fall or demand rise. They certainly exalt prices chalked on the boxes as the new enforcers.

For economists, the world is a flurry of dollar signs, mixed with yuan, yen, euro, dram, franc, peso, krone, gourde. If economists catch sight of what appears to be food—pork bellies, live cattle, soybeans, coffee, sugar . . .—it is a commodity. The value of land is abstracted. Even people turn into populations, occupations, and percentages. As Joan Robinson

(1933, 1) admitted, someone inquiring about ticket prices would find it "a poor comfort to be told that it will depend upon the relative concavities of the demand curves."

Early on, money took tangible form in cowry shells, later rare metals, then coins, notes, and IOUs, all of which the digital age has confirmed are unnecessary. So what is money? Many thinkers—from before Adam Smith through Karl Marx to Georg Simmel, John Maynard Keynes, Friedrich Hayek, Keith Hart, and beyond—have endeavored to pin down receipts and deceits.

Following earlier, and more sensible, Enlightenment liberals, I understand money as having entered economies as a replacement for physical sustenance. With economies held together by the circulation of food and drink, money arose as a flexible intermediary. Traders no longer had to directly exchange chickens for apples. The earliest states' reliance on food tithes, tributes, and distributions gave way to money taxation and payment. Eventually, money turned into a frightening antithesis of food, given how its preservative qualities enabled accumulation. Gold and silver treasures did not "decay and perish," unlike John Locke's more evanescent "food, raiment, and carriage." But there's still nothing there, physically—just a "fancy or agreement" (*Treatises* 2.5.46, 50). Food is perishable; whereas money's rational solidity, backed by fiat or algorithm, ensures its shelf-life is theoretically eternal. Food is tricky to accumulate (mold and mice get at it); whereas money stacks up. Money is so metaphysical that it cannot be seen, smelled, or touched but can be counted, enjoying the certainty of sums. Wrongly associated with grubbiness, money is an unsullied force. As perfectly as $2 + 2 = 4$, its tokens grant wishes.

Money as a means of exchange brought more and more items onto the market, until economists egged on *commodification*. As economic historian Karl Polanyi (1977, 10) wrote, even labor and land have been "treated *as if* they had been produced for sale," and the audacity of this step, requiring major government intervention, could be gauged, he said, by remembering that "labor is only another name for [people], and land for nature." Commodification is money's grab for power, eroding the commons, public service, and civility.

Now education is sold, pollution rights are traded, genes are patented, human organs are trafficked, and surrogacy bought. Train passengers, hospital patients, and university students are "customers," and corporations reintroduce road tolls. Chicago practitioner Gary Becker (1981) opened up orthodox economics to something previously as priceless as love, pointing to the marriage "market." With everything, including your movements and other personal data, having a price, everything becomes manipulable. The price system is a highly rarefied meal reflection, restructuring power relations, so that money greases gross inequality, estrangement within nature, and the capture of the state. Aiding the sophisticated division of food and its labor, money's ubiquity cries out for caution. It is a symbol, with no materiality.

Whereas food might be judged on taste, satisfaction, nutrition, and cultural benefit, no one can live on money until it is exchanged back into nourishment. To quote Karl Marx (1977, 123): "If I long for a particular dish . . . , money fetches me the dish . . . that is, it converts my wishes from something in the realm of the imagination, . . . into their sensuous, actual existence."

Money would seem to be pinned to *value*, although the nature of value has remained elusive. Perhaps value is intrinsic—think of land, or maybe gold. But then value can also respond to the amount of labor required—the labor theory of value. Perhaps value measures usefulness. Given that diamonds are essentially useless, and water cheap (until scarce), Adam Smith supplemented use-value with exchange value. Establishing Market value, economists shunted use-value off as the purchaser's "subjective" desire for "utility." Circling back, we find that money measures utility, and then money is value.

Given that price eclipses all, economists have neglected other values—whether religious, political, ethical, nutritional, hedonistic, or aesthetic. In elevating price to the "common denominator of all values," to quote German sociologist Georg Simmel (1971, 330), money "hollows out the core of things, their peculiarities and their uniqueness." To borrow from English playwright Oscar Wilde, economists know "the price of everything and the value of nothing" (*Lady Windermere's Fan*, 1892, Act 2).

People agree to the make-believe, backed by force, of money. Being so conveniently banked, loaned, stolen, and transmitted (and faked), money grants an exquisite means to order people about, including by purchasing their labor, or not. Social power has been wielded through persuasion, through physical force, and, latterly, through a fierce but "invisible" hand. Money has proved handy, economically, but its use has gone well beyond a joke. In viewing the world as a system of prices, chrematistic economists have not merely simplified daringly, they have also prioritized one specific enforcer.

Economists boosted a brave new world of the "cash nexus," a phrase credited to Scottish essayist Thomas Carlyle. Writing on "laissez-faire" in *Chartism* (1840, 61), he deplored: "Cash Payment has become the sole nexus of man to men!" In 1843 Carlyle rejected the new "Gospel of Mammonism": "We call it a Society; and go about professing openly the totalest separation, isolation. Our life is not a mutual helpfulness; but rather, cloaked under due laws-of-war, named 'fair competition' and so forth, it is a mutual hostility. We have profoundly forgotten everywhere that *Cash-payment* is not the sole relation of human beings." People now believed that the cash system "absolves and liquidates all engagements of man," he wrote. A rich mill-owner might shrug: "My starving workers? . . . Did not I hire them fairly in the market? Did I not pay them, to the last sixpence, the sum covenanted for? What have I to do with them more?" Carlyle was dismayed: "Verily Mammon-worship is a melancholy creed" (87).

In delightfully sarcastic tone, in 1850, Carlyle (1860, 57) assured "Respectable Professors of the Dismal Science" that the "Laws of the Shop-till are indisputable to me: and practically useful in certain departments of the Universe, as the multiplication table itself." Economists were making the Universe, "wholly a Shop." Carlyle objected that "the chief end of man being now, in these improved epochs, to make money and spend it, his interests in the Universe have become amazingly simplified. . . . 'To buy in the cheapest market, and sell in the dearest.' "

In recent years, as neoliberalism confirmed the "invisible hand" as supreme ruler, commanding the entire globe, capitalism multiplied its strength through financial accumulation, sovereign wealth funds, and money-managing elites—so-called financialization, which shifted capital from both redistribution and production into debts and bets.

On May 5, 2019, the *New York Times* reported how one bad bet of a lone Norwegian futures trader "shook the world's financial system." The near-miss was arguably saved by the expansion of "central counterparties"— more than eighty clearinghouses worldwide, intended to protect against contagious, global losses. In one year, according to the report, the large London Clearing House processed contracts that covered "the risk of a quadrillion dollars' worth of derivatives trading—that's a thousand trillion dollars. By comparison, the total annual economic output of everyone on the planet is worth about $80 trillion" (Ewing and Schreuer 2019).

Economists imagine that such ferocious capitalism exerts a more peaceful push than armed gangs and the state. Individuals seek gain by serving others, or so the theory goes. However, capitalism might often more accurately be portrayed as perfect exploitation. That is, people might be not so much rational dynamos as manipulated through purse strings, often forced to work inordinately, and eat badly. Capitalism uses the market, not the other way around. With money substituting for food, "Life itself appears only as a means to life," as Marx put it (1977, 68). The "absolute means" of money becomes the "absolute purpose," as Simmel explored (1982, 232). Fantasizing that "money itself *is* a good. . . . We tolerate fabulous capitalists who think a bet on a debt is an asset," U.S. farmer-poet Wendell Berry wrote (2010, 55).

Accelerating over the past two centuries, the enormous press of money-making has reshaped the world, often in useful, progressive ways. The elevation of "freedom," "rationality," and "property" as heavenly truths might have played a part lately in reducing sexism and racism, opening up definitions of the family, and bringing humanity closer to one world. However, Market aggression has eroded "equality" and so democracy and social welfare, along with natural supports.

Money's mirrored funhouse has twisted our language. *Growth* no longer suggests greenery. *Wealth* has lost linguistic ties with well, weal, wellness, and welfare. The *market* as a distributor of nutrients and associated goods, services, relationships, and pleasures has become a lever of power.

In its Latin origins, and lasting into the nineteenth century, *competition* was "seeking together," although Adam Smith already used the rivalrous sense. *Profit* has become a specific accomplishment. *Redistribution* seems only to mean robbing the rich to pay the poor. The word *liberalism* has been systematically deprived of its material moorings. "Liberal" once meant "befitting a free man"—that is, a person with economic responsibilities both as a citizen and as head of a household. That person was more likely renowned for generosity than merely looking after themselves. Above all, *economy*, once the running of a home, applied to other "homes" and then rose up into merely capitalism.

In this book I object not just to the lust for money but to its capture and overvaluation. Money-directed processes, such as commodification, rationalization, fetishism, alienation, and financialization, undermine meals. And with that, they have colonized our language, and so us. Such forces go terribly wrong because, to amend the classics (1 Timothy 6:10), it's the love of money *more than meals* that's the root of evil, and no one is more infatuated than the Market makers. Despite Market metaphysicians' self-presentation as hard-nosed realists, they proved themselves idealists of high-flying capitalist rule.

Embedding Economies?

Other social scientists have frequently chastised economists for their blinkers. Critics have borrowed Karl Polanyi's complaint (e.g., 1944, 57) that the economy is necessarily *embedded* in society. They say that, for example, the market's very existence relies on social matrices of trust, convention, and formal law. I have some sympathy for the economists, however. From the dining table, economic considerations appear fundamental. Certainly, the market economy requires laws, but lawmakers must eat. Laws are based in society, but society has to provide meals, which necessitates an economic base—"economic" in a full sense. All cognition, culture, social action, and political negotiation must ultimately be embedded in the productive interchange with nature.

The real mistake has been to think of one, single *"the* economy," narrowing concern to money, particularly the Market. Economists have talked of only one "invisible hand"—prices—and yet society relies on a plethora of hands—the hand rocking the cradle, dab hand at cooking, handiwork of God, hands on deck, charity handouts, handshakes, and lending a hand. Even the originator of the "invisible hand" phrase, Adam Smith, wrote about another, nonmarket example. In the *Theory of Moral Sentiments* (1759, 4.1.10), he found that the "proud and unfeeling landlord" still had only the same basic needs as his magnificent estate's poorest laborers. Since his "stomach bears no proportion to the immensity of his desires," once he had taken his share of life's necessities, he left much of the earth's bounty for his people. The fantasy of opulence had led the lordly master as by "an invisible hand" to leave his dependents a share, thereby advancing the interests of society, "without intending it, without knowing it."

Polanyi (1944, 249) actually revised his "embeddedness" argument later in the same work, saying that the "true criticism of market society is not that it was based on economics—in a sense, every and any society must be based on it—but that its economy was based on self-interest."

Also taking up the "self-interest" complaint, anthropologists and sociologists have found mainstream economics to be individualistic. Even the most selfish individual depends on long-established languages and techniques; and government is unavoidable, even if only to ensure security, property rights, contracts, regulations, and picking up the pieces. Young, old, infirm, and nonrational individuals require domestic and political support.

Again, I have some sympathy with the economists. Individuals have a fundamental responsibility to themselves. Eating and drinking might be shaped by norms or status, but social and cultural factors emerge from the "natural law" of self-preservation. It's just that individuals look after themselves best by joining with others. This paradox, which underpins much of the discussion, returns explicitly as the "diner's knot" in chapter 8.

Economic theorists of most stripes have accepted, at least initially, that individual interest is best served through cooperation. According to hardline belief, selfishness binds individuals tightly through the Market. The real problem was that mainstream practitioners forgot that their "methodological individualism" was only a method, not a prescription. Worse, as I show later, they adopted such an alienated "individualism" that it applied to corporations more accurately than persons.

In truth, economic science is far from monolithic, and nonmainstream or "heterodox" schools have included Marxists, Schumpeterians, Keynesians, feminists, environmentalists, complexity theorists, and personalists. Seeking to distance themselves from capitalist apologetics, some continue under the rubric "political economy"; and so-called institutional economists study some social aspects.

New York Times economics columnist Paul Krugman (2014) accepted the usefulness of an "idealized vision of capitalism, in which individuals are always rational and markets always function perfectly," although "starting in the 1980s it became harder and harder to publish anything questioning these idealized models in major journals." In a manifesto, economics students protested against the "dramatic narrowing of the curriculum" under which economics was "often presented as a unified body of knowledge" (ISIPE 2014). By 2016 even economists at the International Monetary Fund admitted that core recommendations of global capital freedom and enforced government austerity had worsened inequality (Ostry, Loungani, and Furceri 2016). Before a short-lived stint as chief economist at the World Bank, Paul Romer (2015; 2016, 15) called out fellow macroeconomists for burying inconvenient assumptions beneath mathematical modeling. He mocked the "mathiness" hiding the equivalent of gremlins, trolls, and phlogiston. Theorists got away with it, he suggested, by possessing tremendous self-confidence, belonging to an unusually monolithic community, and shutting themselves off from other experts. Lately, amid mounting disciplinary turmoil, progressive economists have banded together under such labels as "Economics for Inclusive Prosperity."

Few internal critics would have denied that, since the 1970s, mainstream or "neoclassical" practitioners had provided world-shaping intellectual cover for the neoliberal putsch. Even these questioners inadvertently demonstrated chrematistics' pervasive grip. In Krugman's lines just quoted, he appeared to accept that a market might be in some way "perfect," rather than intrinsically messy, and life-giving. The protesting students accepted that "maths and statistics are crucial to our discipline" (ISIPE 2014), forgetting that Adam Smith's venerated tome included a sprinkling of pounds signs but certainly no differential equations. The IMF economists warned that inequality slowed "growth."

Borrowing from psychological sciences, behavioral economists feared selfish calculations "crowd out" higher motivations. Recognizing people are not "entirely self-interested and amoral," Samuel Bowles (2016, 1–5) warned that the assumption of self-interest, while aimed at "perfecting" markets, might actually make markets "work less well" and corrode "civic-mindedness." In *The Moral Economy: Why Good Incentives Are No Substitute for Good Citizens*, Bowles gave an example from Haifa (Israel), where imposing fines on parents for late day-care pick-ups transformed lateness into "just another commodity," so parents "purchased" more, and lateness increased. Worse, abandoning fines had no immediate effect, the introduction of market principles having "undermined the parents' sense of ethical obligation to avoid inconveniencing the teachers." But what to do? Some proposals to balance selfishness with a social commitment have tended toward the authoritarian, by overrating love of country, civic virtues, or communitarian rights.

Confirming that financial competition can become self-fulfilling, in an often-quoted paper, "Does Studying Economics Inhibit Cooperation?," three New York researchers (one economist and two psychologists) confirmed that "exposure to the self-interest model commonly used in economics" seemed to make "economists behave in more self-interested ways" (Frank, Gilovich, and Regan 1993, 159). Yet there was hope. The researchers argued that experimental games, such as the prisoner's dilemma, turn out differently once the players were assured that everyone would cooperate so as to maximize everyone's returns. Their conclusion: "With an eye toward both the social good and the well-being of their own students, economists may wish to stress a broader view of human motivation in their teaching" (170–71).

While this chapter's criticisms of economics have been raised elsewhere, and often by economists, I want in this book to make a perhaps surprise sally, throwing a sweet *bombe*, demanding the meal-lovers' economies back, and, with that, the study of living, breathing, eating individuals, who make and share meals in a respiring, photosynthesizing world. In comparison with high finance and big industry, meals might feel modest, "merely" scrabbling in the soil, steaming vegetables, lifting spoons, laughing. But don't be fooled—actual economies revolve around family tables, market counters, city banqueting halls, sacrificial altars, farms and factories, ports and palaces, all within the ripe sufficiency of paradise. Liberalism starts from self-interest, but sustenance sharing brings individual interests gratifyingly together.

Why?

Throughout the second half of the twentieth century, *The Worldly Philosophers* "lured" tens of thousands of students into courses in economics, its author Robert Heilbroner confessed in his final preface in 1999. First publishing in 1953, Heilbroner (1980, 11–12, 14) introduced the "great economic thinkers," who had shaped and swayed people's minds and thereby "shaped and swayed the world." They had pursued "an inquiry as exciting— and as dangerous—as any the world has ever known." They had discovered how people created material wealth and "trod on the toes of [their] neighbor to gain a share of it".

Acceptance of the competitive market, given that society "hangs by a hair," had required "nothing short of a revolution." Economists had had to persuade people to "abandon . . . security for the dubious and perplexing workings of the market system." It was "hard to wring a livelihood from the surface of this planet." Nevertheless, whereas "primitive society" had looked the "spectre of starvation . . . in the face every day," advanced society lacked "this tangible pressure of the environment" (Heilbroner 1980, 16–17, 19). Historically, as gathering and hunting societies lost out to pyramid-building states, the management of material life moved to the "new force of Command," meaning autocratic rule. Then, gaining the acquisitive drive and markets, the modern "social order would in time be called *capitalism*; its means of organizing material life an *economy*, and its new explanation system *economics*" (1999, 312–13).

Far from their proclaimed worldliness, Heilbroner's pie-in-the-sky philosophers were actually in awe of "Order and Design . . . Consistent Laws and Principles." His succession of heroes—an admirable range of voices (albeit all male), including Adam Smith, David Ricardo, Karl Marx, Thorstein Veblen, John Maynard Keynes, and Joseph Schumpeter—had transformed a "humdrum or a chaotic world" into an "ordered society" (1980, 14).

So why had economists done it? Heilbroner (1999, 313) was typically to the point, accepting in his seventh edition that "the worldly philosophy is the child of capitalism and could not exist without it." Karl Marx had used colorful language, referring to "hired prize fighters" (*Capital*, afterword). No less an authority than Chicago's Gary Becker (1976, 11) confirmed why economists danced to dollars. This winner of the Sveriges Riksbank Prize in Economic Sciences in Memory of Alfred Nobel declared:

> There is no obvious reason why intellectuals would be less concerned with personal rewards, more concerned with social well-being, or more intrinsically honest than others.
>
> It then follows from the economic approach that an increased demand by different interest groups or constituencies for particular intellectual arguments and conclusions would stimulate an increased supply of these arguments.

Becker was not writing particularly about economists, but he had just recommended applying his economic approach "relentlessly and unflinchingly" (5).

So there we have it: economists meet demand. Maximizing their own selfish rewards, they supply rational arguments for greed. Economists have been feted by the likes of Sir Antony Fisher, who made his fortune by introducing battery chickens to Britain. Inspired by reading and meeting Friedrich Hayek, Fisher did not enter politics; instead he set out to sway opinion by establishing think-tanks throughout the world, starting with the Institute of Economic Affairs in London in 1955. Money wants the economists who want money.

Blowing away the gold dust, economics must start afresh, or at least resume from where capitalism took over. It means reimagining people as wanting not rational gain but table-pleasure, not rewards and expenditures but complex communities, not disposable resources but a precious world. Devotion to vegetable plots, laden benches, enticing spreads, and conversations regrounds the "incomparably powerful tool for understanding society." Economics is fundamental—that's why it's been captured by money and must come back. It *is* the economy, stupid—and that means meals.

In the next chapter I introduce meals advocate Jean Anthelme Brillat-Savarin. He wrote when "economists" were drifting from political economics. Not enraptured by the profit dream-world, Brillat-Savarin preferred to make, share, taste, relish, and discuss reality. Unlike many contemporaries, he remained convinced that appetite (not greed) was good. His unparalleled classic of gastronomy, *Physiology of Taste*, published in Paris in 1825, contains delightful aphorisms, evocative anecdotes, and a stylish example of a more full-blooded, liberal economics that makes the neoliberal version look thin indeed.

3

BRILLAT-SAVARIN'S QUEST FOR TABLE-PLEASURE

"... and You Will Behold Wonders"

"For a long time now you've been boasting of your *fondues* . . . , and you always keep our mouths watering. We must put a stop to this. The captain and I are coming around." And so Doctor Dubois, who would have been aged seventy-eight, and his brother, seventy-six, arrived at ten sharp one morning in 1801 at their relative's apartment in the center of Paris. They were spry and healthy, freshly shaven, their hair well-powdered, and they found the white linen set with two dozen deliciously fresh oysters and a golden lemon, with a bottle of Sauternes at each end. After the oysters, their host organized *rognons à la brochette* (grilled kidneys), *une caisse de foie gras aux truffes* (truffled goose liver in pastry), and then the fondue (Brillat-Savarin, §76).[1]

The host had picked up the fondue recipe in Switzerland in 1794, when fleeing postrevolutionary violence: beat eggs well in a saucepan and add one-third their weight of grated Gruyère cheese and one-sixth as much butter; put the saucepan on a lively fire and turn the contents with a spatula until thick and soft; add salt according to the age of the cheese and a good amount of pepper; finally, "serve it on a gently heated plate; call for the best wine, which will be roundly drunk, and you will behold wonders."

The phrase "you will behold wonders" has become one of the celebrated phrases in the gastronomic classic *Physiologie du goût* (*Physiology of Taste*), published in 1825 by that day's host, Jean Anthelme Brillat-Savarin (1755–1826). He revealed the fondue recipe in a section entitled "Varieties 16" and described the lunch in meditation 14, "On the pleasure of the table." Brillat-Savarin also used "*on verra merveilles*" to sum up the effect of a favorite tuna recipe, the Curé's Omelet: "Let it be floated downward on a fine old wine, and you will behold wonders" (varieties 1).

After some fresh and candied fruits, a cup of real mocha coffee and two kinds of liqueur, Brillat-Savarin led the brothers on a tour of his spacious apartment, inspecting his guns, musical instruments, first editions, reproductions of ancient sculptures, a bust and miniature of renowned beauty Madame Récamier (another relative, and wife of a professor of medicine), and such new-fangled kitchen gadgets as the economical stockpot, roasting shell, clockwork spit, and steamer.

They returned to the dining room as the clock struck two, the guests remembering that their sister expected them home at the already unfashionably early dinner hour of three P.M. But Brillat-Savarin prevailed on them, sent a messenger across the River Seine, and exchanged a word with his master cook, who enlisted the help of neighboring restaurateurs. Dinner included two novelties lately imported by Prince Talleyrand, who would soon employ illustrious chef Marie-Antoine Carême. These were Parmesan cheese to go with the soup and a glass of dry Madeira. Rather than piquet (a card game), they preferred a nap, and then conversed over another new experience for the old men, cups of tea. Was anyone bored? No, because the guests watched the making of the fondue, toured the apartment, and made food discoveries. In turn, the doctor passed on Parisian genealogy and gossip, and the captain reminisced about Italy.

"Long practice has taught me that one pleasure leads to another, and that once headed along this path a person loses the power of refusal," Brillat-Savarin observed, and so he called for lemons, sugar, and rum to concoct a bowl of punch, which the old men had never experienced either, and for some beautifully thin, delicately buttered, and perfectly salted toasts. Against the brothers' protests, their host called for another plateful. It was after eight o'clock when the old men left to share a bit of salad with their poor sister. They had the sweetest of sleeps and arose refreshed, according to their letter of appreciation.

This was the longest meal that Brillat-Savarin ever ate, its description popped as a bonbon into his reader's mouth for reaching halfway through *Physiology of Taste*. He had just listed twelve requirements for peak table-pleasure. The maximum number of guests should be twelve, so that conversation might remain "general" (everyone sharing the one thread); the room temperature should be between 13 and 16 degrees Réaumur (16–20 degrees Celsius or 61–68 degrees Fahrenheit); the dishes should progress from the most substantial to the lightest; and so on. But that was for fashionable dinner parties, and Brillat-Savarin also appreciated simplicity. Therefore his longest meal illustrated the four minimum requirements for total table-pleasure—"at least passable food, good wine, agreeable companions, and sufficient time." The most careful preparations and sumptuous accessories were to no avail, he knew, "if the wine be bad, the guests assembled without discretion, the faces glum, and the meal consumed in haste" (§76).

Brillat-Savarin sprinkled his classic text with many two- or three-page evocations of, typically, a few simple dishes with wine enjoyed calmly with a few companions at an inn or, frequently, a private house. These anecdotes interlard a series of discussions from the apparently trivial to the deceptively profound—from the "verrition" or sweeping action of the tongue to the sweep of history. Perhaps a little disorganized from decades of work rushed into publication, the book consists of thirty "meditations" on a range of topics, followed by nearly as many miscellaneous scraps entitled "Varieties," encased in some prefatory and linking sections. At first sight, Brillat-Savarin might seem a surprising choice to illustrate the more grounded predecessors of recently high-flying economists. His conversational style might be appropriately convivial, but the mix of wit, anecdote, social observation, and scientific finding has tended to hide his meal-centered theory of economics. More off-putting than his deceptively light touch was that his economics was quickly becoming unrecognizable, as such colleagues as Jean-Baptiste Say promoted antigastronomic rationalization.

In this chapter I show that Brillat-Savarin's *Physiology of Taste* might equally, or even better, have been entitled *Economics of Taste*. That is not

FIGURE 3.1 Poster advertising Brillat-Savarin's 1848 edition in Paris. https://gallica.bnf.fr / Bibliothèque nationale de France.

only because the words "physiology" and "economy" were still largely inter-changeable. More particularly, he established the basis for gastronomic economics. He explicitly started from the *jouissances* or *plaisirs du goût*, the pleasures of taste, which brought people together for *le plaisir de la table*, table-pleasure, whose improvements marked human history. He presented economies as driven by physical appetite, which is satiable, not financial greed, which knows no end. By the time *Economics/Physiology of Taste* appeared in 1825, his lifelong, late-Enlightenment concern with rounded human beings seemed a little old-fashioned. Other economists had switched decisively from corporeal individuals to the moneymaker playing in a mathematical wonderland.

A Full Life

Jean Anthelme Brillat-Savarin was born on April 1, 1755, in a well-to-do family at Belley, an attractive town about 500 kilometers southeast of Paris, on the edge of the Alps. From 1774 he studied law and some medical subjects at Dijon University. As a provincial lawyer, he became mayor of his hometown and was elected to the National Assembly with the Revolution in 1789. He had to flee the Reign of Terror (1793–1794) to the United States, where he spent two years teaching French and playing violin in a theater orchestra. His Stradivarius, made in 1721, is now known as the Macmillan. Returning to France in 1796, he was briefly an assistant at army headquarters, and in 1800 he was appointed to the court of final civil and criminal appeal, the Court of Cassation in Paris, a senior judicial position he held for the rest of his life.

Brillat-Savarin collected material for his book throughout his entire adulthood; "Often, in the midst of the most luxurious festivities, the pleasure of observing my fellow banqueters saved me from my own possible boredom." He was carried along, he said, by curiosity, not wanting to fall behind the times, and "a desire to converse, without hindrance, with savants, among whom I have always liked to be found" (preface). He dined frequently with leading philosophers, scientists, doctors, public officials, and salonists. His Parisian contacts included, as mentioned, the influential free-market economist Jean-Baptiste Say (Teulon 1998, 43).

In a prefatory "Dialogue between the author and his friend," Brillat-Savarin revealed that his good companion, Anthelme Richerand, a successful physiology textbook author, entreated him not to leave publication of so much labor until after his death. But people who only know the title will think me trivial, Brillat-Savarin protested. He relented, he wrote, only to reveal publicly Richerand's sole vice. Here it is: "You eat too fast!" Brillat-Savarin published *Physiology of Taste* at his own expense at the end of 1825 (dated 1826) and died several weeks later in Paris, on February 2, 1826, at the age of seventy. He had remained unmarried.

The gastronomic meditations provide evidence that meals lead to charming encounters, fond memories, poetry, and deep thought. "Tell me what you eat, and I shall tell you what you are" is the fourth of twenty opening aphorisms, intended as a "lasting foundation to the science" (gastronomy). Revealing "what you are" required wide knowledge. "To fulfil my self-appointed task, I had to be physician, chemist, physiologist, and even a little erudite" (preface). All those collations, all those conversations, all those observations. . . .

Unfortunately, gastronomy soon shrank to fine-food promotion. Brillat-Savarin therefore warrants a full introduction, because he set out the scope, style, and method of an all-encompassing gastronomy. "Gastronomy governs the entirety of life," he wrote (§18). Having imbibed eighteenth-century economics, which was grounded in meals, Brillat-Savarin will help restore liberal knowledge of the distribution of sustenance (that is, meals) and their containing organizations (economies). With his gastronomy placing meals well before money, I quote him in almost every chapter in this book.

Brillat-Savarin commented dolefully: "Humanity is incontestably, among the sentient beings that populate the globe, that which is inflicted with the most suffering." People had unprotected bodies, poorly shaped feet, an inclination to war and destruction, and a mass of maladies such as gout, toothache, acute rheumatism, and strangury. The fear of all this pain, he said, pushed people to give themselves up to the "small number of pleasures which nature has allotted" (§70). Behind it all, and explaining Brillat-Savarin's dedication to increasingly out-of-favor, sensual concerns, he left clues to a world-shaking love story, with which this chapter ends.

Ironies in the Fire

Highly appreciative French introducers of *Physiology of Taste* include novelist Honoré de Balzac in 1835, Brillat-Savarin's physiologist friend Anthelme Richerand in 1838, "king of the gastronomes" Charles Monselet in 1879, and literary theorist Roland Barthes in 1975. Four English translations are readily available, the most annotated and endearing, if not most accurate, being that by American enthusiast M.F.K. Fisher, in 1949. Nevertheless, many readers remain perplexed, complaining of a hodge-podge of scientific-sounding observations and garrulous reminiscences, reflecting privilege and sexism.

Three decades after publication, and writing as "Jules Paton," banker and columnist Jules Fleurichamp (1853–1860, 715) wondered how "to pronounce on this fine mixture of gravity and amusement that confounds both those who would want to mock it and those who would want to take it all seriously." Admittedly, theoretical headway is almost lost amid Horatian satire, interjections, and snippets of solemnity. The biggest problem would seem to be his semiserious science and puckish profundity. Should coffee be pounded or ground in a mill? He purchased some good mocha and tested two samples on devout connoisseurs, who supported pounding (§46). The suspicion that the truffle contributed to sexual pleasure necessitated other, "undoubtedly indelicate" questioning of friends (§44). As a founding member of the Society for the Encouragement of National Industry, he once demonstrated his invention of the "irrorator"—a pocket pump for perfuming the air. With droplets raining, the learned heads bowed "under my irroration," he marveled (author's preface).

Nearly two centuries later, philosopher of taste Carolyn Korsmeyer (1999, 69) declared the book a "monument" to "amateur research and thoughtful introspection." Neuroscientist Gordon Shepherd (2012, 125) dotted his work on flavor with such statements as: "Amazingly, Jean Anthelme Brillat-Savarin already knew this." Yet his commitment to natural science was ambiguous. "Playing the savant," was Roland Barthes's (1975, 14, 28) take, "serious and ironic at the same time."

Brillat-Savarin was light but never glib, jokey but never disparaging, and left numerous clues on how to be read. Monsieur Greffulhe invited him to dinner and to choose whether his fellow guests should be scientists or literary types. "My choice is made," our man replied, "Let us dine twice!" While that might sound evenhanded, according to a footnote, the "meal with the literati was notably subtler and more delicate" (preface). He had studied the greatest literary stylists, he announced; and he has, in turn, been held up as a model. For Charles Monselet in 1879, Brillat-Savarin had command of the anecdote's "real secret, elegance, and tone" (in Brillat-Savarin 1948, xix). Barthes (1975, 18) decided: "His attention to language is always meticulous, as behoves the culinary artist." Yet, liberal arts professor Michael Garval (2001, 659) warned, "to see Brillat-Savarin solely as a stylist is to underestimate the philosophical depth of the work." Brillat-Savarin had fun in a world not only of appetite, gourmands, and restaurants but of thirst, obesity, fasting, exhaustion, sleep, death, and the world coming to end, all topics allocated a meditation.

After contented sleep, a person "goes back to society without once regretting the lost time," he wrote (§98), and dreams usually lacked taste and smell, so that we see feasts without tasting them (§87). Devoting many pages to obesity, he saw the challenge: "Philosophers have praised temperance, princes have made sumptuary laws, religion has preached against gourmandise; alas, we have swallowed not one mouthful less, and the art of overeating flourishes more each day!" (§103). And he observed that the more rigorous a diet, the less efficacious, "because it is followed badly or followed not at all" (§111). In meditation 10, "On the end of the world," he suggested filling idle moments by imaging what would happen if, say, a stray comet caused global warming. His only hint was that "real danger tears down all social ties," as when husbands closed doors on their wives during a yellow fever epidemic in Philadelphia in 1792 (§54).

Perhaps the best example of Brillat-Savarin's sly wit is meditation 29, depicting the model host, Monsieur de Borose, whose advice would be valued by a Palais-Royal restaurateur. Just being invited to a Borose dinner was such an honor that even people who had never attended praised the delights. His dishes were never numerous, but his watchfulness and exquisite taste ensured perfection. His piano playing drew applause; he paid a scholar in an attic to supply conversation topics; and, belonging to a charity committee, he delivered leftovers to the deserving poor. Borose's daughter Herminie was so beautiful and talented that her veiled face at Sunday Mass drew crowds of extraordinarily handsome, newly devout young men. Although M. F .K. Fisher decided that Brillat-Savarin must have "despised" Borose, other readers appear not to notice that he is *irritatingly* perfect. This was a satire of the lifestyle influencer, recognizable today, to whom merchants aspired to sell at moderate prices, knowing that their delicacies would be "discussed in social circles." Even the gourmand's death was impossibly neat, struck by lightning.

Political Economist

As to a revealing political comment, in October 1794 Brillat-Savarin and a friend went hunting wild turkey in its native habitat. A Connecticut farmer called Bulow greeted them with a table "plentifully laden" with a handsome piece of "korn'd beef," a "stew'd" goose, a magnificent leg of mutton, and root vegetables of all kinds, along with enormous jugs of excellent cider. The visitors "proved to our host that we were genuine hunters, at least in our appetite" (§38). Brillat-Savarin, who was thirty-nine and unmarried, flirted with Bulow's four daughters, aged between sixteen and twenty. "Buxum lasses" he called them to show off more English, "radiant with freshness and good health." The eldest, Mariah, sang the national song, "*Yankee dudde.*" Overall, he spent an idyllic couple of days.

As the companions were saddling to leave, having fluked bagging one turkey, the yeoman farmer recited a political lecture: "You see in me, my dear sir, a happy man, if such there be on earth." Everything came off the farm—his shoes and clothes from his own sheep and his stockings knitted by his daughters—"and what makes our government so admirable is that here in Connecticut there are thousands of farmers just as happy." Taxes were almost nothing, he said; government supported agriculture; liberty was founded on good laws; "I am master in my own house"; and no one ever saw uniforms or bayonets except on the glorious Fourth of July. Brillat-Savarin was "plunged into profound thought" during the whole trip back to Hartford. Dinners sponsor powerful meditations. "It may be believed that I was pondering the parting speech of M. Bulow," he recorded, "but I had something quite different on my mind: I was considering how best I should cook my turkey" (84).

Brillat-Savarin's punchline was not meant as a put-down of Jeffersonian democracy, let alone its yeomanry. Quite the reverse, it confirmed that republican theory arose out of life's fundamentals. Joyfully caring for dinner was a lightly put restatement of bottom-up Epicureanism.

Even before this jumble of jest and solemnity, the book's title can be off-putting. For modern readers, *Physiology* suggests biology, and *Taste* narrows that to the mouth. Publishers of English translations have tried such improvements as *Handbook of Dining* (1865), *Gastronomy as a Fine Art* (1876), *Handbook of Gastronomy* (1884), and *The Philosopher in the Kitchen* (1970), although it is more than a matter-of-fact "handbook," speaks of more than "fine art," and rarely enters the "kitchen." He signed off as "L'auteur des *MÉDITATIONS GASTRONOMIQUES*," and *Gastronomic Meditations* might have been more appropriate.

Nevertheless, his title had resonances that were subsequently lost. Deriving from *phusis* for "nature" in ancient Greek, the word "physiology" was similar to "economy" in connoting organized natural systems. Eighteenth-century French *économistes* were eventually known as *physiocrates*. The English title of the textbook from 1801 by Brillat-Savarin's close friend Richerand combined both words in *The Elements of Physiology: . . . to explain the actions of the animal economy*. Brillat-Savarin's book twice used *économie animale* for *physiologie*.

On top of that, he declared that his gastronomy intersected with political economy and commerce. Given that these made up two of only six nominated disciplines (along with natural history, physics, chemistry, and cookery), economics loomed large (§18). Political economy had been a long-term interest. In the year of the fondue party, 1801, Brillat-Savarin published *Vues et projets d'économie politique* (Prospects and proposals for political economy), mentioning Adam Smith, and informed by his experiences in the local and national administration of public households. He proposed, for example, that with positions no longer handed down father-to-son, the public service should adopt a system of internships, and that local businesses might help with the upkeep of roads.

The meanings of economics and physiology were separating as he wrote; the nonbiological logic of corporations was taking hold. While political economists were becoming increasingly hooked on the ascetic Market and dropping the "political," he held together the animal, domestic, market, political, and natural economies. A lifetime of sensual, conversational satisfaction informed an economics not of financially gainful *Homo economicus* but of *Homo gastronomicus*. Reading the work as *Economics of Taste*, what is its basic proposition?

Brillat-Savarin's Economic Theory

The next four sections explicate Brillat-Savarin's economic theory, which, distilled into one sentence, runs something like this: In the service of the *stomach*, the exceptional taste abilities of humans support the quest for *taste-pleasures*, and this activity of *gourmandise* drives people to cooperate on complex *table-pleasure*, reliant on *trade and industry*, whose progressive refinements throughout history require the *sciences*, the peak of which is *gastronomy*.

Starting, then, with the stomach: some people are inclined to follow their head, putting their faith in some truth or cold reasoning, and others obey their heart, trusting their passions. A third option is the stomach. Among the ancient philosophers, while Plato put the head first and Aristotle the heart, a member of the next generation, Epicurus, taught that the starting point for morality, wisdom, and culture was "the pleasure of the stomach" (Bailey 1926, 135). While Brillat-Savarin made only two passing references to Epicurus, his *gastro*-nomy literally catered to the *gaster* (ancient Greek, stomach). As Brillat-Savarin opened: "The universe is nothing without life, and all that lives nourishes itself" (aphorism 1).

The name *Homo sapiens* suggests *sapienta* (Latin, wisdom), but materialists have argued that people distinguish themselves from animals not "by consciousness, by religion or anything else you like. They themselves begin to distinguish themselves from animals as soon as they begin to produce their means of subsistence" (Marx and Engels, *German Ideology*, 1.1.A). Rather than the *production* of food, as in that example, Adam Smith (*Wealth of Nations*, 1.1.2) emphasized its *distribution*—the human "propensity to truck, barter, and exchange one thing for another." But why sapiently produce? Why distribute? Brillat-Savarin explained.

Introducing the senses, and supplementing the standard five with the "genesic" sense that drew the sexes together in "reproductive or physical love" (§1), he said the most insistent was taste, with human beings having exceptional abilities (§4), and the other senses coming to its support. Devoting meditation 2 to taste, he invented words for three movements of the tongue "unknown to animals," and according human taste "supremacy." The tongue's "*spication, rotation*, and *verrition* (*verro*, Latin, I sweep)" ensured that every "single particle, a drop or atom" was "submitted to the appreciative power" (§14). He repeatedly emphasized the enjoyments or pleasures of taste (*jouissances* or *plaisirs du goût*)—hereby systematized as taste-pleasures.

By far the oldest of the senses, smell is extraordinarily subtle and closely entwined with the brain's emotional and mood centers and memory. Brillat-Savarin thought of smell and taste as a single sense, "of which the mouth is the laboratory and the nose is the chimney" (§10). His finding, now validated, was that the "number of flavours is [effectively] infinite, since every soluble body has a special flavour that never entirely resembles another" (§9). In comparison to the other senses, which often occasioned sadness, taste was the only pleasure that everyone could enjoy, once, twice, or possibly three times a day; that could be combined with others; that was "not followed by regret"; that was more lasting and more subject to our will; and that, contributing to feelings of well-being, reminded "that, by us eating, we replace our losses and prolong our existence" (§13). Empirical studies of taste were merely the start, he warned, for this restorative sense's cultural journey led through the development of civilization to the emergence of gastronomy (§15).

Heart, head, and habit supported the power of taste through gourmandise—"a passionate, reasoned, and habitual preference for whatever pleases the palate" (§55). He begged any translator of his "instructive book" to retain the French "*gourmandise*," partly out of respect for the French development of both "*La Coquetterie* and *La Gourmandise*, those two great improvements which extreme sociability has brought to our most imperious needs," and to avoid the misleading implications of the English "gluttony." He was clear: "When gourmandise turns into gluttony, voracity or debauchery, it loses its name and its compensations, and it escapes from us and falls into the hands of the moralist, who will treat it with advice, or the doctor, who will cure it with drugs" (§60).

Never having received "the sacred fire," some eaters "regard meals as hours of enforced labour, put on the same level everything that might nourish them, and sit at table like an oyster on its bed" (§33). Napoleon was among those who "eat only to fill their bellies." Others were denied discriminating organs, were distracted, garrulous or preoccupied with business or other ambitions (§61), or "exist only for cards and sly gossip." By contrast, gourmands gratefully "accept everything that is served to them, eat slowly, and enjoy reflectively what they have swallowed" (§62).

Gourmands obeyed, he declared, the "rule of the Creator, who, having ordered us to eat in order to live, invites us to do so with appetite, encourages us with flavour, and rewards us with pleasure" (aphorism 5, §55). With dominion granted human-beings—the "gallinaceous race" (fowl) were "created for the sole purpose of filling our larders and enriching our banquets" (§34)—"Why not take advantage, at least with suitable moderation, of the good things which Providence offers, especially if we continue to acknowledge their ephemeral existence, and they arouse our thankfulness to the Author of all things" (§67). The epidemiological research of Dr. Villermet (presumably Louis René Villermé) showed that life expectancy increased in direct proportion to the standard of living, proving that "good living is far from being deleterious to good health." Other things being equal, "gourmands live much longer than other folk" (§69).

Table-Pleasure

In a further step, Brillat-Savarin recognized that individuals experience not just taste-pleasures but a fuller *plaisir de la table*," with his preface announcing table-pleasure as the concern of the book. Meditation 14 differentiated the pleasure of *the table* from the pleasure of *eating*, which was a direct response to need satisfaction. Largely independent of the drive for food, the pleasure of the table, known only to the human race, was the "*sensation réfléchie*"—"reflective" or "considered" sensation (a concept associated with English philosopher John Locke)—born out of the various circumstances of the meal (§73).

Table-pleasure did not involve ravishments, ecstasies, or transports, Brillat-Savarin felt, but gained in duration what it lost in intensity. Physically, as the diner's brain was refreshed, the face lit up, color heightened, eyes shone, and a "sweet warmth" spread through the body (§73). Morally, the diner's spirit grew more perceptive, the imagination flowered, and clever phrases flew from the lips. "Effectively, as the result of an appreciated meal, both body and soul enjoy a special well-being" (§73). At Brillat-Savarin's longest lunch, his aged relatives "smiled with pleasure when they saw the table ready," "exclaimed with delight" at the fondue, resumed with "poise and aplomb, . . . pulled nearer to the table, spread out their napkins, and prepared for action," and so on (§76).

English translators have usually rendered "*Du Plaisir de la table*" in the plural, "On the pleasures [*sic*] of the table." But this was not some incidental collection of pleasures so much as a singular, emergent *table-pleasure*. Table-pleasure was a state of affairs that might be compared to, say, Aristotle's "good life." In a perhaps closer example, ancient Greek philosophers also talked about *eudaimonia*—"happiness" or "human flourishing"—with the Epicurean version turning up, still in the singular, in John Locke and, later, Thomas Jefferson's "pursuit of happiness."

Roland Barthes drew attention to table-pleasure being a *concomitance*, by which he meant a "coming together," a "coexistence," or even a "companionship" of the sensual pleasures. He underlined table-pleasure as a *plaisir composée*—"composite" or "composed." A French *salade composée* is more artful than "mixed salad," and Barthes (1975, 30, 33) found it significant that Schubert's quartet, *Death and the Maiden*, was composed the same year, 1825, in which Brillat-Savarin demonstrated, "indirectly as befits a good witness," the still underappreciated importance of cultures and histories *composées*.

Table-pleasure is something greater than taste-pleasures, and so what is added? Brillat-Savarin listed four essentials but gave two versions. The first encompassed "*des diverses circonstances de faits, de lieux, de choses et de personnages qui accompagnent le repas.*" In mechanical translation, the meal requires facts, places, things, and protagonists (§73). Brillat-Savarin's longest lunch illustrated the second version: "*chère au moins passable, bon vin, convives aimables, temps suffisant,*" that is, "at least passable fare, good wine, agreeable companions, sufficient time" (§76). Reconciling the two versions, table-pleasure depends on four elements: 1. the setting (including both the location and physical accoutrements); 2. food and drink; 3. companions (and their conversation); and 4. no haste.

Whereas taste-pleasures belong to an individual, table-pleasure belongs to people coming together as one, sharing materially, culturally, and soulfully. Long history has transformed self-centered taste-pleasures into mighty conviviality. Brillat-Savarin was convinced that "all human industry is concentrated on augmenting the duration and intensity of table-pleasure." Throats and stomachs might have limits, but people could throw themselves into improving the accessories. So they ornamented goblets and vases, invented the charms of music, and sprayed exquisite perfumes. Dancers, jugglers, and other entertainers amused the eyes, so that every sense joined in (§75). His contemporaries had contributed dishes that were so delicate that people would never have to get up from table except that other business intruded (§76).

Diners Drive Trade and Industry

Brillat-Savarin inscribed the word "economy" and its variants thirteen times—three of them to specify the "political economy," concerning national matters, particularly taxable resources and international trade. For him, commerce was "buying at the best possible price . . . and selling most advantageously" (§18). In addition, much of the book bubbled with trade and industry. As he declared: "The destiny of nations depends on the way they nourish themselves" (aphorism 3). As well as adding "great opportunities" for public revenue from "licences, duties, indirect taxes" (§56), gourmandise turned the wheels of industry.

Gourmandise sustained the "hopes and ambitions and performances" of fishers, hunters, horticulturists, and such. It supported secondary manufacture through an "industrious multitude" of food preparers, who "employ still more workers of every kind." So gourmandise was "the common bond which unites peoples through the reciprocal trade of goods serving daily consumption," and not merely superior or delicate products. He noted a "proportionate price to mediocre, good or excellent things," no matter whether the qualities were added by nature or art, so that industry aimed at both the "fattest fortunes" and the "commonest daily human needs," stimulating an inestimable "circulation of capital" (§55).

The numbers of *cuisiniers* (cooks), *traiteurs* (caterers), *pâtissiers* (pastry-makers), *confiseurs* (confectioners), *magasins de comestibles* (provision merchants), and new craftspeople, such as the *petit-four* makers, kept multiplying, he said, "without hurting their prosperity" (§134). The pastries of Monsieur Achard were so delicate that they came from some "enchanted land." Queues formed outside Brillat-Savarin's even nearer neighbor, baker Monsieur Limet, who benefited from the advice of some "first-rate experts" (varieties 26). Brillat-Savarin lived in rue des Filles-Saint-Thomas near rue de Richelieu and so a five-minute walk to the Palais-Royal, the center of the new consumer society, where a bundle of very early and very fat asparagus, costing forty francs, would have a potential market of the richest three hundred—the new class of bankers, capitalists, and big merchants—along, he said, with reckless lovers and exuberant revelers. He watched a bundle of asparagus walk off from Madame Chevet's shop with two beefy Englishmen whistling "God Save the King." Honored by always being greeted personally, Brillat-Savarin was Madame Chevet's regular visitor, and occasional purchaser (varieties 15).

Following Napoleon's defeat at Waterloo in 1815, the victorious nations extracted reparations. But rather than collapse, the French economy prospered. "What power came to our aid? What divinity worked this miracle? It was *gourmandise*." Before long, "the Queen of Cities was no more than an immense refectory. These invaders ate in the restaurateurs, in the cookshops, in the taverns, in the street-stalls, and even in the streets." Among food businesses, restaurateur Véry increased his fortune, Beauvilliers made a third lucky one, and Madame Sullot sold twelve thousand tiny tarts a day from her tiny shop in the Palais-Royal (§57).

Gourmandise carried everything worth knowing from one country to another, he wrote, so that a "learnedly planned feast is like a summation of the whole world, with each part represented" (§19). Culinary art was an "enchanter" that "brought together the Old and New Worlds, confounded political rule, and reconciled all distances" (§147). Wines, spirits, sugars, spices, pickles, and salted goods traveled from one pole to the other, along with the "swarm of food workers, who, for several centuries, have left France annually to exploit foreign gourmandise," and have returned with their earnings. No one had more right than the French to "raise for gourmandise a temple and altars" (§56).

The relatively lengthy meditation 27, "Philosophical history of cuisine," chronicled the quest to improve table-pleasure. Of all the arts, cooking (as transformation) had been of most service to civilization, fire having tamed nature itself (§122). By revolutionary times, coffee had become popular in the morning as a food and after dinner as a stimulant. Horticulture made enormous progress with hothouses for tropical fruits, and new kinds of vegetables were bred or imported (§134). A general spirit of conviviality had seized everyone, he wrote, invitations had multiplied, and hosts beguiled friends with the best dishes from the next social level up. His long-term history culminated in the individualized meals of restaurateurs (§135).

With the sciences directed at refining table-pleasure, distinguished savants had not felt it "beneath their dignity to study our basic needs," he declared (§134). The science of cookery divided into three branches: the preparation of foods (cookery proper), the analysis of its elements (chemistry), and their use in reparation (pharmacy) (§123). The sciences were freed from "the danger of regression" once captured in print, as he now did for the ultimate science, gastronomy. Civilization evolved to cater to the imperious needs of the stomach, until a "new science has suddenly appeared that nourishes, restores, conserves, persuades, consoles and, not satisfied with strewing armfuls of flowers in the path of the individual, contributes even more powerfully to the might and prosperity of empires" (§15–17).

"Gastronomy" was still a relatively novel word. It had been rare in ancient Greece—Archestratus was reported to have called his largely lost work either *Gastronomy* or *Gastrology* (Athenaeus 3.104b). It really came to the fore only with Joseph de Berchoux's long poem, *La Gastronomie*, in 1801. While not always understood, the word put a merry smile on every face, Brillat-Savarin found (§36).

Brillat-Savarin defined: "*La gastronomie est la connaissance raisonnée de tout ce qui a rapport à l'homme, en tant qu'il se nourrit*" (§18). Gastronomy was the "systematic knowledge of everything that relates to human-beings insofar as they nourish each other," and the "everything" (*tout*) really meant "everything." By watching over "the preservation of people by means of the best nourishment possible," gastronomy ruled the entire lifespan, from the newborn's cry for the breast to the dying person's final drop, which would give pleasure while being, sadly, too late to digest. The science also looked after every social class, directing the banquets of assembled monarchs and prescribing the minutes to boil an egg (§18). Brillat-Savarin's work demonstrated that "everything" encompassed the biggest questions of life.

U.S. sociologist Priscilla Parkhurst Ferguson (2004, 99) found that Brillat-Savarin turned "the science of human nourishment—gastronomy—into something more—a science of society." For her, the value he placed on sociability went a long way to explaining why his book had never gone out of print. Not lecturing his readers, "Brillat *talks with* them," Ferguson said. Elsewhere, in her many writings on French gastronomic culture, she decided that Brillat's "pleasure of the table is an inherently social pleasure. It sustains the body, and it sustains the body politic" (2003, 9). It also sustains the market for fat asparagus, critically appraised bread, and enchanted pastries.

Gourmandise, Not Greed

Gastronomy's purpose was the "conservation of individuals," Brillat-Savarin wrote (§18). He was also clear: meals made us social beings; table-pleasure was a collective activity. For him, solitary dining was "disastrous for the social order." Accustoming individuals to think only of themselves was worse than overindulgence (§140). The need to eat, merely instinctual at first, became a "powerful passion which has a marked influence on everything connected with society" (§15). Meals originated when the human race stopped helping themselves to fruit in the Garden of Eden. Heads of households apportioned to the children the results of the hunt, the children later doing the same for their aged parents. Meals gradually extended to include neighbors and friends, and then, hospitality provided for travelers. Languages must have been born and perfected during meals, through both necessity and relaxed loquacity, he decided (§72). The epicurean hunt brought the great meal: "Gourmandise is one of the principal bonds of society; it's what gradually spreads the spirit of conviviality that every day brings together the various classes [*états*], melds them into one, animates conversation and smooths the sharp corners of conventional inequality" (§59).

In his *Economics of Taste*, as we might understand it, Brillat-Savarin drew a valuable portrait of the individual faced by the world's puzzles and complexities. For him, the individual was driven not by avarice but by physical needs, involving the senses, and utterly reliant on material circumstances, including the treasured companionship of others. Linking the stomach's demands through gourmandise and gastronomy, he promoted a liberal self-conception in harmony with Enlightenment ambitions, and the approach adopted in this present book (to the extent even of some methodological decisions). Unfortunately, massive financial forces with "sumptuous tables and strong-boxes" (§63) were already converting *Homo gastronomicus* into *Homo economicus*, and suppressing dinner.

Three times he used the phrase "*l'extrême sociabilité*" (extreme sociability), seemingly to suggest dense interactions, especially of urban living. In one use, he wrote: "one often finds gathered around the same table all the improvements that extreme sociability has introduced among us: love, friendship, business, speculation, power, solicitations, patronage, ambition, intrigue: that is why conviviality touches everything; that is why it bears fruits of all flavours" (§74).

Brillat-Savarin devoted a half-century to the close observation of extreme sociability. He proposed that gourmandise was good. He might have been immersed in some of the world's best conversations, but his contemporaries abandoned material economics. Something predisposed him to embrace gastronomy with extreme intensity.

"Louise Weeps"

While Brillat-Savarin remained a bachelor, women evidently found him excellent company, and vice versa, and his family reportedly destroyed records of affairs (MacDonogh 1992, 178–82). He left appreciative observations of, for example, a young woman nibbling on a partridge wing—"her eyes shine, her lips are soft and moist, her conversation is pleasant, and all her gestures are full of grace." This led to his affirmation: "The penchant of the fair sex for gourmandise is something of an instinct, for gourmandise is favourable to beauty" (§58). His enjoyment of the female appetite, and form, was neither a flippant indulgence nor simple chauvinism but arguably the source of his book. *Physiology/Economics of Taste* can be read as a love poem, its publication commemorating a gastronomic tragedy exactly fifty years earlier.

In 1776, as a law student in Dijon, Brillat-Savarin became friendly with "one of the loveliest people I can ever remember," a young woman, whom he names simply Louise—perhaps the daughter of a councilor (Boissel 1989, 37). They enjoyed "endless whisperings," although, sadly, his "strong feeling of friendship . . . must be taken for what it was and not for what it might have become." It is central to the story that Louise "possessed in perfect proportions that classical shapeliness that charms the eyes and contributes to the splendour of the imitative arts" (§109).

One evening, Jean Anthelme realized that Louise had lost weight. She replied: "I feel perfectly well, and if by chance I have lost a little weight, I really would not miss it." "Lose weight!" he replied. "You have no need either to lose or to gain any! Stay as you are." As the days went by, he watched "her face grow pale, her cheeks become hollow, and her charms dwindle." Finally, he called her aside at a ball. She admitted that, tired of jokes about her weight, she had taken a glass of vinegar every morning for a month. Brillat-Savarin spoke to her mother, and together they tried to stop the regimen (which killed many young women annually, he said). However, Louise's life forces had already been undermined, and she died, barely eighteen years old, in his arms, lifted up, at her request, to watch the dawn.

Brillat-Savarin described the corpse's "look of radiance, almost of ecstasy," and noted that such a facial expression was not unusual: "Lavater mentions it in his TREATISE ON PHYSIOGNOMY." Fisher admitted to being especially moved by this narrative shift. She was not fooled by the matter-of-fact, quasi-scientific tone and suspected that here is the "most intimate and revealing moment in the book. . . . This may or may not be a love story, but the abrupt transition seems very emotional to me" (Brillat-Savarin 1971, 258–59, n.7).

None of us should overly romanticize the effect of Louise's death on the young man without another provocation. The name "Louise" reappears toward the end of the book as "this loving friend," who sorrows for Brillat-Savarin in a poem entitled "The Deathbed: Physiological Ballade" (varieties 24). In this, he described his own death—which he presumably did not expect only weeks after the book appeared, and exactly a half a century after hers:

> Louise weeps, and this loving friend,
> trembling, puts her hand on my heart.

Perhaps this referred to a later servant of the same name mentioned by a biographer (Boissel 1989, 241). Yet I suspect that Louise's death had sufficient impact to stimulate his extraordinary, life-long research and to be commemorated with the publication of the book (we can assume it wasn't really to expose his friend's eating "too fast").

Brillat-Savarin led an often charmed life—education, good job, a Stradivarius, overseas travel, distinguished associates, his own cooks, invitations to and from learned gourmands, the world's best shops around the corner. In his words, "for thirty-six years [since the Revolution], I have witnessed from a front seat the parade of people and events" (preface). But not everything went the gastronomer's way: he began adulthood with a horror that would have put the subsequent Revolution and its ensuing terrors into perspective. As a law student he held a young woman, watching the sunrise, as she died. Brillat-Savarin blamed the vinegar, but biographer Giles MacDonogh (1992, 33) reasonably raised anorexia nervosa. Neither Fisher nor MacDonogh tied together the two Louises, but that assumption explains much.

Brillat-Savarin would turn to some medical topics at university; "I am above all an amateur physician. It is almost a mania with me," he admitted (preface). Many of his best friends were doctors (they often make great companions), and he cited several medical texts, including Jean-Louis-Marc Alibert's *Physiologie des passions* (1825) and close friend Richerand's

Nouveaux elémens de physiologie. Among strikingly accurate physiological observations, obesity, thinness, dieting, fasting, and their cure occupied a string of four out of thirty meditations (nos. 21–24). This was such a concern that an abridged translation in 1865 enjoyed the title *The Handbook of Dining, Or, Corpulency and Leanness Scientifically Considered.*

If Brillat-Savarin had graduated in medicine, he would have written a monograph on obesity—in fact, he commenced writing it around 1805 (§106n)—and would have set up in practice, enjoying the twin advantages of having the healthiest of patients and being "besieged daily by the prettier half of the human race" (§99). Speaking on behalf of the citizens of the old and new worlds, "who believe ourselves to be the finest flower of civilisation, it is plain that we eat too much" (§102).

Louise's death was recounted in meditation 22: "Preventative or curative treatment of obesity." Thinness was a horrible calamity for women, he believed; "beauty to them is more than life itself, and it consists above all of the roundness of their forms and the graceful curves of their outlines." He could not see why healthy women should be "more difficult to fatten than fowls" and asked to be forgiven the comparison, because of his "praiseworthy intentions" (§113).

Jean Anthelme Brillat-Savarin knew from indelible experience that we must "eat, drink, and be merry for tomorrow we may die." One of his contemporary admirers wrote: "He left the world like a satisfied diner leaving the banquet-room" (quoted in Brillat-Savarin 1971, 19). Louise's death had forced Brillat-Savarin to confront the material basis of the human enterprise. He studied meals physiologically, psychologically, socially, creatively, and economically. He portrayed taste-pleasures as driving individual action within the social provision of table-pleasure. Economics was just then raising its sights above the body to ascetic, rational gain, which failed Louise.

For a twenty-year-old to have a woman of eighteen die in his arms out of anorexic desperation would have sharpened his interest in the Parisian food supply's exciting era. Fascinated, he built on the Enlightenment's by now considerable advances in science and philosophy. Confronting the big questions, for fifty years, he studied and, in 1825, published his findings in the deceptively breezy *Physiology of Taste.* By retaining meals at the heart of economics, his "gastronomic meditations" provide an unmatched foundation for our own.

In summary, in these two opening chapters I have set off moneymaking *Homo economicus* against meal-making *Homo gastronomicus*. Modern economists have zeroed in on the competitive striver within the price-setting system. As a gastronomer, Brillat-Savarin also gave primacy to individuals, but still with flesh, blood, and feelings, sharing sustenance within an increasingly refined civilization. Where economists imagined the economy as scarcely more than capitalist sums, Brillat-Savarin explored natural, national, international, productive, bodily, retail, culinary, domestic, tasteful, and pleasurable content. This was a life of material loss and pain, and discovery, debate, kindness, and delight.

PART 2
LIBERAL ECONOMICS

4

EPICURUS AND THE PLEASURE OF THE STOMACH

The Garden

Just inside the largest of ancient Athens's fifteen city gates, the Pompeion building contained banqueting rooms for sharing large beasts that had been sacrificed—that is, publicly divided, in those days before mechanical refrigeration. That building's name—Pompeion—relates to "pomp," because this was also the assembly point for religious processions. Outside this Dipylon gate, potters long congregated for the clay of the Eridanos stream, which had just run through the Agora or city market. In this area, called the Kerameikos (from *kéramos* for "pottery clay"—giving "ceramic"), they made amphoras to store wine, olive oil, and funeral ashes. The area was also the city cemetery.

Philosopher Epicurus (341–270 BCE) and his associates lived and worked just further out than the potters, in a school called the Garden. Plato's Academy was further out again along the Dromos road, as was Aristotle's Lyceum. At least, one ancient description placed the Garden there. Following another clue, historians have also located it inside the city walls.

According to Roman philosopher Seneca, an inscription at the Garden's entrance read: "Stranger, here you will do well to tarry; here our highest good is pleasure" (*Moral Letters to Lucilius*, letter 21:10). To call this a commune might not be entirely appropriate, given that Epicurus argued that pooling property indicated mistrust. The name, the Garden, would later conjure up images of philosophers strolling in flowery glades. However, the Garden was a large kitchen garden of vines, fruit trees, including olives, and vegetables (e.g., Hammond and Scullard 1970, 457; Rist 1972, 9). Later Epicurean poet Horace (*Odes*, book 2, ode 15) would complain about the wealthy substituting useful with decorative crops. Violets and other sweet perfumes replaced olive groves; "our princely piles will leave but few acres to the plough."

Epicurus reportedly purchased the property for eighty minae or eight thousand drachmae (Diogenes Laertius [DL] 10.10). However that might be interpreted, opponent Timocrates of Lampsacus would complain that Epicurus spent as much as a mina a day on food (DL 10.7; Clay 2009, 9). The meals here are historically important but tricky to piece together, especially given how the community's once abundant records would be neglected, or actively destroyed, during centuries of vilification. Hostile reports tended to survive, but at least they sometimes quoted the originals.

Although scandalously high food expenditures must be taken with a grain of salt, Athens had gone relatively food mad. Archestratus and others had been traveling the region and writing up culinary findings. Playwrights talked food. In his play *Heroes*, Timocles posed the riddle: The nurse of life, the foe of hunger, the guardian of friendship, the physician of famine . . . What am I? The answer was: a table (Athenaeus 10.455f). In Alexis's comedy *Linus*, Heracles was invited to improve himself by choosing from a library of classics. Upon selecting *Cookery*, he is recognized: "You are a philosopher, that's very plain" (Athenaeus 4.164c). The cook was a stock character, and, in the *Foster Brothers* by Damoxenus (3.102af), one boasts that, as a follower of Epicurus, he follows the laws of nature.

Plutarch would describe the Garden as sharing "common meals" or *trapezai*, literally, "tables" (Clay 2009, 23). A typical meal of this time and place might open with tasty small dishes, resembling modern *mezedes* (appetizers). A main course combined *sitos* (the staple of wheat bread, barley mash, or a pulse) with *opson* (the relish of fish, meat, vegetable, cheese, or just olive oil). *Oinos* (wine) was the universal drink, famously taken after the food in a drinking party or symposium.

But our interest is not particularly the food so much as its central importance. The emblematic activity of the Epicureans was the feast on the twentieth of every Greek month, earning them the nickname *eikadistae*, "Twentyers." From a partly obliterated text from a later Epicurean, Philodemus, Epicurus's custom was to celebrate "the Twentieth with distinguished companions after decorating the house with the fruits of the season and inviting everyone to feast themselves." The head of Plato's Academy in the second century BCE, Carneades, would reproach Epicurus for wasting time by anticipating and recollecting pleasures; according to Plutarch, Epicurus kept a gastronomic record, as if in an official journal, on "where I drank Thasian wine" or "what twentieth of the month I had the most sumptuous dinner" (Festugière 1955, 70n.56).

Classicist Diskin Clay (2009, 24) has translated a written invitation by Epicurus welcoming all sympathizers to the feast—"all those who are members of his household and he asks them to exclude none of the 'outsiders' who are well disposed to him and his friends." In the normal Greek household, men and women ate separately, especially with guests present. The word for dining room, *andron*, was literally "men's room." At sacrifices and open-air meals, men and women divided into their respective

FIGURE 4.1 Ancient Greek philosopher of stomach pleasure Epicurus (341–270 BCE). Photo by Marie-Lan Nguyen, 2011. Courtesy of Wikimedia Commons.

circles (Dalby 2003). Philosophical gatherings were generally all-male affairs. Strikingly, the Epicureans dined together. The community's main writers included Leontion, who some commentators would suppose had been a courtesan, and therefore well-educated. At least seven names of women original members would be handed down to posterity.

Radically, Epicurean meals were the deliberate reason and means for philosophizing. The key to Epicurus's achievements, subsequent disrepute, and semiclandestine rediscovery is that he based his observations, writings, and Garden way of life on the "pleasure of the stomach." With meals as philosophical rationale and practice, the Epicureans worked together, took meals and discussed together, and set out their detailed findings in letters and books. In the one long, surviving record, Roman poet Lucretius interpreted Epicurus's study of nature in poetic form, *De rerum natura* (*On the Nature of Things*). Understanding Epicureanism helps appreciate gastronomic basics, along with the liberal origins of modern economics.

The "Pleasure of the Stomach"

Epicurus's people lived and worked together, while avoiding larger institutional structures. They were guided by pleasure and pain and observant of nature, both studying it and obedient to its laws. The world comprised invisibly tiny particles, they presumed, and their atomic theory, especially the unpredictable "swerve" of atoms, warranted Karl Marx's doctoral dissertation (1975). Their theories of natural and social evolution, promulgated by Lucretius, seem very modern. Epicurean empiricism, appreciation of finitude, and reliance on friends contributed, they anticipated, to happiness. A key concern was to banish vain and unhelpful worries, so that they did not seek the gods, fame, or power.

Few modern interpreters would disagree too strongly with that quick summary. Almost as certainly, however, many would deny Epicurus had much to do with table-pleasure. Yet his close companion, Metrodorus, is quoted clearly: "It is indeed the belly, the belly and nothing else, which any philosophy that proceeds according to nature makes its whole concern"

(Athenaeus 7.546f). Epicureanism's intrinsic connection with meals had remained obvious to all interpreters until the past two centuries. The problem became modernity's intensive financial, technological, institutional, and personal rationalization. Under a ruling asceticism, to be discussed further in chapter 10, academic philosophers sought to protect Epicurus from lowercase epicurean satisfaction from dining.

As a recent example of the complications that set in, historian Catherine Wilson (2015, 1) opened her introductory book on Epicureanism by claiming that it had little to do with an "Epicurean Village" being established in the Marais district of Paris with an "organic bakery, an oyster bar, a fishmonger, ethnic restaurants." By the end of the book, however, Wilson's final sentence summed up the ancient philosophy this way: "It invites us to take pleasure in what is near at hand: in warmth, food, and drink, in moderation; in the company of those we happen, for whatever reason, to like; in the recurrence of spring after winter; and in the surround of foliage and flowers, and the appearance of new life" (119). Other than assuming a philosopher's garden of flowery glades in place of a productive one, Wilson's description sounds like Brillat-Savarin's four essentials for a good meal. As I showed in chapter 3, Brillat-Savarin was an enthusiast for warmth, moderation, good company, scientific findings, *and* local food shops.

Epicurus taught: "The beginning and root of all good is the pleasure of the stomach; and wisdom and culture must be referred to this" (Bailey 1926, 135). If modern specialists have bothered even mentioning the "pleasure of the stomach," they have cast it as a calumny started by an apostate and spread by philosophical rivals. Yet Epicureanism holds together as a belly-oriented philosophy, which had a powerful influence on especially liberal thought. More will be said, including on how high-flown ideas can supplant everyday knowledge, because many ordinary people know "gut instincts," are quick to reach a person's heart "through the stomach," and appreciate the necessity of pleasing the "first brain" or gastrointestinal tract, now scientifically endorsed (Enders 2015, 122–41); and Epicurus's ideas can be shown to derive from, and point persuasively back to, such material basics.

In Athens's remarkable development of philosophy, which gained from contestation among schools, Plato had developed an idealist, explicitly meals-last philosophy. He taught that the everyday realities of farming, cooking, and eating were lowly and corrupting, in comparison to the contemplation of a supreme "world of forms," of which ours was an inferior copy. Plato was brilliant, fascinating, and wrong, so that his scheme really only required putting back on its feet, and meals were restored to pride of place. Sometimes Epicurus can seem simply to have reinverted Plato's priorities and reconnected with common human experience that plants grow toward the heavens, whereas mere decrees come from on high.

Sticking with empiricism, hedonism, and practicality, Epicurus avoided ideology, creed, and even, in a way, philosophy. Disputation most usefully revolved around living, and the best way to do it. "We must not pretend to study philosophy," he wrote, "but study it in reality: for it is not the appearance of health that we need, but real health" (Vatican fragment 54; Bailey 1926, 115). His findings were therapeutic—getting rid of silly ideas that might block happiness. To help with this, Epicurus spoke of reality of no consequence. Death was nothing to a dead person. Likewise, he taught that gods never bothered to get involved. He praised ataraxy—lack of anxiety, or contentment. The less substantial needs included wealth, power, and status, and aspirations could prove hazardous. In summary, Epicureanism was what any sensible person would come to when taking higher authority with a grain of salt.

In a snippet from a lost book (all his books are lost), Epicurus replied: "As for myself, I cannot conceive the good if I exclude the pleasures of taste, and those of sexual intercourse, and of the pleasures of listening, and of the pleasures of a beautiful form" (Bailey 1926, 123). As that quotation affirms, Epicurus took seriously the primary reality of the senses and feelings. Pleasure belonged to the here-and-now, although he also accepted the delights of recollection and expectation (e.g., DL 2.89).

In his "Letter to Menoeceus," Epicurus explained that his hedonism was thoughtful, and not wanton: "When, therefore, we maintain that pleasure is the end, we do not mean the pleasures of profligates. . . . For it is not continuous drinkings and revellings, nor the satisfaction of lusts, nor the enjoyment of . . . luxuries of the wealthy table, which produce a pleasant life, but sober reasoning, searching out the motives for all choice and avoidance" (Bailey 1926, 89 [*Menoeceus* 131–32]).

Few acknowledged writers on gourmandise have taken many pages before also extolling moderation, along the lines of Brillat-Savarin's aphorism 10: "Those who stuff themselves or who intoxicate themselves know neither how to drink nor how to eat." Luxury was incidental, which was not to say that the occasional indulgence should be avoided. Believing in moderation, Epicurus said: "Frugality too has a limit," and he compared the errors of stinginess and excess (Bailey 1926, 117). Likewise, Brillat-Savarin wrote in his sixth aphorism that gourmandise "is an act of our judgement" and elsewhere assumed the need for "considered," hedonic choices. He spoke of "reflective sensation."

"Send me some preserved cheese, that when I like I may have a feast," Epicurus wrote in a letter (Bailey 1926, 131). Twentieth-century interpreters used this as evidence that he was not concerned with the pleasure of the stomach and was perhaps, some inferred, a vegetarian. Yet undisputed gourmands often specify simplicity. The London inventor of "aristology" (study of dining), Thomas Walker, wrote in *The Original* (August 12, 1835): "Some good bread and cheese, and a jug of ale, comfortably set before me, and heartily given, are heaven on earth."

With the stomach foundational, Epicurus gave integrity to the individual. We shall keep finding, nonetheless, that the individual requirement to eat, and to labor to achieve that, necessitates conviviality. Epicurus recognized self-interest as the soundest basis for social relationships: "All friendship is desirable in itself, though it starts from the need of help" (Vatican saying 22; Bailey 1926, 109). Epicurean self-interest meant working with others—not slaving for some higher authority or ideal—so that removing Epicurus from the table destroys the argument. "Friendship has its origin in needs," he wrote, "but it crystallizes only in the course of close association among those who have come to enjoy the fullness of pleasure" (DL 10.120, end; quoted in DeWitt 1954, 102).

Epicurus was irrepressibly social, advising: "You must reflect carefully beforehand with whom you are to eat and drink, rather than what you are to eat and drink." He went on: "For a dinner of meats without the company of a friend is like the life of a lion or a wolf" (Bailey 1926, 101 [*Principal Doctrines* 27]; Seneca *Ep Morales* 19, 10). Gastronomic authorities have similarly decried solitary dining. Ancient Romans said, "I have eaten, but not dined today," and Plutarch explained that a *dinner* requires sociability as seasoning (*Moralia*, 697C; 1961, 9:5). "Solitary dinners," advised student of dining Thomas Walker in 1835, "ought to be avoided as much as possible, because solitude tends to produce thought, and thought tends to the suspension of digestive powers" (*The Original*, August 12, 1835).

Being convivial enabled a person to live comfortably, and vice versa— that is the intent of one of Epicurus's so-called *Principal Doctrines*, in which he declared: "It is not possible to live pleasantly without living prudently and honourably and justly; nor to live prudently and honourably and justly, without living pleasantly" (*PD* 5; Bailey 1926, 95). That seeking pleasure (living pleasantly) went hand-in-hand with considering others (living prudently, honorably, and justly) developed into social contract theory.

Joining others, Epicurus was nevertheless wary of institutions, that is, of religious, political, and commercial structures. With advice on escaping the "prison of affairs and politics," Epicurus offered the simple injunction: "Live unknown." Rather than work in purposive organizations, he urged companionship: "Of all the things which wisdom acquires to produce the blessedness of the complete life, far the greatest is the possession of friendship [*philia*]" (*PD* 27; Bailey 1926, 101).

Living "unknown" in a large *household* did not stop him founding a highly successful network, extending throughout the ancient world for several centuries until suppressed by Christianity. For example, Jews, Christians, and Muslims know an Epicurean book framed as Ecclesiastes/Kohelet, whose verse 3:13 repeats "that all should eat and drink and take pleasure in all their toil." While publishing many books and letters, Epicurus and colleagues basically networked around tables, the likely meaning of the statement: "Friendship goes dancing round the world proclaiming to us all to awake to the praises of a happy life" (Bailey 1926, 99, 115, 139 [*PD* 7, *PD* 14, *Vatican* 58, Plutarch *Adv Col* 1125D, *Vatican* 52]).

"We must not violate nature, but obey her," Epicurus wrote (*Vatican* 21; Bailey 1926, 109), suggesting humility toward soils, seasons, and juicy figs, and eventual Enlightenment versions of "natural law." The sunlight makes the wheat grow to energize its producers, while poultry finds spilled grain, before being sacrificed—observant diners might decide that ecological cycles conserve matter, in support of Epicurus's findings on indestructibility. Diners might sniff out, literally by olfactory means, some notion of atoms, and thereby his surprisingly modern-seeming physics. When Roman poet Lucretius put otherwise lost Epicurean science into poetic form, he explained the sense of smell in atomic terms. Differently shaped particles emanating from deep within foods attracted a bee to its honey or vulture to its corpse, he wrote (1951, 4.675–80).

Epicurus placed importance on limits: the limits to life, the limits to nature, the limits to pleasure and pain, the limits to human needs. "It is not the stomach that is insatiable, as is generally said, but false opinion that the stomach needs an unlimited amount to fill it" (Bailey 1926, 115). Pertinently, material needs were finite, unlike fantasies of wealth and power. "The wealth demanded by nature is both limited and easily procured; that demanded by idle imaginings stretches on to infinity" (*PD* 15; Bailey 1926, 99). Epicurus conceived a matrix of desires, depending on whether they were natural or not, and necessary or not. The appetite for food was both natural and necessary. The desire for luxury food was natural but not necessary. And the desire for wealth, power, and fame, a vain ideal (*PD* 14; Bailey 1926, 101, 103).

Epicurus has been consistently misrepresented, and his writings often suppressed. In particular, his "pleasure of the stomach" philosophy has been rejected as scandalously irreligious. Christian apologists resolutely rejected his ideas of limits, for example; God's "economy" was infinite, so that the seeker embarked on a never-ending journey, Gregory of Nyssa argued in the fourth century (Leshem 2016, 92). Although often portrayed as an atheist, Epicurus was happy to think that the gods kept their distance. Epicureanism has flourished when orthodoxies break down, exemplified by the Renaissance and Enlightenment returns to basics, largely discarded during two recent centuries of Market institutionalization.

Luminary for Enlightenment

In this short chapter I introduce Epicurus and his companions because they grew, shared, and talked about meals, because their philosophy opened up useful theories about joining with others and constructing knowledge about natural and social evolution, and because ideas about the "pleasure of the stomach" have inspired perhaps surprisingly many thinkers appearing in this book.

The epic scientific poem *De rerum natura* by Lucretius (Titus Lucretius Carus, c.99–c.55 BCE) just managed to survive until the Renaissance, when Epicureanism influenced Desiderius Erasmus, Thomas More, and Lorenzo Valla. Again, in the seventeenth and eighteenth centuries, leading philosophers identified with Epicurean science, deism, and quietism, and the dignity accorded the individual. Standard lists of these sometimes closet Epicurean sympathizers include, on the Continent, Baruch Spinoza, Pierre Gassendi, Julien Offray de La Mettrie, Claude-Adrien Helvétius, and Jean-Jacques Rousseau; and in Britain, Thomas Hobbes, John Locke, Joseph Priestley, David Hume, and Jeremy Bentham (Wilson 2009; Abramovici 2013).

Further afield, Thomas Jefferson was declared by his biographer to be both an uppercase (philosophical) Epicurean and a lowercase (fine dining) epicurean. "A gourmet and a connoisseur, he could be correctly termed an epicure," wrote Dumas Malone (1981, 198). Jefferson's special fondness for French cuisine lay behind him taking his late wife's half-brother, the slave James Hemings (1765–1801), to Paris to learn in French kitchens. As to uppercase Epicureanism, in a student notebook, Jefferson copied Horace's dictum: *Carpe diem, quam minimum credula postero* (Seize the day, and put little trust in the morrow, *Odes* 1.11). After dinner on November 3, 1807, John Quincy Adams recorded Jefferson declaring Epicureanism to be the superior ancient philosophical system. At the age of seventy-six, Jefferson still followed Epicurus. Hastening to add that the doctrines had been much misrepresented, Jefferson set them out in a letter for his former secretary William Short (Monticello, October 31, 1819).

Joining those who have got the philosophy wrong, Adam Smith wrote in *The Theory of Moral Sentiments* in 1759 as if Epicureanism were purely self-centered. Smith complained that Epicurus reduced all "natural desire and aversion to the pleasures and pains of the body," with no intrinsic desire for anything else—"such as knowledge, such as the happiness of our relations, of our friends, of our country" (7.2.70). Plainly, Smith wrote from ignorance. Historian Pierre Force (2003, 1, 201) opined in *Self-Interest*

Before Smith that, although Smith might have preferred civilized "self-love" (or *amour-propre*) over natural self-interest in bodily sustenance (*amour-de-soi*), "economic science is a neo-Epicurean doctrine."

Philosopher and economist Henry Sidgwick (1907, 48, 84, 86, 89) made much the same mistake in his classic defense of utilitarian ethics in 1874. He contrasted happiness for the individual, which he labeled as "Epicureanism or Egoistic Hedonism," with happiness for society, which was "Universalistic or Benthamite Hedonism to which I propose to restrict the term Utilitarianism." He spoke of, for example, Thomas Hobbes's "audacious enunciation" of Egoistic Hedonism, in which a person "maintains throughout an epicurean mood, keeping his main conscious aim perpetually fixed on his own pleasure." Admittedly, Sidgwick acknowledged that this Epicureanism was as commonly understood, rather than its reality, and that for Hobbes, the aim could be "Preservation rather than Pleasure, or perhaps a compromise between the two."

French philosopher Jean-Marie Guyau amplified the bond between diners in his *La Morale d'Epicure* (*The Ethics of Epicurus*) in 1878. Starting out from the "fundamental pleasure: that of the stomach," he picked up on English utilitarian Herbert Spencer's observation that society inculcated "ego-altruistic sentiments," in which living together became its own positive reinforcement. For Guyau, "even the most selfish pleasures, because they are entirely natural, like the pleasure of eating or drinking, only acquire their full charm when we share with others." Any moral system would have to recognize this. "No doctrine, indeed, can turn off the human heart." No one was willingly going to disempower themselves: "pure selfishness would be a nonsense, an impossibility." The self was "an illusion . . . my pleasure does not exist for me without the pleasure of others." Not working together "would be contrary to my *interests*" (283).

Lately, with some abatement of twentieth-century asceticism and escalating crises requiring another return to basics, scholars have shown signs of rediscovering Epicurus. Yale historian Thomas Kavanagh (2016, 100) even described Brillat-Savarin's *Physiology of Taste* as "written as a response to the [French] Revolution's systematic denigration of the Epicurean tradition." Perhaps Brillat-Savarin did not set out *specifically* "to rehabilitate and redirect the premises of Lucretian materialism and its focus on the subjectivity of the pleasured self." Nonetheless, many prerevolutionary philosophers appreciated the relevance of pleasure, companionship, and living with nature and read Lucretius, as Brillat-Savarin would have done. Some of those Enlightenment philosophers whose economic thinking was highly influential reappear over the next three chapters.

Individual Interest

Not the most studied ancient Greek philosopher, Epicurus was neverthe-less the most influential on the authorities populating this book. He talked neither money, markets, nor national debt and yet installed the intellectual framework for economic science, from European Enlightenment versions to nineteenth-century perversions. At first sight surprisingly, the admir-ers of Epicurus have ranged from Karl Marx, undoubtedly on the left, to such rightist libertarians as Ayn Rand and Friedrich Hayek.[1] Individuals needed to go about eating and drinking free from autocratic and ideologi-cal impediment, all have agreed, but then many too quickly abandoned the shared table.

Epicurus was "the greatest representative of Greek Enlightenment," Marx (1975, 73) declared in his doctoral dissertation, which pinpointed the introduction of indeterminacy—through the *clinamen* or unpredictable "swerve" of atoms—as the telling Epicurean advance on Democritean atomism. Marx (1977, 136) would soon consider human action within a "metabolic" universe, acknowledging each person as a *"corporeal*, living, real, sensuous, objective being full of natural vigour." Pursuing "eating and drinking, housing, clothing and various other things" would generate the wonders of society. While Marx avoided portraying the future communist state, he mentioned dreaming of an ability to "hunt in the morning, fish in the afternoon, rear cattle in the evening, criticise after dinner, just as I have a mind" (Marx and Engels, *German Ideology*, 1.1.A). Marx contrib-uted all that before he got to the *Manifesto* as a "twenty-nine-year-old with a taste for epicurean hedonism" (Varoufakis 2018, viii).

While Marx and Marxists have added enormously to human under-standing, and still do, class struggle became a trap. Rather than individuals working together around the table, they had to form tight organizations to prosecute "war"—theory seemed to build-in permanent, rather than instrumental, enmity. Political urgency meant losing sight of individuals and coalescing as owners and nonowners of the means of production. The *Communist Manifesto* found that the "unceasing improvement of machinery" reduced workers to the same, "equalised" condition. With continuing development, the proletariat "becomes concentrated in greater masses, its strength grows, and it feels that strength more" (chap. 1). The forging and defending of revolutions provided for a new division, all repressing the radical power of individual appetite.

I devote chapter 9 to Ludwig von Mises, the mid-twentieth-century "godfather" of neoliberalism and the closest to this book's villain. Like Marx, he acknowledged Epicurus as the classical enlightener of humanity and said that British political economists completed "the spiritual, moral and intellectual emancipation of mankind inaugurated by the philosophy of Epicureanism" (1966, 147). Mises, too, initially accepted liberalism's primary focus on "material welfare . . . food and drink, shelter and clothing" (1985, 4). In a further quotation that might well have come from Marx, Mises (1966, 174) declared that "final decisions rest with acting men." Liberalism was accused, he wrote elsewhere (1981, 37), of "considering only what is earthly, of neglecting, for the petty struggles of daily life, to care for higher things." However, such critics were "merely picking the lock of an open door," because liberalism had only ever been a philosophy of earthly life. Other economic theorists have joined Mises in finding, however, that individuals cooperate through mathematical mechanisms, cut and polished into brilliant orthodoxy. To run earthly life, Mises abandoned actual living, breathing individuals for financial heaven.

Mises (1981, 38) wrote that human action "knows only *one* end, the greatest pleasure of the acting individual." However, with just a few waves of his hand, he transmuted meal seeking into profit seeking. In successive sentences, he turned appetite into greed, arguing that, universally, people "want to eat and drink," and then they believe that "more food, clothing, and the like, is better than less." In turn, an individual chose action "based on reason"; therefore action was "only to be understood by reason." Since "pleasure" really just meant any preferred condition, chosen *rationally*, "exchange" to that condition was only visible using the rationality of money (96–100). Audaciously, the utmost materiality became high idealism.

The next chapter stays with the big impact of Epicurean ideas on the intellectual upheaval of the Enlightenment. Following any collapse of meaning, self-confidence, goals, or gods, as occurred in Europe into the eighteenth century, individuals nevertheless retain their senses, feelings, and observations and can join conversations. They still cater to the stomach, implying the primacy of the individual's search for contentment, and yet they also recognize that everyone's "pleasure of the stomach" is served through social networks and cultural wealth. Shared humanity opens up trust in others, sensible cross-checking, and discussion, while avoiding mystical authority, doctrine, slogan, or promises of fame, riches, and supremacy. The great seventeenth- and eighteenth-century philosophers advocated emancipation, and participatory democracy, "from below."

Taking eyes off the next meal—that's the mistake. Individuals must, together, work on merriment. As I will demonstrate in later chapters, the Epicurean commitment to individual well-being, adopted across the political spectrum, was betrayed in the modern economic calamity by, for one thing, inviting ascetic corporations to participate as "persons."

5

CAVENDISH, HOBBES, LOCKE, AND LIBERAL POLITICAL ECONOMY

Material Margaret

In seventeenth-century England, an "olio" was a stew; "fricassee," pieces of meat in a thick white sauce; "hodgepodge," many ingredients—especially mutton broth with vegetables; "marchpane," almond paste or marzipan; and "posset," a spiced milk drink, curdled with ale or wine. Such were the materials for extraordinary poems published in 1653.

Often disparaged as a reclusive and eccentric aristocrat, and nicknamed "Mad Madge," English poet, playwright, and scientist Margaret Cavendish (1623–1673) has been reclaimed lately by feminist scholars as valiantly asserting a woman's voice in a male milieu. "Spinning with the Fingers is more proper to our Sex," she admitted in her poems' dedication, rather than "writing Poetry, which is the Spinning of the braine." I introduce her because *Poems, and Fancies* made a meal of the world. Composed in her late twenties, the rhyming couplets boldly paired Epicurean atomism (the *Poems*) with the immanence of food preparation and consumption (the *Fancies*). I have not modernized her spelling.

In lengthy prefatory matter—self-confessed "chirping" about her fledging "Childe"—Cavendish further protested her naïveté. She could not speak French, "although I was in France five yeares" (the first of long periods in exile). Nor did she "understand my owne Native Language very well"—merely the "Vulgar part, I meane, that which is most usually spoke." So writing in verse would let her get away with errors, she claimed, "since Poets write most Fiction, and Fiction is not given for Truth, but Pastime." She could not offer golden plates, crystal glasses, agate tables, and Persian carpets, she admitted, nor feast us on ambrosia and nectar—that is, the ancient foods of the gods—"yet perchance my Rye Loafe, and new Butter may tast more savoury" ("To Naturall Philosophers"). With her Royalist husband's estates confiscated under Oliver Cromwell's austere regime, she had no house "but what my Mind is lodg'd in," and so no use for "Huswifery." After seven years of marriage, she had no offspring to employ her care. So her book was her unattractive child, deserving praise as "not being wanton, nor rude."

Despite the apologies, Margaret Cavendish also anticipated that her work would ensure her fame among later generations ("To the Reader"). Perhaps she recognized that she drew powerfully on experiences that subsequent industrialization and rationalization would alienate modern readers from. With little expectation that she remain unduly deferential to ancient literature, scientific exactitude, sophisticated expression, God, nor high ideals, and yet with the license of an aristocrat, Cavendish also had no need to disguise her earthiness.

At the age of twenty-two, when in exile in Paris with her English queen, Margaret married William Cavendish, the Earl and, later, Duke of Newcastle, who was thirty-one years her senior. Together with his younger brother, Sir Charles Cavendish, Newcastle hosted the so-called Cavendish Circle, the network of scientists and philosophers who led the Epicurean revival in Europe. Especially during long exiles on the Continent, the Earl's table provided an unmatched forum for René Descartes, Baruch Spinoza, Pierre Gassendi, Walter Charleton, William Petty, Sir Kenelm Digby, and, importantly here, Thomas Hobbes. Presumably joining at least some discussions, Margaret Cavendish introduced the Circle's ideas, relatively unmediated.

Her book's first part, *Poems*, explained the formation of the world out of atoms. Variously shaped and in constant motion, they locked into more complex forms that took on lives of their own. Small atoms "dance about,

FIGURE 5.1 Composer of *Poems and Fancies* Margaret Cavendish (1623–1673). Painting by Peter Lely, 1665. Courtesy of Wikimedia Commons.

fit places finde / Such Formes as best agree, make every kinde" (1653, 5). Although they were too tiny to see, "All things are govern'd by Atomes," she wrote, including "Sicknesse, Health, and Peace, and War" (16). Their gyrations produced the natural world, in which "the Earth to all gives Forme, and Feature, / Yet the Sun is Nurse to every Creature." The same short poem concluded: "Just as a Childe is got, and born of Man, / It must be fed, or't will soone dye agen" (37). Cavendish mentioned William Harvey's recent work on circulation: "Some by Industry of Learning found, / That all the Blood like to the Sea runs round" ("The Motion of the Blood," 42).

The book's second part, *Fancies*, was like a household manual, made up of distinct mental images or inventions—known at the time as "fancies." Cavendish conjured up many fancies as similes—"similizing" the brain as like a garden "full of delight," for example, or anger like pepper, and revenge like hot ginger. In a fancy entitled "Similizing the Heart to a Harp, the Head to an Organ, the Tongue to a Lute, to make a Consort of Musick," she wrote: "In Quavers of Similizing lies great Art" (137).

The brain was like an oven, she said, burning thoughts as "wood," so that "all sort of Fancies, low, and high," would be extracted by the "Tongue a Peele" (a "peel" being a baker's flat wooden implement for sliding loaves in and out of the oven). She warned that thinking too hard, the brain overheated; allowed to get too cold, and "Thoughts are Dough" (128). Elsewhere, the head was like a "Barrell of Wine," with "Wit" working away, and bursting forth, unless "a Pen, and Inke do tap it out." Strong Malaga wine, once broached, turned straight to "Heroick Verse"; and "all high Fancy is in Brandy Wits" (133–34).

Frequently, fancies resembled culinary recipes. The ingredients for thought included "A Braine that's wash'd with Reasons cleare," before some "Judgment hard, and sound is grated in." Then, add herbs: "A Bunch of sent [scent], sounds, colours, tied up fast," stewed a long time (for memory). The resulting "Meat is good, although it is not much" (131).

Life baked "A Tart" out of bodily parts—with "Floure made of Complexions white," and a filling including "Cherry Lips that's red." "A Dissert" [dessert] comprised "Sugar of Beauty which melts away soon," and "Bisket [Biscuit] of Love, which crumbles all away." Balancing that, "Creame of Honour, thick, and good, / Firm Nuts of Friend-ship by it stood" (131–32).

Beauty relied on health: "A body plump, white, of an even growth"; but beware that "Life scummes the Cream of Beauty with Times Spoon" (128–29). She often talked ugliness, disease, and death. In "Natures Cook," Death appeared as a cook. "Some Meates shee rosts with Feavers" [roasts with fevers]; "Some Flesh as Sage she stuffs with Gouts, and Paines"; "sometimes she stues [stews] with savoury smell, / A Hodge-Podge of Diseases tasteth well." Not squeamish, Cavendish was clear: "Death cuts Throats, for Blood-puddings to make, / And puts them in the Guts, which Collicks rack" (127–28). Death strove "to fill the Minde with black despaire." Its servants, Sloth and Sleep, "get halfe of the time," although "Sleep, a friend to Life, oft disobeyes," and rests weary limbs, and gently locks up the senses (5).

Socially reticent, and on the fringes of scholarly ferment, Margaret Cavendish moved in an Epicurean universe of atoms, household routines, and bodily behaviors that she turned into fancies. Confiding to the page, she conjured up raw economies—the domestic, physiological, and natural, and the mind, working away at self-understanding. Like a spinning wheel or an oven, thinking was also like a physical market. "The Mind's a Merchant, trafficking about / The Ocean of the Braine, to finde Opinions out" (143). She decided elsewhere that "In Natures Market you may all things finde"—especially "Carts of Sicknesse" and "soure Orange sores" (140).

From the mid-seventeenth through the eighteenth century in Scotland, England, France, Germany, America, and elsewhere, aristocratic and church hierarchies could no longer suppress social, scientific, and commercial ferment, or, as Cavendish would say, "wit." With Levellers and Diggers demanding rights for the common people, the economic upheavals forced intellectuals back to basics. Who on earth are we, and how should we behave? Scarcely yet corralled within disciplinary boundaries, Enlightenment philosophers tangled with moral, medical, political, physical, and other ideas. The physical world pressed heavily on these people, with only their fancies as a protection.

The most influential member of the unrepentantly materialist Cavendish Circle proved to be Thomas Hobbes. He devoured the material world as a hodgepodge, olio, and posset, and reported back. His careful observations and analysis made him an exceptional contributor to political economy.

Before turning to his findings, I draw attention to the topic of "natural law," sometimes also "natural order" or "natural right." Although the terms have shifted meaning, Hobbes and others around that time understood, like Epicurus, that nature was not to be violated, but obeyed. Too many interpreters of Hobbes and his successors have neglected their concern with basic requirement for self-preservation through subsistence, but not here, as Margaret Cavendish has helped explain.

The "Problem" of Natural Law

Descending through a range of thinkers that includes ancient Greek philosopher Aristotle and Italian theologian Thomas Aquinas, the topic of natural law is not without fuzziness. Hobbes did not necessarily help, dramatizing the natural state as a "warre of all against all." John Locke (*Treatises* 1.9.86) would appeal to Christian texts, calling, for instance, an individual's senses and reason their internal "voice of God." Yet Locke also declared that the law of nature is "plain and intelligible to all rational creatures" (2.9.124). For present purposes, natural law referred to the material realities of the natural economy, to which individuals belong—whether they are being born, snatching some sleep or a drink, or spinning fleshly thoughts.

Amid turmoil, when verities collapse, the natural economy could seem a more immediate and firmer source of authority than God's monarchs and mediators. Getting back to basics, philosophers would resort to self-analysis as a material being and thus discover themselves as an "in-dividual" or "in-divisible" in the sense of being a living, breathing, moving, natural whole or "animal economy." Using the senses (empiricism), plus a spin of reason, it would be "plain and intelligible" that natural law applied to themselves. Individuals knew intimately the imperative of self-preservation ("Thou shalt eat"), the implications of which Epicureans have explored.

As Locke put it, God had endowed reason to work out "the best advantage of life and convenience" (2.5.26). The word "natural" derived, as did "innate," from the Latin for "be born." That is, the word "natural" suggested ontological priority to socially constructed or "civil," "legitimate," or "positive" law. For an obvious plan was to come together with other "indivisibles," each enhancing their self-preservation by working together within the political economy (the city as household). In this, a sensible assumption would be the natural equality of persons; there were no good grounds on which to assert any superiority/inferiority. Shakespeare's Shylock reminded that everyone was "fed with the same food." Later, for Brillat-Savarin, the necessity of digestion was "the leveller, ruling over poor and rich, shepherd and king" (§79).

Leading physiocrat François Quesnay published a short work on the *Droit naturelle* (On *Natural Rights*) in 1765. Natural rights would apply to "those things necessary for an individual's happiness [*jouissance*]" (3). He also said that a child had an undoubted "natural right to subsistence" (7). Yet individuals cooperated in society, whose foundation was material subsistence, and the wealth necessary for society's defense. Thus it would only be "ignorance" that might favor "positive laws" contrary to a land's production and distribution (33); that is, Quesnay argued that good legislation would be consistent with "natural law."

A decade later Adam Smith (*Wealth of Nations*, 4.2.42) decided that the "exclusive privileges of corporations" were a serious encroachment on "natural liberty." In the same year, 1776, the American Declaration of Independence set out from "the Laws of Nature and of Nature's God."

This is all intrinsically radical liberalism, emphasizing rights to eating and drinking, enforced by nature. Recourse to "the natural" hung on but lost its gastronomic grounding. The right-wing response has generally been to find some higher authority, most blatantly God, King, and Country. The proponents of laissez-faire or "classical" liberalism, who transferred their allegiance from monarchs to money, had trouble with "the natural." The founder of utilitarianism, Jeremy Bentham (1843, 501), exploded at the French Declaration of Rights: "simple nonsense: natural and imprescriptible rights, rhetorical nonsense,—nonsense upon stilts." An agitator for capitalism, and its necessary inequalities, Ludwig von Mises (1966, 174, 761–62, 841) denied any claim by "eminent Virginians" (led by slaveholder Thomas Jefferson) that people were "biologically equal." Mises scoffed at "alleged," "metaphysical," and "quite arbitrary" natural law, which biological science had "unmasked as a fallacy." Yet Mises was not without inconsistency (more in chapter 9), since he also spoke about the "reality of natural law" and frequently about "biological" law. As he wrote: "Only the insane venture to disregard physical and biological laws." Perhaps he was thinking of Newton's laws, but life absolutely requires feeding.

From a mid-twentieth-century vantage point, historian of economic analysis Joseph Schumpeter (1954, 107, 110, 112) found natural law to be "beset with difficulties and an inexhaustible source of misunderstandings," so that "many of the best economists" now felt "distaste" for natural law, which became a "byword for unhistoric and unscientific metaphysics." Yet for mainstream economists, private property became a "natural right" in some sense of absolute, inherent or "normal," to quote Schumpeter. Antirepublican economist Friedrich Hayek (1967) declared the market to be "self-adjusting," "natural," "organic," and "not of human design," so that its "spontaneous order" should not be upset. The Market's "naturalness" became the basis of the Chicago school's free-market advocacy (Harcourt 2011, 30–31). The connotations of "natural" had been lifted from the living world to suggest money as untouchably sacred.

But that is to leap ahead, when the real need is to step back to those for whom individuals were unquestionably natural bodies, each belonging equally to the human species, and living together within the natural economy. Human survival depended, as Margaret Cavendish put it, on hodgepodge and Malaga wine, therefore property, incorporated through labor. The intricate customs generated by living together within the natural order have formed etiquettes, which are generalized as ethics, and points highlighted as rights. As elevated as rights might sound, they are proclaimed with reference to nature, as Thomas Hobbes and others wanted.

Hobbes's "Concoction"

Having been left in the care of a well-to-do uncle, Thomas Hobbes (1588–1679) gained a good education, including at Oxford, and became a tutor, spending many years with the eventual Duke of Newcastle, William Cavendish, whom Margaret Lucas married. Cavendish companionship took Hobbes on long visits to Europe, especially France, often fleeing war, and meeting philosophers and scientists, especially those with an Epicurean bent. If ever a person had to return to first principles, it was during nearly a decade of political, religious, and military turmoil of the English Civil War or English Revolution (1642–1651). This was the contest between men with short hair (the Roundheads, supporters of Parliament, often Puritan, and led by Oliver Cromwell) and men with ringlets (the Cavaliers, supporters of Charles I and, after his beheading and the republican Commonwealth, Charles II), who employed Hobbes.

In 1651, after eleven years as an émigré in Paris, Hobbes published the mighty *Leviathan: Or, the Matter, Forme and Power of a Common Wealth Ecclesiasticall and Civil*. He offered no sudden revelation, nor noticeably much reliance on others' findings, so much as worked systematically through the world as he found it—that is, worked his way from the physical world of space, time, and body, through the human person with senses, motivations, and deliberations, to the citizen avoiding war and actively cooperating with others. Like other Enlightenment thinkers identifying with the philosophy of Epicurus, Hobbes (*Leviathan*, chap. 11) voiced an "eat, drink, and be merry" case, denying any ultimate goal or highest good, and instead treating happiness as a process. "Felicity is a continuall progresse of the desire, from one object to another," he wrote, "to the assuring of a contented life."

Throughout his inquiries, often conducted on walks with a notebook or paper pasted on a board for jotting down ideas, Hobbes recognized the pressing need for individuals to keep themselves going. In an early work, *Elements of Law, Natural and Politic* (hand distributed in 1640), he had presented self-preservation as a *"right of nature"* (1994, chap. 14). Hobbes further explained the all-important "Desire of Food" in *Leviathan*'s chapter 6. He distinguished two types of motion of an individual, both with "Interior Beginnings." The first were the internal or *"Vitall"* motions, such as the pulse, breathing, concoction (digestion), nutrition, excretion, etc. Then, the *"Animall"* or *"Voluntary"* motions were *"going, speaking,* and the like." Guiding these conscious actions, individuals experienced "AVERSION" away from something and "APPETITE, or DESIRE" toward something. "Desire" was a general term, including no doubt sexual desire, but "Appetite" featured, being "the Desire of Food, namely *Hunger* and *Thirst*."

In preserving their body, the individual was guided by pleasure and grief. Two sorts of pleasure affected the sensual body, "the greatest" being an invitation "to give continuance to our species; and the next, by which a man is invited to meat, for the preservation of his individual person." Generally, "appetite is the beginning of animal motion toward something which pleaseth us." In addition to sensual pleasure, he found a "delight of the mind, and is that which we call JOY" (chap. 7).

The individual had natural rights and responsibilities for sustaining their own life, and obtaining "such things as are necessary to commodious living" (chap. 13). In his words (not modernized): "The Right of Nature, which Writers commonly call *Jus Naturale*, is the Liberty each man hath, to use his own power, as he will himselfe, for the preservation of his own Nature; that is to say, of his own Life; and consequently, of doing any thing, which in his own Judgement, and Reason, hee shall conceive to be the apt-est means thereunto" (chap. 14).

Cognizant of the little force required to take another's life, individuals ought to admit equality, he argued. Given the default assumption of equal-ity, then each required the means to keep themselves "both from death and pain." His frequently quoted "warre of every one against every one" makes *Leviathan* sound desolate, but this was to accept the desirability of good government, because "to endeavour Peace," individuals would be "contented" with only so much liberty as they would allow others (chap. 14). Talk of "warre" introduced the beauty of the social contract, which was an at least notional agreement by which people joined in collabora-tive social economies. When individuals transferred their natural right to an authority with powers of coercion—the "sword of justice that keeps them all in awe" (chap. 20), then this *union* (a coming together of wills) was a body politic, or what the Greeks called a "πόλις [*polis*], that is to say, a city" (1994, 1:chap. 19). A political system's members cooperated as one body under a head, which was the Leviathan.

Although *Leviathan* contained only one use of "œconomy," referring to fiscal officials (chap. 23), the topic was the management of the great econ-omy or "Common-wealth." Just as people lived in "small Families," they also lived in "Cities and Kingdomes which are but greater Families" (chap. 17). Hobbes devoted chapter 24 to a commonwealth's "nutrition," or "the Plenty, and Distribution of Materials conducing to Life." Even his use of "procreation" in the heading "Of the NUTRITION, and PROCREATION of a Common-wealth" referred to the "Children of the Common-wealth" called "Plantations, or Colonies."

Importantly, Hobbes theorized money as "concocted" food. Since the medieval scholastics, if not before, money had been accepted as the "blood" of the social body, circulating as substitute food for converting back, where and when needed. Adding the new knowledge of William Harvey's *De Motu Cordis* (On the Motion of the Heart) of 1628, Hobbes considered that the human stomach "concocted" food into chyle for the liver to con-vert into blood, circulating goodness through the body. So, too, the social body *concocted* excess food into the more portable "food" of gold and sil-ver. Money was *preserved* food, kept for another time or place.

By Concoction, I understand the reducing of all commodities, which are not presently consumed, but reserved for Nourishment in time to come, to some thing of equall value, and withall so portable, as not to hinder the motion of men from place to place; to the end a man maye have in what place soever, such Nourishment as the place affordeth. And this is nothing else but Gold, and Silver, and Mony.

(chap. 24)

As food's substitute, money "passeth from Man to Man . . . and goes round about, Nourishing (as it passeth) every part thereof." Thus "Concoction" was the "Sanguification of the Common-wealth" (from Latin *sanguis* blood). In circulating, the flexible stand-in for sustenance assisted in the stewardship of a kingdom, being collected as taxes, before redistribution for (preferably) the common good. Hobbes described two types of redistributive functionaries under the Leviathan—one that collected and the other that dispersed the digested food: "One, that Conveyth it to the Publique Coffers; The other, that Issueth the same out againe for publique payments" (chap. 24). As well, and as Hobbes's successors would feature, the food substitute greased market exchange, buying and selling food, and its labor. Being less prone to decay, money was also more accumulable, so that its amassing both appealed to ambitious governments and opened the way for market capitalism.

Hobbes's most significant contribution, some have held, was prompting reasonable individuals to join together explicitly through a social covenant or contract. I will return to this, after introducing John Locke's expansion of Hobbes's intrinsically liberal gastronomics.

Locke's Liberalism

The liberalism label is much disputed, yet tenacious, and few commentators would fail to put English philosopher John Locke (1632–1704) at the head of the class, his direct influence recognizable, a lifetime later, in American and French revolutionary documents. Like Hobbes, Locke attracted aristocratic sponsorship and studies at Oxford, and he practiced medicine.

Leviathan had just appeared when Locke entered university during the Cromwellian interregnum. He became physician to, and also coauthor with, a political leader, the Earl of Shaftesbury, and spent years in France, with a later exile in the Netherlands. The bulk of the writing was not published until after his return to England in 1688, accompanying Protestants William and Mary, who were "invited to invade" to take the throne. His key outputs were *An Essay Concerning Human Understanding* (abbreviated here to *Essay*) and *Two Treatises of Government* (*Treatises*).

While not adopting the label himself, Locke gained the "liberal" tag from such claims as this: "The natural liberty of man is to be free from any superior power on earth, and not to be under the will or legislative authority of man, but to have only the law of nature for his rule. The liberty of man, in society, is to be under no other legislative power, but that established, by consent, in the commonwealth" (*Treatises* 2.4.22).

Such liberalism made no mention of money, and note, too, that it had deeper connotations than unbounded "liberty." Even the original Latin *liber* did not denote abstract freedom but referred to a man who was not an enslaved member of a household, that is, to an actual person responsible for their own welfare, which related, in turn, to being both a good citizen and good head of household. Locke's liberalism was not high-flown philosophy but thoroughly grounded; it was soundly economic, and gastronomic.

Fundamental to establishing liberal philosophy, as Locke recognized, "we cannot be all devotion, all praises and hallelujahs and perpetually in the vision of things above." As he explained in a letter in November 1678, during more than three years in France: "We are not born in heaven, but in this world, where our being is to be preserved with meat, drink, and clothing and other necessaries that are not born with us, but must be got and kept with forecast, care, and labour" (quoted Bourne 1876, 396).

In *An Essay Concerning Human Understanding*, published anonymously in December 1689, Locke spoke of a person's never breaking out of the world of "sounds, tastes, smells, visible and tangible qualities" (2.2.3). Then, "sensation and reflection" furnished "simple ideas, the materials of all our knowledge." As he pointed out, "I would have any one try to fancy any taste which had never affected his palate; or frame the idea of a scent he had never smelt" (2.2.2). In addition to external sensations, people experienced the world hedonistically. Without pleasure and pain, "we should neither stir our bodies nor employ our minds" (2.7.3). Lying behind the will to act, "our all-wise Maker . . . has put into us the uneasiness of hunger and thirst, and other natural desires, . . . wills, for the preservation of themselves, and the continuation of their species" (2.21.30). Inquiring further into what moved desire in a chapter entitled "Of Power," he answered, "happiness, and that alone" (2.21.41).

Individuals had different palates or preferences, he acknowledged, so that not everyone was delighted with "riches or glory," nor with "cheese or lobsters" (2.21.55). Separating minds and bodies, some were made happy by knowledge, and others by sensual pleasures. Nonetheless, each needed some of what attracted the other. The person finding happiness in knowledge needed to satisfy hunger and thirst. From the opposite direction, knowledge was needed to find "good cheer, poignant sauces, delicious wines," so that "the epicure buckles to study." Pointing to the mundanity of pleasure, he said "a succession of ordinary enjoyments" could provide happiness (2.21.43–44).

The interactions of appetitive individuals occasioned Locke's *Two Treatises of Government*, dated 1690, although probably written several years earlier. He suspected that "folly or craft" had inaugurated religions, governments, and manners. What fashion then established, "custom makes it sacred," until it seemed "impudence, or madness, to contradict or question it." By comparison, an observer might decide, "the woods and forests, where the irrational untaught inhabitants keep right by following nature, are fitter to give us rules, than cities and palaces" (1.6.58). Accordingly, Locke started out from the "fundamental" law of nature "that all, as much as may be, should be preserved" (2.14.159; 2.16.183). The plain fact was that people, "once born, have a right to their preservation, and consequently to meat and drink, and such other things as nature affords for their subsistence" (2.5.25). And people sought self-preservation in cooperation with others, occasioning serious political consideration.

The fundamental law of self-preservation encouraged an assumption of universal equality. Perhaps, as he said, each person was made in God's image (Genesis 1:27), and the New Testament commanded: "You shall love your neighbour as yourself" (Mark 12:31). Locke preferred a materialist principle—"an equal right" of everyone in common to "provide for their subsistence" (*Treatises* 1.9.87). They had the right "to use any of the inferior creatures, for the subsistence and comfort" of survival. However, population pressures would reveal limits, necessitating government intervention for the "good of the governed" (1.9.92).

Property rights followed from the requirement, already quoted, for "necessaries that are not born with us"—primarily, subsistence to be incorporated, because even when sharing a meal, we are not swallowing exactly the same food: what's mine is mine, yours is yours. The word relates, after all, to the French *propre* in the sense of "one's own." After that, the claims become trickier, depending on the labor expended, the necessary land, need, and availability. With "nature, the common mother of all," the self-nourisher "certainly appropriated" the acorns picked up from under an oak, or the apples gathered in the wood, Locke thought. "Nobody can deny but the nourishment is his. I ask then, when did they begin to be his? when he digested? or when he ate? or when he boiled? or when he brought them home? or when he picked them up?" For Locke, the person's labor made the foods "more than nature, . . . and so they became his private right" (2.5.28).

Developing what others have called his "labor theory of property," Locke argued in the *Second Treatise* under the heading "Of Property" that something beyond simple "enclosure" was required; after all, gatherer-hunters did not fence off fruit or venison for themselves (2.5.27). "Though the water running in a fountain be every one's yet who can doubt but that in the pitcher is [only that person's] who drew it out?" (2.5.29). Labor added value—"more useful commodities: for whatever bread is more worth than acorns, wine than water, and cloth or silk than leaves, skins, or moss, that is wholly owing to labour and industry." Some "food and raiment" was furnished by "unassisted nature," and the other prepared by "industry and pains" (2.5.42).

A person would starve if having to ascertain everyone's agreement (2.5.28). Instead, civilization relied on "positive laws to determine property." Such general agreements were required when sharing the land, and also the fish from "that great and still remaining common," the sea. A key qualification involved satiability. A person could take only as much as they could "make use of to any advantage of life before it spoils." More than a person's share "belongs to others." The next paragraph has often been read expansively: "As much land as a man Tills, Plants, Improves, Cultivates... so much is his property." But the ellipsis midsentence, "and can use the Product of," implies just sufficient land to maintain life. Besides, a person cannot appropriate land "without the consent of all his fellow-commoners, all mankind." Such matters meant adopting the rule of law, "which is not to be violated" (2.5.30–35).

Furthermore, not merely seeking the protection of the law, individuals worked together to obtain sustenance. Locke was struck by the "Conveniencies" brought by society. Why would individuals subject themselves "to the dominion and control of any other power?" The great end of commonwealths might be seen as "the mutual preservation of their lives, liberties, and estates, which I call by the general name, property" (2.9.123). Not just protection, individuals "enjoy many conveniencies, from the labour, assistance, and society of others" (2.9.130). In the simple, communal cluster of the family, "the general rule, which nature teaches all things, was self-preservation," and this went along with the preservation of the young (1.6.56). Children repaid "nourishment and education" by taking care of their own children, so that reciprocal benefit down the generations led to a "natural right of inheritance to their fathers' goods, which the rest of mankind cannot pretend to" (1.9.89–90).

The use of money further increased cooperation. Where plums "would have rotted in a week," people found that they could give "nuts for a piece of metal," and "sheep for shells, or wool for a sparkling pebble or a diamond," and then "heap up as much of these durable things as [they] pleased." Hence the use of money, "some lasting thing that [people] might keep without spoiling, and ... would take in exchange for the truly useful, but perishable supports of life" (2.5.46–47). People played around with "the intrinsic value of things, which depends only on their usefulness," agreeing that a "little piece of yellow metal, which would keep without wasting or decay, should be worth a great piece of flesh, or a whole heap of corn" (2.5.37).

Having granted property, but only so much "food, raiment, and delight" as a person might require to survive (2.5.41), and allowing that personal labor intensified ownership, Locke did not discuss money's accumulation without limit. Money, he said, "introduced (by consent) larger possessions, and a right to them" (2.5.36). That little phrase, "by consent," asks many questions. So, too, do the complexities of property law for those living simultaneously in different economies. For example, does a fruit tree belong to the orchardist or to their heirs, mortgagee, nation, birds nesting there, or bees? By what rights might a corporation patent the tree's genetic code? French anarchist Pierre-Joseph Proudhon declared "property is theft!"

Thinking of property less abstractly as some God-given right, and more materially as "a living," might work better, as actually flowing from the soil through the trunk, photosynthetic leaves to beehives and birds' nests and to apples, thence from the orchardist's hands to eaters, and sewerage, back to the soil. That is, Locke's was not some truth but a complex of arguments, keeping in mind the fundamentals of the shared table.

Almost by definition, liberal principles remain endlessly debatable, and corruptible. A recurring idea in this book, as for Locke, is that, remaining true to the world of "sounds, tastes, smells," liberal concepts never become things in themselves. Freedom is not simply there to be borrowed for money but, like equality, is grounded in shared human needs. A "formal" or "procedural" equality might be a sound starting point for mutual care and imply steps toward a "normative" or "substantive" equality, including "equality of outcomes," but it never warrants an abstract equivalence between humans and other entities (corporations, say), floating free of socially organized nourishment, requiring no food, raiment, and delight.

Liberal principles enable individuals of good spirit to take sensible decisions, all *based on bodily necessity*. As Locke said in the *Second Treatise*: "Thus the law of nature stands as an eternal rule to all men, legislators as well as others. The rules that they make for other men's actions, must, as well as their own and other men's actions, be conformable to the law of nature . . . the fundamental Law of Nature being the preservation of Mankind" (2.11.135).

Social Contract

In *An Enquiry Concerning the Principles of Morals* in 1751, Scottish Enlightenment philosopher David Hume was scathing about pure greed theorists, who assumed that "all *Benevolence* is mere Hypocrisy, Friendship a Cheat, Public Spirit a Farce, Fidelity a Snare to procure Trust and Confidence." Either "so pernicious a Theory," which depicted their own species "under such odious Colours," had to be ascribed to the perpetrators' own "corrupted Heart," or they were "Superficial Reasoners" (11–12).

Nonetheless, Hume welcomed the *modified* self-interest of joining with others, calling it the Epicurean principle that "no Passion is, or can be, disinterested; that the most generous Friendship, however sincere, is a Modification of Self-love." The Epicurean strand of philosophers, Hume said, exhibited "as generous and friendly Dispositions as any Disciple of the austerer Schools," and "*Hobbes* and *Locke*, who maintain'd the selfish System of Morals, liv'd irreproachable Lives" (12–13). The Epicurean self-love can be understood as modified by a *diner's knot*: nothing is more self-interested than appetite, which urges individuals toward the table with others. Saying that true self-interest lies in cooperation might sound glib but is self-evident in everyday dining. Few survive by collecting acorns and apples.

Enlightenment philosophers typically opposed government by God-decreed monarch or self-appointed gang, let alone invading power. Instead, they advocated a political household by general agreement of all citizens, that is, a "social contract." People either literally sign up to constitutional arrangements or behave as if by general consent. A social contract for a political community might require oaths of allegiance at citizenship ceremonies, like the marriage contract—"tying the [diner's] knot"—of a domestic economy, and the midwinter, spring, monsoon, and harvest festivals that acknowledge a deal with nature. Mutual restraints to neither harm nor be harmed lead to a protective compact, but the fuller economic version formalizes actively working together. That is, individuals agree not merely to respect others' water but to collaborate on installing and maintaining a community supply. Think of an invitation and

FIGURE 5.2 The great body politic rules town and country. Frontispiece to Thomas Hobbes's *Leviathan*, 1651. Courtesy of Wikimedia Commons.

acceptance to the banquet, through which individuals contribute to mutual benefits.

Thomas Hobbes declared in *Leviathan* (chap. 24) that people's lack of complete self-sufficiency necessitated "exchange, and mutuall contract." Given the contradiction that people "naturally love Liberty, and Dominion over others," they required a covenant, mutually submitting to authority, whether "an Assembly or a Monarch," supported by force. "Covenants, without the Sword, are but Words, and of no strength to secure a man at all" (chap. 17). Hobbes specified that a commonwealth had to move beyond an affective "concord" (such as a family) into a rational "union." This differentiated the commonwealth as economy and its management structure, the body politic. He even set out a sample contract for "more than a Consent, or Concord; it is a real Unitie of them all; in one and the same Person, made by Covenant of every man with every man": "*I Authorise and give up my Right of Governing my selfe, to this Man, or to this Assembly of men, on this condition, that thou give up thy Right to him, and Authorise all his Actions in like manner.* This done, the Multitude so united in one Person, is called a COMMON-WEALTH" (chap. 17).

The commonwealth was worth joining, because, as Hobbes observed, covenanters gave up a life that was "solitary, poore, nasty, brutish, and short" and gained "Culture of the Earth . . . Navigation . . . commodious Building . . . Instruments of moving . . . Knowledge of the face of the Earth . . . account of Time . . . Arts . . . Letters . . . Society . . ." (chap. 13). All that, on Hobbes's account, from individuals pursuing self-maintenance, together.

John Locke expected the state, preferably democratic, to exert a light touch. Beyond mutual protection, finding "every man his equal," a person reasonably "seeks out, and is willing to join in society with others" (*Treatises* 2.9.123). Each person was "to part also with as much of his natural liberty, in providing for himself, as the good, prosperity, and safety of the society shall require" (2.9.130). And so to the democratic compact: consenting "to make one body politic under one government" obliged everyone "to submit to the determination of the majority" (2.8.97). As Locke said, "government . . . is for the good of the governed," and the "magistrate's sword" forced the observation of the "positive laws of the society, made conformable to the laws of nature, for the public good" (1.9.92).

As Margaret Cavendish showed, individuals confront a world of pleasure and pain, health, and disease, in which they must enter a dialogue with nature, most satisfyingly by connecting with others in a fricassee, olio, hodgepodge, marchpane, and posset, while dishing out stories, some more credible than others. Cooked up "from below," her "Rye Loafe, and new Butter" leaves a savory taste.

Further pursuit of the social contract now crosses the Mor Breizh (Breton, "Sea of Brittany"), otherwise known as La Manche (French, "The Sleeve") or English Channel. French *philosophes*—notably Jean-Jacques Rousseau—theorized great conviviality.

6

THE CITY SACKS VERSAILLES

From *Grand Couvert* to *Souper Intime*

A crowd of nobles of the highest rank waited late every evening near the staircase to French king Louis XV's rooms at the Versailles palace. An usher read out the names to ascend, and those not on the list would retire graciously to their rooms. In his journal, the Duc de Croÿ (1906, 71–73) recorded the king's "charming" dining room for a supper that was "congenial, without any stiffness." At his first such occasion, after a day's hunting in early 1747, the duke noted that only two or three valets placed what was necessary before each person and then withdrew. "We were eighteen at the table," Croÿ recorded. The king sat next to his mistress, the Marquise de Pompadour, along with various other counts, countesses, and a prince or two. One of the king's favorites, the Marshal of Saxony, did not sit but helped himself to morsels, "being a great gourmand." After two hours, Louis XV led them to a drawing-room, where he warmed and poured his own coffee, for no servants appeared. They played a card game, which the king loved, but which Madame de Pompadour loathed, and she eventually managed to get him away.

At another *souper intime* (intimate supper) in 1754, the Duc de Croÿ sat modestly at a table in the corner by the window, along with Monsieur de Lameth. Louis XV was already seated and sent over dishes. After supper, the king inquired of Croÿ about architect Ange-Jacques Gabriel's renovation plans for the Hermitage, where Pompadour would spend much of her life. The king organized the diners to unpack a fine blue, white, and gold dinner service, recently shown off in Paris. Although cost cutting has been suggested for the king's switch from silver, the delicate appearance of the porcelain tureens, platters, and dishes fitted the rococo style. Catching up with Chinese and Japanese techniques, porcelain manufacture was just then transferring from Vincennes to the village of Sèvres, near Pompadour's Bellevue mansion (Croÿ 1906, 230–31).

The *souper intime* might no longer appear dramatically small-scale, informal, and individualistic. For several thousand years, however, monarchs had dined in state, typically in an elevated position, although sometimes at the apex of such a social pyramid that they literally disappeared behind a screen. These great banquets remained the hub of the political economy of citywide and nationwide food contribution and reallocation, increasingly supplemented and replaced by money collections and disbursements.

The "Sun King," Louis XIV (1643–1715), had expanded the palace at Versailles as a dining room, utilizing locations through the garden and, during the royal household's *voyage*, through the French countryside. Court feasts were elaborately orchestrated over a few days with sets, music, dance, and delightful themes. This was changing in the eighteenth-century, possibly through the differences of personal style of Louis XIV's great-grandson and successor, Louis XV, but undoubtedly also because of economic upheaval, requiring court officials to pay more attention to the increasingly centralized and complex, nationally redistributive banquet.

Ascending to the throne as a five-year-old, Louis XV (1710–1774) relied initially on a regent, the Duc d'Orléans, who was acclaimed for replacing huge pieces of meat by delicacies, each costing ten times as much (Mercier in Mennell 1985, 33). Taking command, Louis XV reduced the *grand couvert*, in which the king and queen dined before a crowd of courtiers, from daily to weekly, preferring something approaching the bourgeois dinner party, the *souper intime*. One of his cooks, named Moustier, was stolen from a private household after several successful try-out suppers in 1738, despite the existing staff's attempts at sabotage. Moust-ier was required to prepare supper only twice a week and was given his choice of three sets of new clothes every year. He cooked the king's suppers for ten years, until dying in 1748 at the age of about forty-two (Luynes 1860, 260).

The influence of Madame de Pompadour (1721–1764) over Louis XV, whom she joined in 1745, is said to have been overestimated, but perhaps on such conventional affairs as losses in the Seven Years War. Representing the pinnacle of French taste, she supervised exquisite royal dining. One writer credited her with such dishes as *filets de volaille à la bellevue* (chicken breasts in the style of her palace), and *palais de boeuf à la Pompadour* (a "taste" of beef her way) (Ellwanger 1902, 63). Ensuring fine food on fine china in the intimate dining characteristic of emerging consumer culture, she helped reshape French meals in further ways, not least by sponsoring ideas about big economic changes.

To attempt a simplification of interwoven economic, religious, politi-cal, and social revolutions in which Pompadour was immersed: the aris-tocrats, with the support of the church, had long held supreme power in European agrarian society. Monarchs boosted riches through monop-oly and foreign plunder, sometimes through chartered corporations. The Reformation having encouraged individual responsibility, the turmoil of incipient industrialization and urbanization opened up liberal dreams of equal and free individuals within republican commonwealths, as I raised in the previous chapter.

This chapter and the next introduce the additional shift of power from those with land toward those with money, most dramatically with the French Revolution turning landed opulence not merely into Rousseau's republic but into city-centered finance. The new bourgeoisie (the moneyed urbanites, or "the City") invested in banking, trade, and manufacture, and this expanded the market, which led to corporate capitalism, taking eco-nomics with it, although that aspect can largely await the next and subse-quent chapters.

The Financiers Push for Control

In France, as elsewhere, the king, as head of the "body politic," had dragged in food and other tribute, and taxes, and put them to such uses as centralized feasts, infrastructure projects, and military adventures. The ruler's personal servants also ran the larger political household, so that the Chamberlain was in charge not merely of the royal chamber but the national "chamber." Even in the seventeenth century, the great ministers of state—such as Sully, Richelieu, and Colbert—still transacted the family affairs of the prince (Funck-Brentano 1929, 146). In *Bread, Politics and Political Economy in the Reign of Louis XV,* historian Steven L. Kaplan (1976, 5–6) explained: "The fatherly monarch was, *d'office,* by his own proclamation and by universal anticipation and acclaim, the supreme victualler. What more solemn duty could a father have than to make it possible for his children to enjoy their daily bread?" Theoretician of absolutism Bishop Jacques-Bénigne Bossuet argued that the king's assurance of subsistence was the "foundation" of his claims. As the head of the national family, he was the "baker-king," whose chief deputy for all domestic affairs, especially provisioning, was the controller-general. Together, they assured food essentially by regulation, enforced by "police," meaning special officials (11–12).

A strengthening of the national *banquet* required increasing sophistication, through more use of money, and centralization. With the king assuming greater command nationally, no longer did the local seigneur lead his men to war; they were taken by the king's representatives. Many public works were centralized. General laws were enacted by parliaments. The ancien régime was morphing into a more bureaucratic nation, with competing democratic and business interests. The monarchical administration was giving way to urban industrial, commercial, and cultural activity. New factories and financial institutions both supplemented and diminished the more agrarian-based palaces, manors, villages, farms, and gardens. The noble households scarcely participated in trade and commerce, losing out to the industrious bourgeoisie (those of the increasingly powerful City). By Louis XV's reign, a large number of aristocrats congregated at Versailles, relying on the king's favors for financial survival (Funck-Brentano 1929, 90–91). In its expansion, the banquet was disappearing.

As the center of French fashion shifted from Versailles to Paris, along with real money and power, remarkable women established alternative courts, or salons. They, too, promoted fine dishes, table talk, settings, and guests, otherwise known as taste, ideas, the arts, and luminaries. Their *soupers intimes* helped establish French dining among the most cultured in history. From 1745 Madame de Pompadour helped the king adapt.

The new financiers, industrialists, and dealers objected to government restrictions, often on behalf of royal monopolies. There were even detectable rumblings from below. As I surveyed in chapter 5, theorists responded with plans for a more rational and republican political economy. The inherited social pyramids—and their lordly banquets—would have to give way to a commonwealth, based on the equality, and sovereignty, of each individual. This required new constitutional relationships to give importance to not just each person but the people as a whole. This all made for peak Enlightenment, the name for the upsurge in intellectualism, emerging from the Renaissance and Reformation and picking up on the more scientific approaches, exemplified by Francis Bacon (1561–1626), along with an often clandestine appreciation of Epicureanism.

The culminating project of the Enlightenment *philosophes* (intellectuals) was the Wikipedia predecessor (although without open editing and access), Denis Diderot's mighty *Encyclopédie*, or *Encyclopédie, ou dictionnaire raisonné des sciences, des arts et des métiers* (Encyclopedia, or systematic dictionary of the sciences, arts, and crafts) (1751–1772), in twenty-eight volumes, plus addenda. As editor Diderot disclosed in the article "*Encyclopédie*," the aim was "to change the way people think." It gathered up the latest from such intellectuals as Jean Le Rond d'Alembert (the early coeditor), Baron d'Holbach, Chevalier Louis de Jaucourt, Abbé André Morellet, François Quesnay, Anne-Robert-Jacques Turgot, Voltaire, and, not least, Jean-Jacques Rousseau. For this last, the baker-king would have to give way to the baker-people, who, together, would express a "general will."

The Republic of Rousseau, Economist

Swiss-French philosopher, composer, and novelist Jean-Jacques Rousseau (1712–1778) contributed mightily through his close analyses and fiction. For a start, his *Discours sur l'origine et les fondements de l'inégalité parmi les hommes* (*Discourse on Inequality*) of 1754 recognized the individual's natural interest in self-preservation, which he knew as the self-love of *amour-de-soi*, to be distinguished from self-respect pursued within society, *amour-propre*. Along with the individual, Rousseau emphasized the greater society as a "moral being with a will."

In *Du contrat social* (*On the Social Contract*) of 1762, Rousseau (1, chap. 2) urged not to lose sight of self-interest—"Man's first law is to watch over his own preservation; his first care he owes to himself." Nevertheless, at the same time, rule by divine right was to be answered by the "general will" of the populace tied in a social contract.

For immediate purposes, I turn to Rousseau's long *Encyclopédie* entry in 1755 on "Economy," which built on the work of Hobbes, Locke, and others. Rousseau opened with the etymology of "economy" as combining the Greek *oikos*, house, and *nomos*, law. Although economy "originally meant the wise and legitimate government of the household for the common good of the whole family," the notion of the "domestic or particular economy" could be extended, he said, to the "government of the great family, which is the state." With members "naturally equal," the "general or political economy" was necessarily a more artificial body, ruled by the *volonté générale* (general will) through its laws (337).

Rousseau's entry drew the other analogy of an "organised, living body"—the body politic—so that the "sovereign power represents the head; the laws and customs are the brain, . . . commerce, industry and agriculture are the mouth and stomach, which prepare the communal subsistence"; public finances were the blood, pumping life and nourishment throughout; and the "citizens are the trunk and limbs that make the machine move, live, and labour." No part could be injured without a "painful impression carrying to the brain, so long as the animal is in a healthy state." The *general will* always worked toward the preservation and well-being of the whole and each part, and was the source of the laws. The whole contained smaller "tacit or formal associations," whose own wills modified the general will, not necessarily for the overall benefit (338)—a complication that returns in chapters 10 and 14.

Rousseau did not hide from the need for a strong central authority. Any despot could mete out punishments, he wrote, but a real leader knew how to conduct the state so peaceably as to make punishment unnecessary. The legislator's first duty was to conform laws to the general will, and then the administrator should abide by not just the law but its spirit. Undue fluidity of rank and fortune among the citizens was "both proof and source of a thousand disorders," requiring government to prevent extreme inequality, "not by taking away treasures from their possessors, but by removing all means of accumulating them; not by building charitable hospitals for the poor, but by guaranteeing the citizens against becoming poor" (340, 342, 344).

The right to property was in some respects more sacred than liberty itself, Rousseau decided, given how crucial it was to individual survival, susceptible to theft and appropriation, and foundational to civil society. As to the secret of the happy economy, and the reason for a good public education: "The nation cannot survive without liberty, nor liberty without virtue, nor virtue without citizens; form good citizens, and you will have everything" (343).

Rousseau dismissed the rich's claim that their luxuries would be superfluous for inferior persons, saying "a grandee has two legs just like a cowherd," and both have "but one belly." He despaired how a rich person could commit a crime with impunity, and, as soon as "the same man is robbed, all the police go immediately into action." Likewise, "inconvenienced by a crowd," a rich person made a sign, "and everyone makes way." Detailed discussion of taxation countered such notions as that burdening peasants would rouse them from laziness. Tax ought not depend on a flat rate for all contributors but be proportionate to "their conditions and the superfluity of their property" (346–47).

Although Rousseau's *Encyclopédie* entry was entitled "Economy or Œconomy (Ethical and Political)," when republished in Geneva in 1758 it became a "Discourse on *Political* Economy." This is because, in addition to the banquet, which Rousseau favored coming under the *volonté générale*, another kind of great meal entirely was coming into view—the market. This was not so much under the general will, but people coming together through distributions, one-to-one, with some guidance from price. French writers, not least Rousseau, had included ideas about government, social contract, and rule of law within *economics*, but the discipline became "political economy" around when Rousseau wrote. In the early nineteenth century, economists strengthened their market orientation and shed the adjective to return to plain "economics." These days, his entry might be read as political philosophy, but preferably as "economics," coming under the specialty of "political economy." But this is rushing ahead. My intention for the moment is to reflect on Enlightenment *political* philosophy, particularly that which would gain the name "liberalism."

Liberal Alternatives

Enlightenment liberalism started with the individual, taken to be a sensual body in possession of appetite, activity, reason, and living in the physical world with others. Sensible participants cared for themselves by caring for one another. Through a social contract, everybody would acknowledge, in principle, other banqueters' *equal* right to act and think *freely* in their pursuit of happiness. Every individual owned their body, labor, and property by way of what they hunted, picked, prepared, and ingested, but their precise property was far from glibly decided, especially once their immediate needs were satisfied.

In accordance with such ideas, in 1776 the U.S. Declaration of Independence carved in stone the liberal ideals of the new, contractual kind of commonwealth that respected the individual: "We hold these truths to be self-evident, that all men are created equal, that they are endowed by their Creator with certain unalienable Rights, that among these are Life, Liberty and the pursuit of Happiness.—That to secure these rights, Governments are instituted among Men, deriving their just powers from the consent of the governed." In drafting this, Thomas Jefferson is generally accepted to have borrowed a phrase from John Locke, but swapping the right to property for the right to seek "Happiness." As I suggested earlier, property might be understand less abstractly, and more dynamically, as "a living," and this would have alliterated as an equal right to "Life, Liberty, and Livelihood."

Property returned explicitly when Jefferson helped the Marquis de Lafayette compose the French Declaration of Rights of 1789, ensuring the "aim of all political association is the preservation of the natural and imprescriptible rights of man. These rights are liberty, property, security and resistance to oppression" (article 2). As with all rights, property was limited by others' same right (article 4).

Beneath mutual protection, the state would organize the positive benefits of the redistributive economy, and Rousseau contributed especially to the collaborative expression of the political banquet's mind, encapsulated in law. The advantages of economic togetherness featured perhaps a little more obviously in the French republican slogan "*liberté, egalité, fraternité.*" Individuals were to be "free" and "equal," and . . . the French played around with *amitié* (friendship), *charité* (charity), and *union* and *unité* (unity). Sexism would also have been avoided with "conviviality" from the Latin *convivium* for "feast" (from *vivere*, to live). It is one of strikingly many *com-* or *cum-* (Latin, with) words—more than three dozen in the English dictionary. Other contenders might be sharing *panis* or bread as in "company," a *munus* or gift in "communion" or well-being in "commonwealth."

Ideas about replacing the monarchical banquet with the people's conviviality thus formed the foundation for modern political philosophy. Meanwhile, however, another type of economy was gaining support. In this case, the plan was to abandon the aristocracy by shifting life-sustaining activity from the redistributive economy toward individuals exchanging in the marketplace. Although later blocking the view, the *market economy* took time attracting sufficient attention from theorists to gain any constitutional backing. Political economists knew trade and commerce, but even when Adam Smith referred frequently to the market, he did not fully conceive this as an alternative great household. In book 5 of *Wealth of Nations*, Smith was inclined, along with the old moral philosophers, to list the individual as "the member of a family, of a state, and of the great society of mankind."

FIGURE 6.1 Groundbreaking market economist François Quesnay (1694–1774). Engraving by J. C. François, 1767, after J. M. Frédou. Wellcome Collection, CC BY.

Yet, led by Madame de Pompadour's personal physician, François Quesnay, a new "cult" of *économistes* argued that the French king might guard against the people's starvation by not regulating the grain trade but letting a healthy population look after their own interests, and exchanging one-to-one. The *économistes*, notably Quesnay, credited the market with systemic qualities, arguing the life-giving naturalness of circulation particularly of primary production. With the market being self-regulating, agriculturally enamored Quesnay advocated its government be left to "nature"—hence to "physiocracy" (from ancient Greek *phusis*, nature). As "baker-king," Louis XV took a historically remarkable, even if tentative, step in the winter of 1763–1764, relinquishing government responsibility for the grain trade, lasting until 1770. As explained by Steven Kaplan (1976, xxvi): "The politico-moral claims of the people were superseded by the natural rights of proprietors in the esteem of the king. Subsistence became a matter for the individual to work out on [their] own."

The *économistes* and market liberalization occupy chapter 7, but before that a little digging uncovers some fascinating background to Pompadour's support for the *économistes*. The market economy can sometimes seem divorced from government—mistakenly, as Karl Polanyi (1944) explained. Certainly, using her influence within the corridors of political power, Madame de Pompadour became instrumental in promoting free exchange—by sponsoring Enlightenment thinkers, supporting consumer culture, and representing City subversion within Versailles.

Pompadour Against Pomp

Throughout the history of banquets, administrators and boon-companions have contributed advice and conviviality. So the novelist Petronius was an "arbiter of taste" in ancient Roman emperor Nero's coterie, just as Pompadour became. She should be seen as principally *mistress* of the household rather than of the bed. In fact, the latter would seem to have been low in her priorities; she and the king severed sexual relations after five years. As well as a string of mistresses, not normally with household responsibilities, Louis XV also kept a queen elsewhere in the palace to produce heirs and alliances—when only fifteen, he had married the king of Poland's daughter Maria Leszczinska, with whom Pompadour remained on good terms.

By all accounts, Pompadour was a charming companion with broad knowledge, desirable talents, wealth of contacts, and the often underappreciated gift of lifting spirits. Pompadour planned meals in their fullest sense. Not merely offering advice on diplomatic and trade matters, she assisted in buying, building, extending, reorganizing, and decorating houses, and surrounding them with gardens. This required wide contacts, not often aristocratic.

When the young Jeanne-Antoinette Poisson became Madame d'Etoiles and gained Etoiles castle upon her marriage in 1741, she had gained

FIGURE 6.2 Agent of cultural change Madame de Pompadour (1721–1764). Painting by François Hubert Drouais, possibly 1763. Stewart Museum, Montréal. Courtesy of Wikimedia Commons.

everything necessary for her own *salon*. The future Marquise de Pompadour sang, played the clavichord, was a good actor, who recited entire plays from memory, and a connoisseur, who knew painters, sculptors, architects, and suppliers. She attracted the king's attention probably before and certainly at a ball in February 1745 and soon shifted her salon to Versailles. She was now twenty-four. As well as members of her family and close friends, she brought in her cook, M. Benoît (Mitford 1968, 87), and welcomed *philosophes* to the center of political power. Pompadour introduced talk of equality, liberty, fine porcelain, and the grain trade.

Just as autocrat Frederick the Great found advantage in promoting aspects of Enlightenment, Pompadour obtained a court posting and pensions for prolific and polemical writer Voltaire, whose favoring of civil liberties definitely required freedom of expression. In 1752 she success-fully defended the publication of Diderot's massive, groundbreaking *Encyclopédie*. Of the several *encyclopédistes* whom Pompadour spon-sored, few became more influential than the "father of economics," François Quesnay. He was her medical practitioner for a quarter of a century. The king's accounts show two of Marquise de Pompadour's staff on relatively vast salaries, followed by her doctor, François Quesnay, on three thou-sand livres, then Benoît, as chef de cuisine on four hundred, the same as three other senior cooks, with several "boys" on two hundred (e.g., Gon-court and Goncourt 1888, 64).

Pompadour's father, François Poisson, had worked for the four enor-mously rich and powerful Pâris brothers. Making money out of feeding the military, banking, and the slave trade, their operations were "clouded in the mysteries and the highly-charged atmosphere of famine pacts and other machinations" (Kaplan 1976, 700). The brothers cultivated intellec-tuals, including Voltaire, helping with his investments. The youngest brother, Joseph Pâris-Duverney, was sometimes said to have been the real biological father of the future Pompadour. Another brother, Jean Pâris de Monmartel, who was court banker, was the girl's godfather.

In 1725, when François Poisson had moved to a grander house and Jeanne-Antoinette was only four years old, he was made the scapegoat for a scandal concerning grain supplied by the Pâris brothers. He escaped over the German frontier, and the family was taken care of by Charles Fran-çois Le Normant de Tournehem, another suggested genetic father. Mon-sieur de Tournehem eventually arranged for Jeanne-Antoinette to marry his nephew and eased their way with a large dowry, all living expenses, and promise of a great inheritance. The now Madame d'Etoiles said she would never leave her husband, except for the king (Mitford 1968, 34–35, 40).

One story is that Madame Poisson had encouraged her daughter to think of herself as a future king's mistress—a fortune-teller predicted as much for the nine-year-old—and her guardian Tournehem also encour-aged her, which awakens a suspicion that the beautiful and accomplished woman was meant to gain access on behalf of her capitalist protectors. Less conspiratorially, having caught the king's eye, Pompadour brought to the court the livelier conviviality associated with the emerging bourgeoisie and market consumerism, as well as the latest economic thinking. She had brought the City into the Leviathan.

After promoting reform, Pompadour died from tuberculosis in 1764, at the age of forty-three, with the *économistes* poised to win many converts, including the first restaurateur.

7

MAKING THE MARKET

Diderot Discovers the Restaurant

Mathurin Roze de Chantoiseau invented the trade of restaurateur in Paris in 1766, as historian Rebecca L. Spang (2000, ix, 255 n.35) has established. Opening on rue des Poulies, Roze soon shifted to the hôtel d'Aligre in rue Saint Honoré but did not remain long in the trade, since his main business was publishing commercial guides. His *Almanach Général* in 1773, which credited the new institution to Messieurs Roze and Pontaillé, provided an early description: "Restaurateurs are those who have the skill of making true consommés, called *restaurants* or the prince's bouillons, and who have the right to sell all sorts of creams, rice and vermicelli soups, fresh eggs, macaroni, stewed capons, confitures, compotes, and other delicate and salutary dishes." That is, *restaurant* originally referred not to the establishment but to the restorative broth (or "restore-ing") that a *restaurateur* (or "restor-ator") offered.

Many food innovations have arrived with health claims, and the restaurant was no exception. Nonetheless, its real novelty was individualization. The "Founder's intention," Roze later explained, was to provide "delicate and healthful foods . . . served not at a table d'hôte, but at any hour of the day, by the dish, and at a fixed price," and within surroundings that ceded nothing "to the most beautiful cafés" (Spang 2000, ix, 67). Customers no longer shared the family's food at a *table d'hôte* (host's table) or the aristocratic *à la française* (impressive array of options). Instead, individual customers called for what they wanted, when they wanted, with offerings separately priced, in *service à la carte* (according to the card). Initially, customers were even served in separate booths (a custom that hung on, suiting lovers' trysts).

Only the year before, Denis Diderot had overseen publication of the basic seventeen volumes of the monumental *Encyclopédie*. Accordingly, the entry "*Restauratif ou Restaurant*" still concerned a "medical term" for any "remedy to give strength and vigour" (1765, 14:193). More fortunately for restaurant historians, however, and making up for any gap, Diderot maintained a nearly three-decade affair with Sophie Volland. Her mother demanded her company on long months away from Paris, forcing Diderot and Volland to correspond. Diderot mentioned restaurant visits in three surviving letters, those dated September 8, 19, and 28, 1767. He did not name the establishment, and already by then a few had opened.

Diderot feared he might get addicted. "What if I have developed a taste for the restaurateur's! Really, yes: an infinite taste," he wrote. "One is served well, if a little dearly, but at the hour one wants." He also explained: "One eats alone. Everyone has their own little booth." Diderot seemed enraptured by the *belle restauratrice* or *belle hôtesse*. She was "truly a very beautiful creature. . . . Beautiful face, rather more Greek than Roman; beautiful eyes; beautiful mouth, neither too much nor too little weight, large and a good size, light and elegant in bearing, but unsightly arms and hands." She would never initiate a conversation with her customers, he said, but would chat as much as they pleased, and she responded well. She did not intrude on the personal booth, although she checked if anything were lacking. He summed up the establishment as "marvellous; and it seems to me that everyone is pleased."

Full of schemes, restorator Roze also became a pamphleteering *économiste*. On January 31, 1783, for example, he wrote to Benjamin Franklin, telling the U.S. ambassador about a plan for reducing national debt without increasing taxation (https://founders.archives.gov/documents/Franklin/01-39-02-0052). In 1791 he pushed the same idea in a text available from the Bibliothèque nationale de France entitled (in translation): "The Wealth of the Republican People, or Mathematical Demonstration of the Possibility of Repayment of the National Debt, Without Drawing Anything Out of the Public Treasury, of the Possibility of Selling Bread . . . at the Most Moderate Price . . . Without the Farmers Dropping the Price of Their Grain." By 1799, still enthusiastic, Roze and a partner launched a private bank, but the United Departmental Bank of Commerce and the Arts failed (Spang 2000, 13). He was left impoverished.

In his first annual gastronomic guidebook to Paris in 1803, Grimod de la Reynière (1810, 212–13) launched a benevolent appeal for "the earliest Restaurateur in Paris," calling on the innovator's "prosperous successors to secure for him, by getting up a subscription, a small pension for life." The man who had occasioned the fortunes "of the Méots, Roberts, Beauvilliers, Naudets, Vérys, Balaines, etc." was now impoverished and deserving of "a small sacrifice on the part of these high-class cooks." Roze died in 1806.

Enlightenment philosophers had returned to economic roots, monarchy having proved inadequate to increasingly sophisticated modes of distribution, involving the weakening of domesticity with the rationalization of redistributive administration, and the strengthening market. Thomas Hobbes, John Locke, Jean-Jacques Rousseau, and others established radical, liberal principles for bringing individuals together for self-preservation through the great banquet under participatory democracy. Having concentrated in the previous two chapters on republican moves, I turn in this one to the French awakening, led by Madame de Pompadour's physician François Quesnay, to the intensifying market, to which the new restaurant belonged, catering, in theory, to every consumer whim.

Food scholars have long held that the first restaurateur benefited from deregulation, particularly the abandonment of guild restrictions on which trades had the rights to sell what items. While Rebecca Spang (2000, 9–10) decided that difficulty was overrated, these were commercially tumultuous times—the restaurant year of 1766, in particular. The restaurant exemplified the giving way of the old hierarchical regime, centered on Versailles, to lively consumer culture, racing ahead in Paris. This was the new world in which James Steuart (1767, 59), the Scottish author of the first work in English expressly on "political economy," observed: "Wants promote industry, industry gives food, food increases numbers." That meant that people were no longer "slaves to others" but "slaves to their own wants," which insisted they sold their labor.

Having examined the mounting feeling in favor of democratic republics, based on the universal need for subsistence, I now turn to complementary ideas about the free market, again from concerns for meals together. At an explicitly policy level, pressure from Madame de Pompadour, her physician François Quesnay, pathbreaking official Anne-Robert-Jacques Turgot, and others persuaded Louis XV to experiment in freeing up the grain trade from 1763 until 1770. In the midst of that, in 1766, the year in which Mathurin Roze de Chantoiseau became the first restaurateur, economically inclined circles gained access to Turgot's manuscript, *Réflexions sur la formation et la distribution des richesses* (*Reflections on the Formation and Distribution of Riches/Wealth*). As it happened, English philosopher Adam Smith also spent a large part of that same year in Paris, gaining inspiration from Turgot and others for his *Wealth of Nations*.

Économistes

François Quesnay (1694–1774) was a peasant's son who rose to become the physician and confidant of Madame de Pompadour. As raised in chapter 6, Quesnay moved into nearby rooms in Versailles, and Pompadour's visitors would call in on him, and she would join the discussions.

In 1736 Quesnay had written about human physiology in *Essai phisique sur l'œconomie animale* (Physical essay on the animal economy). In 1747 he expanded the book's coverage of the constituent physical elements, humors, temperaments, organs, and nerves and moved his discussion in a more discernibly market direction. The body was an organism in motion, which, for Quesnay, raised the question of liberty—the right to undertake considered actions. "People have the power to make their decisions according to their interests, by means of their freedom," he wrote. Anticipating gain, a merchant would consider such complications as the cost and additional expenses, possible deterioration, promptness of payment, and likely sales and prices. Beyond market calculations, reasoning led to agreements about reciprocal restraint. Quesnay thus distinguished people's "natural" and their "legitimate" (or legislated) rights—that is, between self-centered physiological needs and the rights when combining with others (1747, 320, 350, 364, 369).

Quesnay's influence widened with his articles in the *Encyclopédie* on "Fermiers" (Farmers) in 1756 and "Grains" in 1757. The latter included a list of fourteen "Maxims of economic government," emphasizing the agrarian source of wealth, the benefits of free trade, and the soundness of exporting primary produce and importing manufactures. The primacy of sustenance, and especially bread grains, made agriculture the source of real wealth. He and colleagues also developed such physiological ideas as William Harvey's circulation of blood to understand the "natural" circulation of grain within the social "body." The French followed the Chinese, Quesnay said, in wanting the greater economy ruled not by the monarch but left to the *phusis* or "nature," which is why his group would eventually be known as *physiocrates* (physiocrats). (Quesnay would explain Chinese ideas in *Le Despotisme de la Chine* in 1767.)

Quesnay used the royal printing press for the first edition of the *Tableau économique* in 1758 (1888). This "Economic Table" modeled the agriculturally based economy with a flow chart, scored in *livres* (the currency of the time). The *Tableau* assumed three social classes, with only the agricultural laborers creating a surplus. Artisans and traders were "sterile" in terms of wealth creation. The landowners did little, so their rental incomes should be taxed.

The *Tableau économique* caused considerable excitement, with numerous versions of the diagram soon circulating. As welcomed by the Marquis Victor Riquetti de Mirabeau (1763, xliv), the "Economic Table is the first rule of Arithmetic . . . to reduce to exact and precise calculation the elementary science and perpetual executing of the Eternal's decree: *you will eat your bread by the sweat of your brow*" (quoting Genesis 3:19). Mirabeau thought that the "calculations are to the economic science what the bones are to the human body." As a person cannot walk without the bones of the legs, nor lift loads or satisfy wants without the bones of the arms, so too with economics: "without the calculus, it would always be an

FIGURE 7.1 François Quesnay's conceptualization of the market economy. *Tableau économique*, Versailles, 1759. https://gallica.bnf.fr / Bibliothèque nationale de France.

indeterminate science, confused and always open to error and prejudice" (xlv–xlvi).

Mirabeau went so far as to call the *Tableau* the third of the three great inventions giving stability to political societies. The first was the written word, which let human beings transmit, without alteration, its laws, contracts, annals, and discoveries. The second was money, binding societies together. Quesnay's "Economic Table" derived from, and completed, the other two (52–53). Adam Smith quoted this evaluation in the *Wealth of Nations* (1776, 1.4.9), where he spoke of the "pretty considerable sect" following Quesnay, a person of "the greatest modesty and simplicity." Smith advised that, "representing perfect liberty as the only effectual expedient" for obtaining subsistence, Quesnay's "system, with all its imperfections is, perhaps, the nearest approximation to the truth that has yet been published upon the subject of political economy." As a medical theorist, Quesnay had believed in "some unknown principle of preservation," a self-correcting mechanism of the healthy human body. By analogy, Smith said, Quesnay assumed that a political body would "thrive and prosper only under a certain precise regimen, the exact regimen of perfect liberty and perfect justice."

Steven Kaplan (1976, 101–3) has drawn attention to the publication of free market ideas elsewhere in France, even as Quesnay set out on his quest. A middle-ranking public servant in Bordeaux, Claude-Jacques Herbert (1700–1758), was the anonymous author of an *Essai sur la police générale des grains*, dated 1753 in London, and expanded, to translate, as "Essay on the public administration of grains, on their prices and the effects on agriculture," dated 1755 in Berlin. Herbert showed that control by the monarch or "baker-king" drove rising grain prices higher, prolonging public suffering. In addition, regulations themselves made cultivation economically unattractive. The land was our "common mother," agriculture furnished the "most real" source of well-being, and the government must realize that "the severe policing of grain never caused an ear to grow." A liberal policy had enabled English agriculture and trade to flourish, he wrote, because people pursued their own interests in the most favorable conditions. "It is the destiny of humanity," Herbert claimed, "to be highly motivated only by personal interest." Yet the sum of interests was inevitably congenial, and their interplay socially profitable. The dynamics of greed excluded waste and inefficiency. Appetite for profit would meet need, and rivalry for clients would ensure a reasonable price and quality.

An anonymous publication in 1759, possibly also written by Herbert, *Sur la liberté du commerce des grains* (On the liberty of the grain trade), opened: "The lack of liberty in the commerce of corn, through the excessive variations it creates in the price of such a necessary foodstuff, ruins both the cultivator and the consumer." When grain was cheap, working for perhaps only three days would provide enough to purchase bread, and the farmer would be ruined; when grain was expensive, all laborers required work, reducing wages too low to afford the necessities of life (1–3). With freedom of commerce, the price would find its natural balance.

In late 1763, when Quesnay and other *économistes* published a journal, held public lectures on "economic arithmetic," formed a "school," according to their friends, or a "sect," according to Smith and others, they persuaded the king to radically liberalize the grain trade. The experiment was supervised by a protégé of Madame de Pompadour, Henri Bertin, who would have been educated by Quesnay and drew his closest advisers from liberal, agronomist, and *économiste* circles. A pernicious doctrine had "infected" the ministry, one opponent soon complained; some persons had become "pupil and proselyte of the flour fanaticism," wrote another (Kaplan 1976, 130–31, 142, 146).

The government abandoned liberalization in 1770, although this did not abruptly stem the crisis (xxviii). Joseph-Marie Terray, the controller-general who supervised the renewed controls, saw liberalization as increasing the leverage of rich over poor, whose wages tended to decline as prices rose. By convincing the people "that the King is incessantly working for their relief by continually overseeing its subsistence," he would restore confidence and tranquility (quoted 542–44).

Joly de Fleury, advocate general of the Paris Parliament, decided the "extremely dangerous" liberal experiment went against the "opinion or, if you wish, the prejudices of the people" about a question on which "their life depends." The economists wanted to subject "a good so necessary to life" to the same commerce as less useful and "even superfluous" things, he said. Since the strong always commanded the weak, government had a responsibility to favor the have-nots. This was not a tussle between city and country, Joly said, observing that the rural majority were as much consumers, "desirous that bread be cheap." Wages could lag behind the higher price of grain. And, even then, employers would profit from the clamor for work by holding down wages. Joly feared that those who controlled the crop would form "monopolies" with those with "influence and authority" (nobles and officers) and financiers. He also wanted to maintain the physical marketplace. Unless grain were visible, the people would be uneasy (quoted 171–73).

Only after the *économistes* gained such conspicuous influence did the word *physiocratie* emerge. In English, physiocracy is usually explained as belief in government "by nature," although it is more like "according to nature." Quesnay had written *Le Droit naturel*, again stressing the importance of living according to nature, in 1765. The first of a two-volume collection of the *économistes'* writings, dated 1768, was entitled *Physiocratie, ou Constitution naturelle du gouvernement* (Physiocracy, or the natural constitution of government, the most advantageous to human kind) (Du Pont 1768), not that "physiocracy" cropped up much in the text. The editor was Pierre Samuel du Pont, a close colleague of Quesnay and known to Adam Smith and Thomas Jefferson. After the Revolution, Du Pont took his family to the United States, where one of his sons, a chemist working with gunpowder, founded the DuPont Company.

The frontispiece to *Physiocratie* included a motto in Latin, "Those who work their land will have abundant food" (Proverbs 28:19), and the editor's introduction recommended that, to extend the enjoyment of their *natural right*, people should become farmers. The *natural order* made individuals the proprietor, first, of their person, then of their movable wealth, and finally of their soil. Then, *natural laws* having led people to secure *properties*, led to mutual protection under an authority, preferably *physiocratic* government, which conformed to the nature of both things and people (xliii–xliv). Historically, ignorance of *"natural right, natural order,* and *natural laws* rendered the despotism of Sovereigns arbitrary and disorderly." They prepared their own ruin by attacking the *properties* of their Subjects and of their neighbors, using the force entrusted to them to maintain peace within and without (lxvii–lxviii). Ignorance of physiocracy enchained liberty, destroyed riches of peoples and kings, and opposed "the progress of the speculative sciences themselves, and the arts of taste and pleasure" (xci–xcii).

Nineteenth-century economists would distance themselves from the quaintly named French "sect" by suggesting physiocrats had clung anachronistically to real surpluses as reliant on agricultural labor. They mocked Quesnay's school for remaining glued to the naturally dictated economics of eating by the "sweat of the brow." Yet for all their commitment to physical survival, the *économistes* had themselves started to lever off market economics and favor mathematical supply-and-demand modeling. As economists oversaw more liberalization, the more sect-like they became. Adding to the irony, two centuries after these hints of modernity, economists took for granted that the "natural" or "spontaneous" Market supported money's "self-organizing" whirl.

Smith's Wealth

Scottish philosopher Adam Smith (1723–1790) lived in Paris for the last ten months of a French tour in 1764–1766, which was the year of the first restaurateur and at the height of the experiment in freeing up the grain trade. There he exchanged thoughts with Quesnay, Condillac, Mirabeau, Condorcet, Du Pont, and, especially, Turgot. Smith recalled in a letter (November 1, 1785) that he "had the happiness of his [Turgot's] acquaintance, and, I flattered myself, even of his friendship and esteem." Turgot's *Réflexions sur la formation et la distribution des richesses*, to which Smith would have had early access, developed *économiste* ideas about the grower creating the most important object of consumption (food); the three classes—cultivators, artificers, and proprietors; and the role of money, gold, silver, and interest, in representing riches. Turgot's work also foreshadowed many of Smith's writings on the division of labor and justifications for market freedom. Smith worked for a further ten years, publishing the hallowed *An Inquiry Into the Nature and Causes of the Wealth of Nations* in 1776.

Wealth? With the idea of "wealth" ascending from wellness, well-being, and welfare toward financial power, what did Adam Smith mean? Should his book title be interpreted as the *Riches*, as Turgot used, or the *Well-being of Nations*? Frustratingly, Smith did not define "wealth," although he provided hints. At one point he rejected "gold and silver" in favor of something akin to "the good cheer of private families" (1.4.1). More technically, in praising French economists for promoting trade, he supported their "representing the wealth of nations as consisting, not in the unconsumable riches of money, but in the consumable goods annually reproduced by the labour of the society" (1.4.9). Some commentators have drawn attention to his writing about "the annual produce of the land and labour" (1.2.3), and Smith explained that his book's five main parts inquired into how the supply of the "necessaries and conveniences of life" depended on, first, the productivity of labor; second, the capital stock setting people to work; third, the relative concentration of industry in town or country; fourth, the application of theories of political economy; and fifth, public revenue and expenditures.

In sum, Smith did not necessarily see wealth as "unconsumable" money. Nor, as his French colleagues had suggested, merely agricultural production. While his "necessaries and conveniences of life" were still much closer to meals than gold and silver, yet "Wealth, as Mr. Hobbes says, is power" (1.1.5). The ambiguity reflected Smith's overall bridging of metabolic and monetary economics. Accordingly, in this section I demonstrate Smith's physiocratic/physiological/natural grounding, leaving his more pecuniary analysis until the next chapter.

Others have remarked on Adam Smith's "obsession with food" (Hill 2013, 13). After all, Smith defined his topic as a "branch of the science of a statesman or legislator" with the twin objects of supplying sufficient revenue for public services and "to supply a plentiful revenue or subsistence for the people, or, more properly to enable them to provide such a revenue or subsistence for themselves" (*Wealth*, 1.4.Intro.). Food and cooking peppered the book's opening discussion of productivity. He contrasted the "lone houses and very small villages" scattered about the Scottish Highlands, in which "every farmer must be butcher, baker, and brewer for his own family" (1.1.3), with the thriving centers, in which the various trades' sharing of products occasioned the "universal opulence which extends to the lowest ranks of the people." He took more than a page to list the victuals, utensils, and associated goods for which a person depended on others—"kitchen-grate . . . the coals . . . the knives and forks, the earthen or pewter plates" (1.1.1).

Wondering at society-wide cooperation, he sought the "*principle which occasions the division of labour*." His finding—"It is not from the benevolence of the butcher, the brewer, or the baker, that we expect our dinner, but from their regard to their own interest"—often opens economics textbooks (the mighty Samuelson, for example), misrepresenting the individual "interest" as "gain." Speaking of the universal interest in "cooperation" for the stomach's sake, Smith imagined the earnest conversation: "Give me that which I want, and you shall have this which you want" (1.1.2). With artisans having more in their shop than the household could consume, they could "truck, barter, and exchange" (no money necessary, let alone profit). With each specialist living by exchanging, becoming "in some measure a merchant," the more thorough division of labor formed "commercial society" (1.1.4).

While recognizing "the higgling and bargaining of the market," he declared the market price remained in approximate accord with a "natural" price, which depended on the labor required, at least sufficiently for "carrying on the business of common life" (1.5.4). The butcher would seldom carry beef or mutton directly to the baker or the brewer "in order to exchange them for bread or for beer." Instead, the butcher took the meat to the market to exchange for money and then exchanged that money for bread and beer. Consequently, and this was a pertinent observation, meat's value came to be seen in terms of money rather than bread and beer (1.5.6). Smith also considered that the market price of any commodity could seldom continue long below its "natural price," so that "the quantity brought to market would soon be no more than sufficient to supply the effectual demand" (1.7.30).

When Smith went on to inquire into the application of capital to the production of wealth, he applauded free enterprise and shifted his attention from the substance of meals. Laissez-faire successors would soon dismiss concerns with the soil, bread, and exchange as "physiocracy" and scarcely notice Smith's "necessaries and conveniences." Quesnay, Turgot, Smith, and others succumbed to market magic and so helped push the world from mercantilism—described by Smith as "in its nature and essence a system of restraint and regulation" (2.4.9)—toward the new Market. In chapter 8 economists have decisively forgotten actual tables for *tableaux économiques*.

Problems to Come

A person's body is a private "temple"; families expect the seclusion of their "castle"; and the borders of national "bulwark" are backed by arms, tariffs, visas, and walls. The market economy appears relatively open—anyone can trade; everyone is equal and free. Money, however, is a fierce enforcer. To redeploy Smith, the market wields a stern, disciplining "hand." The market fails the weak, most obviously in the case of children, the frail, disabled, and the culturally and socially disadvantaged. Price only incidentally supports the common good, restricting the market to an, at worst, disruption and, at best, complementary role to domestic and political decision-making. Without question, money is power for those with it.

Once money greases exchanges, it is readily accumulated, which can fund large-scale, coordinated activities—whether the Pâris brothers' manipulations or plastic packaging manufacture. Well-capitalized organizations offer many advantages but much can go wrong, especially when private capital aims at profit above all else. Given that "money makes money," the sheriff of Nottingham robs the poor to pay the rich, blames the victim, and cuts high-end taxes to "expand the whole cake." Make no mistake: capitalism, whether public or private, is not the market. Capitalism uses markets, but not the other way around, and Pompadour helped capitalism on.

Furthermore, running society collaboratively through the general will's expression in constitutions, laws, regulations, and institutions has proved progressive. But a big gap opened, historically, with the emergence of moneymaking machines. The republic's individuals faced cashed-up rivals. To gain legal, political, and economic rights, in the absence of special provisions, business corporations often came to be conceived as individuals, with enormous real-world ramifications.

After the French Revolution, taken to be a decade of upheaval from 1789, the rule of law under democracy had its successes, even if universal suffrage took another two centuries. Many peasants were granted land, contributing to culinary pleasure. Along with republican property rights, the importance *économistes* accorded agriculture must have helped develop French culinary standards.

As the Pâris brothers and successors gained political clout, Karl Marx and Friedrich Engels said the capitalist class had "pitilessly torn asunder the motley feudal ties that bound man to his 'natural superiors'" (1952, chap. 1). Brillat-Savarin (1826, §63) used even more ironic terms, speaking of the financiers as "the heroes of gourmandise. Here, *hero* is the right word, because there was combat, and the noble aristocrats would have crushed the financiers under the weight of titles and heraldic shields, if they had not been met by sumptuous tables and strong-boxes." Since each person's basic needs were equal, financiers had to spend their riches on the *art* of the table, he suggested.

Those pushing Enlightenment economics had split by then, with one stream remaining sympathetic to the original, social liberalism, leading to American left-liberalism, and the others moving selectively toward Market abstraction and inversion, the so-called classical liberals or neoliberals committed to liberty and property, but who fumbled collaboration and denied equality and democracy. Much power shifted from the monarch not to the joyful masses and a popular banquet replacement but to money. By the opening of this present century, political philosopher Ronald Dworkin (2000, 1) recognized: "Equality is the endangered species of political ideas." Importantly, for him: "Equal concern is the sovereign virtue of political community."

From Roze to Rose

As I examine in the next chapters, economists would continue to model exchange between allegedly "free" and "equal" bakers, brewers, and butchers, even though a few of these "individuals" would be so free and unequal as to bloat into giant corporations. Fortunately, as we will explore, actual artisans and their domestic households would also survive.

Consider, for example, Daniel Rose running the restaurant Spring in the narrow rue de la Tour d'Auvergne in the ninth *arrondisement* of Paris. His tiny establishment was a half-hour walk northward from, and 240 years later than, that of the original restaurateur, Roze. From Chicago but trained in France, and eventually expanding to include New York, the young Rose was unquestionably cook-host-restorer at what amounted to a dinner party for just sixteen guests at effectively his own home of one and a bit rooms.

His front door was set into a full glass wall onto the street (so that the venue would later be taken over by La Vitrine—the Shop Window). It meant that Daniel Rose spotted arrivals and took a few steps from his workbench to greet them. At close quarters, facing his guests, he improvised four courses from perhaps little fish, sous-vide veal, the pick of the vegetable crop, raspberries. From among the diners, and in front of her proud parents, a girl helped plate the desserts.

Quite the reverse to Roze, Rose offered no choice, simply what had excited him at the market. Yet Spring was still intimate, a little restaurateur's household, and also wide open to the world—receptive to the morning's best, visible to passers-by, and taking bookings from the other side of the globe. This was an open, studio home in a free market. All those present were "in some measure a merchant," exchanging bits of gold and silver for sustenance. And who could have wanted more?

PART 3

THE CAPTURE

8

THE DISMAL SCIENCE

Escape to a Berlin Garden Suburb

German sociologist Georg Simmel (1858–1918) was a popular lecturer, prolific newspaper contributor, and scholar, writing on a long list of topics, including the nature of society, culture, and art. His often fragmentary, darting, and surprising "impressionism" of such topics as "The Stranger" and "Flirtation" was arguably ahead of his time, because he was passed over for academic postings, and translators would take another lifetime to introduce him to English readers. An early major work, *Philosophie des Geldes*, originally 1900, only became available as *The Philosophy of Money* in 1978.

Georg's wife, Gertrud, was also a noted philosopher, publishing such titles as, to translate into English, *Reality and Legality in Sex Life* and *About the Religious*. She was the "pinnacle" of what a woman could be, said their friend Marianne Weber, who was herself a leading feminist, writer, and wife of economist-sociologist Max Weber (who features in later chapters).

To imagine the Simmels entertaining the Webers at dinner, Max Weber's complaint about tiresome German potatoes presumably applied elsewhere. From contemporary cookery books, well-to-do, cultured hosts would have proposed not just meat soups and dumplings but possibly caviar or soufflés, not just sausages and beef stews but hare pies or goose under aspic, and not just cabbage but asparagus or mushrooms. With coffee, they could have ordered cakes and perhaps pastries or chocolates from the *Konditorei*.

Georg Simmel did leave some general clues about contemporary dining. His search for a civilized existence on the edges of Berlin's moneyed commotion led to an essay, "The Sociology of the Meal," in a newspaper in 1910, and untranslated for most of the century (Symons 1994a). This included advice on table settings, food presentation, and appropriate conversation, suggesting that the Simmels would have ensured a calm dining room, unobtrusive family portraits on the wall, and white linen on a table with identical settings in silver. The talk would have mixed wit with depth.

Simmel supported such recommendations with a fascinating argument that meals were sufficient to explain human society. Answering brutish hunger created even the heights of culture. In particular, Simmel pointed to what I have termed the *diner's knot*, based on the realization that the stomach's demands are so intensely self-interested that human persons are bound irrevocably with others. Arguing this way, Simmel harked back to the social contract idea, before economists promoted the selfish individual, a model of the human that, to an unsettling degree, persuaded Simmel's colleague Max Weber.

Simmel often opened essays with a paradox. In "The Handle," for example, Simmel (1959) asked readers to imagine a fine vase displayed in an art gallery. The gaze of admirers reinforced an aura of beauty, keeping an apparently sacred object on the pedestal. But what, asked Simmel, if the vase had a handle? In inviting the observer to pick up, and conceivably use, an inviolable object, the handle connected transcendent beauty to the mundane.

"The Sociology of the Meal" presented the meal as the comprehensive link between the *high* and *low*. In this paradox of the table, Simmel (1994, 346) pointed to the basic selfishness of eating—no two people could eat physically the same food (the starting point of Locke's argument for property). Yet egoistic eating was shared like nothing else. Furthermore, the commonality, constancy, and exceptional self-interest of thirst and hunger necessarily gathered people more firmly and frequently than "higher and more spiritual motives." With illustrations of ancient sacrificial cults,

Arab hospitality, and the Eucharist, he observed how communal eating and drinking "releases a tremendous socializing power," sufficient to transform "a stranger who was recently a deadly enemy into a friend." Binding individuals so forcefully endowed the meal with "immense sociological significance."

The meal is the link—the handle or *axis mundi*—between earth and heaven. The tension is contained in the word "gastronomy," which binds each individual *gaster* (stomach) with the supraindividual *nomos* (law), a coupling captured in Brillat-Savarin's concluding exhortation: "profess, for the good of the science; digest, in your individual interest." It's the dialectic of the table, intrinsic to Epicurean dependence of the "pleasure of the stomach," intrinsic to many of my arguments in this book.

From this, Simmel decided that the art of meal giving was to balance crude individualism with cultural refinement. Participants should never let a meal remain unduly animalistic nor become too mannered. A flagrant display of raw hunger would be wrong; conversely, setting the table using the highly fashionable, "broken," and "nuanced" colors of Impressionistic art would let style dominate over substance. To balance imperatives, the dinner table should offer "simple, shiny colours which appeal to quite primary sensitivities: white and silver." Since style should not overwhelm actual dining, furnishings should avoid "extravagant, lively, provocative shapes and colours and should seek instead those which are calm, dark, heavy." The pictures on the wall should not be attention seeking but preferably family portraits, which "give the feeling of the customary, the reliable, that which harks back to ancestral roots."

As to table manners, Simmel argued that eating with the hands would be excessively individualistic. Clasping the knife and fork with whole fists would be ugly, because it hindered freedom of movement, unlike sophisticated, "nimble and free" gestures. The use of separate dinner plates encouraged individualism, he wrote, but using identical plates then elevated that individualism into a formal community. In the same way, conversation should blend the light and heavy. With care, the physicality of nourishment could become "more stylized, more aesthetic, and more supraindividually regulated" (347–48). With such etiquette becoming ethics, don't underestimate what Simmel was saying here.

In part 2 of this book I examined Enlightenment thinking about two great meal-sharing economies—the political economy, based on redistribution under government that preferably would move from monarchical to democratic, and the market economy, based on one-to-one exchange. Now, in part 3, I demonstrate corporate capitalism's capture and expansion of the market economy, pushing for laissez-faire rights with the support of a new science, calling itself "economics," and hanging from a simple simulation of buying and selling. In chapters 10 and 11 I will explain corporate appropriation with the help of Max Weber's guiding theme of "rationalization." Where he suppressed appetite and pleasure, as rationalization would want, I bring them back in, replacing his Protestant asceticism with profit's antigastronomic rationality.

This chapter starts with the story of the "classical," followed by the "neoclassical," economists, who, over Simmel's lifetime, transfigured the world into sublime mathematical expressions that put money in unrivaled command, quite detached from earthly needs. French economists had helped set the path, discerning a "natural" market mechanism, which attracted Adam Smith's attention. Following Smith's death, Jean-Baptiste Say's strong support for the *Wealth of Nations* switched David Ricardo and others on to wages, profits, and rents. Rather than their predecessors' medical science, the now pathbreaking, predominantly English economists were typically involved in business and debated not so much human needs as free trade, corn laws, poor relief, and the stock market. They generally cheered on profit's free-for-all. Then, around the 1870s, marginalists in different parts of Europe—Stanley Jevons, Carl Menger, and others— explained "value" in terms of the differential calculus.

Georg Simmel's Metropolis

In his most-read essay, "The Metropolis and Mental Life," originally published in 1903 and translated in 1948, Simmel (1971, 326–27, 329) found that, having left behind the slower rhythms of rural life, people struggled no longer with nature, but now with money. Abolishing all values but price, commerce had transformed the world into "an arithmetical problem."

As well as the demands of moneymaking, the necessity for "punctuality, calculability, and exactness" suppressed an individual's "irrational, instinctive, sovereign" impulses. With domestic production and barter "eradicated," buyer and seller no longer even knew each other.

This was heart-felt, because Simmel had been brought up at the corner of Friedrichstrasse and Leipziger Strasse, right in the center of Berlin's new retail, cultural, and industrial clamor. Then, in 1901, having recently published *The Philosophy of Money*, Georg, along with wife Gertrud and son Hans, moved to Berlin's new garden subdivision of Westend, where streets were named after trees. The Simmels turned from life as an "arithmetical problem" toward the forsaken abundance of nature and calm of rural life, in a comfortable home in Nussbaumallee or "Walnut-tree Avenue." Georg and Gertrud researched and wrote, and lived on inheritances (Georg Simmel's father had been involved with what became the Sarotti brand of chocolates, and his later guardian owned music publisher Peters Verlag). The couple also hosted cultivated gatherings of artists, critics, writers, students, and scholars during the so-called Wilhelmine era, which was Germany's Belle Epoque or Gilded Age.

Simmel's discipline of sociology had sprung up as a reaction to the massive technical and organizational changes through disruptive consumerism, city anonymity, and academic rationalization. Among important contributors, Karl Marx had expressed simultaneous dismay and hope in the rearrangement of social classes for the capitalist mode of production. Other sociologists were now worried by the loss of traditional, community bonds. Among Simmel's friends, Ferdinand Tönnies wrote about agrarian (*Gemeinschaft*) community giving way to total (*Gesellschaft*) organization along corporate lines.

Simmel and colleague Weber would react in different ways to laissez-faire's market society, with economic theorists characterizing cooperation as primarily "hungering" for financial gain; the technicians of Thomas Carlyle's "dismal science" pushed "mutual hostility" in a world that is "wholly a Shop." Rejecting the new "exactness," Simmel took some refuge in sophisticated inquiries into detailed interactions, while Max Weber simultaneously embraced, and feared, the overwhelming rationalization of life.

Some might regard Simmel's concern with dinner parties in a green suburb as privileged escape. Nonetheless, in retaining an allegiance to table satisfaction, Simmel's "sociology of the meal" was an urbane rebuke to the new calculus of price, with which Weber, as a professor of economics, tried to come to terms. Preferring the healthy individual's engagement with a healthy society, Georg would have directed hints about dining's irreplaceable joys across the table toward the perceptive but deductively seduced Max, whom Gertrud and Marianne might have ribbed for never entering a kitchen. What immensely influential economic ideas had taken hold through the nineteenth century?

Adam Smith's Liberty

Economists have long hailed the name of Adam Smith and his *Inquiry Into the Nature and Causes of the Wealth of Nations* in 1776. This was not the writer in my chapter 7, however, for whom the baker, butcher, and brewer shared tasks for dinner, and who supported the "liberal plan of equality, liberty, and justice" (4.9.519). Instead, modern economists seized on Anne-Robert-Jacques Turgot's friend—the free-market convert—found once Smith had laid out his book's groundwork.

Smith lived at the time of mercantilism—government policies that installed customs duties and export restrictions and supported international adventurism, including warfare, aimed at accumulating bullion. As Smith glossed the mercantile rationale: "A rich country, in the same manner as a rich man, is supposed to be abounding in money," and such a nation would "heap up gold and silver." For Smith, however, attempting to increase the wealth of a nation by detaining an "unnecessary quantity of gold and silver, is as absurd as it would be to attempt to increase the good cheer of private families, by obliging them to keep an unnecessary number of kitchen utensils" (*Wealth*, 1.4.1).

Besides, government intervention did not necessarily help commerce, Smith wrote, then introducing the example later developed by David Ricardo into the theory of "comparative advantage." Using "glasses, hot-beds, and hot-walls," good grapes could be raised in Scotland, Smith said.

However, employing thirty times more capital making claret and burgundy than somewhere better suited was "a manifest absurdity" (1.4.2). Just as people trusted that "freedom of trade, without any attention of government, will always supply us with the wine which we have occasion for; we may trust with equal security that it will always supply us with all the gold and silver which we can afford" (1.4.1).

Despite the "profusion of government" having "retarded the natural progress of England towards wealth and improvement," private capital had been "silently and gradually accumulated" (1.2.3), and private individuals were "continually exerting" themselves to find the "most advantageous employment for whatever capital" they could command. The capitalist, intending "only his own gain," was "led by an invisible hand to promote an end which was no part of his intention," frequently promoting society's interest effectively and unintentionally, and Smith backed the capitalist's judgment over that of "any statesman or lawgiver" (1.4.2).

Smith welcomed the "simple system of natural liberty"—natural, because it "establishes itself of its own accord. Every man, as long as he does not violate the laws of justice, is left perfectly free to pursue his own interest in his own way," and in competition with others. Foreshadowing the "calculation problem" confronting centralized control (later highlighted by Ludwig von Mises and Friedrich Hayek), Smith pointed out that no sovereign could ever have sufficient "wisdom or knowledge" for "superintending the industry of private people" (2.4.9). Nor, we might add, would money's subsequent wielders prove extraordinarily wise superintendents or their boosters universally civilized.

Harking back a century, Smith hailed "Mr. Colbert, the famous minister of Louis XIV" (Jean-Baptiste Colbert, in charge of French finances from 1665 to 1683); and yet Colbert "unfortunately embraced all the prejudices of the mercantile system" and "bestowed upon certain branches of industry extraordinary privileges, while he laid others under as extraordinary restraint." Quoting the proverb about straightening a rod by bending it as far back the other way, Smith said, since Colbert had favored town over country, French philosophers came to represent "agriculture as the sole source of the revenue and wealth of every country." Now the rod bent again, so that in a chapter "Of the Agricultural Systems," the *Wealth of*

Nations stood for commerce over agriculture. He cited the case of Holland, which, drawing "a great part of its subsistence" from other countries, demonstrated that a "small quantity of manufactured product purchases a great quantity of rude produce" (2.4.9). Smith found a land's success lay not in its weight of resplendent metals, nor even its productive soils, but in its efficient capital investments.

The popularity among English speakers of the slogan "laissez-faire" has been credited to American all-rounder Benjamin Franklin in a coauthored pamphlet in 1774, entitled "Principles of Trade," and which also used "*pas trop gouverner*: not to govern too strictly" (Franklin 1978). Earlier, in 1759, Smith's friend Turgot wrote that French merchants had gone to Colbert, advocating "*laissez nous faire*" (1844, 288). Without employing the phrase himself, although picking up the associated ideas, Smith nevertheless became the great wealth-making authority for the flurry of early nineteenth-century, "classical" economics and "classical" liberalism.

In 1776 Smith had retained clear references to actual human interests, but the meaning of the "wealth of nations" now rose further from general well-being toward private capital. Indicative of the strengthening capitalist milieu of these next writers, the Philadelphia Stock Exchange opened in 1790, Wall Street in New York in 1792, and London's first regulated exchange in 1801, and Napoleon asked architect Alexandre-Théodore Brongniart to design the Paris Bourse in 1807.

Say's Advocacy

Adam Smith's correspondent and admirer British politician Edmund Burke (1800, 4, 32, 46) urged Prime Minister William Pitt, in a lengthy memorandum in 1795, not to be tempted to alleviate "scarcity." Setting the style for the conservativism of recent decades, he argued that no government had the power to provide the necessities of life. Laboring people, Burke wrote, were poor because they were numerous. "Patience, labour, sobriety, frugality, and religion, should be recommended to them." The laws of commerce, he claimed, were "the laws of nature, and consequently the laws of God" (while workers were commercial commodities, to be recommended opiates). The State's responsibilities, recognized by Burke's *Thoughts and Details on Scarcity*, were merely "restraint," namely: "the exterior establishment of its religion; its magistracy; its revenue; its military force by sea and land; the corporations that owe their existence to its fiat; in a word, to every thing that is *truly and properly* public."

Conclusions drawn from Smith's major gathering of ideas were widely boosted by French economist Jean-Baptiste Say (1767–1832), who had worked for some months for sugar merchants in London and later spent some years editing a journal in Paris, *La Decade philosophique, litteraire, et politique*, in which he expounded Smith's doctrines. In 1803, Say published *Traité d'économie politique* (*Treatise on Political Economy*). Well before translations appeared in German in 1807, and English in 1821, serious economists were familiar with the work. Largely dismissive of Quesnay's "sect" of economists, although defensive of Turgot, Say (1821, xlviii, xxii) declared that the "science of Political Economy did not exist" until Smith's *Wealth of Nations*. Say credited Smith with confining *political economy* to wealth, separating this study from *politics*, which examined the "relations existing between a government and its people, and the relations of different states to each other."

Wealth might consist of forests, streams, farms, clever artisans, feasting townsfolk, wise elders, and grand city dining halls; it might result from hard work; it might be bulging bank vaults; or it might be decreed by the market. Claiming this last, Say praised Smith for having "demonstrated that wealth was the exchangeable value of things" and could be "created, preserved, accumulated, or destroyed" (xlvii). This was not "natural wealth" but "social wealth," which was "founded on exchange and the recognition of the right of property, both social regulations" (xxii n.). Wealth was "essentially independent of political organization," he wrote: "Nations have risen to opulence under absolute monarchs, and have been ruined by popular councils" (xxi).

Say's development of Smith's political economy, relegating politics, was taken up by, among others, David Ricardo (1817), Jean Charles Léonard de Sismondi (1803, 1819), Thomas Malthus (1820), and John Stuart Mill (1836, 1848), each running through increasingly standard questions of wealth, value, market price, labor costs, profits, trade, and taxes. Often business people or having close contacts with them, this new generation employed the circular argument that declared wealth to be what capitalists wanted. Often under the title *Principles of Political Economy*, the authors believed they enunciated scientific laws. "Political economy, in the same manner as the exact sciences, is composed of a few fundamental principles, and of a great number of corollaries or conclusions, drawn from these principles," claimed Say (xxxii).

Ricardo's Principles

David Ricardo made a fortune on the stock market, much through brazen manipulation based on couriering news from the Battle of Waterloo in 1815. Given the enemies he made, he was safer writing a book, *On the Principles of Political Economy and Taxation* (1817). Ricardo's preface opened: "The produce of the earth . . . is divided among three classes of the community; namely, the proprietor of the land, the owner of the stock or capital necessary for its cultivation, and the labourers by whose industry it is cultivated." Depending on the stage of society, the relative allocations differed between "each of these classes, under the names of rent, profit and wages." Political economy sought the laws that regulated this distribution, about which the "writings of Turgot, Stuart, Smith, Say, Sismondi, and others" afforded "little satisfactory information" (iii–iv). Instead, with tedious rigor, Ricardo analyzed political policies, price movements, and the laborer's requirement for mere "subsistence" to purchase "food, necessaries, and conveniences" (90). For example, in chapter 6, entitled "On Foreign Trade," he introduced "comparative advantage" by estimating the work required for producing wine and cloth in Portugal and England to indicate the profitability for each to specialize, even if production costs for *both* commodities might be cheaper in one country or the other.

As to its flavor (or trendsetting lack thereof), Ricardo's *Principles* was, to quote Robert Heilbroner (1980, 92, 99), "dry, spare, and condensed; there is none of the life, the lively detail of Adam Smith . . . nothing but principle, abstract principle. . . . we watch a model puppet show in which the real world has been stripped everything but its economic motivations." Yet unreality was a strength: "Ricardo gave the powerful tool of abstraction to economics," Heilbroner said, piercing the "distraction of everyday life" to expose its "underlying mechanism." Something becomes scarce, its price goes up, and the world becomes explicable! Another interpretation is that Ricardo entrusted well-being to money.

Ricardo enjoyed a famous friendship with cleric and professor of history and political economy, Thomas Malthus, although their personalities and ideas contrasted. Ricardo's *Principles*, which praised Malthus for having recently explained rent, nevertheless spurred Malthus (1820, 23) to respond with his own *Principles of Political Economy*. Malthus had a high opinion of Ricardo's sincerity, and his "talents as a political economist . . . while I have remained unconvinced by his reasonings." The core issue was Ricardo's embrace of the deductive method. Malthus accused him of promulgating "laws" that might appear beautifully logical, rather than inferring principle from numerous factual observations.

Political economy might "partake more of the certainty of the stricter sciences" than some other branches of human knowledge, and yet, Malthus warned, given the variability of people and soil, "we should fall into a serious error if we were to suppose that any propositions . . . lead to the same certain conclusions, as those which relate to figure and number." He said "a precipitate attempt to simplify and generalize" had "occasioned an unwillingness to acknowledge the operation of more causes than one" (1, 6). Malthus cited "great differences of opinion" on "the definitions of wealth and of productive labour—The nature and measures of value—The nature and extent of the principles of demand and supply—The origin and progress of rent—The causes which determine the wages of labour the profits of stock—The causes which practically retard and limit the progress of wealth [etc.]" (4).

While Malthus accepted that every person, adhering to the rules of justice, should pursue their own interest, it was also "universally acknowledged" that the sovereign still had much to do: "To what extent education and the support of the poor should be public concerns? What share the Government should take in the construction and maintenance of roads, canals, public docks," and colonization with forts in other countries (3, 18–19)?

Malthus worried that Ricardo's science lost contact with political realities. For Malthus, political economy still bore a "nearer resemblance to the sciences of morals and politics, than to the science of mathematics." That might detract from its certainty but "not detract from its importance." The science involved questions with the "nearest connection with the well-being of society," and principles "carefully founded on an experience sufficiently extended" would rarely disappoint (517–18). Malthus understood: "There are few branches of human knowledge where false views may do more harm, or just views more good" (12). Ritual warnings like Malthus's were ritually ignored, as ingenious ideology took hold.

Marcet's Conversations

Jane Marcet's account of chemistry in 1805 launched her series of popular introductions, called *Conversations*. A daughter of a wealthy merchant and banker, she had a thorough knowledge of the main economics texts, and experts liked her summary, *Conversations on Political Economy*, in 1816 (e.g., Say 1821, lvx n.). In these conversations, "Caroline" confesses to "Mrs B." to yawning at the mention of political economy. Adam Smith's name was "never uttered without such a respectful, and almost religious veneration," and yet "religion and morality teach us that . . . inordinate love of wealth is the source of all crimes." Mrs B. replies that laissez-faire principles "all tend to promote the happiness of nations, and the purest morality." Political economy shows that "the surest means of increasing national prosperity are peace, security, and justice," and a "liberal system of commerce" ensures that individuals, "far from growing rich at each other's expense, . . . mutually assist each other" (1817, 16, 24–25).

Mrs B. urges that "no productive enterprise can be undertaken without capital." Gathering mushrooms on the common or nuts or wild strawberries are "small remnants of a savage state," and even fishers needed capital for nets and boats; besides, they "must have something to subsist on, when the weather will not allow them to venture on the water." Requiring profit, capital might economize with an "abridgment of labour," Mrs B. accepted, but the savings will be applied to some other purpose—"an advantage both to the proprietor and the public, and eventually affords employment for the labourers thrown out of work" (98–99, 118).

Laissez-faire vs. Limited Liability

After a stormy political career in England and France, the staunchly liberal Thomas Cooper (1759–1839) emigrated to the United States in 1794, along with fellow chemist Joseph Priestley. Thomas Jefferson supported Cooper's appointment as professor of chemistry at South Carolina College (later university) in 1819. Picking up a second professorship in political economy, Cooper published *Lectures on the Elements of Political Economy* in 1826 (preface, 2, 5), lamenting the "manifest ignorance or neglect" among American politicians of "a branch of knowledge, on which human happiness so much depends." In Europe, the recent disquisitions of Malthus and Ricardo had alerted governors to the "great truths of Political Economy." Acceptance of the principles hinted at the "dawn of a new day; and of peace on earth." Replacing the "wicked and destructive" maxims of mercantilism, ideas of less expensive government let people and nations "gain in prosperity, in proportion as their neighbours gain also." Cooper recommended that "acquiring and accumulating what we call WEALTH" enabled the emergence from barbarism to the "comforts and enjoyments of civilised life."

Cooper called government the "most wantonly extravagant and ill managed establishment that the people have to support," and "apt to engage in foreign wars, and to incur a national debt." The best government was "effective at the least expense to the people," and the English public finally understood the reasonableness of Colbert's request, "*laissez nous faire*; let us manage our own business . . . no government has knowledge enough to interfere. . . . Every individual in the nation better knows how to employ his industry, skill, and capital to the best advantage for himself and his family" (preface, 22 and n., 50–51).

As a liberal, Cooper vigorously opposed corporations. Such "institutions are founded on the right claimed by government to confer privileges and immunities on one class of citizens not only not enjoyed by the rest, but at the expense of the rest." Corporations were hangovers from the mercantilist system, which had "contributed to the splendor of courts, the extension of patronage and power, and the poverty of the people." The old system had made "war, plague, pestilence, and famine" seem inevitable (18).

As Cooper saw it: "The object of the companies, apparently, is, first to obtain large profits by exclusive privilege and monopoly. Secondly, to be licensed to run in debt to an indefinite extent, under a limited liability of payment. A mode of swindling, quite common and honourable in these United States."

The Constitutional Convention had specifically ruled out the U.S. Congress from granting incorporation, unfortunately accepted under state governments. Accordingly, the country had "glutted itself by incorporating banking companies, insurance companies, canal companies, and manufacturing companies of various descriptions. All these are increasing daily" (206).

Cooper had "no objection in great and expensive undertakings to joint stock companies, who can by joint effort, manage a concern that an individual fortune is not competent to undertake." The principle, however, had to be that of partnership, "viz. those who claim a dividend of unlimited profits, are liable to the loss." No special government protection should be involved, abiding by the rule, "let us alone." In Great Britain, all shareholders were "individually responsible in their separate and private fortunes for the debts of the concern of which they are partners" (210, 212), although that would change with the Joint Stock Companies Act of 1844 and Limited Liability Act of 1855.

Cooper was far from the only economist to find limited liability incorporation contrary to laissez-faire ideals. Adam Smith (*Wealth*, 1.4.2) had wanted to "break down the exclusive privileges of corporations" of the mercantilist era, and Jean-Baptiste Say (1821, 256) complained: "An exclusive privilege, a species of monopoly, is created, which the consumer pays for, and of which the privileged persons derive all the benefit . . . the prosperity of the corporation is mistaken for that of commerce and of the nation." Thomas Jefferson translated French theorist Antoine Destutt de Tracy's *Treatise on Political Economy* in 1817 (several years after its composition, although before its publication in French). In his introduction, Jefferson commended the work of Smith, and Say for condensing and improving on Smith, and he also hoped that "diffusing sound principles of Political Economy" would "protect the public industry from the parasite institutions."

That this intense liberal opposition to corporations might be surprising to many modern readers points to a mighty illusion—economists having transferred arguments about natural individuals, whose appetites are served by economies, to artificial corporations, which pursue gain. Actual individuals might share subsistence, comfort, or even luxury, but the new "individuals" obsessed about "rent, profit and wages" (Ricardo). The once universal problem of the next meal became incidental, suppressed in favor of a simplistic value. As Georg Simmel found, the struggle was no longer with nature but with money, the world as a mathematical problem.

Karl Marx described this historical elevation of economics in the afterword to the second German edition of *Capital,* volume 1, in 1873. The "vulgarising and extending of Ricardo's theory" went along with modern industry's emergence from childhood, he observed, when "the class struggle was as yet undeveloped." After 1830 in both France and England, when "the bourgeoisie [business owners] had conquered political power" and beaten off the landowning aristocracy, the class struggle took "more outspoken and threatening forms" and "sounded the knell of scientific bourgeois economy." "It was thenceforth no longer a question," Marx wrote, "whether this theorem or that was true, but whether it was useful to capital or harmful, expedient or inexpedient, politically dangerous or not. In place of disinterested inquirers, there were hired prize fighters; in place of genuine scientific research, the bad conscience and the evil intent of apologetic."

Marginalization

For decades, economists debated the source of value. Among the possibilities, value might be intrinsic to an item, depend on the labor required, or respond to usefulness. Anne-Robert-Jacques Turgot would have shared with Adam Smith a manuscript proposing that value was actually decided by the market. As Turgot (1795, 33) also explained, the "value of the wine and corn is not fixed by the two proprietors with respect to their own wants and reciprocal abilities, but by a general balance of the wants of all the sellers of corn, with those of all the sellers of wine." Smith (*Wealth*, 1.1.4) went on to distinguish "use value" and "exchange value," using the example of water and diamonds. "Nothing is more useful than water; but . . . scarce anything can be had in exchange for it. A diamond, on the contrary, has scarce any value in use, but a very great quantity of goods may frequently be had in exchange for it."

In the same year as the *Wealth of Nations*, 1776, philosopher Étienne Bonnot de Condillac (1714–1780) contributed *Le Commerce et le gouvernement considérés relativement l'un à l'autre* (Commerce and government, relatively considered), writing about water being worth little more than the price of its cartage, and yet it was a "primary need" worth carting. On the banks of a river and on a desert, its price would be different, requiring a distinction between a good's value and its *"utility"* (14–16). Later Ricardo (1817, 388–89) explained that production cannot create, only "reproduce matter under another form—we can give it utility." That is, production created not a glass of water but "utility." In turn, this was estimated by market exchange of certain quantities of one commodity for another. "This valuation . . . constitutes what Adam Smith calls value in exchange; what Turgot calls appreciable value; and what we may more briefly designate by the term *value.*"

After almost a century of economists trying to nail value, brilliant English exponent W. Stanley Jevons took one of the discipline's biggest leaps, coming up with "marginal utility." In a paper, delivered in 1862 under the title "Brief Account of a General Mathematical Theory of Political Economy," Professor Jevons (1866) still spoke of individuals experiencing, and anticipating, pleasure and pain. For him, satisfaction required calculations, balancing the pain and pleasure to be gained. Then, an even bigger step: "Every appetite or sense is more or less rapidly satiated," he said. After immediate hunger is satisfied, the necessity of extra nutrition diminishes. Accordingly, he argued, the calculating consumer knew that every bit of *additional* food provided less benefit or "utility". Inversely, the seller's labor became increasingly painful. Pleasure tailed off for the pleasure-seeker until in balance with the laborer's pain, when it occasioned an exchange.

This principle of diminishing returns was already familiar to mathematicians. By his *Theory of Political Economy* in 1871, Jevons was determined: "Economics, if it is to be a science at all, must be a mathematical science." Given how the "nature of Wealth and Value is explained by the consideration of indefinitely small amounts of pleasure and pain," the secret was the application of the "differential calculus" (viii, 3–4). "Repeated reflection and inquiry have led me to the somewhat novel opinion," Jevons announced, "that *value depends entirely upon utility*" (2). Value was not intrinsic to the item, not what the king decreed it to be, not the amount of labor it had cost, nor any other option but what a calculator would pay. The marginality came in because purchasers found decreasing utility—cost worried them more and more toward their limit. Water was exceedingly valuable if in short supply, but someone with plenty would pay next to nothing for more (4). He introduced the marginal theory of utility with a series of graphs to show that the first part of someone's food was essential for life, but as more food was added, the less necessary the extra was to a person's happiness. Food's diminishing utility might therefore be investigated through the mathematics of "infinitesimally small" changes of variables reaching equilibrium (52–63).

Thomas Hobbes (1994, chap. 15.2) had alluded to such a principle when writing: "I define ENDEAVOUR to be motion made in less space and time than can be given . . . motion made through the length of a point, and in an instant." Prussian economist Hermann Heinrich Gossen had published marginalist ideas in 1854, unnoticed. Gaining greater recognition, founder of the Austrian school Carl Menger published *Principles of Economics* in 1871, and French-Swiss Léon Walras came out with *Elements of Pure Economics* soon after. After the "classical" revolution, led by Say and Ricardo, this decisive leap around the 1870s became the "neoclassical" or "marginal revolution." The centerpiece was still supply and demand, but the marginalists found prices responding on a sliding scale, which suggested how to handle variables hovering around equilibrium. After the revolution, typically now ascribed to Jevons, Menger, and Walras, the mathematical elegance seemed so compelling that market price outshone any concern with actual satisfaction. Economists became convinced that the differential calculus unlocked not only the laws of economics but those of the whole social world.

That's a condensation of the marginalists' sleight-of-hand that banished material needs in a puff of gold dust. Henceforth, already a simple sum, "utility" became a residual category, food's pleasure losing out to price. Eaters now paid disappearingly tiny attention to infinitely small accretions of pleasure or pain. They no longer preferred white to yellow peaches, merely cheaper. A clever mathematical device had brought out the mystery of the Market.

Modernity's "Overconfidence"

W. Stanley Jevons (1871, 85) accepted that the shift in concern from actual wine and corn to their price was tied up with market capitalism. "By a *Market*," he wrote, "I shall mean much what commercial men use it to express." As he recognized: "Originally a market was a public place in a town where provisions and other objects were exposed for sale; but the word has been generalised." That is, Jevons abstracted the Market from community exchange—involving growers, cooks, and diners—to an overarching, organizational power under "commercial men." Here was the Market, which he capitalized, and that set prices, which both responded to and determined activities and had the authority of science.

In the much-read *Principles of Economics* of 1890, English synthesizer Alfred Marshall set out: "Economics is a study of men as they live and move and think in the ordinary business of life." He meant "business" narrowly, explaining that "definite and exact money measurement of the steadiest motives in business life . . . enabled economics far to outrun every other branch of the study of man." It was incomparably the most scientific human science because "the force of a person's motives—*not* the motives themselves—can be approximately measured by the sum of money, which he will just give up in order to secure a desired satisfaction" (1.2.1). The economist "does not claim to measure any affection of the mind in itself, or directly; but only indirectly" (1.2.3). That is literally superficial, however:

FIGURE 8.1 Panic at the New York Stock Exchange, May 5, 1893. Library of Congress reproduction of *Frank Leslie's Illustrated Newspaper*, May 18, 1893, 322.

a physicist measures heat expansion with little pretense that a number is the actual iron rod, whereas economists tended to mistake their equations for the economy.

"Money valuations pervade all our thinking," marveled Herbert J. Davenport in *The Economics of Enterprise* in 1913. Under this "competitive order," he delighted that "market price" had become "the central and unifying problem of present-day economics." An economics professor at Missouri and later Cornell University, Davenport enthused that winning in the new "régime of price" was to have "scored in the most widespread and absorbing of competitions." Now a great artist was judged not by any intrinsic merit, he said, but by "what do his pictures sell for?" He celebrated that "all great political issues, and almost all absorbing social problems, and almost all international complications rest upon a pecuniary basis" (21–25). Mind you, educated at Harvard, Chicago, Leipzig, and Paris, Davenport had returned to academia after losing mightily on real estate.

Over the decades, economists removed inconvenient realities. They ignored the original *oikos*, brushed off politics as noneconomic, pushed aside material needs and desires as "utility," and abandoned all values but Market price. Deliciousness, satisfaction, civility, reverence, and survival were irrational, therefore unscientific, and so unreal. A technical, otherworldly model came to rule our lands. Greed moved from some limited, predictive power to a law of the universe.

Sounding the Alarm

By the early nineteenth century, wide-ranging philosophy split into many academic responsibilities, including those for animal, domestic, market, political, and natural economies. This multiplied scientific knowledge but weakened gastronomic cohesion, so that Epicureanism became philosophically unimportant, and Brillat-Savarin genially eccentric. Money also pushed the newly constricted "economics" of wages, profits, and rents into greater and greater command.

In 1832 Oxford professor of "political economy" (and later archbishop of Dublin) Richard Whately supported Say's advocacy of dropping the "political." He cautioned that *"Political-Economy"* was "most unfortunately chosen"—being based on two almost contradictory Greek terms, the *polis* and *oikos*, "the one treating of the affairs and regulation of a Commonwealth, the other, originally at least, of a private family." He also worried that a "man is called a good economist" for merely "prudently regulating, so as to prevent waste, all the details of his household expenses."

Forget all that, Whately urged, because the science was more interested in the person "making his fortune by a judicious investment of his capital in some successful manufactory or branch of commerce." Although the ultimate interest might be profit, the science was now "concerned, universally, and exclusively, about exchanges." People might be defined as the "animal that makes *Exchanges*." Accordingly, Whately suggested a new name, "catallactics," for the "analysis of market phenomena" (5, 6, 9). "Catallactics" did not catch on, despite Austrian school support more than a century later (e.g., Mises 1966, 3, 233–34; Buchanan 1964, 217; Hayek 1976, 108–9). Instead, the "political" was let drop.

The imperialism of self-proclaimed "economists" would seem to have frightened *animal* and *natural* economists into becoming physiologists and ecologists and undermined *political* economists, although the most poignant casualty was the original *oikonomia*. By 1861, in London, a book on the original economics had to be called *Beeton's Book of Household Management*—"household management" being a direct translation of *oikonomia*. The first meeting in the United States of scholars of the now tautological "*home* economics" was held in Lake Placid, New York, in 1899, attended by nine women and one man. The study was seriously *humble* (Latin, *humus*, soil), so that the adoption of scientific methods initially seemed progressive, and created professional openings for women teaching other women. Corporations, however, co-opted the field's "original message of women's liberation through control of the domestic environment" for selling to housewives, decided American food historian Megan Elias (2008, 2). An "intellectual movement" became "product-focused."

Mainstream economics suited moneymakers but attracted major criticism. Early on, some German materialists rediscovered sustenance. Among them, Ludwig Feuerbach reiterated the pun *Der Mensch ist was er isst* (People are what they eat). Reared on roast beef, the English worker was superior to the lazy Italian with a predominantly vegetable diet, he said. Blaming the failure of the 1848 revolution in Germany on sluggish potato blood, Feuerbach recognized "the pledge of a better future, which contains the seeds of a slower and more gradual, but also of a more thorough, revolution. It is beans" (quoted Hook 1933, 127).

Materialism could never remain as "medical" or "vulgar" as that, and Karl Marx inserted social organization. That is, potatoes would generate characteristic behaviors not directly but through associated economic activities. As Marx put it in *Grundrisse* (1973), hunger is different when "gratified by cooked meat eaten with a knife and fork," rather than flesh bolted down raw with tooth and claw. The starting point of Marx's economics was expressly "metabolic," although early English translators hid references to *Stoffwechsel* (metabolism) in such literal guises as "exchange of matter." The *production* of subsistence distinguished humans from other animals (Marx and Engels, *Manifesto*, 1.1.A). Food production produced our social relationships, technology, consciousness, history and estrangement, Marx (1977, 96) said. "The forming of the five senses is a labour of the entire history of the world down to the present."

Examining production picked out historical stages, such as gathering, followed by agrarianism and then industrialism, and found capitalism simplifying Ricardo's three classes to two: the owners of the powerful new organizational, technical, and coal-fueled means of production, and those who had only their labor to sell. Marx's *Capital*, volume 1: *The Process of Production of Capital* (1867) was a heavyweight entry and remains among key texts for continuing "political economists." None of these inheritors could be accused of neglecting material welfare, but enshrining *production* shifted the focus from meals. Workers would sweat blood in steelworks, often without dinner, nor much family life. Exalting production demoted nature, too.

Georg Simmel, a public intellectual in Wilhelmine era Berlin, showed civilized concern with both money and meals that took him beyond simple disciplinary boundaries. His friend and the far more accepted scholar Max Weber recognized that capitalism relied on rational organization, which blurred social classes. Weber features in the largely sociological critique that supports chapters 10 and 11, although, he returns with his own indefensible narrowness.

Depression "Scarcity"

Having introduced political economy as the study of "public or national wealth," early American exponent Daniel Raymond argued in 1820 that, according to "the sum of human happiness" involved, his science must be the most "interesting and important" (9). He was right, but economists already idealized profit seeking, or, as Aristotle knew it, chrematistics; they were seduced by the laws of market price, or catallactics; and, seemingly without shame, they appropriated the name, economics. Nevertheless, money is power, and its contours pressed further and further into human affairs.

Then, the Great Depression rattled economists into internal debates and public defenses. Progressive British economist William Beveridge had launched the London School of Economics's journal, *Economica*, in 1921 by defining economics as "the study of the general methods by which men co-operate to meet their material needs" (2). In a doctrinaire defense, however, the head of economics at that same institution, Lionel Robbins, insisted in 1932 that those still studying "the causes of material welfare" were lazily repeating outdated ideas, which he insulted as "the last vestige of Physiocratic influence" (4, 9). His definition of economics as choosing between "scarce means" became the most quoted, and this "scarcity" was a mathematical abstraction, rather than a material reality, and his *Essay on the Nature and Significance of Economic Science* (1932, 87–88) advocated the concern be "maximisation." While admitting that "I may be interested too in the happiness of my baker," and that "certain liens" might make that baker's more expensive bread preferable, nevertheless explaining *why* people valued something was not "part of our problem." Fair enough. Yet after disregarding "individual valuations and technical facts" as "the *irrational* element in our universe of discourse" (98), he still claimed that economic analysis enabled people "rationally to choose between alternative *systems* of society" (138). Such was the power of money.

While human beings could never afford to ignore the "irrational elements" of satisfaction, survival, and suchlike, the inconvenient fact remains that the rational pursuit of profit distinguished business corporations. To hide this elephant in the room, economists accorded the corporation selected human rights, so that they still might pursue, from Robbins's definition, their "science which studies human behaviour." In an expanded edition of the same work, Robbins accepted that judging "the different satisfactions of different individuals" went "beyond the scope of positive science." Yet he was affronted that others read that admission as meaning economic science had to stand aloof from the political fray (1935, vii–viii). For him, extreme abstraction actually *endorsed* political prescription. The more abstract, he argued, the more scientific. Robbins wanted to pursue starry-eyed simplification to find the "laws" of a hard science that should run government, and then to deny outrageous self-contradiction.

With other economists' certitudes shaken by the stock market crash of 1929, one of Robbins's economics challengers down the road at Cambridge University, the innovative Joan Robinson, produced an introductory booklet, *Economics Is a Serious Subject: The Apologia of an Economist to the Mathematician, the Scientist and the Plain Man* (1932), in which she emphasized the unreality of the necessary assumptions. She understood that this irritated both the "mathematician," who wanted to follow logical rules, and the "plain man," who would question such audacity. For a hundred years, economics had become "at once primitive and over-confident" and so had "done more harm than good in the sphere of political life." Economists should continue to advise governments, she believed, but should "explain frankly" the considerable limitations of their knowledge (13–14).

The standard assumption of *perfect* competition had "some aesthetic charm," Robinson noted in her subsequent *The Economics of Imperfect Competition* (1933, 3–4), although "somewhere, in an isolated chapter, the analysis of monopoly had to be introduced." Nonetheless, she remained fearful that economists had convinced themselves that their logic actually had "importance in the real world." Their duplicitous "optimism" led them "to hope that no one will notice quite how unreal their assumptions are," and to not quite know themselves what the assumptions were (1932, 8; 1933, 3). Amid the disillusionment with economics, in 1936, English economist John Maynard Keynes contributed his magnum opus, *The General Theory of Employment, Interest and Money*. Economists had to widen their vision from the microeconomics of exchange to make macroeconomic room for government involvement.

Given life's intricacies, thoughtful simplification is unavoidable, and price performance indicates something. Flexible, and platonically enduring, money provides a convenient handle on certain metabolic activities. It is a compelling power (for those that have it). Unfortunately, while actual material welfare might depend on taste, observation, conversation, and more, big money never lacked the wherewithal to control people and resources.

Many critics concede that profit-pursuing capitalism has come up with goods, but, with human happiness at stake, economics has to get back to roots, to reground thinking. A more gastronomic economics appreciates life from humus through hummus to humor. The next chapter harkens to a truly humorless economist whose political agenda, vehemently reasserting mainstream economic models, has devastated our world.

9

LUDWIG VON MISES, NEOLIBERAL GODFATHER

"The Evening Was a Disaster"

In Margit von Mises's memoirs, *My Years with Ludwig von Mises* (1976), she fondly recalled meals with her husband throughout Europe and the Americas. When Ludwig taught in Geneva during the 1930s, for example, the couple would take Sunday drives across the border to restaurants in France (40). While he might never have consulted sightseeing guidebooks—"a Baedeker or a Fodor, [for] these things he knew"—he used the *Guide Michelin* for restaurants (49). At Alfredo's in Rome, the owner himself prepared the fettuccine, "mixed them, whipped and beat them with a golden spoon and golden fork, and only after this imposing ritual was the waiter allowed to give everyone his portion" (151). During two months in Mexico City in 1942, they saw street people "in rags, with naked, dirty feet," while the couple were regularly feted by a former secretary of the Mexican treasury in his sprawling mansion and exotic gardens (76–79).

On other evidence, however, one of the twentieth-century's most influential economic thinkers, Ludwig von Mises (pronounced "Meezez"), was no lover of the table. He never learned even to boil an egg, according to Margit, and repeatedly called instant coffee the "greatest invention of the twentieth century" (85). His own memoirs mentioned no dining, and his wife intimated why.

As a widowed actress, age thirty-five, with two children, Margit had met Ludwig, age forty-four, at a dinner party in Vienna in 1925, when his posture "indicated the former army officer" (21). She found him talking economics, deeply unhappy, and living with his aristocratic mother, who had "a will of iron, showing little warmth or affection for anyone" (24). Ludwig's father had died more than two decades earlier, and mother and son sat opposite at a long table, "always set immaculately," with his mother never speaking one word. Margit learned about these austere dining habits from her husband's long-term colleague, Friedrich Hayek, because Ludwig was never prepared to introduce the two women, and only finally married Margit after his mother's death in 1937 (25). Margit believed that her husband's upbringing accounted for his extraordinary punctuality, invariably arriving first at any lunch or dinner engagement, and his unfailingly wearing a jacket at a meal, even when unbearably hot and just the two of them (143).

A major figure in the Austrian school of economics, Ludwig von Mises (1881–1973) used meals to make contacts and converts—the French restaurant jaunts belonged to his many years courting the highly cultured Margit. French economist Jörg Guido Hülsmann (2007, 847) reported in his 1,160-page appreciation that Mises's private seminar in Vienna routinely moved from his offices in the *Kammer* (chamber of commerce) "to Ancora Verde for dinner, then to the Café Künstler to continue the conversation late into the night." Borrowing well-known Viennese tunes, that original Mises Circle sang about their beloved marginal utility and its proponents and opponents. Keeping up the tradition, participants in Mises's New York University seminars from the late 1940s would repair to Child's Restaurant, followed by the Café Lafayette, and adherents sing the original verses to this day.

Fleeing Europe to New York with his now wife in 1940, Mises struggled to find academic work. Nevertheless, he gained an influential circle of admirers, including finance journalist Henry Hazlitt, marketing executive Lawrence Fertig, and the head of Coty cosmetics, Philip Cortney

(Philippe Cotnareanu), who was a pamphleteer for wealth and who, for many years, invited "the family" of the Miseses, Hazlitts, and Fertigs for dinner at the Plaza Hotel, where Cortney permanently reserved the "round corner table, number 1," Margit reported (1976, 91–92a).

Ludwig remained unhappy. His "astonishing temper" drove his wife to tears (44); he could be "unbelievably stubborn" (143), and he "could never talk about his feelings" (148). One thing she never understood: "In thirty-five years of marriage he never, never—not with a single word—referred to our life together during the thirteen years before our marriage" (43). She associated his continued sadness with his fears for the end of civilization. Having lived through the violent rise of Communism and National Socialism, and as a minor aristocrat and secular Jew, Mises longed for the peace and order that capitalism promised. But he fretted that "the world would turn its back on capitalism and liberalism (in the old sense of the word)." Already, Margit added, the fight against the "foes of liberty and the free market had broken the spirit" of the Austrian school founder Carl Menger, "had thrown a dark shadow over the life" of Ludwig's teacher and friend, sociologist Max Weber, and "had destroyed the vitality and the will to live" of Mises's original collaborator in Vienna, Wilhelm Rosenberg (45).

As I investigated in chapter 5, Enlightenment political philosophy resisted autocracy by emphasizing the universality of material needs. From the mid-eighteenth century, however, French *économistes* initiated the study of a separate market economy. As found in chapter 8, in the nineteenth century David Ricardo pushed market deductivism, and although Thomas Malthus (1820, 2) still objected that political economy should be nearer to "the science of morals and politics than to that of mathematics," Adam Smith's successors dropped the "political," implicitly announcing a new science. The attendant "classical" liberalism of laissez-faire became the antithesis of Enlightenment liberalism.

In the 1930s macroeconomist John Maynard Keynes moved the other way, reasserting the importance of politics in economics. Hot on his heels, however, Ludwig von Mises insisted on Market rule under government protection. In his appreciation, Hülsmann called Mises the "last knight of liberalism," meaning "classical" liberalism. Better to understand Mises as having established the arguments of *neoliberalism*, a fiercely probusiness interpretation.

For geographer David Harvey (2005, 2), neoliberals claimed that human well-being was best advanced "by liberating individual entrepreneurial freedoms and skills within an institutional framework characterized by strong private property rights, free markets, and free trade." While Harvey scarcely mentioned him, Mises had led the way by openly declaring the Market's antagonism to democracy and equality, to welfare and the family, and the environment. "Nothing" was as "ill-founded," Mises (1985, 28) declared, as the "alleged equality of all members of the human race. Men are altogether unequal." Instead: "No deviation from the unhampered market economy is thinkable without authoritarian regimentation" (1966, 729).

Only widely acknowledged after his death, Mises inspired many economists, as well as business leaders, politicians, and activists. Numerous right-wing commentators adopted his contemptuous tone (although, admittedly, often with some feeling for irony). Neoliberals demanded Market solutions at almost any cost—and much has indeed been spent promoting Mises's ideas through the Heritage Foundation, American Enterprise Institute, Liberty Fund, Cato Institute, Youth America's Foundation, and other think-tanks and activist bodies. Following a split in the Cato Institute, anarcho-capitalist Murray Rothbard was a principal founder of the Ludwig von Mises Institute in 1982.

Mises's scientific capitalism turned up in government when, a month before his death in 1973, the U.S.-supported coup against socialist Chilean president Salvador Allende ushered in Augusto Pinochet's military dictatorship, and the neoliberal formulas of Milton Friedman and the "Chicago boys" (graduates of the University of Chicago). This was soon followed by Reaganomics in the United States, Thatcherism in the United Kingdom, and the Washington Consensus more widely—policies favoring privatization, outsourcing, corporate-adjusted regulations, reduced government services, increased security expenditure, tax cuts, and financial wizardry.

Many present-day economists might consider that their mathematical sophistication has pushed Mises to the margins, but he recognized clearly the extent to which their rational postulates signposted an idealistic program. By extending the "frigid" calculus of maximizing behavior (Becker 1976, 4–5), economists had joined Mises in projecting competitive exchange as a total solution. He asserted the present "greed is good" order that has shape-shifted from free enterprise through neoliberalism to autocracy.

Removing all nonfinancial characteristics of the individual while making corporations invisible was such a severe task that Mises crashed through with self-contradictions. Unabashed Market fundamentalist Mises revealed how economists had mathematically laundered capitalist principles, initially claiming that was for approximation, and then presenting them as panacea.

In summary, the Mises that I find in this chapter represented modern economics as highly abstracted—alienated, even—from human needs. He set aside human sustenance as "subjective." He recognized that the power of money necessarily suppressed egalitarianism and participatory democracy. The *Homo economicus* model did not permit any collective action, although an exception was made for protecting business. Finally, according to the new science's core model, corporations did not exist.

In chapters 10 and 11, I will employ the sociological concept of rationalization to show why meals were dismissed from not only economics but almost all serious consideration for two centuries. Mises's own discomfort at dining did not necessarily predispose him to antigastronomic rationality but did not bode well.

Neoliberal Triumph

As the leading economist of the Austrian school in the first half of the twentieth century, Ludwig von Mises studied under Eugen von Böhm-Bawerk, who had been an immediate disciple of school founder Carl Menger (introduced in chapter 8 as an inventor of marginalism). Mises influenced not only his eventually more famous student, Friedrich Hayek, and others identifying with the Austrian school but also other leading economists, including Lionel Robbins at the London School of Economics and Frank H. Knight and Milton Friedman at the University of Chicago.

FIGURE 9.1 Ludwig von Mises among leading "Austrian school" economists. Artwork by Krapulat. Creative Commons Attribution-Share Alike 4.0 International. Courtesy of Wikimedia Commons.

In his early career with the Vienna Chamber of Commerce, advising government, Mises had backing from the Rockefeller Foundation, and his American exile was supported by individual business leaders and the William Volker Fund, which also set up Friedrich Hayek at the University of Chicago. In turn, supporters have pinpointed his influence not only directly on the Austrian, German, and U.S. governments but also on the British through Robbins, Italian through Luigi Einaudi and French through Jacques Rueff.

Bedazzling students, associates, politicians, and business leaders with uncompromising talk of epistemology, praxeology, and apriorism, Mises promoted market capitalism in such works as *Socialism* (originally 1922, expanded 1932), *Liberalism* (1927), *Epistemological Problems of Economics* (1933), and his magnum opus, which he worked on in Geneva from 1934 and published as *Nationalökonomie: Theorie des Handelns und Wirtschaftens* (National economy: theory of action and economics) in 1940, and which he expanded into the more than nine hundred pages of *Human Action: A Treatise on Economics* in 1949. In a review for *Newsweek* magazine, business journalist (and friend) Henry Hazlitt (2011, 141) hailed *Human Action* as "at once the most uncompromising and the most rigorously reasoned statement of the case for capitalism that has yet appeared." The text was the "counterweight of Marx's *Das Kapital*, or Lord Keynes's *General Theory*."

A gathering of intellectuals discussing Walter Lippmann's ideas on liberal democracy had used the term "neoliberalism" in Paris in 1938. However, that meeting's acceptance of a strong state alongside the price mechanism was rejected by participants Mises and Hayek, who went on to launch the hard-line Mont Pelerin Society in 1947. The initial meeting warned that the "most precious possession of Western Man, freedom of thought and expression," was imperiled, requiring a commitment to "private property and the competitive market." Mont Pelerin meetings have continued to attract leading right-wing economists, a string of whom would win Nobel Prizes.[1]

The most influential economic theorist in the other half of the twentieth century, Milton Friedman (1991, 18), who attended Mont Pelerin from the first meeting, acknowledged that "no one has done more to spread the fundamental ideas of free markets than Ludwig von Mises." Speaking to libertarians, Friedman added: "nobody has done more to develop a popular following for many of these ideas than Ayn Rand." Both theorist Mises and popularizer Rand were "extremely intolerant," he said. This was personally, as well in their writings, both of them advocating "absolutely certain knowledge," thereby converting "an asserted body of substantive conclusions into a religion." When the Hazlitts invited Ayn Rand and her husband Frank O'Connor to dinner with Dr. and Mrs. von Mises, "The evening was a disaster."

Espousing Misesian doctrine with Nietzschean overtones, novelist Rand promoted "rational selfishness." Like Mises, Rand attracted an intense New York circle in the 1950s. Her self-declared "Collective" included Alan Greenspan, who became the head of the U.S. Federal Reserve for two decades. Upon Rand's death in 1982, Greenspan was among eight hundred mourners at a Madison Avenue funeral parlor. As reported in the *New York Times*: "Ayn Rand's body lay next to the symbol she had adopted as her own—a six-foot dollar sign" (Chira 1982). Libertarians filed past, testifying to the reporter that they had been intellectually "lost" until finding Rand's advocacy of individuality, rationality, and free-market capitalism.

As Hülsmann (2007, xii) noted, Mises died in October 1973 at the age of ninety-two, with "only a small circle of admirers and disciples, but this group became the nucleus of a movement that has grown exponentially. Today his writings inspire economists and libertarians through the world." Within months, his former protégé Friedrich Hayek leapt to prominence by sharing a bankers' Nobel Prize.

With funding flowing from wealthy business people, many economists joined proliferating think-tanks as "senior fellows." Under a banner of "Austrian Economics, Freedom, and Peace," the Mises Institute promoted "a profound and radical shift" from statism and political correctness "toward a private property order." When last checked, all twenty-two senior fellows of the institute were male, and mostly professors of economics, along with lawyers. Such think-tanks fed statistics and arguments to sober business commentators, economics bloggers, and Australian-British-American media magnate Rupert Murdoch's staffs.

"In this present crisis, government is not the solution to our problem; government *is* the problem" was not an auspicious inaugural address by a U.S. president. When Ronald Reagan listed six intellectual heroes on March 20, 1981, four of them were economists already mentioned in this chapter: Hayek, Hazlitt, Friedman, and Mises.[2] Prime Minister Margaret Thatcher went further in a *Woman's Own* interview in 1987: "There is no such thing as society." Complaining about people recasting their problems as society's, she demanded: "and who is society? There is no such thing! There are individual men and women, and there are families. And no government can do anything except through people, and people must look to themselves first."

Operating in oil, fertilizers, cattle ranching, plastics, and packaging, America's second largest private company, Koch Industries (pronounced "Coke"), includes, among its numerous brands, Lycra and Dixie Cup. After building oil refineries for Joseph Stalin and Adolf Hitler during the 1930s, entrepreneur Fred Koch turned to libertarianism and became a founding member of the anticommunist John Birch Society. In 1983, after a family struggle, Charles and David Koch took over. At one stage ranked equal sixth richest individuals in the world, the pair funded so many activist organizations that even friendly forces have labeled them the "Kochtopus." The Kochs have opposed antipollution measures, for example, not without self-interest, since Koch Industries scored in 2012 as the biggest U.S. producer of toxic waste (Mayer 2016, 168–69).

The Kochs backed populist campaigns that centered on the Tea Party and then unloosed Donald Trump. They linked with the likes of hedge-fund pioneer Robert Mercer and daughter Rebekah, backers of such right-wing actions as Breitbart news and big-data manipulator Cambridge Analytica. With the Trump ascendancy in January 2017, the billionaires gained allies in key cabinet posts. Once Stephen K. Bannon returned from working with Trump to Breitbart, he and the Mercers pushed hard to shift the Republicans further right, and to boost populism in Europe.

In his book *The Science of Success* (2007, x), Charles Koch credited his thinking to Mises's *Human Action*: "As an engineer, I understood that the natural world operated according to fixed laws. Through my studies, I came to realize that there were, likewise, laws that govern human well-being." Mises (e.g., 1966, 761) had extrapolated these laws of "human action" into "laws of the universe," available to economics, Koch said.

Spreading well beyond Viennese coffeehouses, Mises's reasoning helped inspire inequality, niggardly action on climate change, mocking of parliaments, enforced austerity in Greece and elsewhere, and demoralizing uncertainty, leading to autocratic takeovers. Enormous street protests, exemplified by "Occupy" camps in more than nine hundred financial centers across the globe, might have represented "the 99 percent," but Ludwig von Mises had backed the money.

Money as God—the Rest Is "Subjective"

Ludwig von Mises wrote in *Human Action: A Treatise on Economics* in 1949 (1966, 2, 285) that market regularities were the "laws of social cooperation," so that people could no longer organize society as they pleased. "One must study the laws of human action and social cooperation as the physicist studies the laws of nature." Separating the "economic" and "noneconomic" spheres of "human life and action" would be a "spurious distinction."

Mises's simplification of life to Market exchange relied on the Austrian theory of "subjective value," meaning that "value is not intrinsic; it is not in things. It is within us" (1966, 96). A person's "preference for water, milk, or wine" depended on neither the qualities of the drink nor its physiological effects, but on the person's "valuation" of those effects. "If my friend prefers to dress, be housed, and eat as it pleases him . . . who can blame him? . . . It is his valuation that counts, not mine or other people's" (1981, 404–5).

The subjectivity was no problem because of the extraordinary fact that all value was revealed in buying and selling. People must value a good to purchase it, and their keenness showed in price. The movement of prices could now be studied, leaving everything else aside. Individuals trying to sell for the highest price and buy at the cheapest produced "not only the price structure but no less the social structure" (1966, 311). By applying mathematical logic, neoclassical economics provided a "more universal science" of human action, called praxeology (3), the only objective way to understand, and therefore run, the world.

Economists' deductions were necessarily correct, Mises (1966, 34–35) explained, because they used the same rationality (the same "logical structure of the human mind") that guided all human action. Mises called this "methodological apriorism." I have difficulty not finding a circular argument trapping economists inside the echo chamber of their own rationality.

Mises scoffed at people talking about extraneous matters. Whereas Alfred Marshall's (1890, 1.1.2) economics textbook had still allowed "two great forming agencies of the world's history . . . the religious and the economic," Mises (1966, 166–67) derided any "fable of the mystic communion," including the many stories of "God's power and love," the "voice of the blood which brings the father close to his child," and "mystical harmony between the ploughman and the soil he tills." He rejected Christian consciences because their "substitution of social justice and righteousness for selfish profit-seeking" would necessitate "authoritarian regimentation" (729). Most especially, he scorned labor union appeals to some "eternal laws of morality" in seeking minimum wages because as soon as wage rates were fixed, "unemployment emerges" (769–70).

Mises delighted in "acquisitiveness," "greed of capitalists," and "greed of the wealthy few" (585, 852). Moreover, *every* human action was selfish because it invariably aimed at the "attainment of a state of affairs that suits the actor better" (735). Wanting to sip cocktails in the vicinity of a duke might seem "ridiculous vanity" but still aimed at an improved "state of satisfaction." Overriding a preference for food "the more appetizingly and tastefully it is prepared, the finer the table is set, and the more agreeable the environment," the individual would still seek "the cheapest market" (241–42).

A succession of economists have cautioned that neoclassical economics of itself did not justify capitalism. John Stuart Mill (1836, 12–13) knew that, by attending to money, the new economics "makes entire abstraction of every other human passion or motive." No political economist "was ever so absurd," he thought, as to actually believe that people were "occupied solely in acquiring and consuming wealth." Studying the possible consequences of "the desire of wealth" was but a branch of a greater science of "*social economy*." Joan Robinson (1962, 25) remained mindful that "economics limps along with one foot in untested hypotheses and the other in untestable slogans." Even greed enthusiast Milton Friedman (1991, 17–18) could advocate "humility.... We do not have all the answers."

Yet for a century theorists had adjusted to money's rule, which Mises now proclaimed as the "laws of human action." He did not seek a *sensible* understanding of the world, involving pleasures, passions, and amities. Hatched in Viennese cafés, New York hotels, and Swiss resorts, Mises's scientific capitalism backed Market logic, hedge funds, and plastic Dixie cups.

Market Rule

Ludwig von Mises (1966, 269–71, 311) was adamant that the economy was run by "merciless bosses, full of whims and fancies." But who were these tyrants? "The captain is the consumers," he explained. "Neither the entrepreneurs nor the farmers nor the capitalists determine what has to be produced. The consumers do that." Entrepreneurs had to "obey unconditionally" the "law of the market, the consumers' sovereignty." Intent on monetary gain, every individual was bound to contribute "most to the best satisfaction of everyone else" because the unimpeded market rewarded only those producers who met consumers' needs.

The owners of breweries and distilleries would have published "devotional books, had the demand been for spiritual and not spirituous substance," Mises observed (1981, 403). Similarly, he absolved armament manufacturers of pressing for war: "It was not Krupp and Schneider who incited the nations to war, but imperialist writers and politicians." The rise of "merchants of death" was the result of people's "warlike spirit, not its cause." If the "principles of the market economy were acknowledged by all people all over the world," wars would cease (1966, 282, 300).

Mises was equally adamant, however, that the "direction of all economic affairs is . . . a task of the entrepreneurs." While capitalism was "the consummation of the self-determination of the consumers," the "striving of entrepreneurs after profits" was the "driving power in the market economy" (1966, 269, 683, 299). On one hand, entrepreneurs were "virtually mandataries or trustees of the consumers, revocably appointed by an election daily repeated"; on the other, the "marvellous economic improvements of the last two hundred years" were "an achievement of the capitalists" (271, 301).

Mises expected producers to induce consumers to act even against their own interests. That the "consumer is not omniscient" necessitated commercial advertising, or "propaganda," as he called it: "Business propaganda must be obtrusive and blatant. It is its aim to attract the attention of slow people, to rouse latent wishes, to entice men to substitute innovation for inert clinging to traditional routine. . . . Advertising is shrill, noisy, coarse, puffing, because the public does not react to dignified allusions" (317). Mises conceded: "Like all things designed to suit the taste of the masses, advertising is repellent to people of delicate feeling." He had heard that advertising "should be forbidden. The consumers should be instructed by impartial experts." But restricting "the right of businessmen to advertise their products would restrict the freedom of the consumers to spend their income according to their own wants and desires" (320).

He argued the superiority of the market "democracy"—consumers voting in continual dollar plebiscites (729). In a political democracy, "only the votes cast for the majority candidate or the majority plan are effective. . . . But on the market no vote is cast in vain. Every penny spent has the power to work upon the production processes." Having no time for "one person, one vote, one value," he wanted plutocracy, saying that the "rich cast more votes than the poorer citizens" only because "this inequality is itself the outcome of a previous voting process." To be rich followed "success in filling the best demands of the consumers. A wealthy man can preserve his wealth only by continuing to serve the consumers in the most efficient way" (271).

Opposed to egalitarianism, except "under the law" (to which I return), he was adamant that the elimination of inequality of incomes and wealth would remove incentives, and "entirely destroy the market economy" (840). It was a fact: "freedom is incompatible with equality of wealth and income" (1981, 287). Those with get-up-and-go were "merely superior to the masses in mental power and energy." These great men—"promoters, speculators, and entrepreneurs"—would be first to pick a "discrepancy between what is done and what could be done" and fill that gap (1966, 336). By contrast, the common person "relies upon other people's authority . . . like a sheep in the herd" (46).

Mises explained his opponents' egalitarianism as "envy" of the "higher income of prosperous businessmen." This "widespread frailty" drove many intellectuals toward socialism. "They believe that the authorities of a socialist commonwealth would pay them higher salaries" (90). Only capitalism opened up the "prosperous development of human society," making private property "not a privilege of the property owner, but a social institution for the good and benefit of all" (1985, 30).

Ultimately, Mises could assert that the Market outweighed government, sense, civility, nature, etc., through resolute commitment to laissez-faire capitalism, which solved everything, full stop. Embarrassingly for mainstream economics, he simply believed its assumptions.

Capitalism, or Else

One of Mises's favorite techniques was to pose a stark choice—the alternatives were "apodictic and absolute" (1966, 196). The two options amounted to the price mechanism or total planning, to capitalism or war, to siding with money or being a soft-hearted, envious dupe. Mises then chose capitalism, and, since the world is complex, this required inconsistency. At one point, greed was a human universal: "Whereas in a capitalist society selfishness incites everyone to the utmost diligence, in a socialist society it makes for inertia and laxity" (677). Elsewhere, a committed communist bureaucrat might actually work hard to "court the favor of those in power" (274).

Little matched his hypocrisy about the state. He dismissed democracy and welfare and overlooked corporate reliance on government for planning, infrastructure, regulation, subsidies, correcting externalities, outsourcing, and so on. Instead, "considerable" taxes for the "government apparatus of courts, police officers, prisons, and of armed forces" were "fully compatible with the freedom the individual enjoys in a free market economy" (282).

In 1920 Mises set out the Austrian school's often-quoted claim that a socialist commonwealth was unachievable because of the "economic calculation problem," that is, the world's complexity made central direction of "rational economic activity" impossible (1935, 130). As quoted earlier, Adam Smith (*Wealth*, 2.4.9) said sovereigns lacked the wisdom and knowledge to superintend the lives of ordinary people. Economics professor Max Weber (1968, 103) found a "planned economy" impossible unless some non-Market way were found to ascribe value. When "self-styled welfare economists" ignored complexity, Mises (1966, 834) suggested, they were trying to hide their "fallacies" behind a word (welfare) that might "disarm all opponents." Society's complicated task could be entrusted only to his alternative. Money did "all that we are entitled to ask of it—a guide amid the bewildering throng of economic possibilities" (1981, 100–1).

Mises toughed out internal contradictions for his own combative reasons. But why am I bothering? Not only have Mises's ideas permeated recent thinking, but he pursued the antigastronomic ideals of neoclassical economics to the bitter end. In deploying key arguments, Mises demonstrated that economics had adapted to, and then advocated, corporate logic. Not that Mises accepted the existence of corporations.

Throughout, Mises remained committed to individual liberty. "Since time immemorial in the realm of Western civilization liberty has been considered as the most precious good....'Rugged' individualism is the signature of our civilization" (1966, 284). This was no everyday individual, however—not marked by dignity, wisdom, compassion, nor that most self-centered of attributes, a healthy appetite.

Extreme Individualism

Standardly, economists have practiced *methodological individualism*— "methodological" because complex economies are studied *as if* they had no systemic qualities. Alfred Marshall (1890, 1.2.6) accepted that: "As a cathedral is something more than the stones of which it is made, . . . so the life of society is something more than the sum of the lives of its individual members." All the same, he recommended that "in most economic problems the best starting-point is to be found in the motives that affect the individual."

The opposite has gone under such names as "organicism" or, in Mises's list, "universalism, conceptual realism, holism, collectivism, and some representatives of *Gestaltpsychologie*" (1966, 146). Accordingly, Aristotle (1932, 1235a) found the city was naturally prior to the household, and to the individual. Just as the human body must exist before the foot or hand, an individual could not exist independently of the city.

Materialists, such as Epicureans, have resolved the chicken-or-egg conundrum through the idea of emergent properties. Two thousand years ago an unknown Latin poet composed *Moretum*, describing a poor farmer cooking a meal before going out to plow. With mortar and pestle, he pounded herbs, salt, cheese, olive oil, and vinegar into a *moretum* or pesto. The ingredients blended into something more than each alone, or, as the poet wrote, *e pluribus unum* (out of many, one) (Kenney 1984). With a whole coming together out of his citizens, the United States borrowed *e pluribus unum* as its motto in 1792.

By 1820, however, America's first dedicated author on political economy, Daniel Raymond (1820, 27–28), bemoaned a "prevailing error." While other writers "profess to treat of national interests, they depart from the subject and treat of individual interests." He spelled out: "A nation is a UNITY," and anyone who "treats of the interests of some constituent part of it, will just as certainly arrive at a wrong conclusion." Raymond knew that "individual wealth is often national poverty."

In 1908, summing up intense debate, in which Max Weber had argued for individual agency over social, a young economist then identifying with the Austrian school, Joseph Schumpeter (1980, 2, 5), pleaded that methodological individualism merely helped explain price phenomena, and not how things *should* be politically. Ludwig von Mises (1966, 43, 143) resolved otherwise. He opened *Human Action*: "Society is concerted action, cooperation"—but only, he stressed, as the gainful action of individuals. "That there are nations, states, and churches, that there is social cooperation under the division of labor, becomes discernible only in the actions of certain individuals." An individual might be born into society as a system of self-interested actions, but in no other sense was "society—logically or historically—antecedent to the individual." A society could not act or have a purpose; it was "a delusion" to search for society "outside the actions of individuals."

Nobel economist Kenneth J. Arrow (1994, 1) later confessed that, while "the actions and reactions of individuals" were "a touchstone of accepted economics," practitioners defied their own strictures by using "social categories" as "absolute necessities of the analysis." That is, "economies" and "markets" were active agents. For example, stoutly individualistic Chicago economist Gary Becker (1976, 5) wrote that "market instruments . . . *constrain* the desires of participants and *coordinate* their actions" (emphasis added). For Mises, while dollar votes might restrain the poor harshly, nothing should interfere with the "*structure* of the market." He was emphatic: "Nothing is left of economics if one denies *the law* of the market" (1966, 758, 761; emphasis added).

Mises differentiated between *hegemonic* bonds, imposed by a third party, and mutual contracts between individuals and found that human history had been a slow shift from hegemonic to contractual cooperation (500). The family and the state relied on the "hegemonic bonds of the older days, slavery and serfdom" (196–98), so that progress required the withering of not merely feudalism and slavery but also the family and state. With the "invisible" visible to economists, "interpersonal exchange of goods and services weaves the bond which *unites men into society*" (194).

And where did Mises find one-to-one contracting "individuals"? The heaviest market hitters would be corporations, which are clearly dedicated to the price mechanism, and without distraction of appetite or affection. Given how corporations form none but contractual bonds, they should be Mises's truly amoral, rational, "rugged" heroes. However, corporations might be far more tightly organized, and militant, than any trade union, and often "too big to fail," but Mises never railed against them, because they simply did not exist. Every producer and consumer was an individual. "Laissez faire means: Let the common man choose and act; do not force him to yield to a dictator" (732). Any joint stock company that did not "wither in bureaucracy" relied for its prosperity on being run by the founder, or by other actual individuals with major shareholdings (1981, 185)

Recall that Mises (1966, 842) scorned equality, except "under the law," which extended freedom of enterprise to all, notably corporations. I keep finding that the economists' "individual" has been a Viktor Frankenstein amalgam, enjoying selected human rights to act like a coldly calculating monster, without appetite.

Uncomfortable at the table, especially the family table, where he expected the father to "supervise everything," Mises (1981, 101, 108) fantasized about a society based not on meals but on purely rational calculations, catallactic deals, and profit targets. For him, the "economic" was "nothing but the sphere in which money calculation is possible." Rather than the dining table, he celebrated the poker table at which corporations became the biggest bankrolled and most fixated cardsharps, dealing unequal hands.

Liberty of Profit

Naming is tricky, but who would credit that the Ayn Rand Institute would disown the tag "libertarian"?—they are "objectivists." Similarly, supporters of the Ludwig von Mises Institute would reject "neoliberalism," wanting "liberalism" or "libertarianism." But who was a "liberal"? Mises himself objected with typical intensity, and proprietorial adamancy, to the confusing uses of the label.

In 1927 he published *Liberalismus*, eventually translated as *Liberalism: In the Classical Tradition* (1985, 10, 19), which made clear that capitalism and "classical" (laissez-faire) liberalism were identical. Condensed to a single word, his liberalism was "*property*, that is private ownership of the means of production." Mises argued that the "brief and all too limited" supremacy of this political program "sufficed to change the face of the earth." The "release of man's productive powers multiplied the means of subsistence many times over," improved living conditions, reduced infant mortality, and lengthened the average span of life. By the eve of the Great War, the ordinary worker could not only "eat and drink according to his desire; he could give his children a better education.... It is thanks to [capitalist] industries that the masses today are far better clothed and fed than before" (1, 11).

In *Human Action* (1966, 153–54), Mises still wrote: "Liberalism, in its 19th century sense, is a political doctrine ... an application of the theories developed ... especially by economics." Speaking generally, that version survived in Europe, but now living in the U.S., he confronted strong support for a Lockean, social liberalism. Mises declared science to have found against the "metaphysical nonsense" of the Declaration of Independence, along with natural rights based on appetite: "Nature is unfeeling and insensible with regard to any being's life and happiness" (174). Nothing separated that eighteenth-century liberalism from his liberalism, Mises acknowledged, as readily as the treatment of equality. But the assumption that "God created all men equal" was "ill-founded." It was "beyond human power to make a Negro white." That left merely equality under the law (28), which permitted *Homo economicus* to be a characterless calculator.

Twentieth-century liberal usurpers had "reversed the meaning of words" (especially in the United States), he said, and they dared complain that the market economy "grants liberty only to a parasitic class of exploiters, the bourgeoisie." Economists had done "a brilliant job in unmasking" the "crass fallacies and contradictions" of those calling themselves the "true *liberals*," but who should really be labeled "advocates of totalitarianism" and "fanatical planners" (284–85).

Caught up in violent political upheavals, Ludwig von Mises took fright at totalitarian political economies and waved capitalism's flag. No constitutions, bills of rights, laws, or statutes directly produced freedom, he said. "There is no kind of freedom and liberty other than the kind which the market economy brings about." Quite simply, freedom was an "effect of competition" under capitalism (283–85). This was, of course, a constricted freedom because, as he claimed elsewhere, price-pursuit controlled everything "more strictly and exactingly than could any government or other organ of society" (1981, 401).

Repackaging Mises's conviction that civilization's great advances had been the "products of individual genius," Milton Friedman (1962, 4) cherished "economic" ahead of political freedom. He saw "freedom as the ultimate goal and the individual as the ultimate entity," but such liberalism had been hijacked, so that the twentieth-century "catchwords became welfare and equality rather than freedom" (5). The new American "liberals" did not deserve the name, he said, because the only two ways to coordinate the economic activities of large numbers were either "coercion" or the "voluntary cooperation of individuals—the technique of the market place" (13). With the enemies of private enterprise having appropriated "liberal," believers in freedom had had to adopt the label "libertarian" (Friedman 1991, 17).

Seemingly also not noticing, Friedman (1962, 15) decried "coercion of a man by his fellow men" on the same page as supporting "economic power." The "great threat" was the concentration of power (2), and yet "in a capitalist society, it is only necessary to convince a few wealthy people to get funds to launch any idea" (17).

From their websites recently, the Cato Institute stood for "individual liberty, limited government, free markets and peace"; the Mises Institute shortened that to "Austrian economics, freedom, & peace"; whereas the Heritage Foundation retained a socially conservative luster, wanting "free enterprise, limited government, individual freedom, traditional American values, and a strong national defense." None of these right-wing ideas factories mentioned equality, democracy, life, or happiness, let alone conviviality, but favoring the Market, as Mises showed, meant rejecting fellow-feeling.

Put simply, the tussle back and forth bequeathed four distinct liberalisms, chronologically: Enlightenment (Epicurean, Lockean, or natural law) liberalism; classical (laissez-faire or rational) liberalism; social (Keynesian or welfare) liberalism; and neoliberalism (Market or Misesian). They alternated between cooperative meal making and competitive moneymaking, between the liberalism of appetite and the antiliberalism of greed.

Once-fashionable German historian Oswald Spengler observed in *The Decline of the West* (1991, 366–67; originally published in two volumes in 1918 and 1922) that power had shifted from the *demos* (people) to *ploutos* (wealth). The original (Enlightenment) liberalism seemed to have been a mere "wish" or "theory" that, in seeking to contest money, only ended up assisting it. For the ideals of "equality for all, natural rights and universal suffrage" had opened up freedom of expression, which required money. He decided: "the freedom of the press brings with it the question of possession of the press, which again is a matter of money, and with the franchise comes electioneering, in which he who pays the piper calls the tune."

I decline Spengler's cynicism and instead, in later chapters, will explain how the liberalism of meals enjoys its fifth, "politically correct" restoration.

Alone Amid Civilization

In 1719 prolific English writer Daniel Defoe published, to shorten the title, *The Life and Strange Surprizing Adventures of Robinson Crusoe, of York, Mariner: Who Lived Eight and Twenty Years, All Alone in an Un-inhabited Island . . . Having Been Cast on Shore by Shipwreck, . . . Written by*

Himself (1831). Defoe's novel forged a new form, in which a solitary writer communicated a protagonist's inner thoughts to a lone reader. Ever since, Robinson Crusoe's adventures have attracted young and old, and economists, who find the true individual. In *Human Action* (1966, 243), Ludwig von Mises was ready to concede that the so-called Robinson Crusoe economics of the isolated or "autistic" (Mises' term) actor was entirely imaginary, but strict individualism, he insisted, was still necessary to theorizing.

Not that the hero of Defoe's novel was actually detached from civilization. Thriving on an island near the mouth of the "Oroonoque," he had brought economic baggage from Europe, including hunting and other implements, rescued from the shipwreck. Relying on age-old experience, he built a table. "I could not write, or eat, or do several things with so much pleasure, without a table: so I went to work" and henceforth "spread my table in the wilderness" (1831, 72, 139).

Even more than that, "Our friend Robinson Crusoe . . . having saved a watch ledger, ink and pen from the shipwreck, he soon begins, like a good Englishman to keep a set of books." In an early section of *Capital*, Karl Marx (1.1.4) also found Crusoe preoccupied not with market exchange but with production. For Marx, Crusoe represented the dignity of labor, with the stranded mariner reporting: "I could not live there without baking my bread, cooking my meat, &c" (Defoe 1831, 189). Economic value came from labor, not exchange, was Marx's argument, and Crusoe himself frequently noted that money was useless.

A preoccupation with the freely exchanging individual remained a ridiculous "Robinsonade" for another reason: it neglected Crusoe's physiological and hedonic needs. His meals were solitary, but they still served the pleasure of the stomach. In the world as an "arithmetical problem," dinner had disappeared, including an Englishman's preoccupation with meat, bread, and pleasure.

In another literary classic, *A Christmas Carol* in 1843, Charles Dickens depicted Bob Cratchit's family living happily together and celebrating Christmas with goose, mashed potatoes, gravy, and applesauce. Then, as beneficiaries of Ebenezer Scrooge's unexpected philanthropy, the family even more joyously shared a great turkey. The miserly Scrooge had rediscovered his humanity when, dining miserably alone, he recalled that his dead, money-lending partner, Jacob Marley, was chained for eternity by his own greed. Dickens wrote that Marley's ghost remained bound by "cash-boxes, keys, padlocks, ledgers, deeds, and heavy purses wrought in steel." The "iron cage" features in the next chapter.

10

RATIONALIZATION AND CORPORATE PURPOSE

Markets vs. *Super*-Markets

Of all the "spectacular" food markets in Italy, the "one near the Rialto in Venice must be the most remarkable," reported English cookery writer Elizabeth David (1987, 142) in *Italian Food* in the early 1950s. She extolled: "every separate vegetable and fruit and fish luminous with a life of its own. . . . Here the cabbages are cobalt blue, the beetroots deep rose, the lettuces clear pure green, sharp as glass. . . . In Venice even ordinary sole and ugly great skate are striped with delicate lilac lights, the sardines shine like newly-minted silver coins, pink Venetian *scampi* are fat and fresh, infinitely enticing in the early dawn." Watching the "gentle swaying of the laden gondolas" and workers "swinging boxes and baskets ashore" and hearing "the robust life and rattling noise," David decided: "the whole scene is out of some marvellous unheard-of ballet."

Confessing a lifelong love affair with the farmers' market in Los Angeles, the French market in New Orleans, and Les Halles in Paris, New York food writer Mimi Sheraton (1997, 25, 29) extolled a market's "magical" sight, "heady" smell, and food that whets the appetite and whose trading requires "mixed undertones of passion and planning." Numerous elements came into play, because "markets deal with food and food is life."

Leading sociologists did not share these positive assessments. Karl Marx and Friedrich Engels (*Manifesto*, chap. 1) complained in 1848 of traditional motivations drowning in "the icy water of egotistical calculation"; Max Weber (1968, 636–37) called the market "the most impersonal relationship of practical life into which humans can enter." Buyer and seller were not interested in one another but in "the commodity and only that," so that the free market seemed "an abomination to every system of fraternal ethics."

Perhaps the food writers were unduly nostalgic or romantic—even "ordinary" fish looked fresher in Venice. Perhaps David and Sheraton were unreasonably charmed as outsiders, sometimes not even speaking the language. Another cynical reaction might be that globe-trotters from East Sussex, England, (David) and Brooklyn, New York, (Sheraton) showed off their privilege.

The key difference, as I have brought out in preceding chapters, is that the gastronomic authors wrote about the "whole scene" (David)—"markets deal with food and food is life" (Sheraton). By contrast, the social scientists lamented the loss of personal connections under the new regime of profit-and-loss. The cries, sights, and face-to-face routines of a growers' market were lost to "impersonal" prices. The one was market as meal, and the other was nearer the economists' abstraction. Economic historian Karl Polanyi (1957, 243–44) described economists as studying *formal* Markets, while people dined in *substantive* ones: "The laws of the one are those of the mind; the laws of the other are those of nature." In the "economistic fallacy," Polanyi (e.g., 1977, 6) said, economists adulated the rational supply-demand mechanism, only remotely connected to an actual economy.

Economists are better understood in a supermarket. On one level, the experience is the same. However, the foodies and sociologists might be more agreed: shrouded fish, hermetically canned vegetables, and silently shouting snacks, lacking smell and taste, jostle for attention. Bottles and boxes line the central aisles or "morgue"; the smallgoods counter, meat cabinets, and warm bread "carts" mimic competition around the perimeter. With conversation replaced by piped tunes and exhortations, shoppers squint at prices and lunge at special reductions. This is no longer a public but a corporate *super*-market, with controlled sales, security cameras, and

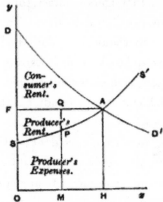

FIGURES 10.1A AND 10.1B The market (Les Halles, Paris, 1879) vs. the Market (Marshall's supply-and-demand graph, 1895). Painting by Jean Béraud. Courtesy of Wikimedia Commons; Alfred Marshall, *Principles of Economics*, 8th ed., 1920, courtesy of Liberty Fund.

mass data collection. Walled in by products in masses of plastic, Marx's scorn and Weber's despair prove more compelling.

In this chapter and the next, I dig deeper into economists' suppression of material imperatives. The explanation: capitalism. More correctly, it is *corporate* capitalism. While even the most hard-nosed capitalist has to eat, corporations concentrate on money, without distraction. Under laissez-faire, single-minded corporations rationalized social life, and ideas about it.

"Corporations," here, are tightly organized, task-oriented entities, ultimately in search of profit. Behind closed doors, such firms as Nestlé, Unilever, Pepsico, Mondelez, Mars, and Diageo employ armies of a magnitude that would have amazed Alexander the Great. Other corporations support with materials, transport, energy, and finance. One recent figure was that thirty-seven of the world's one hundred largest financial powerhouses were not states but corporations. Another was that Walmart's revenues compared with the twenty-fifth largest national GDP. These interests and actions reshape economies, and the supervisory science of economics.

I present business corporations in this chapter as *purposive organizations*. Other instances include criminal gangs, orchestras, and government departments. Such teams engage in what Max Weber encapsulated as "rationalization"—the relentless application of systematic methods for achieving a clear objective, increasingly the purest. With profit as their end, corporations rationalize the world, measured in weights, volumes, times, percentages, targets, ratings, remunerations, prices, and dividends. To a large degree, substantive markets belonged to an irrational world in which people were intimately familiar with seasons, and cooking qualities, techniques, and lore, whereas David and Sheraton themselves contributed to the post-Enlightenment condition, in which literacy enabled reading both the packaging and their books about what was being lost.

Overturning corporeal appetite, corporate greed reengineered the world and its people, in conformity with business models. Moneymaking machines twisted the liberalism of equality and democracy into money's freedom, and economics with it. Yet business firms have remained unnatural members of any economy.

Profit as Pure Purpose

Aristotle separated the natural community of the city and its constituent fraternal, religious, and business associations (1935, 1241b), and such distinctions have been used since. Tweaking that, Thomas Hobbes (1994, chap. 19.9) spoke of the overall body politic, within a commonwealth and under a sovereign, as a union, itself instituting "subordinate" unions "for certain common actions" for the benefit of either the subordinate union or the city, and usually called a "corporation." Hobbes also devoted chapter 22 of *Leviathan* (1651) to "systemes," or "any numbers of men joined in one Interest, or one Businesse," acting like the "Muscles of a Body natural."

In his *Encyclopédie* entry on economics, Jean-Jacques Rousseau (1755, 338) differentiated between economies and *sociétés particulières*. He wanted the control of the economy to come under the combined opinion of citizens, the *volonté générale*, seeing this "general will as the first principle of public *economy*, and the fundamental rule of government." Expressed in the rule of law, for Rousseau, "the voice of the people is in fact the voice of God." Opting for better citizens, he advocated public education, preferably along Enlightenment lines. That was especially necessarily, given the worrying despoliation of the general will by the little general wills of *sociétés particulières*, that is, of small, private, "special societies" or "partial associations" (*Social Contract* 2.3). Membership of special societies could compromise the public economy. "An individual might be a devout priest, or a brave soldier, or a zealous patrician, and a bad citizen," Rousseau said. "One deliberation may be advantageous to the small community, and very pernicious to the great," a caution still worthy taking seriously.

To understand economies, follow the food. Distinctive circulations of sustenance animate bodies, kitchens, markets, cities and other political communities, and the living planet. Whether known as a "household," "home," "body," "organism," "physiology," or "food system," an economy remains a cooperative organization of comprehensive life support—that is, the members, first, work together, and, second, the whole addresses the range of members' basic needs. In healthy economies, every component is valuable. Internal controls can make them relatively "natural," "spontaneous," or "self-organizing." In turn, trying to specify a "purpose" would be misleading. Not mere tools nor instruments, they are to be assured a measure of freedom.

To understand corporations: follow the money. They are a subcategory within a lately highly successful class of organizations, whose essence is tool-like. For, as well as participating in economies, people work in *purposive organizations*. These are the separate category of organization picked out by Aristotle, Hobbes, Rousseau, Tönnies, and others as "associations," "unions," or "*sociétés particulières*," and by more recent writers as "hierarchies," "institutions," and "organizations." U.S. social theorist James S. Coleman (1990, 584) depicted a modern industrial society "composed of purposive corporate actors wholly independent of the family." Whereas an economy might be judged in such general terms as "life," "health," or "naturalness," the performance of government agencies and business corporations is often subject to exact measurement.

Systematic labor can be highly useful, but purpose's punch can be hazardous, encouraging impersonality, secrecy, arbitrariness, self-perpetuation, and overreach. As tools, purposive organizations *must* be directed from outside; left alone, they keep doing their thing like the budding sorcerer's brooms. With the ability to raise its own funds, a corporation does not even require shareholders, which, anyhow, are often "institutional," that is, other corporations. Whereas a family is a life-giving bonding of persons "as one," a hedge fund is designed to convert everything endlessly into money. At best, smart investments indirectly assist. At worst, they chew up real wealth and corrupt legal and economic thinking.

Purposive organizations fail one or both of the two criteria for an economy: that is, they serve nonmembers and/or they do not address basic needs. As an example, some institutions can meet alimentary and related needs but not mutually—such as a hospital with separate staff and patients. In other cases, such as a golf club or sclerotic government department, they might serve members but not across life-preserving needs. Not that the distinction is always clear: monasteries aspire to being single-purpose households (so becoming, in their Weberian routines and obedience, prototype corporations).

As blurred as the economic/purposive distinction might become, it nevertheless assists in clarifying the gap between the market and Market. Essentially, the former operates without purposive intrusion. The participants are individuals or, often more exactly, families, who open an aspect of their production to exchange. In treating a market as money-based, purposive organizations degrade the "free" in free market. In the name of the "self-regulating" market, neoliberal theorists campaigned against (non-compliant) governments and trade unions but, hypocritically, rarely worried about corporations.

Arch-economist Ludwig von Mises announced in *Socialism* (1981, 261–63; originally 1922) that "organism and organization [*Organismus und Organisation*] are as different from each other as life is from a machine, as a flower which is natural from one which is artificial." An organism was a spontaneous creation, based on "mutuality," whereas an organization depended on "authority" imposed from outside. So far good, except Mises then limited his organisms to market society—"in the living body there is no longer leader and followers"—whereas the socialist dictator would "tear a living plant to bits," ensuring that "collectivist movements are doomed to failure." As well as exaggerating government malevolence, Mises studiously ignored profit-seeking firms ripping a "living plant to bits."

Making Monsters

Corporations have existed for centuries as guilds, hospitals, universities, municipalities, scientific societies, and traders. In *A Treatise on the Law of Corporations*, London barrister Stewart Kyd (1793, 13) covered the main points, including that this "body" had a name and was "acting, in several aspects, as an individual," except that, as he also wrote, as "merely a political institution, it can have no other capacities than such as are necessary to carry into effect the purposes for which it was established." This "artificial form" was not a "moral agent," not "subject to personal suffering," nor "capable of personal action" (70–71). Corporations were only occasionally commercial, notably the bank and insurance companies, and "others for the regulation of trade, manufactures, and commerce, such as the East India Company" (28–29). Under government charter, the East India Company ruled large areas of India, and its undercutting of American tea merchants triggered the Boston Tea Party in 1773, and thus the American Revolution. Corporations often got a bad press.

In Adam Smith's day, "workmen desire to get as much, the masters to give as little as possible," and Smith knew which side had the upper hand.

The "masters, being fewer in number, can combine much more easily." Backing that, many acts of parliament actively prevented workers combining. The landlord, farmer, master manufacturer, or merchant could also hold out for perhaps a year, whereas many workers "could not subsist a week," Smith wrote (*Wealth*, 1.1.8). Even back when mercantilist agents were more clearly a combination of individual employers, Smith wanted to "break down the exclusive privileges of corporations, and repeal the statute of apprenticeship, both which are real encroachments upon natural liberty," along with the "law of settlements" that inhibited a "poor workman" seeking work in another trade or parish (1.4.2).

Upon its foundation in 1801, the London Stock Exchange was still "widely viewed as a locus for morally indefensible gambling," according to economic historian Paul Johnson (2010, 2, 110). The joint-stock limited liability company was "still a disputed, legally suspect and morally dubious organizational form." A series of acts during Queen Victoria's reign created the legal framework for incorporation and share ownership, until, by the 1880s, for-profit corporations had become the primary form in Britain.

In the United States, the scanty records of the Federal Convention of 1787 indicate widespread opposition to incorporation, especially of banks (Farrand 1911, 2:615–16; 3:325–26). Thomas Jefferson had envisaged a democratic republic of yeoman farmers, witnessed by Brillat-Savarin during a stay at Bulow's Connecticut farm. But "coal was still an oddity," as financial historian Bray Hammond found (1957, 7). Four decades after bestowing the phrase "Life, Liberty, and the Pursuit of Happiness," its author wrote to George Logan: "I hope we shall . . . crush in its birth the aristocracy of our moneyed corporations which dare already to challenge our government to a trial of strength, and bid defiance to the laws of their country" (November 12, 1816). Jefferson was rightly alarmed, because corporate apologists would turn the "Liberty" cry, once used against autocracy, against democracy. Railroads required a strong state, for example, to forcibly access land. As Karl Polanyi (1944, 139–41) put it, the heroic period of laissez-faire was itself enforced by the state, including through enclosures, poor laws and surveillance, and a central bureaucracy. He decided: "the concept of a self-regulating market was utopian." The *super*-market was coming.

In 1833 President Andrew Jackson (1835, 179) complained that the Second Bank of the United States had devoted funds to becoming "a permanent electioneering engine" and asked whether people were "to govern through representatives, chosen by their unbiased suffrages" or by the "money and power of a great corporation." It was "objectionable" that the bank sought to control public opinion through newspapers "known to have been sustained by its money."

As large organizations increased in sophistication and power, social critics sought to restate the value of natural-seeming "community" against artificial "organization," as historian of political thought Sheldon S. Wolin (1961, 354, 363) categorized them. He mentioned big government, large trade unions, giant corporations, impersonal universities. "Everywhere there is organization, everywhere bureaucratization; like the world of feudalism, the modern world is broken up into areas dominated by castles . . . the castles of Kafka."

In the words of political theorist Wendy Brown (2015, 10, 43, 151), given how "all spheres of existence are framed and measured by economic terms and metrics," corporations gain the power "to fashion law and policy for their own ends" and overtly demote the public interest. So, too, law has been co-opted as a "medium for disseminating neoliberal rationality beyond the economy," so that, not merely "securing the rights of capital and structuring competition, neoliberal juridical reason recasts political rights, citizenship, and the field of democracy itself."

Ruling Class or Corporations?

Corporations get things done: they marshal resources, gain production-line efficiencies, and invest in innovation. They have also adorned homes with consumer trophies, including saucepans designed to fail after eight years, and filled freezers and empty moments with snacks, liquid breakfasts, and meal powders. The marketing *spectacle* has broken into homes through labels, magazines, radio, television, and palm-held devices. With domestic work dismissed as mindless time wasting, and sustenance portrayed as, at best, some kind of reward, many households with double incomes still only scraped along. This has not always been pretty. To give an irritating instance, an industry campaign removed public drinking fountains and sold water in plastic bottles—a wasteful disruption introduced, as so often, under the guise of health.

Vance Packard gave early exposure to psychological manipulation in *The Hidden Persuaders* (1957) and planned obsolescence in *The Waste Makers* (1960). Nutritionists proved vulnerable to bribes (as tied funding might be interpreted). In 2015 the *New York Times* obtained emails revealing Coca-Cola sponsored studies minimizing the effects of sugary drinks on obesity. The Associated Press then obtained emails showing how a trade association sponsored evidence that sweet-eating children have healthier body weights. A new order of nutritionists then located correspondence from 1967, revealing payments to Harvard University for research that shifted blame for coronary heart disease from sugar to saturated fat. "But science is not supposed to work this way," New York nutritionist Marion Nestle (2016) observed wryly.

In the so-called McLibel case, an expensive legal team took on two obstinate young members of a tiny London political group for publishing a pamphlet, *What's Wrong with McDonald's: Everything They Don't Want You to Know*. Many of group's claims were eventually accepted by the courts, after ten years of bad publicity for the brand, the longest case in English legal history (Vidal 1997). Confirming state complicity, investigative journalists found that the offending pamphlet had been cowritten by police spy Bob Lambert, who took his undercover role so seriously that he also fathered a child with a group member (Lewis and Evans 2013).

"No One Knows More About Fruit & Vegetables," declared the website of the Dole Food Company, also billing itself as the "world's largest producer and marketer of high-quality fresh fruit and fresh vegetables." Among legal tangles, Dole fought for years against claims that DBCP, a pesticide banned in the United States, had made Nicaraguan banana workers sterile. Dole's legal and public relations teams sought to sabotage Swedish director Fredrik Gertten's documentary about this, persuading the Los Angeles Film Festival to remove *Bananas!** (2009) from competition. Gertten's sequel *Big Boys Gone Bananas!** (2011) documented Dole's use of "Slapp writs" (not necessarily winnable legal actions as a deterrent), "strategic communications" (planting unfavorable media stories about perceived enemies), and "astroturfing" (creating fake "grassroots" campaigns, especially on the internet).

Reacting at more than the journalistic level, sociology arose with studying the hefty transformations behind economics' elevation of care into mathematical laws. Under such forces as capitalism, industrialization, urbanization, individualization, and rationalization, ordinary households lost the means of production. Where farmworkers suffered patriarchal hierarchy, proletarians were now city-dwellers, paid wages, and immediately "set upon by the other portions of the bourgeoisie, the landlord, the shopkeeper, the pawnbroker, etc." Globalizing its "naked, shameless, direct, brutal exploitation," capitalism used "cheap prices" as the "heavy artillery with which it batters down all Chinese walls" and "compels all nations, on pain of extinction, to adopt the bourgeois mode of production; it compels them to introduce what it calls civilisation." That was according to the *Manifesto* of Karl Marx and Friedrich Engels (chap. 1). But were the brutal exploiters a ruling class or capitalist *corporations*? When David, Sheraton, and other foodies valued person-to-person markets over impersonal aisles, they rebelled against the corporate food industry.

In more traditional times, people learned at society's heart, the hearth, grew most ingredients within a short walk, and knew seasons, cooking qualities, and tastes. Closeness to the soil, hands-on preparation, and neighborly sharing hint at *Gemeinshaft* relationships. German sociologist Ferdinand Tönnies (1974, 223, 227) wrote about these in 1887, associating *Gemeinschaft* with kinship, and which were being replaced by *Gesellschaft* relationships, associated with technical achievement. Having studied Hobbes's distinction between the body politic and its "muscles," Tönnies found the family to be the prototype *Gemeinschaft* relationship, and the clearest contrast was the business corporation, which "represents, in its exclusive concentration on profit making, the perfect type of all legal forms for an association based on rational will."

Although often translated as *Community and Association*, Tönnies's *Gemeinschaft und Gesellschaft* suggested something more. The issue is not with "community," although some scholars have spoken of a "moral economy," but with "association," which only hints at business responsibility.

After all, *Gesellschaft* provides the "G" in German firm abbreviations GmbH and AG. Economists have typically opted for "community and commerce," although Deirdre McCloskey (2006, 254) spoke of the dichotomy of "homely *Gemeinschaft*" and "businesslike *Gesellschaft*." We're on the track of purposive organizations, and their rationalization of society, which became Max Weber's core theoretical contribution. He remained ambivalent about life's increasing rationality, both despairing that it destroyed beauty and spirit, and also (as hinted in chapter 8) determined to stick with the economists in denying the obvious.

Weber's Rationalization

So much as they existed, early written recipes had contained such obscure quantities as "a little bit of this—a handful of that—a nip or pinch of t'other,—do 'em over with an Egg." These archaisms were quoted by English author Dr. William Kitchiner to claim that his *Cook's Oracle* in 1817 introduced scientific precision. Writing for the "rational Epicure," he set down quantities in number, weight and measure, and times requisite for dressing. "This precision has never before been attempted in Cookery books," he boasted, although not entirely accurately (1821, 30–31). Cooks no longer relied on their experience, judgment, and senses but, with the spread of literacy and new ways of eating, could follow written instructions.

As well as reading and writing, by the late nineteenth century schools taught arithmetic, so that ordinary people could do the household budget and weigh out ingredients. The character of time changed in Europe, too, with calendars replacing the annual saint's days and weekly round that had previously been imposed on the firsthand experience of the seasons, and regular market circuits. Church chimes, which could scarcely coordinate between neighboring towns and villages, were now supplemented by domestic clocks, personal watches, and a more rigid day. Such rationalization seemed so scientific, so reasonable.

German economic sociologist Max Weber (1864–1920) greeted *rationalization* across modern society, whether law, music, science, or religion. By a clear margin, an international association of sociologists voted Weber's large bundle of manuscripts, published posthumously as *Wirtschaft und Gesellschaft: Grundriß der Verstehenden Soziologie* in the early 1920s, as *the* sociology book of the twentieth century. A complete two-volume, English translation appeared as *Economy and Society: An Outline of Interpretive Sociology* only in 1968. The title's original *Gesellschaft* has generally been rendered as "Society," as if to balance "Economy," but again removing suggestions of systematic purpose. Weber (1968, 40–41, 973, 1376) argued that *Gemeinschaft* had relied on "subjective feeling" that might be "affectual or traditional," and now *Gesellschaft* obeyed "rational agreement by mutual consent," the exemplar being a commercial contract. One of Weber's own lists referred to rationalized offices running on: "Precision, speed, unambiguity, knowledge of the files, continuity, discretion, unity, strict subordination." He cited "rational free market exchange." That is, rationalization related to neoclassical economics, by which Weber was heavily influenced.

Weber was apprehensive about rationalization, worrying, for example, about the loss of religious beauty or "disenchantment" in the face of soulless modernity. Yet he was supportive of rationalization, striving in his writings to approach society scientifically, and an advocate of methodological individualism. This was an illusory individualism—seemingly advocating for persons, while pushing for corporations, and leaving their hazards out of view. For the *Gesellschaft* world belonged to corporations. It was how they operated.

Corporations insist on rationality, as Adam Smith (*Wealth*, 2.5.1) already knew, finding that the "only trades which it seems possible for a joint stock company to carry on successfully . . . are those, of which all the operations are capable of being reduced to what is called a routine." Just a quick example: a key discovery of McDonald's was enforced standardization among franchisees. In March 1958 entrepreneur Ray Kroc taped a message telling the McDonald brothers that he, too, distrusted nonconformists. "We will make conformists out of them in a hurry," he said. "You can't give them an inch. The organization cannot trust the individual; the individual must trust the organization [or] he shouldn't go into this kind of business" (quoted in Love 1986, 144). In the 1970s McDonald's guaranteed teenage personnel would say "Thank you."

Rationalization is what clarity of purpose does to life. Setting a definite objective, especially a measurable one, encourages systematic actions, and, as Weber (1968, 86) observed, "money is the most 'perfect' means of economic calculation. That is, it is formally the most rational means of orienting economic activity," so that Weber paid special attention to the "most fateful force in our modern life, capitalism." As a student of the "capitalistic rules of action" (1976, 13–18, 54), he also appreciated that nothing comprehensively worthwhile has a purpose, at least in the tool-like sense. Economies have no purpose in a narrow, instrumentalist way, as Weber accepted at least in the case of domestic households, which "appear 'irrational' from the economic point of view" (1968, 377).

Rationality is not wrong in itself, just a false God, taken too far. The wisdom of happiness through conviviality cannot be pushed aside. Far from fretting about time costs, the Slow Food movement celebrated lack of rush. Meals are life, and life cannot be rationalized without "disintegration," as Weber called it.

Economic Disintegration

Under the heading of the "disintegration," Weber (1968, 375–80) spoke of the "internal dissolution of household communism" through the "growing sense of calculation," linked to "the rise of the calculative spirit and the modern capitalist enterprise," and the export of activities to new, rational sources of goods, education, entertainment, and employment. Governments had a "fiscal interest in a more intensive exploitation of the individual taxpayer," thereby depleting households "for the sake of military self-equipment." Where the baker's wife sold from a counter in front of the oven, with the children upstairs, the "old identity of household, workshop and office fell apart."

Distributing food and tasks more widely and intricately brought tremendous advantages. The household became "open" to the market, a concept that returns in chapter 12. For many, working outside the home proved liberating. Transferring formal education from home to school furthered Enlightenment. Was entertainment the worse for moving from the fireside to the public theater and digital screen? Was the plethora of restaurants less, or more, convivial?

Tortured by inexorable rationalization and its associated intellectual-ization, disintegration, and disenchantment, Weber confronted a "*stahl-hartes Gehäuse*," literally, a steel-hard casing or housing, although translators have preferred to lock life into a "shell as hard as steel" or, more commonly, an "iron cage." Human society was trapped in machine production "until the last ton of fossilized coal is burnt," he warned (1976, 181). Eliminat-ing "the ever more bureaucratic organizations of private capitalism . . . becomes more and more utopian" (1968, 988). Despite Weber's brilliant identification of corporate logic, he had blind spots, having joined econo-mists in their stern individualism, and their suppression of gastronomic concerns.

Weber's highly systematic writings fatally furthered rationalization. For how complete was the iron cage? Weber's "ever more bureaucratic" capitalism relied, ultimately, on everyday collaboration. The rational turn that Weber both feared and furthered depended on actual, material economies—the elevation of profit seeking is self-defeating and never complete, so that people can prize apart rationalization's mesh. Shopping malls deliberately obscure exits, but they exist. The Elizabeth Davids and Mimi Sheratons who treat life as a meal rather than a financial opportunity have recognized pleasure over power, collaboration over competition, living over expansion. Chat to the grower. Invite someone around.

While Weber linked profit to asceticism, he unfortunately remained trapped in the steel casing of rational economics, whose methodological individualism sought not to notice the monsters in the room: for-profit corporations.

The Real Ascetics

Along with hard-line economists who refuse to acknowledge corporations, Weber (1968, 14) declared that collectivities such as "a state, a nation, a cor-poration, a family, or an army corps" should be treated as "*only* a certain kind of development of actual or possible social actions of individual persons." Accordingly, he searched for the carriers of capitalism among individuals. In *Die protestantische Ethik und der Geist des Kapitalismus*, published in parts in 1904 and 1905 and translated into English as *The Protestant Ethic and Spirit of Capitalism* in 1930, Weber (1976, 41, 48, 157) proposed that capitalism was an unintended by-product of the ascetic ways and beliefs of Calvinist Protestants. No bodily impulses were involved: "the English, Dutch, and American Puritans were characterized by the exact opposite to the joy of living." He found English theologian Richard Baxter's belief, "Waste of time is . . . the first and in principle the deadliest of sins," reflected in Benjamin Franklin's business-friendly "Remember, that *time* is money."

Being a "body" (Latin, *corpus*) with brains and brawn, but no life, a corporation acts much more ascetically, chasing "the earning of more and more money, combined with the strict avoidance of all spontaneous enjoyment of life." To borrow further from Weber's description of Calvinist behavior, corporate activities are "completely devoid of any eudaemonistic, not to say hedonistic, admixture." Corporations promote "rational business book-keeping" and "legal separation of corporate from personal property" (21–22, 53). As corporate romances show, larger-than-life entrepreneurs might have started out working at home alone, but they soon purchased land and equipment, hired accountants, engineers, graphic artists, digital engineers, and conferred with bankers, politicians, and economists.

Corporate rationalization was made clearer in adaptation of Weber's ideas in American sociologist George Ritzer's *The McDonaldization of Society* (1993). Activist Jim Hightower (1975, 237) had already directly blamed "food profiteering" by giant food firms for the "McDonaldization of America"; now Ritzer blamed implacable, McDonald's-style "efficiency, calculability, predictability, and control." Individual consumers might opt for speedy rather than pleasurable eating (efficiency), cheapness rather than taste (calculability), routine rather than delight (predictability), and a managed rather than open-ended experience (control). Consumers can disavow the natural world, shun bodily impulses, and postpone enjoyment by choosing a "complete" dietary drink, "Soylent—free your body." Promising "maximum nutrition with minimum effort," the web page proposes: "What if you never had to worry about food again?" Variations include

"Soylent Cafe: Breakfast and caffeine in a bottle." However, even the most monomaniacal consumer could not compete with a corporation.

As we have found, even the most convinced economic rationalists can scorn the natural and also appeal to the "natural" of the Market. Ludwig von Mises (1981, 263) wanted the Market left alone, like a "living body," to run the whole world. His protégé Friedrich Hayek (1967, 162) declared the market "self-adjusting," "natural," "organic," or the creation of "human action but not of human design," so that its "spontaneous order" should not be upset. "Liberalism," he wrote, "derives from the discovery of a self-generating or spontaneous order in social affairs." But corporate involvement was never "natural" in any substantive, self-preservation sense. As shown already, far from safeguarding any free market, corporations thwart it; they "grow" the market to death, so that economic theorists had to hide them somewhere. Weber, Mises, and others were loath to speak of them as disintegrators, so they had to be given no meaningful existence.

Magical. Heady. Infinitely enticing. The market is indeed a marvel, a collective catering. John Stuart Mill (1836, 8) believed in the 1830s that the primary "law of mind" was that "man *desires* to possess subsistence." Appetites tangled up human beings in multiple economies. The problem was rationalization. Money articulated the incessant search for efficiency, through rational calculation, judged by profit. Greed-directed corporations rationalized economies with one purpose.

Just as a billionaire has one thousand times the power of a millionaire, many corporations are the equivalent of one thousand billionaires. These highly organized virtuosi of profit have rationalized and financialized domesticity, government, and nature, until derivatives derive from derivatives, and credit cards are repaid by loans. With the explosion of efficiencies over the past two centuries, big business, and supportive big government, have uprooted the seemingly eternal ways of the ancestors, with no promise catchier, or deadlier, than the eternal *more*. Corporate logic—the "business model"—infects government. Politicians talk "productivity," "efficiency," "innovation," "reform," "jobs," and "growth" that leverage financial power. Money-power is shifted from the political to the market economy through increased outsourcing, including of infrastructure, healthcare, pensions, and education.

Corporations automate, contract out, and casualize work, until with "gig" disintegration they text teenagers last-minute to labor at the drive-thru. These "bodies" lack bodily functions. They are no animal economies. They live on, and live for, the forceful food substitute, money. They are disemboweled wallets. Yet as we discover in the next chapter, the power-houses of rationalization have relied so far on that pretense that each is a person. From a Wikipedia check of the world's biggest companies, Adam Smith's trio would become "JBS S.A., the Butcher," "AB InBev, the Brewer," and "Grupo Bimbo, the Baker." These multinationals, based in Brazil, Belgium-Brazil, and Mexico, respectively, are behind such well-known brands as Swift, Corona, and Sara Lee. Termed "greed," their motivation sounds almost human.

Sting in the Coda

This chapter has concerned the rationalization of the world. Hitherto, social economies had responded to material needs. Certainly, this has been with some moderation, given how princely and religious patriarchies have seized and held power for their own interests. But post-Enlightenment, liberal economies were intended to serve the *common-wealth* or *welfare*, as glimpsed in such other terms as "the common good," "pursuit of happiness," and *"fraternité"* (conviviality). Purposeful organizations rationalize often usefully. However, increasingly dominant enterprises reorganized society in the interests, most ostensibly, of profit. Neoliberal apologists argued that the market mechanism would push corporations to respond to material demands. Money, however, had emerged as an end in itself. With the self-reinforcement of power, the whole point of the world became making money and would be rationalized to suit. Among consequences, rationalization downplayed gastronomic interests and marginalized meals.

The concluding image is simplistic, paranoid, and fascinating.

Writing on the "Economic Possibilities for Our Grandchildren" in 1930, the great British economist John Maynard Keynes (1931) estimated that incomes would grow four to eight times over a century because of continued capital investment. This prediction has largely been borne out. But Keynes assumed this would reduce the working week: by 2030 a fifteen-hour week would maintain the standard of living. The "economic problem" would be solved. Keynes acknowledged *technological unemployment* as "our discovery of means of economising the use of labour" outran finding new uses for labor. In the 1960s the threat of automation occasioned books and newspaper headlines. With computers and robots, people would no longer have to work and instead faced the "problem" of leisure.

So what went wrong?

First, economists anticipating increased productivity and scientists predicting widespread automation neglected a continuing bulk of producing, serving, conversing, cleaning up, and other economic actions. Economists mistook their charts for the living world, just as scientists mistook technical achievement for civilization. Second, despite Keynes's quaint conception of money as a mere tool, it was worshipped for its own sake, until it has accumulated to the point of diminishing returns. Third, modified to extract money, corporations developed an iron grip. Instead of machines doing our bidding, we did theirs.

Corporations constructed the military-industrial-financial-surveillance system behind a consumer spectacle. Bulking up in size, and sloganizing freedom, they ran national and global economies through government and industry committees, exchanging personnel, sponsorship, and opinions. Under neoliberalism, governments transferred capital, labor, and power to corporations (and their cronies) by privatizing and outsourcing functions, including transport, military, and policing, and planning, policy making, and law drafting. Corporations got big by squeezing wages and abandoning them for "self-employed" junk jobs. Through salaries and bonuses, they *bribed* senior management to do profit's bidding. This became a vicious spiral in that bigger corporations gained more to extract more.

In the absence of ready statistical comparisons of big and small business, *New York Times* columnist David Leonhardt (2018) compiled his own. Measured by total numbers employed, in the United States, the smallest companies had been shrinking in importance, while the biggest, especially with more than ten thousand workers, got bigger, so that, for example, the "supermarket is Whole Foods, which is now owned by Amazon." The big corporations "can create jobs, take on ambitious projects and compete around the world." They can also raise profits by getting bigger. "Larger companies simply have more power—to compete with other giants, to restrain workers' pay, to influence government policy and, in the long run, to increase prices."

Rather than live, we work. Leisure has become an industry. We dine in irrational, "free" time. Rather than become cultivated sovereigns, we work harder and borrow more. Rather than be *educated* for living (with humanistic knowledge and arts), we are *trained* for profitable work. Rather than participate in an informed, sensible, complex democracy, we are run by metrics and mottos. The profit motive extracts the utmost from workers, shoppers, and future generations. Some commentators have recently tried to stimulate a fight between the lucky "baby boomers" and the deprived "millennials"; this new gap is an artefact of capital intensification. Some outcasts blow resources on space travel, while others molder on sugar-coated pills. The answer is not some new class war but the debunking of assertive profit.

Profit-directed corporations have seized economic science, redefined success, and demeaned human beings as like them. With artificial intelligence, algorithms, big data, and constant intrusion into the very palms of people's hands, machines have seized control. Yet the expropriation might have already neared its limits, and new generations might abandon the self-perpetuating, command-and-control lust for money, to again love eating together.

11

THE CREATION OF
HOMO ECONOMICUS

Deep-Fried Things on a Stick

At the Iowa State Fair, the self-proclaimed "true heartbeat of the Midwest, unequaled and unduplicated," citizens learn about agriculture, admire the life-size cow sculpted in butter, and eat a fatty item on a stick. U.S. presidential candidates join the ritual, seeking photo opportunities. They have avoided the deep-fried Oreo on a stick, although contender Jeb Bush once tackled a Snickers. Barack Obama had a fried corn dog and a beer, but the usual preference is posing with a grilled pork chop on a stick. Visiting the pork producers' barbecue, Republican candidate Mitt Romney flipped a chop onto the ground. The crowd groaned as he returned it to the grill (Gonyea 2015).

As well as eating things on a stick, presidential candidates take turns orating from the "soapbox" of hay bales, trading points with ordinary folks for twenty minutes (except for Donald Trump, who arrived by name-emblazoned helicopter, took two bites of a pork chop, and flew off). Obama seemed in his element in 2011, whereas Romney fought hecklers hard and issued a fateful truth: "Corporations are people, my friend. . . . Everything corporations earn ultimately goes to people. . . . Where do you think it goes? Whose pockets? Whose pockets? People's

pockets" (August 11, 2011, e.g., https://www.youtube.com/watch?v=KlP
Qkd_AA6c).

As head of Bain Capital, Romney knew his firm as a bunch of smart
people, with big pockets. He was also not alone: the predominant legal and
economic view has long allowed corporations as people. However, while
Romney suggested that corporations consisted of actual people, the more
prominent treatment has been that each corporation is a single, autono-
mous person. He knew that version, too, because Bain Capital was in the
business of buying, stripping back, and selling slimmed-down units—
including Burger King, Domino's Pizza, and Dunkin' Donuts. Legally,
such a corporation owns property, sues and is sued, and so forth, as if an
ordinary human being. In basic economic theory, a corporation buys,
sells, and gains like the rest of us.

So corporations are people, but in two mutually inconsistent ways—an
aggregate of actual people (perhaps shareholders, managers, workers),

FIGURE 11.1 "Corporations are people, my friend." Presidential candidate
Mitt Romney, Iowa State Fair, August 11, 2011. Photo by IowaPolitics.com.
Creative Commons Attribution-Share Alike 2.0 Generic. Courtesy of
Wikimedia Commons.

or a distinct legal "person" or economic "individual." Whether a mere aggregate of persons or a distinct individual depends on immediate requirements. On some occasions, the law pins a crime on an individual board member, manager, or worker. On others, the law fines the corporation as if it were, singularly, the criminal. This legal equivocation is no match for the tenuousness of the economists' conceit: their model buyer and seller is almost always disguised as an individual.

In ordinary language, corporations are not people but something else again—large and perhaps even frightening monsters. An incessant spectacle of logos, packaging, and product launches, and internet urging, cloak black-windowed offices of single, named entities, boasting a tight hierarchical structure, organizational culture and memory, and clear corporate purpose, pure profit. As we shall see, corporations have long been granted "bodily" integrity. A "charter," "concession," or "creature" theory applied in Thomas Hobbes's day, when corporations obeyed the "Soveraign." These "Bodies Politique" and their "Representatives" had to observe the bounds set by the "absolute Representative of all the subjects" through two means: "One is their Writt, or Letters from the Soveraign; the other is the Law of the Common-wealth" (*Leviathan*, chap. 22). However, they abstracted their purpose to money's high ideal not much longer than two centuries ago, that is, after political philosophers had endorsed the sovereign individual.

In the previous chapter I introduced corporations as purposive organizations, distinct from economies in having definite tasks. Clarity sharpens systematic actions, but such rationalization can be hazardous, and corporations set about making the world suitable for profit. In this chapter I find supporters helping naturalize enterprises by disguising them as individuals. In numerous legal steps, profit-directed capital formations were freed from charters, acquired political influence, appealed to the courts, and promoted new legal and economic ideas, gaining a respectable veneer of citizenship.

After considering the powerful forces behind the weird rationalization of corporations as "persons," I reverse direction, examining the elevation of actual persons as rational maximizers. Taken together, these explain

Homo economicus as a for-profit entity, operating in a Market utopia, whose imposition disintegrates earthly existence.

In summary, in this chapter I find that legal systems granted corporations property, market, and political rights in liberal democratic commonwealths by treating them as individuals. Alongside, economists accommodated corporations as simply further individuals in rational pursuit of gain. Amalgamating corporations and persons as *Homo economicus* might have suited corporations, but corporations don't eat.

Citizens Disunited

In 1819 Chief Justice John Marshall (*Trustees of Dartmouth College v. Woodward*) declared a corporation an "artificial being, invisible, intangible, and existing only in contemplation of law. Being the mere creature of law, it possesses only those properties which the charter of its creation confers upon it." Nevertheless, for the next two centuries the U.S. Supreme Court shifted from one foot to the other and often decided that corporations were persons. This depended on whether the majority of justices favored profit over people and so, perversely, granted human rights to corporations. As an early example, the Supreme Court found that the Fourteenth Amendment of the U.S. Constitution, designed after the Civil War to ensure full citizenship for black Americans, also applied to corporations. In *Pembina Consolidated Silver Mining Co. v. Pennsylvania* (1888), the Court had "no doubt" that a corporation, as merely "individuals united for a special purpose," would be included as a "person."

Assuming a formal "equality before the law," the Supreme Court reinforced the equality of a corporation and an employee during the probusiness *Lochner* era from 1905 until 1937. The *Lochner v. New York* (1905) decision was that "liberty of contract" meant that an employer could expect an employee to work unhealthily long hours. In a sharp dissent, Oliver Wendell Holmes, Jr., opined that "a constitution is not intended to embody a particular economic theory." The activist Court had followed the laissez-faire doctrine, which Holmes associated with Herbert Spencer's book

Social Statics (1851), "an economic theory which a large part of the country does not entertain."

Lawmakers pushed back against business with consumer legislation, among the first being the Pure Food and Drug Act of 1906, in part aroused by Upton Sinclair's *The Jungle* (1905), which exposed abuses in the meat-packing industry. An even more humanistic post-Depression interregnum, linked to the era of President Franklin D. Roosevelt and Keynesian mixed economies, was answered forcefully by Ludwig von Mises, Ayn Rand, and others, who pushed capitalism as the one true response to Soviet communism. Economist Friedrich Hayek's *The Road to Serfdom* in 1944 even got a *Reader's Digest* condensation, while General Motors reproduced a *Look* magazine cartoon version. The latter's eighteen antigovernment pages illustrated how "Planners" never "delivered, never will," and cautioned: "If you're fired from your job, it's apt to be by a firing squad. What used to be an *error* has now become a *crime* against the state."

In 1971 Virginian corporate lawyer Lewis F. Powell advised the U.S. Chamber of Commerce that the political power of corporations "must be assiduously cultivated." Reacting to 1960s unrest, Powell panicked at the "impotency of business"—few elements of society had "as little influence in government." Not only recommending probusiness think-tanks and the "constant surveillance" of textbooks and television networks for anti-business sentiment, Powell urged that "the judiciary may be the most important instrument for social, economic and political change." Within weeks, President Richard Nixon appointed Powell to the Supreme Court, where he wrote the majority decision in *First National Bank of Boston v. Bellotti* (1978) in favor of a corporation's freedom of political speech.

When the arguments were rehearsed in *Citizens United v. Federal Election Commission* (2010), the right-wing majority of five judges overturned the Court's decision twenty years earlier in *Austin* v. *Michigan Chamber of Commerce* (1990) and granted a corporation the right as "an individual American" to directly fund political campaigns. Citizens United was a right-wing organization kicked off with Koch brothers funding (Charles Koch appeared in chapter 8), and for which Steve Bannon directed several sensationalist documentaries before becoming President Trump's early *éminence grise* and later an activist in Europe.

According to the majority author in *Citizens United*, Justice Anthony Kennedy, corporations were nothing more than "associations of citizens" and so covered by the Constitution's free-speech amendment. Kennedy said the disputed legislation exempted the speech of media corporations as individual Americans. Already, "executives and employees counsel Members of Congress and Presidential administrations on many issues, as a matter of routine and often in private."

Justice Antonin Scalia added that the First Amendment's free-speech clauses might not apply to the "trees or polar bears": "But the individual person's right to speak includes the right to speak *in association with other individual persons*. Surely the dissent does not believe that speech by the Republican Party or the Democratic Party can be censored because it is not the speech of 'an individual American.'" As well as giving rights to an entity because it isn't an entity (but an aggregate), Justice Scalia ignored any differences between political parties being (at least theoretically) designed to represent individuals in the political economy, and market organizations that intrude there.

Representing the liberal minority of four, Justice John Paul Stevens stressed the artificiality of corporate "personhood." The "activist" judges will next be asserting the right of corporations to vote, he scoffed (33–34). Stevens argued that corporations were sufficiently different from natural persons to claim "limited liability" and "perpetual life"; they had "no consciences, no beliefs, no feelings, no thoughts, no desires." Their "personhood" often served as a useful legal fiction. "But they are not themselves members of 'We the People' by whom and for whom our Constitution was established" (75–76).

Corporations were not even necessarily domiciled in America, Stevens said, so that foreign interests would enter the political fray. Corporate resources enabled them to "grab up the prime broadcasting slots on the eve of an election" to "flood the market with advocacy," not necessarily in accord with the ideas of natural persons or a notion of the public good (80–81). Stevens concluded: "While American democracy is imperfect, few outside the majority of this Court would have thought its flaws included a dearth of corporate money in politics" (90). And more money flooded in, as "super PACs" spent extraordinary sums, eventually electing Trump.

Free speech for corporations might seem distant from gastronomic issues. That is the point, however: the justices, along with legal and economic theorists and the wider political system, had lost the plot. Inculcated with the preciousness of political rights, learned persons forgot how rights served the "pleasure of the stomach." As shown in earlier chapters (and gestured toward by Justice Stevens), Epicurean-inclined philosophers derived rights from the fundamental "Desire of Food, namely Hunger and Thirst," to quote Hobbes (*Leviathan*, chap. 6). God had endowed humans, as all animals, with a "strong desire of self-preservation, and furnished the world with things fit for food and raiment, and other necessaries," to quote Locke's *First Treatise of Government* (1.9.86). But custom soon detached civil rights as "sacred," as Locke also understood (1.6.58), with an increasingly sacred freedom to make money.

Those extending "liberty" beyond the human might look again at Locke's *Essay Concerning Human Understanding* (1690). Individuals were motivated by either "delight" or "uneasiness," Locke wrote. As well as a "fantastical uneasiness" in quest of honor, power, or riches (which Epicureans warned against), human motivation concerned "ordinary necessities," and so "the uneasinesses of hunger, thirst, heat, cold, weariness, with labour, and sleepiness." With numerous uneasinesses jostling to be acted on, a person had to examine, and weigh up, their objects. "In this lies the liberty man has," he found, and then expanded: following "fair examination," each person could proceed, or not, and "daily may experiment. This seems to me the source of all liberty" (2.21.46, 48). In that picture, the liberty of corporations would align with the "fantastical." The justices should have asked: Do corporations have appetites, or are they simply avaricious?

The right-wing Supreme Court soon made an even more outrageous decision. Remember economist Milton Friedman's declarations that businesses had no social consciences? (Liberal Justice Stevens was just quoted similarly.) In 2014 (*Burwell v. Hobby Lobby, Inc.*) the Court decided that artificial "persons" could hold religious beliefs; in this case they could object to covering female reproductive health costs. The purpose of a for-profit corporation was not "simply to make money," claimed the justices, citing corporate support for charity and other "worthy objectives" (http://www.supremecourt.gov/opinions/13pdf/13-354_olp1.pdf). Yale law academic

Amy Kapczynski (2019) has since drawn attention to mounting pressure on the courts to shift the balance of free speech from protecting "public discourse," and therefore citizens' need for information, to protecting corporate publicity. Requiring nutritional disclosures on food labels, for example, undermined a marketer's right to convey a happy image.

Living indefinitely, never going to jail, and fed on money, corporations are not flesh-and-blood persons. With inhuman drive and unequal clout, they dislocated cultures, subjugated many, rewarded few, and exploited the planet within an inch of its life. Playing American states off against one another, corporations drifted to friendly jurisdictions, and a high proportion of major American corporations are still registered in Delaware, with its deliberately weak oversight and taxation. Not requiring passports, many straddle the globe, made "safe for freedom," transferring costs between their various arms to minimize tax and demanding "free trade" to minimize government restraints (especially global). In July 2014 Burger King's share price jumped 19.5 percent when its purchase of Tim Hortons of Canada promised "tax inversion," moving accounts to a lower-taxing regime (Sommer 2014).

Government has proved necessary to control much in the corporate interest, including "intellectual property," such as brand and identity. In a typical case, when McDonald's arrived in the Philippines, the hamburger corporation forced a fast-food shop operating as MacJoy to change to MyJoy. People have had occasional wins. McDonald's Family Restaurant was sufficiently established in Fairbury, Illinois, for a human Ronald McDonald to keep that name. The corporation not only lost out to a MacDonald's Restaurant already serving West Indian food on Grand Cayman but was prevented from using the name there (many examples collected on en.wikipedia.org/wiki/McDonald's_legal_cases).

In summary, families, market systems, communities, and other economies exhibit qualities of *Gemeinschaft*, which disintegrates under organizations with *Gesellschaft* purpose. This distinction helps interpret many themes in this book, especially liberal defenses of the "natural" or "spontaneous," appropriated selectively on behalf of constructed bodies, which are meant to be useful, and not capital-accumulating machines disguised as "persons."

Artificial bodies for which profit is the "absolute purpose" measure much and savor nothing. In quest of bullion (from *bouillon* as in "boiled-up" metal), these exalted machines rationalize all economies to fit. As "creative destruction" and "disruption" race to the heavens, corporations have marshalled individuals into shopping malls. Without human characteristics of care, civility, and empathy, corporations have pushed crass, sugary food. Their frozen dishes have proved comically unlike the food stylists' "pack shots." Hard chairs and bouncy music speed customers through. Now new factory foods are launched through problematic environmental benefits (the vegan Impossible Burger and other genetically manipulated, cell-grown meats). In 1967 the one word of advice to the protagonist in *The Graduate* (a movie starring Dustin Hoffman) was "plastics." Lately, big money can be made from big data, robotics, high-tech biology, and tissue engineering.

Economics for Corporations

Through such artifices as personhood, corporations gained legal rights to property, market freedom, and political influence. Simultaneously, economists' models became so abstract as also to accept corporations as "individuals." Textbooks expressly committed to methodological *individualism*, with exchanges between "persons" or "individuals", and the concept encompassed any profit-seeking entity. W. Stanley Jevons (1871, 85–86) defined: "By a market I shall mean two or more *persons* dealing in two or more commodities" (emphasis added here and below); Herbert J. Davenport (1913, 21) wrote in an "era of free *individual* initiative under private property for private gain"; economic analysis came into its own, explained Lionel Robbins (1932:18–19), when "independent initiative in social relationships is permitted to the *individual*"; Friedrich Hayek's (1948, 79) big question was "whether planning is to be done centrally, by one authority . . . , or is to be divided among many *individuals*"; and Milton Friedman (1962, 133) saw no system approaching the efficacy of the "*individual* in pursuing *his* own interest." Despite muttering about "firms," Paul Krugman's textbook resorted quickly to such statements as

"Each *individual* producer makes what *he or she* thinks will be most profitable; each *consumer* buys what *he or she* chooses" (Krugman and Wells 2009, 3).

Economists could speak blithely of the "exchange" between grossly non-equivalent entities because they adopted formal equality, by now quite detached from liberalism's meal-sharing roots. In the nineteenth century Jevons (1905, 60) had proposed a "Law of Indifference" or "Substitution" that envisaged total abstraction, so that "one man's labour may serve in place of another's," except Jevons accepted that applied more to "the lower the class of labour" because at the level of "barrister, engineer, author, etc. little or no comparison is possible." Nonetheless, a century later, for Ludwig von Mises (1981, 95), all human action was to be understood through "the rationalization inherent in economic calculation based on the use of money."

Liberal theory derived from an appreciation of the mutual meeting of needs. Steadily through the nineteenth century, so-called classical and then neoclassical economists detached their science from gastronomic considerations in favor of the price system or Market. Capitalism was not the market but exploited it. This ran alongside profit-centered corporations' rationalization of production, distribution, and consumption, along with ideas about them. The simple reality is that corporations never share meals. Therefore where chrematistic economists might genuinely have thought they advocated for individuals—and "individualistic" became a common criticism—they actually acted against actual living ones.

Modern economics makes more sense once recognized as having abandoned human needs to suit corporate profit-making logic. With the alienation of economics, one single "the economy" subordinated the animal, domestic, political, market, natural, and other economies. With no concern for these other levels, neoliberalism—policies based on chrematistic assumptions—was bound to damage human welfare and conviviality, democracy, and the environment. It is to be hoped that recently renewed interest in the growing, preparing, and sharing of meals, associated with foodies and food activists, provides the necessary framework to recover a liberal economics of meals, not money.

Giving People Purpose

Assuming financially *identical* players permitted business corporations to become like human beings, so that liberal philosophy was ransacked in the interests of alien profit-maximizers. Even more devastatingly, the corollary was that economists made believe that humans were merely "hungry" for money, that is, were identical to corporations. Lawyers and accountants organized the world to suit persons in pursuit of profit. In particular, they dressed up rich individuals and households as family trusts, private companies, and other financial instruments to facilitate capital multiplication and avoidance of obligations. In parallel, economists imprinted the language of *Homo economicus*—the imaginary "individual" merely maximizing financial gain—throughout society.

The neoliberal policy framework of the 1970s and onward—elevating citizens to buying, selling and contracting *Homo economicus*—pressed commodification and financialization. No longer housing the banquet of the people, with no living collaborators at the feast, government was merely to get out of the way. Principles like "user pays" shoved people into the competitive Market of tax-minimizers and opportunistic bargain-seekers, of winners and losers.

As circumstantial evidence of economic theorists in the process of reimagining people as rational calculators, at least two Victorian-era leaders, W. Stanley Jevons and Alfred Marshall, were fascinated by thinking machines. Jevons made a prototype computer, called a "logic piano," to perform mathematical operations (Maas 1999). Hinting at a world as profit machine, he spoke of "the principle of competition which underlies the whole mechanism of society" (1905, 60). In about 1870 Marshall's essay, "Ye Machine," explained the human brain as innumerable cog-wheels, taking in impressions and processing them, and developing sympathy for other machines (Cook 2009). These baby money-machines, without digestive tracts, would grow up as *Homo economicus*.

The mechanical player was already known as *Homo economicus* to Italian professor Maffeo Pantaleoni, in *Principii di Economia Pura* in 1889 (translated as *Pure Economics*, 1898). However, by clearly separating "pure economics" from the real-world "art of economics," Pantaleoni was explicit that *Homo economicus*, maximizing results with minimum means, was a "pure" abstraction (5).

Amid their fantasizing, economists homogenized all needs as the non-financial benefit of exchange, "utility." Laissez-faire pathfinder David Ricardo (1817, 388) wrote: "This faculty, which certain things have, of satisfying the various wants of mankind, I call utility," and he used a "pair of stockings" as an example. Paul A. Samuelson's textbook, *Economics* (1998), which outsold all others for several decades, declared, as a fundamental premise, that "people tend to choose those goods and services they value most highly," so that "*utility* denotes satisfaction." But "utility" became the name for the unconsidered, too personal for rational science, merely drained of all qualities, and balancing the economists' "value" on the other side of the equation.

Blurring the person/corporation distinction, Max Weber (1976, 17) had warned it was "naïve" to identify capitalism with greed. The insatiable demand for money "has in itself nothing to do with capitalism." Greed was, he said, the impulse of "waiters, physicians, coachmen, artists, prostitutes, dishonest officials." Leaving aside Weber's insult to waiters (equivalent to "dishonest officials"), his objection was that greed was too carnal for the necessarily ascetic programming for the eternal more. The pursuit of profit through "continuous, rational, capitalistic enterprise" might even require restraint, he said. Only metaphorically "hungry," corporations converted our lifeblood into theirs, reorganized the table, smiled at the rich, plundered Paradise, and rationalized "greed," removing carnal connotations.

In urging pathological "greed" back onto human persons, self-styled cool heads came, politically, to encourage what E.A.G. Robinson (1941, 276), a colleague of Keynes, explained as "the nastiest motives of nasty people for the ultimate benefit of society." To add to earlier examples, writing for Ayn Rand's *Objectivist Newsletter* in 1963, eventual "rock star" economist Alan Greenspan celebrated "the 'greed' of the businessman or, more appropriately, his profit-seeking" as the "unexcelled protector of the consumer," because developing a "reputation for honest dealings and a quality product" was "in the self-interest of every businessman." In more mature reflections, with greed popularized, Greenspan worried: "An infectious greed seemed to grip much of our business community . . . the avenues to express greed have grown so enormously" (Goldstein 2002).

The internet carries a two-minute extract, entitled "Greed," from the *Phil Donahue Show* in 1979, in which Milton Friedman suggested all societies, capitalist or communist, ran on greed. "You think Russia doesn't run on greed? . . . The world runs on individuals pursuing their separate interests." Some greed was more equal than others, however, because history was "crystal clear" that no other way of "improving the lot of the ordinary people" compared with "the productive activities that are unleashed by a free enterprise system." Individuals had become free enterprises.

Economists have spoken of individuals as like corporations in further ways, such possessing moneymaking assets or *Human Capital*, as Gary Becker entitled his 1964 book. Such "capital" accrued through schooling and higher studies. Who could possibly object to "investing in human capital?" Becker's arguments, however, led logically to training for salable skills, while accruing student debt. Becker (1981) went on to theorize the individual in terms of investments, utility, time-budgets, depreciation with age, and more.

Adopting profit's purpose, "self-help" authors promoted "logic pianos," often with a Protestant gloss. The classic of "get rich" entrepreneurship literature was New York pastor Norman Vincent Peale's *Power of Positive Thinking* (1952). His inspirational anecdotes showed businessmen's fortunes turned around by the self-belief coming from a secure spiritual life. Before President Trump credited Peale's influence, Robert Schuller cited Peale's sway when founding the Crystal Cathedral in California to push the "prosperity gospel."

Adopting modern management techniques, megachurch pastors then returned the favor, providing motivational courses for business. The Willow Creek megachurch ran an annual Leadership Summit and frequent Blue Sky events, "Where Business, Leadership and Ministry Meet." Pastor Rick Warren's forty-day study program stimulated twenty-one million book sales of *The Purpose-Driven Life* in its first two years, and Coca Cola, Ford, and Walmart adopted Warren's *Forty Days of Purpose* program. Mark Stevens wrote *God Is a Salesman: Learn from the Master*, and *Rich Is a Religion: Breaking the Timeless Code to Wealth*, both in 2008.

"You're the boss," Mars Inc. told its workers. Fully owned by the Mars family, the corporation makes Milky Way bars (called Mars bars outside the United States), M&M's, Snickers, Wrigley's gums, Uncle Ben's, and numerous other snack foods, and Pedigree, Whiskas, and other pet foods. Except that Mars has no workers, only "associates." That's because, the corporation website explains, each "associate" runs the business as their own. "It's about how you can grab everything within your reach here and use it to pursue mutual, long-term gain." The company boasts "Five Principles" that "unite us across geographies, languages, cultures and generations," with the fifth principle being "Freedom. We need freedom to shape our future; we need profit to remain free."

Into this century, "inspirational" speakers on the "purpose economy" had so fused people with for-profits that they appealed to executives' desire to seem to be "doing good" so as to catch the next profitable wave and bring onside millennials, who were otherwise turning against business. Addressing the "Power of Purpose," the "Founder and Chief Purpose Officer of Conspiracy of Love," Afdhel Aziz, declared that "corporations have seven times the resources of government and non-profits combined . . . so the power is in those companies and, by extension, you!" No longer think of yourself as leaders in corporate social responsibility but as "catalysts of corporate social opportunity," he said. Shift your mindset "from transactional to transformational," and "let your values drive your value" (https://insights .benevity.com/blog/2019-trends-csr-conference).

In *Weconomy: You Can Find Meaning, Make a Living and Change the World* (Kielburger, Kielburger, and Branson 2018, 11), three "thirty-somethings" of the business, charity, and nonprofit worlds promised CEOs they would learn how to "embed purpose into the DNA of their business to inspire their employees and boost the bottom line," while newcomers would "get a crash course on purpose that will help them climb the corporate ladder." An investigator in *Nation* magazine called the movement a "new scam" (https://www.thenation.com/article/big-business-has -a-new-scam-the-purpose-paradigm/). In actuality, trying to keep up, each individual human enterprise must work more and more desperate hours; some invest furiously in pension funds, shares, scams, and Bitcoin, and a tiny minority get rich.

The unavoidable conclusion remains that modern economic theory better fitted corporate behavior than human. Step by step, economists edged away from individuals' concerns with labor, marriage, children, bread, clothing, pleasure, affection, and government on behalf of their next dinner. The need to eat, once obviously core to human existence, came to seem irrational, and near irrelevant. Spinning on the pinhead of earning ratios, yields, and trending metrics, economic theorists came to believe that, because their mathematics was rational, individuals do and *should* behave like the ideal, profit-purposed corporation.

Set a corporation in motion, order it to seek its fortune, and off it goes, systematically. If the world gets in the way, change the world. Corporations are the real, unfeeling, superhuman *rentiers* on jet fuel. With selected human rights suitably rationalized, economic theory relied on the simplistic, machine-like image of *Homo economicus*, the rational accumulator never lingering over a meal. In a fraud pulled on the human species, *Homo economicus* found political, cultural, and spiritual purpose in profit.

But individual persons are complicated, dignified beings, who *live* rather than *maximize*. Mature persons seek a full, *good life*. They want bustling towns in lands of milk and honey. People run on much more than mission statements, self-management by objectives, market research, input-output analysis, annual reports, and corporate ladders. Individuals and corporations are ontologically distinct—natural members of economies, and rights-claiming imposters. One implication is that speaking of a "capitalist" refers more accurately to a business enterprise than to a person, who has a whole life to lead.

Winners attend the lavish party thrown annually by the World Economic Forum at the Swiss resort of Davos. There, world political leaders mix with celebrities, CEOs, hedge-fund billionaires, Russian oligarchs, and influential economic theorists and commentators. The most exclusive parties lately have been thrown by Russian billionaire Oleg V. Deripaska. But this is not merely the rich entertaining the rich. The mission: "The Forum engages the foremost political, business and other leaders of society to shape global, regional and industry agendas." This is "a platform for the world's 1,000 leading companies to shape a better future."

In this chapter I have pointed to pressures to treat corporations, legally, politically, and economically, as individuals, and, worse, individuals as corporations. Corporations and persons have been conflated as the rational devourer, *Homo economicus*. If individuals were identical to corporations, then individuals would have to abandon feelings, pleasures, conviviality, and, indeed, life—they would have to leave the table. They would have no need for economics.

Indeed, with its concern being money and not meals, corporate rationalization would appear to have contributed to the two-century relegation of eating and drinking economically, politically, socially, and culturally, and among scholarly disciplines. In this book's final part I introduce what can be done, and what is already being done.

PART 4

RESTORING ECONOMICS

12

FREE THE MARKET! (IT'S BEEN CAPTURED BY CAPITALISM)

"Garçon, la Carte!"

"Really, my dear friend, I would advise every rich epicure to fix his residence in this city." This was the recommendation of a London visitor to Paris at the opening of the nineteenth century, writing when restaurants, invented only four decades earlier, were in full swing. Conversely, the visitor warned, "without money, Paris is the most melancholy abode in the world" (Blagdon 1803, 437). If journalist Francis William Blagdon were, as usually supposed, the anonymous author of *Paris: As It Was and as It Is, . . . in a Series of Letters, Written by an English Traveller, During the Years 1801–2, to a Friend in London*, he never had much money, so that the advice about its necessity was heartfelt. Nevertheless, this person—let's assume Blagdon—visited the greatest of the early restaurateurs, Beauvilliers.

Establishing many characteristics of the classic French restaurant, Antoine Beauvilliers (1754–1817) learned his skills in the extravagant kitchens of the future Louis XVIII, before opening Le Grand Taverne de Londres in perhaps 1782. With mixed fortunes, he would appear to have shifted address twice but remained in the Palais-Royal (renamed the Palais de Tribunat temporarily after the Revolution). As Blagdon (1803, 209) described the complex, a young man could purchase smart clothes on the ground floor, dine on the second, ascend to a brothel on the third, join a gaming table, and descend to pawn his watch, before climbing again to a lodging in the garret. Add a theater and numerous food retailers, and the Palais-Royal was the center of the new consumer society.

Beauvilliers's elegant decorations, large mirrors, lighting by the bright new "Argand" oil lamps, and warming by ornamental stoves impressed Blagdon, as did the waiters, "neatly habited in close-bodied vests, with white aprons before them" (457–59). On a kind of throne inside the entrance sat a woman of "majestic gravity and dignified bulk," Madame Beauvilliers, to whom the waiters would bring the cash.

At five o'clock it was quiet, but by six scarcely a seat would be vacant. Headed "*PRIX DES METS POUR UNE PERSONNE*" (Prices of dishes for one person), the *carte* would take a half-hour to scrutinize, the English traveler said, and he reproduced it from pages 444 to 452 of his book. He also appended a summary:

> Let us see; Soups, thirteen sorts.—*Hors-d'œuvres*, twenty-two species.—Beef, dressed in eleven different ways.—Pastry, containing fish, flesh and fowl, in eleven shapes. Poultry and game, under thirty-two various forms.—Veal, amplified into twenty-two distinct articles.—Mutton, confined to seventeen only.—Fish, twenty-three varieties.—Roast meat, game, and poultry, of fifteen kinds.—Entremets, or side-dishes, to the number of forty-one articles.—Dessert, thirty-nine.—Wines, including those of the liqueur kind, of fifty-two denominations, besides ale and porter.—Liqueurs, twelve species, together with coffee and ices.

The *carte* annexed a price to each article, so that "you have it in your power, before you give the order, to ascertain the expense." Within ten or fifteen minutes, you would have the "most dainty or troublesome dish . . . smoking on the table," although Blagdon cautioned that a "pompous, big-sounding name sometimes produces only a scrap of scarcely three mouthfuls." He further advised, when dispatching each dish, to order the next to avoid long delays. If you ordered both Champagne and Burgundy and "do not reduce the contents below the moiety, you pay only for the half bottle" (453–54).

The establishment was highly organized: "Each cook has a distinct branch to attend to in the kitchen, and . . . each waiter has a distinct number of tables, and the orders of particular guests to obey in the dining-rooms" (454). The waiters were so quick that "no scouts of a camp could be more on the alert" (459). And look over there:

> Remark that portly man, so respectful in his demeanour. It is BEAUVIL-LIERS, the master of the house: this is his most busy hour, and he will now make a tour to inquire at the different tables, if his guests are all served according to their wishes. He will then, like an able general, take a central station, whence he can command a view of all his dispositions.
> To pay, you said: "*Garçon, la carte payante!*"
>
> (459)

Jean Anthelme Brillat-Savarin, who was an almost exact contemporary of Beauvilliers, did not provide the immediacy of Blagdon's report. Nevertheless, meditation 28 of the *Physiology of Taste* (1826, §143) reflected on the new restaurateurs, including "the most famous," Beauvilliers, the first to have "an elegant dining room, smart waiters, immaculate cellar and first-rate cuisine." When others followed, Beauvilliers stayed ahead. With a prodigious memory, he could recognize customers who had only eaten there once or twice twenty years earlier. He knew all the military heads during occupations and spoke their languages, "as much as necessary for his business."

Brillat-Savarin remarked on a characteristic practice. When a wealthy group had assembled in his rooms, Beauvilliers came up with an obliging air, kissed the women's hands, and seemed to give his guests special attention. He would advise on which dishes to avoid and which to order immediately, organize something not on the *carte*, and call for a wine from the cellar to which he alone held the key. He appeared so friendly that all these extras seemed like so many favors on his part. This would not last: he would vanish before the arrival of the swollen bill, when the bitterness of the *"quart d'heure de Rabelais"* would amply demonstrate having dined *"chez un restaurateur"* (§143). The "quarter-hour of Rabelais" referred to the penniless Renaissance author François Rabelais, who could not pay a bill and instead orchestrated his own arrest to be hauled back to Paris, also free of charge.

With his own cook and private dinner invitations, Brillat-Savarin might not have been overly committed to the new, marketed elegance, requiring overt payment. Nevertheless, his doubting of Beauvilliers's motives raises a key question. Was Beauvilliers a greedy business operator only affecting a generous manner? More generally, did the brave new world require restaurateurs to be dedicated to money?

A modern economist is meant to respond: "Financial self-interest drives all transactions." Sociologist Max Weber assumed (as quoted in chapter 11) that waiters epitomized greed. Possibly, the founder of *the* French restaurant lived in bad faith, his primary purpose to make a fortune, which he could never keep, making and losing three (§57). But had human relationships evaporated into abominably "impersonal" cash? A restaurant lover could well deny that payment necessarily sullies hospitality, arguing: Beauvilliers joined the human enterprise in the best way he knew—elegant service. Besides, he enjoyed sharing food, human interactions, stylish surroundings and customers' happiness, to the extent of a bit of pandering: he loved life. In defending him, I reprise key strands of this book and set out a more gastronomic reappraisal of markets.

The price mechanism became, for two centuries, the more mesmerizing prong of the fork in economic thought. Not that conventional economics went entirely wrong, merely oversold a handy approximation, and snubbed gastronomic wisdom. Experienced by Denis Diderot (and described in chapter 7), restaurants are tell-tale remnants of the big bang at the origin of market society and the diminution of aristocratic and church power. The restaurant inventor in 1766, Roze de Chantoiseau, was a champion of the new economics, then thrilling the Parisian circles joined by Scottish sojourner Adam Smith. All that was before the American and French Revolutions, and those were before the real rise of corporations and the laissez-faire doctrine. Corporations would develop the mechanisms, summarized by sociologist George Ritzer as "McDonaldization," to fake the meal experience. Economic historian Karl Polanyi (1944, 162) located the "great transformation," inaugurating what he saw as capitalist market society and its utopian economics in the "critical eighty years (1834–1914)." Over that period, economists fell head-over-heels for moneymaking.

Fortunately, and running as a thread through this book, true restaurants stayed with the actual free market and so potentially provide lessons. Unlike corporations that exploit the free market for profit, but like Smith's butcher, brewer, and baker, restaurateurs truck, barter, and exchange the "necessaries and conveniences of life." Restaurateurs, their suppliers, and loyal customers now have the appetite, experience, and life-giving imperative to restore the market and, with that, economics. We need our language back, including words whose distortions I listed in chapter 2, such as "economy," "wealth," "liberal," "redistribution," "growth," and "market," along with more delight in those *com-* words, from "conviviality," "commonwealth," "company," and on. We also deserve a thorough regrounding of scholarly disciplines, bringing sustenance back in.

Rethinking market economics reveals, before anything, that the actual free market, along with ideas about it, has been appropriated on behalf of capitalist corporations. In this chapter, by inquiring into Beauvilliers's alleged lack of true hospitality under the moneymaking imperative, I find lessons in the particular restaurant tradition that emerged alongside Parisian consumer culture and economic thought. The key is to conceive restaurants as *open domestic households*, with representatives exchanging in the marketplace. That is, they are meal sharing, quite unlike corporations. Let's again treasure face-to-face exchanges.

The Restaurant Explosion

Contemporaries pinpointed several factors for the proliferation of Parisian restaurants from fewer than a hundred in 1789 to around five hundred by the time of A. B. L. Grimod de la Reynière's early guidebook in 1803. Grimod (1803, 163–64; 1810, 213–14) credited fine dining in a more public space to, first, "the mania for imitating English customs," given London's earlier emergence as a political capital with associated tavern dining. As corroboration, Beauvilliers had named his establishment the Grande Taverne de Londres (Great London Tavern). Second, when fine cooks lost the patronage of well-to-do households, they sold their skills on the market, or, as Grimod expressed it, the revolutionary tumult threw the wealthy patrons "on a diet" and "cast all the good cooks on to the pavement." Again, Beauvilliers had trained at a palace. The third cause was the capital's "sudden inundation" of republican representatives, who "led through their example all Parisians to the cabaret." In broad terms, Grimod credited restaurants to the intensification of both democracy and City.

In 1825 Brillat-Savarin (1826, §135, §137) saw restaurants as the finishing touch to the millennia-long sophistication of economies. Until around 1770, unless invited to a wealthy household, visitors to Paris left knowing nothing of the city's culinary delights. They had to rely on *aubergistes* (innkeepers), whose meals were generally bad, on *hôtels* (hotels), whose table d'hôte, with few exceptions, offered no more than the essentials and only at a set hour, and on *traiteurs* (cook-caterers), who did not provide individual serves, only an entire joint, say, ordered well in advance.

The significant innovation, Brillat-Savarin (§136–37) said, was meals "served in separate portions and at set prices, on the demand of the consumers." Two pieces of paper opened and closed the occasion, he observed: the *carte* listed the dishes on offer and their prices; and the *carte à payer* showed the dishes actually taken and their cost. Among culinary improvements, the individualization of serves let restaurateurs divide the chicken, or cut off a slice of a roast, in the "obscurity of the kitchen" without "dishonouring the whole," he wrote. Also, many restaurateurs credited their prosperity to specialties, the division having already happened in the market: the Veau Qui Tette owed its celebrity to sheep's trotters; the Frères Provençeaux, to garlic cod; Véry, to truffled entrées; and Balaine, to great care with fine fish. As soon as some ragoût made a fortune for its inventor, Brillat-Savarin (§141–42) wrote, everyone was doing it, such was the emulation among restaurateurs.

While this culinary refinement could add to the cost, the quest for gain also provided a contrary movement. Brillat-Savarin (§143) found some restaurateurs sought to provide good food on a budget and appeal to the more numerous people of modest fortunes. By careful purchasing, good cooking, and watching the size of serves, they could still earn a profit of between 25 and 30 percent on a dinner costing two francs and even less. (By way of comparison, most individual dishes at Beauvilliers cost between one and two francs; one of the most expensive was *Demi-poulet aux Truffes ou aux Huitres*—half-chicken with truffles or oysters—for four francs.)

As to disadvantages, Brillat-Savarin (§140) worried that individualization was "disastrous for the social order." He feared that solitary refection reinforced self-centeredness, accustomed people to think only of themselves, isolating them from everything going on around them, and taught them to dispense with attentive politeness. He could discern, by observing a person's conduct before, during, and after a meal, a restaurant *habitué*.

Visiting Beauvilliers in a thronging center of consumption in 1801–1802, Francis Blagdon (1803, 164) emphasized the novelty of prices on the menu, that Madame Beauvilliers ostentatiously collected cash from a "throne" near the entrance, and that, without money, an epicure would find Paris the world's "most melancholy abode." Grimod believed that many restaurateurs made a good profit: "Once obscure cooks, today almost millionaires," he wrote. Brillat-Savarin was impressed how market forces shaped restaurants.

The central innovation, nevertheless, was the "host's table" being replaced by amazing choices, "according to the card." While this was not the typical communism of the family, and individualization raises crucial questions about consumer society, the provision of choice might be defended as extraordinarily hospitable. Also, in marketing high-level dining, restaurants made refined art more popularly available. As Blagdon (1803, 455) observed, the "commodiousness and elegance of their rooms, the savouriness of their cooking, the quality of their wines, the promptitude of their attendants, all are minutely criticized." Such guides as Grimod's put evaluations in print. Together, in the bustling marketplace for meals, hosts and guests constructed "a public sphere of gastronomic discourse" or "cultural field" (Ferguson 1998 and 2004, 104–6; Mennell 2003).

Despite all this, the key feature is that restaurants remained open family households. In each of Brillat-Savarin's meal options before restaurants—whether a wealthy display, table d'hôte of an inn or hotel, or cook shop's enlarged hearth—the guest essentially paid for a domestic meal. Market meals are ancient, but did some new sophistication of the market economy, now extending to individualization and the fine arts of the table, require a new greediness? My answer is that happened only later, as households gave way to business corporations.

The Market for Dining

In traditional, settled societies, relatively few people traveled. When they did, they relied on the local population. An army seized supplies as it moved, forcibly where necessary. Other travelers would expect to lodge in a household of a matching social class, perhaps at a court, and characteristically without payment. Such *hospitality* became legendary: a seventh-century Irish king, who was "so constantly giving away that his right hand grew longer than his left," once hosted a crowd of 150 poets and their retinue and only hinted they should leave after a year and a day (Zeldin 1994, 437–38).

Welcoming strangers sheltering from the storm and feeding needy widows gained religious endorsement. Upon his conversion to Buddhism in the third century BCE, the Indian emperor Asoka became shiningly benevolent by assisting travelers, installing wells, planting shade trees, and establishing medicinal gardens, along with abolishing animal sacrifice. The Hindu Scripture the *Tirukural*, written around 150 BCE, proposed that the purpose of gaining wealth was to entertain guests. Much has been made of the Abrahamic religions' shared instruction to care for strangers—the Torah reminded Israel: "You shall not wrong or oppress a resident alien, for you were aliens in the land of Egypt" (Exodus 22:21); Jesus said: "when you give a feast, invite the poor, the maimed, the lame, the blind, and you will be blessed, because they cannot repay you" (Luke 14:12–14); and the people of Yathrib (Medina in Saudi Arabia) have been celebrated for according Muhammad exemplary refuge (Switzer 2007, 314–16).

Archaeological digs have confirmed, however, that certain domestic households in busier towns and trade routes evolved into inns and taverns, charging for care. Larger urban centers accommodated workers away from home and developed markets for specialized dining. In concentrating in this book on Europe as the launchpad of liberal economics, I have not wanted to deny Eastern parallels and influences. As an example, nine centuries ago, Meng Yuanlao left memoirs of the numerous eating houses in Kaifeng, which was the capital of the Northern Song dynasty and the world's greatest city. Among Meng's descriptions, he said Kaifeng customers were "extravagant and indulgent. They would shout their orders by the hundreds," each ordering differently. Carrying the orders in their heads to the kitchen, the waiters were called "gong heads" or "callers." The waiter returned quickly with "three dishes forked in his left hand, while on his right arm from hand to shoulder he carried about twenty bowls doubled up, and he distributed them precisely as everyone had ordered without an omission or mistake" (quoted in Freeman 1977, 161).

In England, the growth of the central state under the Tudors brought the elite from their country homes to London to pursue influence and fashion (Heal 1990). They also frequented taverns. In 1771 Scottish-born writer Tobias Smollett (1825, 178) found the English now "totally destitute" of the "old English hospitality." Blaming the rise of taverns, he complained that the same Londoner, entertained in a gentleman's house in France, Italy, or Germany, when returning the favor, would invite the visitor to dine "at the Saracen's Head, at the Turk's Head, the Boar's Head, or the Bear," and then expect the guest to "pay his share of the reckoning." By contrast, man-about-town Samuel Johnson remarked in 1776 that, at a private house, the master "is anxious to entertain his guests—the guests are anxious to be agreeable.... Whereas, at a tavern, there is a general freedom from anxiety. You are sure of a welcome; and the more noise you make, the more trouble you give, the more good things you call for, the welcomer you are" (Boswell 1848, 485).

Certainly, the French aristocracy lamented hospitality's shift into the marketplace. Chevalier Louis de Jaucourt's entry on *"Hospitalité"* in a 1765 volume of the *Encyclopédie* complained: "The spirit of trade, by linking all nations, has shattered the bonds of benevolence between private individuals." Now that "all Europe has gone travelling and trading," he wrote, the love of profit replaced more natural and intimate associations. Nonetheless, Jaucourt accepted that commerce provided innumerable conveniences, greater understanding between people, and much luxury. The rich were looked after "in proportion to their expenditure." Brillat-Savarin presumably retained some of his privileged circle's hesitation about paying for fine dining.

What Is Hospitality?

Even some present-day hospitality management researchers have fretted that "hospitality industry"—in which they place restaurants—might be an oxymoron, in that the capitalistic imperative creates "tensions and contradictions" (Lashley 2000, 13). Recourse to an age-old concern for guests' well-being or "hospitality" was "an early attempt at *spin*," Conrad Lashley decided (2008, 69, 76–77). Another professor accepted that the name "hospitality," redolent of the "tradition of service" of innkeeping, was embraced in the 1980s "as the way hoteliers and caterers would like their industry to be perceived" (Jones 2002, 1).

Whether money corrupts depends on what is meant by hospitality. The dictionary's "reception and entertainment of guests, visitors, or strangers, with liberality and goodwill" (*OED*) elevates hospitality toward a moral virtue, which often carries over to scholarly definitions. In providing hospitality, especially toward immigrants, philosopher Jacques Derrida (2002) urged the self-negation of saints. Equally sternly, philosopher Elizabeth Telfer (1996, 87–90) saw domestic hospitality sullied even by such "ulterior motives" as the hosts' desire to impress, their love of cooking elaborate dishes, or even their "pleasure from feeling that they are pleasing others." On the other side, trying to skirt questions of generosity, hospitality academics have required the recipient merely to be "away from home," or posited, with acknowledged circularity, that "hospitality is what the hospitality industry offers." Industry consultant Paul Slattery (2002, 21, 25) banished benevolence with bluster: "The buyers are not guests, they are customers. The relationship is not philanthropic; it is economic." Conversely, foodies have often reported favorably on expensive meals, as if money scarcely came into it.

The suggestion here is that, whether interpreted as generosity, obligation, interpersonal skill, right, or pleasure, hospitality has always depended on something substantial: a household provides food, shelter, or other comfort to an outsider. The ascribed motivations have been secondary to the extending of physical care beyond that economy. Even traditional hosts would often have resented guests. So, to offer a relatively straightforward definition, based on the concept of an economy in the preceding chapters: *hospitality is an economy's meeting of basic needs of a nonmember.* Given that an economy involves care that is (1) mutual and (2) full, hospitality becomes the exception in which members extend comprehensive support outward.

Hospitality emerges when religious communities open their doors to the poor; when householders invite overseas students to dinner; when cities host the Olympic Games; and arguably when a planet continues to support life. In each case, hospitality is provided by an economy, whether domestic ("shelter from the storm"), national ("Give me your tired, your poor / Your huddled masses") or natural ("land of plenty"). As a corollary, households are not prevented from charging. The traditional triviality of payment/nonpayment is suggested by the mix of words deriving from the Latin *hospes*, which include "host," "hotel," "hostelry," "hostel," "hospital," and "hospice." Each provides full care to an outsider. In the fourteenth century, English writer Geoffrey Chaucer used "host" in the sense of a seller of good cheer, as, later, did William Shakespeare.

Adopting this definition of hospitality—households catering to outsiders—shifts the question. It becomes: Are restaurants households or not? In particular, did Beauvilliers operate as a domestic economy?

Home or Factory?

Significantly, Beauvilliers's wife was no longer at the stove, and cooks and waiters were employed as (male) wage labor. Blagdon (1803, 459) reported: "An establishment, so extremely well conducted, excites admiration. Every spring of the machine duly performs its office; and the regularity of the whole might serve as a model for the administration of an extensive State." Yet, again, this tight organization is not a clinching argument, because Beauvilliers's restaurant was scarcely any more rationalized than the well-run grand household where he had learned his trade. His master, the

Comte de Provence (who would return as Louis XVIII in 1814), maintained a palace with a staff of hundreds.

Physically, Chez Beauvilliers was like a domestic household with dining room and adjoining kitchen and storeroom—centered on a hearth, if you will. People spoke of going to a "restaurateur's," and not for a few decades did the word *restaurant* transfer decisively from the broth to the business. Diners entered the *salle* or *maison de restaurateur* (dining room or house of the restorator). They went *Chez Véry* (to the Véryses' place). Beauvilliers might have opened La Grande Taverne de Londres, but it was more usually known by his name, as were other "grands Restaurateurs" listed by Grimod (1810, 212–13): Méot, Robert, Véry, Léda, Brigaut, Le Gacque, Naudet, Tailleur, Nicolle, Balaine. Perhaps Grimod thought of them as artisans or artists, but that did not stop them being heads of households.

As Brillat-Savarin (1826, §139, 312) observed, many customers acted as if at home, and some regulars would be seated at a central table as if decoys to attract wild ducks. It had also been Blagdon's (1803, 458) impression that, to save trouble, "many single persons, and even small families now scarcely ever cook at home; but either dine at a restaurateur's, or have their dinners constantly furnished from one of these sources of culinary perfection." Both Brillat-Savarin and Blagdon reported that Beauvilliers, working with his wife and later their sons, greeted customers as if long-lost friends.

In Brillat-Savarin's account, Beauvilliers was cynically overattentive, but it would be hard to remain a top restaurateur for fifteen years unless genuinely proud of your home-away-from-home. Commending Beauvilliers's "first-rate cuisine," Brillat-Savarin (§137) also admitted the profession of *restaurateur* was always successful if the practitioner had "good faith, a sense of order, and ability." Beauvilliers's dedication in his book, *L'Art du Cuisinier* (The Art of the Cook) (1814, vi), argued the benefits of conviviality. At the shared table, he told the Marquis de la Vaupalière, "moral forces are renewed, the bonds of society strengthen, and rivals or bitter enemies end up being friends or companions." Strangers participated "with the intimacy of family," differences of rank were eclipsed, manners were polished, and spirit given new life. "I can say that the most amiable epicurean is also a model of reason and philosophy."

Many moralists have considered that charging money blocks hospitality. Many social scientists have portrayed the market as coldly antisocial. Many economists have preached a permanently corrosive "greed." But money turned out to be not Beauvilliers's primary concern, or at least not his primary skill. Brillat-Savarin (§43) did not know how death surprised the chef-patron but said his beneficiaries would not have been left much. Today many restaurateurs declare they would choose another, less demanding trade if they were just in it for the money, and seemingly endless books, columns, and blogs judge a restaurant's individual stylishness and comfort. Many customers express desperation to return for handcrafted dishes, attractive environments, and the servers' panache and charm. With regulars expecting their meal to be prepared and served by owners they know, highly valuable "goodwill" can disappear overnight upon the sale of a business.

As a clincher, the real destroyer of hospitality has proved to be not the market itself but purposive organizations. While it remains possible to quibble about the degree to which he rationalized his operations, Beauvilliers threw himself into the caring tasks of a household, a thousand things done right, quite unlike an efficient profit-seeking machine with perpetual life. The real change came with the corporate production line, aimed explicitly at profit, and businesses bought and sold through the love not of the underlying trade but of spreadsheets. The rationalization of dining only really took hold toward the end of the nineteenth century, and McDonaldization even later.

The success of social economies is to be judged by their richness of culture, quality of internal relationships, overall level of material comfort, and assurance of future generations. By contrast, purposive organizations are judged by their effectiveness in meeting targets, with profit the most self-reinforcing. Corporations can be useful but not hospitable.

McDonaldization

The Industrial Revolution, in which handcrafts gave way to machine production using fossil fuels and harnessed labor, is usually dated around the

1760s until the 1840s, initially in Britain. Massive social and cultural shifts made key commodities more readily available. The complexities of table-pleasure, however, were not readily industrialized. Even rudimentary mechanization did not arrive until well after restaurants. The first mechanical refrigeration got going only with such work as James Harrison's ice making in Australia in the 1850s and 1860s. Gas ranges were adopted around the 1880s, electric cookers from 1900, and then cool rooms. Marketing joined in the last decades of the nineteenth century, making sugar and other "packaged pleasures" (Cross and Proctor 2014). No one had rushed to mass produce human concern and comfort.

By then, French visitors were already astonished by the lack of conviviality among American office workers. In 1892 writer Paul de Rousiers reported "crimes against gastronomy" because of a "dread of wasting time." A worker might send out for sandwiches to devour at the desk. Advertising signs, "Try our quick lunch," should really have boasted, "Eat to live and do not live to eat." Once inside, de Rousiers described: "Gentlemen, with their hats on, stand in a long line beside the counter, on which are cold meats, piles of sandwiches, cakes, beer, iced-water, all within arm's length. In five minutes they manage to gulp down a certain amount of food, pay and go." Quality scarcely mattered: "what is most desired is something that will not hinder business, that does not cut the day in two" (314).

America's pioneering fast-food chain, White Castle, sent out hamburgers in 1921 (Hogan 1997). It took until the highway era, in 1948, before the McDonald brothers, Dick and Mac, sacked their "carhops" (women who waited on vehicles), slashed the menu, abandoned china and cutlery in favor of paper bags, wrappers, and cups, and adopted industrial equipment and rigid procedures to "eliminate the principal obstacle to fast-food service—the human element." The brothers put an "industry that prided itself on extremely personalized procedures" on the assembly line and halved the price of hamburgers, reported corporate chronicler John F. Love (1986, 12–18). Taking over from the brothers, Ray Kroc and Harry Sonneborn turned McDonald's into a globe-straddling giant. A distant management team imposed strict, moneymaking formulas. McDonald's Operations referred in a blog in 2009 to its "600-page operations and training manual" and inspectors carrying a "500-item checklist and a standardized 27-page inspection form." So much for "deregulation."

Factory-farmed, -prepared, and -served meals were garishly uncivilized. Food was predictable ("Do you want fries with that?") and interactions stilted ("Have a nice day"). Guests were no longer welcomed by an actual host but by clown "Ronald McDonald" or KFC's trademark image of founder Colonel Harland Sanders. Speed was dressed up as "customer service," while uncomfortable seating ensured no hanging about. By minimizing human contact, McDonald's eliminated generosity. An outlet in the Netherlands sacked an employee in March 2009 for selling a hamburger to a colleague and then adding a slice of cheese. Calling on McDonald's to reimburse the worker for wrongful dismissal, the court found that a written reprimand would have sufficed (BBC News 2010). In 2016 McDonald's experimented in Canada with "guest experience leaders," who greeted customers at the kiosk digital screen and helped them order. Without Beauvilliers's watchful eye, and no actual appetite of their own, new "bodies" rationalized meals one-dimensionally. The results attracted continuous reproval (e.g., Hightower 1975; Vidal 1997; Schlosser 2001). In comparison to real restaurant hospitality, only sarcasm sufficed, so Canadian sociologist John O'Neill (1999, 49) hailed America as "the only country in the world where the rich eat as badly as the poor. . . . Such is the democratization of taste."

To "enhance guest satisfaction and develop repeat business" was a rational objective, U.S. hospitality industry academic Carol A. King (1995, 229, 231) argued, reasonably. "In a free market, a company that exploits its customers will not last long. When guests are paying for hospitality, generosity is what they are willing to pay for." Many jurisdictions oblige corporations to provide appropriate goods and services—if they advertise comfort and luxury, the law requires some semblance of comfort and luxury. Furthermore, management can provide a platform for talented, personable, and highly professional staff. Staff can break out of their role and become human.

Just as a commercial organizations might mimic hospitality, a family business might obsess about money. While their domestic grounding can make restaurants caring workplaces, the necessity for high inputs of relatively common skills and reliance on family members have often meant low status, poor pay, and menu prices beyond the reach of employees. In the United States, in particular, low wages meant dependence on tips.

Tipping can seem highly "irrational" in the economists' sense. A charitable payment, which a canny "free rider" would avoid, is sufficiently embarrassing for economists that they might hurumph that, without tipping, "as was the case in communist countries, we'd get lousy service." For social anthropologists, such as David Sutton (2007, 191–92), tipping blurs the boundary in a modern capitalist economy between the "commodity and gift." Nonmonetary explanations include the communication of gratitude, social superiority, and solidarity, as when waiters leave big tips for their fellows. Social psychologists have also linked the size of the gratuity to server self-introductions, sexual dynamics, and the weather. Rules differ across cultures, so that a tip might be an insult in Japan. The question could therefore be reposed: Why do American businesses pay such poor wages?

Despairing of finding a Ph.D. topic, anthropologist John Burgess (2013, 207–8) went drinking and was admonished for not leaving a tip. Why were expectations so different in American bars from those in his own country, Australia? He now had a question, requiring further "participant observation." When tipping took hold in the late nineteenth century, Burgess decided, Australians enjoyed strong unions and labor protections, unlike America's "asymmetrical power relations in favour of employers." Employers would "seek to reduce their risk exposure to lower than expected custom by transferring that risk onto their employees, who will respond by seeking tips." Yet from bartenders' stories, Burgess also decided that tipping empowered them, with job security and work autonomy bolstered by strong bonds with regulars, forged through the payment of tips. If this suggests the truly free market of person-to-person exchange, then reducing the dependence on gratuities might purchase even closer bonds.

Whatever the reality of tipping, the chances of empathetic experiences are higher with on-the-spot owners, sharing sociably with staff and customers. Good taste might start with the spoon but encompasses the balance of the cutlery, politics of the drinks, murmur of a congenial room, semiotics of signage, charm of the grammar. Good restaurateurs get on top of each aspect, responsibly. They support good suppliers and restore spirits, and lately they publicly advocate good causes (some even paying proper wages!). That has happened because, fundamentally, restaurateurs are human householders.

In an autobiographical novel and later film, *Au petit Marguery* (Bénégui 1991), the chef has lost his sense of smell, so that the son organizes one last meal to celebrate the interwoven life histories of his parents, their staff, and regulars, publicly commemorating the obvious affection. At an equally neighborhood restaurant in the United States, ethnographer Karla Erickson (2009, 20) found that a waiter might initially approach a table in a friendly manner but, if the warmth were not returned, adopt a different frame. In such an establishment, "servers, managers, and regular customers *cooperate* to create a friendly, cozy ambience . . . service interactions are intersubjective performances."

Having grown up in and around her mother's *puestecito* near the Mexican-American border, Meredith Abarca (2007) learned that, in such "little public places" or small food stands, "communities were simmered, loyalties kneaded, and families blended." Using her later studies of such "public kitchens," Abarca urged that business success be gauged less financially and more by "collaboration and community gain." These businesses promoted social and cultural, "familial wealth."

Sometimes with abusive or neglectful partners, women sought financial independence by putting home-cooking on sale, but Abarca found much more than an income; the stands might incorporate at-work childcare, pride in a local specialty, shared lives with regulars, and support for a homeless person. From her ethnography ("culinary chats"), she found the *puestecitos* providing "a meeting hall where the current local politics are discussed or romances unfold." Raising eleven children primarily by selling burritos, Severa Ochoa de Castaña had designated one of her four tables as "the lovers' table" (185–87). Although Abarca distinguished home-based, "public kitchens" from professional restaurants of celebrity chefs, this is surely a matter of degree, not matching the qualitative gap between the *puestecitos* and globalized Tex-Mex chains like Taco Bell and On the Border.

Throughout the ages, domestic partners have opened their front door to offer home production. Domestic economies ensured genuine hands-on, person-to-person dealings, close to material realities, providing something more genuinely complex than possible from a six-hundred-page manual. So long as hosts retain household characteristics, their exchanges can employ money as an intermediary, and the market can remain free.

Open Eating Houses

A purposive team might beat a family in providing something tiny, such as a pin, whose division of tasks introduced Adam Smith's book, or tackle something major like a metro system. But, as if to confirm a record of despoliations, Ludwig von Mises (1985, 12) boasted that capitalism had placed "a delectable luxury as well as a food, in the form of sugar, at the disposal of the great masses," overlooking both slavery and obesity.

Good restaurants are not merely *small* businesses, which jurisdictions distinguish arbitrarily on the number of employees, varying (recently) from fewer than five in Cuba, fifteen in Australia, fifty in Europe, up to fifteen hundred for "small" manufacturers for the U.S. Small Business Administration. Nor are they a private (as in unlisted) company, which might be Mars with confectionery and pet foods, Walmart with shops, Cargill with global agricultural trade, or Koch Industries with its array of paper towels and plates, cattle ranches, oil refineries, pipelines, and political operations.

Instead, they are *open domestic households*, typically artisanal. When customers enter and leave a small shop with a greeting, this formality acknowledges the boundary of an essentially private space. *Eating houses* retain features of cooking on the spot and personal interaction, and these encompass taverns, roadhouses, diners, greasy spoons, . . . and, so we come, clarifying terminology, to *restaurants*. From its original reference to a restorative food, the word broadened over time until, especially in the United States, it stretched far enough to become its antithesis. Strictly, restaurants individualize choice through à la carte. However, that underrates associated connotations because, certainly in original intent, restaurateurs

FIGURE 12.1 Restaurant as open domestic household. Jennifer Hillier serving at Cantina di Toia, Bacchereto (FI), Italy, 1979. Photo by author.

restored the full person. That meant providing high levels of ambience, taste, and time for conviviality.

Admitting to some personal experience here, both of the restaurants in which I have been involved (Cantina di Toia in Tuscany and Uraidla Aristologist in South Australia) were so domestic that they used the household kitchen. At the Aristologist, opening the private kitchen for customers eventually disconcerted health authorities sufficiently that, while reassuring us that new restaurant kitchen regulations were based on McDonald's specifications, they restricted any eventual sale of the business. (We never worked out whether domestic use of the public kitchen might compromise public health or vice versa.)

The benefits of an eating house over its simulation can be illuminated from another direction. Family households became the place to dine in a communist state, Cuba. Called *paladares* from the Portuguese for "palate" (and borrowed from a restaurant name in a Brazilian soap opera), these eating houses, run by a "self-employer," multiplied in size with successive economic liberalizations. Starting in 1993, the first legal *paladar* was permitted to serve up to twelve customers, then twenty, quickly becoming fifty.[1]

The unmediated exchange between domestic economies (of individuals and families) makes the market fruitfully "free," and so the hospitality of open households provides clues, and motivations, to improve economics. Good economics needs to comprehend markets as interpersonal transactions involving intelligent pleasure and material support, with people collaborating on life, not exploiting each other. Family farming and artisanal manufacture can be welcomed into the open household idea. Major manufacturing and infrastructure works require separate consideration, away from the free market, and necessitating close political engagement. Rewriting economics is a huge task that relies on many subspecialties. But those *opening* their households and those celebrating in and with them understand, at the core, the market's complex exchange of food and its labor, person-to-person.

Restored by Restaurateurs

Tourists can stroll Parisian boulevards, market streets, arcades, parks, cemeteries, and old palaces converted into museums, but they cannot wander, uninvited, into a lacework of privileged mansions, bureaus, and private gardens. On Brillat-Savarin's telling, those walls used to secrete all the delights of fine Parisian cuisine. Then, restaurateurs opened their doors. Beauvilliers adapted aristocratic forms with clever cooks and waiters. Visiting in 1801–1802, Francis Blagdon acknowledged the city's triumphs, at a price. Great restaurateurs put the finishing touch to civilization, Brillat-Savarin decided. Tying natural and social economies together in the interest of meals, could restaurateurs save us?

Recognizing the corporation as "an alien entity with one goal: to reproduce money" within a global economic system "gyrating far beyond human control," progressive management academic David C. Korten (1996, 10, 13, 97) concluded that "collective salvation" required tapping into "an inner spiritual wisdom." That makes improvement sound elusive, until we accept the hearth as the true crucible of poetry, song, storytelling, and enlightenment. Wise restaurateurs might help us understand that meals have evolved through countless iterations, and civilization with them. The Beauvilliers of the world are exceptionally close to actual (biological) growth, hands-on trade, pleasure, conviviality, and culture. They are dedicated to free-market hospitality.

At this point, I need to reassure that fine restaurants are far more defendable than superyachts, private jets, and rocket jaunts. Not only is an expensive meal still a relatively small indulgence, but gastronomy needs its temples, given that improving social justice, peace, and sustainability demands more attention to meals, not less. Not that all plates need sprinkling with gold.

In recent years chefs emerged from their dens and went on show in spotless whites. They became celebrities, and appliance brands, and opened branches in Nice, Las Vegas, Dubai, and Tokyo. Their food traveled far in pixels. Customers snapping plates coincided in the early twenty-first century with the rise of intriguing "molecular gastronomy." Chef Ferran Adrià gained fame for El Bulli on the Costa Brava, Spain, by borrowing foaming, syringe-filling, and flash freezing with liquid nitrogen from food technologists. Unilever scientists had invented spherification, for example, encasing liquid in small balls in the 1950s. This might have leapt beyond realistic *household* bounds.

Elevating picture-perfect plates risked unbalancing meals, according to Georg Simmel's logic introduced in chapter 8, denying their roots in soil, and our animal natures. Camera-readiness threatened to outshine *Gemüt-lichkeit* (German, friendly coziness), chattiness, and occasional sublimity. Culinary art coated over the core of cooking, household sharing. Fortunately, chefs soon reacted against factory-inspired showpieces with named suppliers, herbs at the back door, and foraged "weeds." Environmental concern could remain intrinsic to a properly embedded task. Three-star chef Alain Passard announced in 2001 that L'Arpège in Paris would henceforth feature vegetables and avoid red meat, and he established three farms with different terroirs and employing twelve gardeners and animal traction.

Note that the last few paragraphs switched from good *restaurateurs* to celebrity *chefs*. As the chef emerged, the restaurateur retreated—the person or, often, couple who clearly owned the place and whose open household *restored* the guests, and not merely aesthetically.

Restaurateurs not only compose nature prettily but also provide welcoming settings, social solace, and good manners. An ebullient boss clears away a corner table while patrolling the kitchen, pausing only to welcome newcomers. Like Beauvilliers, many chefs greet customers, sometimes quietly inside the door, like some airline pilots. Guy Martin has welcomed guests in this way to Le Grand Véfour. Even while Guy Savoy put his name to a string of houses, he had Hubert Schwermer as front-of-house in Paris. The defiantly impeccable Mietta O'Donnell, having handpicked chefs from France, presided over a grand Melbourne dining room with the occasional murmur to staff. The strengths of Copenhagen's Noma were not just the food but also the port-side location, lazy Riesling sunset, and young chef, René Redzepi, smiling so sweetly from the open kitchen that he shouldn't mind grateful mention of the humanity of the floor staff.

Saved by restaurants. As unlikely as that might sound, engaging people with the actual free market, real restaurateurs open up civilization's meal. Against power structures, they and their customers network convivially, animating liberal care for individuals cooperating, healthily. Good eating houses build local community, showing off the work of designers, craftspeople, and growers, and finding ways to replenish and recycle (caring for the otherwise discarded, people included). Good *restaurateurs* are the ultimate economists, knowing growing, style, and civility, so that chapter 14 returns with more on this. Restore the restorators, and they might yet restore us!

13

VALUE FAMILIES! (ECONOMICS BEGINS AT HOME)

Behind White Picket Fences

A procession of sixteen "Andy Hardy" movies gained a special Academy Award in 1943 "for representing the American Way of Life." The movies portrayed nuclear families comfortably ensconced behind white picket fences. From *A Family Affair* in 1937 to *Andy Hardy Comes Home* in 1958, the hero of the series, Andy Hardy (Mickey Rooney), gained gradual maturity, all the while joining his father, the tough but understanding Judge Hardy (Lewis Stone), and his "swell" mother (Fay Holden) at dinners that verged on Thanksgiving feasts.

Hollywood kept up the cheery complacency after the Second World War with domestic comedies on television, the earliest and longest-running being *The Adventures of Ozzie and Harriet* (1952–1966). The actual two-story house of popular music stars, the Nelson family, was re-created in the studio. Harriet Nelson wore the apron and solved the problems of husband Ozzie and teenage boys David and Eric ("Ricky") Nelson with milk and cookies. In *Father Knows Best* (1954–1962), Robert Young played father, while Margaret Anderson (Jane Wyatt) shelled peas and called Princess, Bud, and Kitten to the table, where a stack of pancakes awaited at breakfast and a four-course dinner promptly at 5:00 P.M.

In *The Donna Reed Show* (1958–1966), the clever, attractive Donna Stone (Donna Reed) wore pearls and frilly dresses with tight waists and served rather than sat with her family: general practitioner Dr. Stone (Carl Betz), Mary (Shelley Fabares), and Jeff (Paul Petersen). Donna farewelled her family at the front door each opening credits, wearing her apron. Much action was based in the kitchen, the studio having a functioning stove, refrigerator, and sink, and at least one scriptwriter, Helen Levitt, called on Donna actually to make toast or scramble eggs (Fultz 1998, 130).

With the "swinging" sixties, such shows were soon derided as emblematic of car-dependent, suburban conformity with gray-suited, white men headed to offices, white women trapped in unpaid domestic labor, and censors demanding separate beds for married couples. Minor scrapes bedeviled sugar-coated family life, when, in reality, fathers could be violent and tyrannical, children become "delinquents," and abused and bored housewives resort to "Mother's Little Helpers," as the Rolling Stones called tranquilizers. Divorce was frequent, teenagers "fell" pregnant, and historian of the family Stephanie Coontz showed in *The Way We Never Were* in 1992 that the nuclear structure beloved of TV shows in the 1950s was always more the exception than the rule. Yet these sitcoms often put face-to-face meals at their heart, which was more than economists did. Economics texts might sometimes have acknowledged familiar households as the original *oikos/ecos* but then proceeded as if they only mattered as buying and selling units. Other commentators promoted families as sexually reproductive, moral bulwarks, anything but meal-sharing communes.

To a degree, the Hollywood depiction early in the long boom could almost be called subversive because they gave children a voice—and these children became the countercultural generation. At a deeper level, while suppressing sex, the shows promoted meal sharing as the real heart of domestic life. By making sexual orientation largely irrelevant, including in marriage, they liberated the family as the kitchen-table commune.

In this chapter I champion the little economies often called society's "building blocks" and variously named "households," "domestic economies," and "families." We know families well—indeed, the Latin word *familia* has given us both "family" and "familiar." Just imagine: if Latin had prevailed instead of Greek, the field of "economics" would now be "family science" or "familiar studies." And yet familiarity would appear to have bred neglect and confusion. Moreover, insistent marketing both stimulated consumption and weakened domestic foundations. When last accessed (August 2019), the long Wikipedia entry on "family" (with no fewer than 172 footnotes) did not include the word "meal," although food sharing was mentioned twice. Chatting around the kitchen table, entertaining guests with elaborate dishes and table linen, watching over a children's tea party ... keeping a window box, plot, allotment, fowls ... making home brew, bread ... let us praise, and practice, domesticity.

The restoration of the communal meals of householders and their guests starts here with Donna Reed, whose family life, both on-screen and off-, was swept by powerful historical tides. Gastronomically, the suburban sitcoms were just that little bit radical, legitimating not a string of children but a number close to replacement level, to give another example. Ironically, the avoidance of sex only made more room for family meals, and couples had moved beyond courtship to animated chatting with children around the table. With sexual reproduction now widely accepted as inessential for married life, it's time to take home communism seriously again.

Donna Reed

Hollywood actor Donna Reed (1921–1986) won her Golden Globe award for "Best TV Star—Female" for her role as housewife Donna Stone in 1963, the year that arguably opened the major social and cultural upheaval of the 1960s. Protest singers Bob Dylan and Peter, Paul, and Mary joined the march on Washington at which Martin Luther King, Jr., said, "I Have a Dream"; Beatlemania took off with the band's televised appearance at the London Palladium; the academy's top movie, *Tom Jones*, contained a notoriously erotic, fig-eating sequence; Betty Friedan's *The Feminine Mystique* appeared; and, also in 1963, Julia Child launched her television cookery show, *The French Kitchen* (Symons 2006).

While the sitcoms' complacency was soon mocked, following the loud and boisterous Andy Hardy, such programs promoted a confident, articulate new generation; children were no longer to be "seen and not heard."

FIGURE 13.1 Cast of Hollywood television sitcom *The Donna Reed Show*, 1960. Publicity still. Courtesy of Wikimedia Commons.

Just as Ricky Nelson became a pop music sensation, Donna Stone's daughter had a crush on visiting teen idol James Darren, and, then, relying on reverb and backing singers, actor Shelley Fabares performed the hit song "Johnny Angel." That is, coinciding with the invention of the "teenager," family television promoted youth culture.

Nor were the women entirely subservient. Donna Stone was intelligent and charming, and she auditioned for the role of Nora in a local production of Henrik Ibsen's play *A Doll's House* (1879), about a woman who walks out on her family to find herself. In another episode, "The Ideal Wife," visitors calling Donna "sweet" left her fuming. The next day she said "no" to everyone, exploding to a delivery man: "I have been used, victimized, and exploited by my children and husband" (Fultz 1998, 131–32). Needing a "mental challenge," in the episode "All This and Voltaire Too?," Donna takes French lessons from local chef Monsieur Voltaire, starts cooking at home with wine, and acknowledges the "divine smell of French cooking." When Donna, Alex, and Jeff dine at the restaurant, Reed proves brilliantly she could handle farce, involving an expensive dress from

Madame Paulette, and French as the "language of love" (season 8, episode 21, February 5 1966).

As to her own story, Donna Reed was first noticed as a rising star in *The Courtship of Andy Hardy* (1942), the series winning the special "American Way of Life" Oscar the following year. Anchoring the perennial *It's a Wonderful Life* (1946), as Mary Hatch, she was often described as epitomizing the "girl next-door." Yet she won her own Academy Award for playing a prostitute in *From Here to Eternity* (1953). On *The Donna Reed Show*, she might have portrayed the stay-at-home wife, but she coproduced and starred in the 275 episodes. When she bowed out of the show after eight years to pay extra attention to her four children, her sons were in line for the Vietnam War, and she joined the leftward slide, licking envelopes for the Another Mother for Peace group, and campaigning for antiwar Democrat Senator Eugene McCarthy.

Reed's life was caught up in tectonic shifts, with the corporatization successively of domestic food production, processing, and, finally, putting it on the table (Symons 1996). By the nineteenth century, and working outward from Europe and North America, industrial capital had begun entering productive fields, forests, and fishing grounds, so that a great bulk of families lost direct access to the soil, sought work in mines, factories, and offices, and became reliant on robust commodities, such as flour, sugar, salted meats, and alcoholic spirits. Reed's family worked on this first step in modern food—growing basic ingredients for the market. The childhood home in rural Iowa had no electricity; water was carried from the outside cistern; and her mother cooked on a wood-burning stove. As her biographer Jay Fultz (1998, 12) reported, "the place was alive with the sounds of chickens and cows, children, and calls to dinner. Old photographs show several barns, a feedlot and a two-story white farmhouse."

By then, on top of agribusiness, the industrialization of storage/distribution replaced household cellars, barns, pantries, and larders with corporate mills, refineries, breweries, preserving works, confectioneries, and bakeries. Fossil fuel took over handcrafts and transport. Fitted with iron stoves and connected to the town pipes and wires, modern kitchens were supplied with basic ingredients for home assembly, along with instruction manuals—the standard cookery books. Women were fulltime housewives, or training to be as servants. With domesticity increasingly car-dependent, Reed's farming family would have collected processed white sugar and flour, cheese, and other stored items from the nearby town of Denison.

During the long boom of the 1950s and 1960s, the food industry reached into every kitchen and around the globe. Supermarkets became complete store cupboards, and the all-electric wonders exhibited in sitcoms replaced "drudgery," but that still left the final cooking. So in this third, televised stage, sophisticated marketing supported food preparation—ready-made meals, with snacks and drinks in-between. McDonald's took off. Lifestyle consumption supplanted domestic production.

The Donna Reed Show's major sponsor, the Campbell Soup Company, advertised canned soups and Franco-American Spaghetti. The internet carries an old commercial of Reed advertising a special offer of soup mugs from Campbell's. Little wonder that pop artist Andy Warhol's first solo exhibition in New York at the end of 1962 featured paintings of enlarged Campbell's soup cans. Meanwhile, competitor H. J. Heinz sponsored *The Adventures of Ozzie and Harriet*. Advertisers using *Father Knows Best* included Kellogg's breakfast cereals, Mazola margarine, Maxwell House coffee, Pillsbury "refrigerated biscuits" (canned dough for baking for breakfast), and Scott Paper products, found "all through the house."

With the capitalist market allegedly abolishing kitchen labor, these shows did their bit in the "disintegration" (Weber) of domestic units. Rather than families growing food, preserving it, and sharing it at regular mealtimes, they could now heat a can for casual consumption in front of the TV, doing Donna Stone and other housewives out of a job. With son Jeff freely raiding the fridge, this was revolution! Shifting women from housework into the paid workforce contributed to a greater measure of equality for women, even if they still did more than their share of the remaining housework.

Popular domestic comedies showed the family meal but also promoted its breakup, amid worsening dining for many. Portraying happy families, Hollywood television invited the food industry in from the garden and out from the cupboard to now take over the table, while other corporations opened "fast" (car-accessible) street-food stops. Business burst through the white picket fences to put food in front of diners everywhere. With families glued to chatty *Donna Reed*, soup mugs in hand, corporate advertising intruded on dinner conversation. As to economists, the logic of the Market had already written housework out of the picture. To think that left-liberals got the blame for "attacks on the family," when hard-right monetarists and "dries" were counting families out or, more correctly, failing to count them in.

Capitalism contradicts itself: the mass marketing of meals replaced decades of puritanical hard work and plain flavors. Nation building gave way to globalization, and homemaking lost out to the "me," countercultural, or consumer generation. The glorification of flavors—from liquid breakfasts to dried noodles—brought the "complete manufacture of choice" (Symons 2000, 339). The cheap thrills of sugar, salt, fat, and flavoring boosted obesity and other diseases. Food scholar Warren Belasco (1989) described a "countercuisine" rebelling against big food business in America, and wanting "healthy" choices. Vegetable oil companies popularized the "Mediterranean diet," replacing dairy foods (Symons 1994b). Many people now ate worse but many better, at dinner parties, fashionable restaurants, and rediscovered, smartly equipped domestic kitchens. Glossy books and specialist magazines circulated an enormous variety of recipes, knowledge, and opinions. Gardening became trendy again.

Since the sitcom era, privileged individuals could explore foods, food destinations, and ideas, including through the relatively free market of old-style family artisans, retailers, and preparers. The marketing stress on enjoyment and sensory temptation finally supplanted dreary fuel for workers.

Sexual Obsession

The twentieth was the sexualized century of Sigmund Freud, physically attractive Hollywood glamour, *Playboy*, Masters and Johnson, and the 1960s sexual revolution, often credited to the availability of the birth control pill (released in the United States in 1960 and scoring a *Time* magazine cover, and legality in France, in 1967). So-called family values enforcement helped hypersexualize love, marriage, and the family. Sexual repression favored the breeding pair and kept priests celibate, women virgins until wedded, and homosexuals in the closet. American religious conservatives would object to welfare for single mothers, picket abortion clinics, make innocent young children pledge premarital chastity, and demand men be men and women be submissive.

Defenders often claimed that the reproductive marriage was "biblical," but, celebrated for his wisdom by all three Abrahamic religions (Judaism, Christianity, and Islam), Solomon boasted "seven hundred wives, princesses, and three hundred concubines" (1 Kings 11:3), and Jesus issued such stark decrees as a disciple having to "hate his own father and mother and wife and children and brothers and sisters" (Luke 14:26). When the New Testament reproduced some excellent thoughts—"Love is patient; love is kind" (1 Corinthians 13:4)—they were not aimed specifically at marriages. More "biblical" might be something like the Church of England's *Book of Common Prayer*, which originated in 1549, and which stated that marriage was ordained, first, "for the procreation of children, to be brought up in the fear and nurture of the Lord," and, second, "for a remedy against sin, and to avoid fornication."

It was not merely the sex-centered family that seemed unchallengeable but the notion of the "nuclear family," which U.S. anthropologist George Murdock went through scholarly contortions to justify. In *Social Structure* (1949, 1) he identified three possible family types—nuclear, polygamous, and extended. The "first and most basic, called herewith the *nuclear family*, consists typically of a married man and woman with their offspring," and this same sentence disclosed his first qualification, "one or more additional persons may reside with them." In Murdock's count of 192 societies around the world, "47 have normally only the nuclear family, 53 have polygamous but not extended families, and 92 possess some form of the extended family." Marital relations could be permanent or temporary, with polygyny or polyandry or sexual license, and so forth. Among numerous variations, the Banaro of New Guinea would not permit a groom to approach his bride "until she has borne him a child by a special sib-friend of his father." Murdock might plausibly have conceded that families have come in various shapes and sizes. Instead he declared: "The nuclear family is a universal human social grouping" (2–4).

Obsessing about sex, Murdock largely neglected the home as economy. His often-quoted, long, and exhaustive-sounding definition of the family included four references to reproductive sex (requiring, for example, "adults of both sexes, at least two of whom maintain a socially approved sexual relationship") but no mention of child-rearing, let alone education, affective relationships, care and consideration, or love. Admittedly, meal sharing might have squeezed in under "economic cooperation" (1).

More effectively, families can be understood as economies based on communal meals. Having obsessed about sexual relations, the *Book of Common Prayer* conceded an economic reality to families with a third reason: "mutual society, help, and comfort." That mutuality meant throwing in one's possessions, future prospects, psychic well-being, and elemental survival with another (or others), and so a lifetime commitment to meal sharing.

In recent times, the better, but less vociferous, "profamily" case remained the social, educational, health, welfare, and affective importance of the domestic table. Surveys by the U.S. Center on Addiction and Substance Abuse since 2001, and reported as *The Importance of Family Dinners*, have consistently shown that the more teenagers dined with their parents, the less likely they were to smoke, drink, or use illegal drugs. Some traditional nuptials might have led to the bed, but sexual symbolism scarcely rivaled table sharing. Wedding feasts have been interpreted as tying together two extended families, but they are primarily the first official meal of a new household. In former times, a flame might be taken from the old to light the new cooking fire. A Hindu bride might carry her own pestle and mortar, ostensibly to save learning the quirks of foreign equipment. At what exact moment are a couple married? Within the European tradition, is at their exchange of rings? The kiss? When they agree "I do"? Sign in front of witnesses? The couple marry, according to a gastronomic calculation, as they cut the cake. They have invited their nearest and dearest to their first official meal as a family and used the cook's quintessential, sharing instrument to divide the centerpiece.

Communal meals make sense. Preparing a meal for two is only marginally more time-consuming than for one, and two can (almost) "eat as cheaply as one." In addition, as an ancient Epicurean set out: "Two are better than one, because they have a good reward for their toil. For if they fall, one will lift up his fellow; but woe to him who is alone when he falls and has not another to lift him. Again, if two lie together, they are warm" (Ecclesiastes 4:9–11).

A pair also suffices for the most immediately powerful division of labor—between food producing outdoors and food distributing indoors (often traditionally relying on a handy male-female coupling, but that is far from a universal requirement). Two is the simplest partnership with the least conflicts. "Two is company, three is a crowd." Higher numbers get increasingly unwieldly.

Just as the notion of family makes more sense when viewed not sexually but gastronomically, the anthropological standby of "kinship" is slippery until referred to meals. Kinship had seemed either *biological*, being "given by birth and unchangeable," or *social*, being "shaped by the ordinary, everyday activities of family life," English researcher Janet Carsten (2004, 5) explained. Yet biological and social "blood" actually blended in domestic economies: "As inhabitants live together in one house over time and eat meals together, their blood becomes progressively more similar." This applied as much to Carsten's own childhood memories as to her fieldwork among Malay people in the early 1980s, where "consumption of rice meals cooked in the hearth not only strengthens existing ties of kinship between household members, it can actually create such ties" (40).

Little in the second half of last century might seem more sexually obsessed than the pulchritudinously illustrated *Playboy* magazine. Yet in *Playboy*'s first issue in December 1953, Hugh M. Hefner imagined his readers: "We like our apartment. We enjoy mixing up cocktails and an *hors d'oeuvre* or two, putting a little mood music on the phonograph, and inviting in a female acquaintance for a quiet discussion on Picasso, Nietzsche, jazz, sex." Chef Sidney Aptekar's monthly recipes were collected in *The Playboy Gourmet* in 1961.

The Nature of Love

Along with the family, love became interpreted predominantly in terms of sex. Plato's *Symposium* showed real love as a higher form of the crude desire for a youthful body. Initiation into the mysteries began by engaging with the physical beauty of another person, and then admiring the beauty of bodies generally, and of souls, then moral beauty and next the beauty of knowledge, and finally contemplating ideal beauty itself. It took a whole, engrossing book to transcend love's origins in animal lust. Sigmund Freud (1963, 40–41) reinverted this, reducing the higher love of philosophers and poets to sexual desire, with sexual union its goal. Either way, "higher" love was tied to sexual desire.

Yet the all-male group in Plato's *Symposium* analyzed love during postprandial drinking. Perhaps they should have noticed that the table had generated civil relationships, and also love, as food writers have long known. Brillat-Savarin (§60) retorted: even married couples "who do not share a bed (and there are many) have to eat at the same table." As to gourmand couples, "they have a topic of conversation that is forever renewed; they talk about what they are eating, and also what they have eaten and will eat, what they have observed in other people's places, about fashionable dishes, new inventions, etc., etc; and everyone knows that convivial conversation ('chit-chat') is full of charm."

M. F. K. Fisher (1990, 353) explained in her introduction to *The Gastronomical Me* in 1943: "our three basic needs, for food and security and love, are so mixed and mingled and entwined that we cannot straightly think of one without the others." In *Alphabet for Gourmets* in 1949, she wrote that "sharing food with another human being is an intimate act that should not be indulged in lightly" (577).

"Love is a product of the pragmatic realities of everyday life," decided sociologist of French family meals Jean-Claude Kaufmann (2010, 221–22). He did not ignore "what goes in the bedroom, or about the cuddles," but the kitchen did much to "create love for both couples and child-centred families. Thanks to the magic of cookery and the relational and sensual alchemy of meals, love sometimes grows as we peel onions or knead dough." None of his interviewees regarded cooking as an "ordinary domestic chore. There is something different about it. This is because family life is built around the dining table." Not that Kaufmann was oblivious to meals as a battleground. Despite the best efforts of family members, the "war goes on quietly, but it goes on all the same" (111).

Renegade U.S. philosopher turned English food journalist Paul Levy and collaborators were clear that marriages were made in kitchens. They wrote that foodies, in search of a mate, did not squander money and time on the theater, concerts, the cinema, or bed: "To a real foodie, love goes hand in hand with food. When they fall in love their first thought is of the meals they will eat, plan or cook" (Woods et al. 1982, 68). Cooking marriages were lucky in that the "rituals of shopping, preparation, eating and loading the dishwasher are so repetitive and comforting that anyone married to or living with a foodie soon feels completely trapped, like a patient in a hospital." And foodie marriages were often homosexual, but that didn't matter: "Being Foodie is so much more important" (Barr and Levy 1985, 20).

Formally, a family relies on a contract, often termed a marriage contract, essentially agreeing to share everything involved with meals, including necessary property. That means that a domestic household can be established by people with no plan or ability for child-rearing, by people of the same sex, and by more than two people, often a large number at a religious community or commune. A heterosexual couple is convenient for sexual reproduction, yet marriage is a contract to love, comfort, honor, and keep each other, in sickness and in health. San Francisco sociologist Christopher Carrington (1999, 29–30) discovered: "Many lesbigay families point to the continuous preparing of daily meals and/or the occasional preparing of elaborate meals as evidence of their status as families." He, too, noticed the "deceptively simple activities that constitute love and care, activities that . . . may entail trips to the store to pick up something special for dinner . . . remembering a couple's anniversary . . . remembering the vegetables that family members dislike" (6).

Economics, the Unfamiliar

In his *Principles of Economics*, the standard text around a century ago, Alfred Marshall (1890, 2.3.2) still fretted whether domestic servants were productive because they were *paid* to do otherwise invisible family work. Marshall could make "no distinction in character between the work of the baker who provides bread for the family, and that of the [domestic] cook who boils potatoes." He even worried that the French housewife was more productive than her English and American counterparts by adding more value to inexpensive ingredients. "Domestic economy is often spoken of as belonging to the science of consumption: but that is only half true" (3.5.4 n.81). Nevertheless, economists kept drifting off.

With the massive transfer to the wider political and market economies over the past two or so centuries, domestic economies seemed mere adjuncts, reproducing labor and lifestyle purchasers. Together with that, the science of economics concentrated on *Homo economicus*, an *individual* without families. It was not as if economists actively disparaged the affective, moneyless economy so much as endorsed capitalist freedom to penetrate.

Lionel Robbins dedicated his influential *Essay on the Nature and Significance of Economic Science* (1932) to his father and yet never once used the words "family" or "families." When he wrote of "domestic production," that was the tariff-protected kind. Further fussing over the Market relegated the original economics to the humiliatingly tautological and linguistically confused "domestic economy" (*domus* being Latin for *oikos* in Greek), or to such guises as "home economics," "household management," "domestic science," "human ecology," or "family and consumer studies." Trying to avoid such clumsiness, I often turn to "family."

And even when economically denied, they were not sacrosanct. Leading economist of the Chicago school Gary S. Becker became a pioneer of the brazenly named "New Home Economics." Having reconceived individuals as businesses through the concept of "human capital," he turned in the *Treatise on the Family* in 1981 to bring families under the selfish calculus, although, as Becker explained, "altruism is less common in market transactions and more common in families because altruism is less 'efficient' in the marketplace and more 'efficient' in families" (194). His mathematical equations supported such new laws of economics as "Complementarity implies that households with men and women are more efficient than households with only one sex" (23). Revealingly, the only use of the word "meal" to be found in his entire book belonged to the dust-jacket writer, who commended Becker for seeing "each family as a kind of little factory—a multiperson unit producing meals, health, skills, children, and self-esteem from market goods."

Market "efficiency" had captured economics as a largely male concern. In recent decades approximately one-third of economics doctorates have been going to women, and one in nine professorships, and in 2009 the first, Elinor Ostrom, won an economics Nobel. Feminist economist Marilyn Waring of New Zealand argued influentially in *If Women Counted* (1988) that the mainstream ignored women's unpaid domestic work, just as it failed to value nature. These lapses showed up in, for example, the reliance on gross domestic product as a measure of business rather than human prosperity—the "domestic" here again referring to national accounts, which value armament manufacture, not washing the dishes. American historian of economic ideas Nancy Folbre (1998, 35; 2009, 325) chronicled assumptions of men as the real individuals, being both lustful and greedy, with women "defined by morality and sentiment." However, "patriarchal rules and norms helped stabilize an emergent capitalist economy." Asking *Who Cooked Adam Smith's Dinner?*, Swedish editorial writer Katrine Marçal (2015, 7, 65, 167) recognized: "How do you get your dinner? That's the fundamental question of economics." Economic *man* was no ideal for feminists to live up to, she wrote. Without "leaking breasts or hormones," he had no body. "A society organized around the shared needs of human bodies would be different . . . lack of healthcare and lack of food would be central economic concerns."

Right-wing political opinion-makers have divided between those who are "rational," being "promarket" and promoting "freedom," and those promoting corporatist, social conservativism. Many politicians have ended up advocating neoliberal cuts to public health and education and seeking to mitigate ensuing disaster by promulgating fundamentalist religion, defenses of the "traditional" family, scarcely disguised racism, nationalistic appeals to established "values," and divisive ridicule of left-liberals as consuming soft, white, and foreign quiches, lattes, champagnes, and chardonnays.

But capitalism is not total, advised social geographers J. K. Gibson-Graham (Julie Graham and Katherine Gibson). In a stirringly titled essay, "Waiting for the Revolution, or How to Smash Capitalism While Working at Home in Your Spare Time," Gibson-Graham (1995, 193–94) argued that, in terms of the numbers involved and output, "the household sector can hardly be called marginal. In fact, it can arguably be seen as equivalent to or more important than the capitalist sector."

Little evokes sentiment like crackling hearths, carefree conversation, and apple pie, golubtsy, or congee. At family meals, people still learn about kindness, pleasure, and the world (Flammang 2016), exercise their palates, enjoy themselves, and join life's adventure. Where more than one are gathered in regular intimacy and regular creation, they find themselves, and restore civilization. Things can go horribly wrong, tempers flare like a tray of burnt vegetables, or relationships turn into spongey, sliced, white bread. But table-pleasure brings people back. And back people must go, according to radical economics.

Fracturing Meals and So Families

Social scientists found modern Western families—those idealized in the 1950s—devoted to definite dining structures or "proper meals." As reported in South Wales in the early 1980s, for example, young wives followed a standard three-course format two or three times a week. The centerpiece was a "cooked dinner," which was a plateful of meat, two vegetables, and gravy, coming between a savory "starter" and "afters" of a "pudding" or "sweets." The use of knife and fork was obligatory, and never a fork or knife alone, or fingers (Murcott 1982). The "proper meal" had gained such a hold that other British scholars saw it could symbolize the family—representing not merely such physical requirements as "meat and two veg" but social necessities, including the woman doing the cooking and the family sitting down together (Charles and Kerr 1988, 226).

However, with corporations pushing fast foods, ready-made serves, snacks, and an array of drinks, "proper meals" often lost out to packets, muffins, carbonated caffeine, and liquid meal replacements. Expensive marketing went into the casual consumption of boxed deals, children's instant treats, and beer and spirits at stand-up parties. Table companions became a clatter of advertising characters. Knife and fork or chopsticks dropped in favor of phones: fast food came with fast friending. Family members ate according to conflicting timetables, away from the table, and often by themselves. By the 1980s social scientists had spoken of the fragmentation or informalization of meals. Corporations engaged in the "devaluation of domesticity" and thereby of the home (Matthews 1987). Family members came and went, learning to "use the kitchen primarily as a larder," with "the fridge as a central organizing principle" (Kaufmann 2010, 87). Delivery-only "ghost restaurants" or "dark kitchens" appeared only an app away.

Over a number of years, sociologist Anne Murcott (1997, 46) queried whether "family meals" were a "thing of the past." Her conclusion largely remained: "Not only do we probably have insufficient evidence either way, but we also may be looking for quite the wrong type of evidence," confusing historical fact and the necessary myths by which humans live. Certainly, Hollywood had portrayed an unrealistically fixed image of the "family" that, in any case, would not apply across rural households in different historical locations and epochs, to working-class families plagued by shift-work, nor to yuppie couples forever dining at restaurants and others' homes.

The epidemic of "no fuss" and "convenience" products, along with "quick" and "easy" recipes, also aroused commentaries about the *deskilling* of domestic cooking. Cookery experts recommended microwave ovens: "Snacks for one or two can be produced in seconds—great for a family with teenagers!" How were the young, frail, and intellectually disabled, those without funds, and the homeless meant to cope with the complexities, and sales onslaught?

This massive transfer from domestic economies was "disintegration" through "rationalization" (as I borrowed from Max Weber in chapter 10). Yet, paradoxically, in snatching meals, marketers drew attention to them. Individuals had to choose and choose again—brands, styles, calorie counts, hamburger add-ons, the blue or red livery of cola drinks. Family members often demanded hearty, refined, slimming, vegan, paleo, or gluten-free. Heightened food anxieties turned into self-diagnosed allergies.

Just as many diners reacted by eating well, many home cooks consumed unprecedented numbers of magazines, books, and television chef shows, covering a bewildering multiplication of recipes. Were cooks giving up, or getting busier? The conflicting evidence can be partly explained by inequalities. Some people, deprived of cultural capital, succumbed to point-of-sale, while others managed more discernment. While *The Donna Reed Show* promoted Campbell's soup, the show's four principals, noted for their ensemble work, continued meeting for many years over lunch at The Bistro, Beverly Hills (Fultz 1998, 157).

Another aspect of "deskilling" was that the necessary knowledge shifted from practical kitchen to fuller consumer skills (Symons 2006; 2009, 234). Having to handle dinner parties and children's treats and virtuously save money, weight, or labor, the cook who dreamed up a last-minute replacement for an empty packet of a child's favorite breakfast cereal might, later in the day, negotiate a sophisticated wine list. Big, glossy books handed on knowledge of Thai ingredients and Italian *cucina*, of restaurants and gardening.

It's an Economy

It was not that profit-maximizers set out to idealize the sexual family so much as to deal conveniently with the pairing of paid, nondomestic worker and paying customer. Along with that, top-down economists lost the alimentary basis to the domestic economy. Natural functions need acknowledgment, nonetheless—more than that, they need enhancing. Enlightenment thinkers from Hobbes to Brillat-Savarin recognized the power of sexual appetite, but, more than that, they understood the appetite for food as the key to economics.

Families are basic economies—the original *oikoi*—with the familiar meals. In essence, they are hands-on distributions of foods the participants have labored to provide. Founded on the garden and hearth, their property is modest. With individuals contributing to, and taking from, the same *mensa* (Latin, table), this is *commensality* (another *com-* "with" word). The intimate economy can be run autocratically and/or through adherence to rules, but its essential mechanism is communism, and the motivations are nonrational—love and affection, with taste-pleasures at the base. With marriage uniting individuals "as one," property is a right.

Families are organizations of care in meeting fundamental needs; members ensure they are housed and fed, done with dignity. Families come in multiple shapes and sizes, so long as two essentials underlie their economic naturalness or spontaneity: first, mutuality—the components work together; and, second, comprehensiveness—the mutual support is life- and pleasure-giving. Can more than two people get married in this scheme?—perhaps that's a case for civil unions, or some other contract.

As German sociologist Ferdinand Tönnies wrote in 1887 (1974, 60–61, 67), the house or home is "the organic cell . . . of life itself," a "community cooperating in work and consumption. The taking of food is repeated with the regularity of breathing." Centered on the table, "everyone has his place there and is given his proper share." Following Tönnies, the family lies on the *Gemeinschaft* side of relationships, based on subjective feelings of belonging. So find your family, and embrace it! Be guided by the wisdom of meals!

Entertaining guests at home is an open family meal. The real contrast is between meals provided by families and those by Heinz, Unilever, and Subway. That is finished food, purchased with no certain knowledge of the contents, and no contact with its producers. Dining becomes *unfamiliar*, and economists favored that.

The late-twentieth-century questioning of the rigid nuclear version also came perilously close to rejecting the family table, thereby supporting business incursions. But since the meal arguably became the real focus of Hollywood sitcoms, less sexual definitions enable the most treasured of meals an exultant return. The original resistance to industrial intrusions, largely organized through churches, trade unions, and (often) home economics classes, had in different ways been neutralized. Given the Market's ostensible sympathy with individual choice, the newer resistance on behalf of the individual's communal pleasure might prove harder to knock.

So take back the family table with long-term partners! Reassert the domestic economy,[1] make it strong and vital, and learn economics on the job. Homemakers can install herbs, fowl, and ice-cream churns, can become involved with the wider economies, perhaps joining the market as family farmers, food and utensil crafters, or restaurateurs, and can engage in the political process. And talk, face-to-face. It means joining the Donna Reeds, and Dons, of the world.

14

GET POLITICAL! (BRING BACK BANQUETS)

Coming Together on the Cours Mirabeau

Waiters in black waistcoats, with long white aprons and impressive memories, hasten with loaded trays, and one brings fresh orange juice, baguette, butter, jam, and coffee. The juice is just squeezed, the baguette could not be fresher, and the butter more delicately scented, and the coffee is, well, French. Other tables already linger over books and newspapers, and a few face out to watch promenaders on the wide Cours Mirabeau with its two double rows of plane trees. Cafés line this sunny side of the wide avenue, while banks have taken over the gracious seventeenth- and eighteenth-century *hôtels* (townhouses) on the shady side. The world makes sense breakfasting at the Deux Garçons in Aix-en-Provence, France.

We could dine better in Aix—on Provençal classics in vine-covered Chez Feraud, a little more ambitiously at Le Mille Feuille, or cook from nearby markets—and the tourist reports on the Deux Garçons are mixed, to say the least. Yet the ingrained routines of this large brasserie/café/restaurant could not be abandoned merely to satisfy internet nitpickers. We return for foie gras at a bargain price at lunch and give the required forty-eight-hour notice for bouillabaisse. Frequent visits are necessary to become immersed in the daily, weekly, and annual rhythms, as several spaces evolve

FIGURE 14.1 Les Deux Garçons, Aix-en-Provence, France, 2011. Photo by J. M. Campaner. Creative Commons Attribution-Share Alike 3.0 Unported. Courtesy of Wikimedia Commons.

and subdivide, and gain and lose tablecloths and customers, according to the hour.

This institution opened in 1792 and was renamed Deux Garçons (Café of the Two Waiters) by new owners in 1840. Generations of illustrious names have sat here—a popular list includes Paul Cézanne, Émile Zola, and Ernest Hemingway. American food writer M. F. K. Fisher lived around the corner in 1954–1955, dropping in for an aperitif while her two daughters had lemonades. She based a chapter in 1964 on people-watching at the "2Gs," as its name is often abbreviated. Other expatriate, gastronomic opinion leaders living hereabouts have included Alice B. Toklas, James Beard, Julia Child, Richard Olney, and Peter Mayle. If Boston were the capital of Puritan America, then "Provence is the capital of hedonist America," observed poet-traveler Patricia Storace (2006).

Once, I set off, like a schoolboy, to follow the whistle and rattle of a pipe and tambour band parading past. The musicians play a thin flute with one hand and predecessor of the snare drum with the other. On another occasion several such groups danced and sang in the old Provençal language of Occitan. In 1849 Scottish essayist Thomas Carlyle borrowed these people's "gay science" (or *gai saber*, the troubadours' art of poetry) to speak of the "dismal science." This was the "rueful . . . Social Science," the "dreary, desolate, and indeed quite abject and distressing" study that "finds the secret of this universe in 'supply-and-demand,' and reduces the duty of human governors to that of letting men alone" (672).

The traditional life was not yet uprooted in Marcel Pagnol's day. That's someone else who probably haunted the Deux Garçons, because he studied literature at the University of Aix-en-Provence until called up for the First World War, after which he depicted regional life in plays, novels, and movies. Pagnol so influenced another Californian visitor that Alice Waters named her restaurant, Chez Panisse, and her daughter, Fanny, after his characters.

Pagnol became widely known outside France for *Jean de Florette* and *Manon des Sources*, a pair of 1986 remakes of a film and then novel he had directed and written. The tragic story was intrinsically economic, I decided, one morning at my laptop at the Deux Garçons. Educated in the city, Jean de Florette has returned to his village with a modern idea: breeding rabbits for the market. But the story more concerns that economic fundamental, water. Water circulates. It can be measured. Its distribution can be inequitable. In Pagnol's story, avaricious neighbors secretly block Jean's stream, ending his farm, his dreams, and, finally, his life. Years later, with the villainous pair having taken over Jean's land and water, his daughter, Manon, who has fled to the hills as a goatherd, discovers how to stop a spring flowing to not just the farm but the village's life-giving fountain. The mayor and local engineer cannot bring the water back. When Manon restarts the fountain, the villagers think it's a miracle.

Aix was founded on thermal springs, its name a contraction of the original Latin, *Aquae Sextiae* (Baths of Sextius). Parisian doctors suggested the warm waters might help the broken wrist of another American visitor, future president Thomas Jefferson. Traveling alone through southern France and Italy, and stealing olive trees and rice for introduction back home, Jefferson took rooms for four nights from March 25, 1787, at the Hôtel Saint-Jacques. The waters did not help, but the sun did. "I am now in the land of corn, wine, oil, and sunshine," he wrote to his secretary. The town's wide roads allowed one, two, or four rows of shade trees (then elm, subsequently replaced by plane trees) and "delicious walks," he reported. "What more can man ask of heaven, and if I should happen to die at Paris I will beg of you to send me here, and have me exposed to the sun. I am sure it will bring me to life again."

Hot springs feed some of the town fountains, and M. F. K. Fisher (1983, 61) became exasperated seeing "people hurriedly carrying one small pitcher to the fountain five times before lunch, instead of two small pitchers or even two large ones in one or two trips." The locals must have had good reason—perhaps they needed more trips to ensure warm water, to carry lighter loads up flights of stairs, or to socialize.

I am not saying that a cash economy never helped. I am pleased to hand some notes to the waiter. Quick as a flash, he feels in the small, leather-piped pockets on the belly of his waistcoat for coins for the little plate, almost without a glance, and leaves us to linger, recognizes us upon each return, and enquires about the book. But a market is fundamentally not cash, so much as many tables with baguettes, cheese, and pastis and accompanying water jug. And a hydrological plot works in any economy, whether the human body or port city of Marseille, whose supply crosses the world's biggest stone aqueduct, the Aqueduc de Roquefavour, just outside Aix.

I have introduced the Deux Garçons as an irresistible illustration of my concluding chapter's topic, politics. This is political not only for finding Jefferson helping French colleagues with liberal principles for their prospective republic, not only for Carlyle objecting to the "dismal science," and not only for the Cours being named after the controversial revolutionary hero Honoré Gabriel Riquetti, comte de Mirabeau, who was the son of the *économiste* Mirabeau, quoted in an earlier chapter. As well, the old man nearby was keeping up with the news, and the young couple flicking their feeds, at tables that would have witnessed considerable political scheming since 1792—revolutions and more have been plotted at coffeehouses. In setting Les 2Gs in context, I alluded to various officials maintaining the town fountains, aqueducts, tree-lined roads, and laws and regulations that watched over businesses from banks to cafes. Other public servants must have stamped the passports of American visitors, who took home recipes and market impressions to civilize overindustrialized polities. Numerous coffee houses, taverns, and restaurants emerged, as with Deux Garçons, when the City launched its "sumptuous tables and strongboxes" (Brillat-Savarin 1826, §63).

So many shared meals, and so many conversations, contributing to the political banquet, so pervasive that it cannot be permitted to remain almost invisible.

A Delicious Revolution

Alice B. Toklas, Elizabeth David, M. F. K. Fisher, Julia Child, Richard Olney, and numerous other visitors to Provence have pulled industrial nations in a foodie direction, although none with such political deliberateness as Alice Waters. Her senses aroused by Provençal cuisine and Marcel Pagnol's passionate nostalgia, she opened Chez Panisse in Berkeley, California, in 1971, to mix French cooking with radical 1960s politics. She wanted her eating house to be "a place for extended political conversations," at which pleasure would "seduce"—after all, "even French communists enjoyed good food" (Flammang 2009, 183–84).

Long back from France, and a busy restaurateur, Waters underwent a "delicious revolution," a fuller awakening to soils and souls. Through physically seeking out and serving good food, she came to discover the benefits of "meeting farmers and learning from them—and influencing them, too." After years of weekly interactions, "I had woven myself into a community." Food brought "deep pleasure ... by connecting us to time and place, the seasons, and the cycle of nature," Waters wrote in *The Art of Simple Food* (2007, 3–5), which recommended a few principles to "reconnect our families and communities with the most basic human values, provide the deepest delight for all our senses, and assure our well-being for a lifetime."

Waters took the hands-on, transformative power of fresh, local ingredients to customers, neighborhoods, and jails. Her Edible Schoolyard project, inaugurated in the mid-1990s, persuaded educators to install kitchen gardens. Recognizing "how we feed ourselves as just as important as—and maybe more important than—all the other activities," Waters (2009) taught: "If we don't care about food, then the environment will always be something outside of ourselves."

The modern era has been revolutionary, repeatedly, so that in this book I have mentioned, at the very least, industrial, market, and consumer revolutions; English, American, and French revolutions, and a failed German one; classical and neoclassical economic, Communist, sexual, and a long-anticipated one. Perhaps the most disturbing, viewed from the dining table, was the disruption of banquet society by money. The great meal might be restored by some brilliant new dictatorship but, according to a liberal understanding, should be in the hands of the people, contributing their metabolic bit with care, consideration, and ingenuity. We need the delicious revolution.

Primarily, economics is rewritten by living well. So not only get into the garden, but express gratitude for municipal water, invite a politician to dinner. Take joyful feasting to the streets. Others have spoken of "reclaiming," "reembedding," or "reconnecting" to gain a more hands-on food supply. Another word might be "restoring," related to the French *restaurant*. Meals are down-to-earth so that their attentive practice literally regrounds liberal theory. Meals are complex, and this book's analysis has many implications. Here are some immediate pointers—from policies to constitutional arrangements.

The Pervasiveness of Politics

In rethinking economics, I have objected to mainstream technical commentary becoming dominant political ideology and have rediscovered liberal foundations. In the past two chapters I welcomed à la carte restaurants in actual free markets, and communal meals in family life. This concluding chapter invites the reinvigoration of the banquet at the heart of politics. Along with that, I would hope for some scholarly reevaluation, too.

Banquets have advanced civilization for thousands of years, since ancient temple-states, as introduced in chapter 1. Organized religion's remnant banquets ("vestigial," according to Goldenberg 2015) are now transfigured into the Catholic mass and the like. Violent and inherited privilege had taken over until, to use the example in chapters 6 and 7, Versailles was sacked by the City. Rediscovering good gardening and sharing would restore natural beings with equal rights to pursue life and happiness, convivially. However, with nationwide meals fully monetized through tax and payment, and moneyed interests holding tight, government hid democracy's festal core (Latin *festus*, joyous), and believers earned such epithets as "elites" and "politically correct."

Look again at the frontispiece of Hobbes's *Leviathan* (figure 5.2). Three hundred people form the arms and chest of the body politic. The citizens have their backs to the viewer, perhaps in awe of the crowned head, carrying a sword and bishop's staff. In a democracy, the people themselves are the ruler. Gastronomically imagined, the citizens join at tables under the reflective gaze of the president. Once this basic redistributive meal or banquet is accepted as the core of the political economy, then other fundamentals become more apparent. One is redistribution's sheer pervasiveness and complexity—politics infuses our lives, and vice versa. Markets must operate within the law of the land, that is, they are subordinate to politics. It's not just voting, or what politicians do—replenishing immediate households, and setting markets free, every opinion and encouragement is politics.

Given the complexity, amounting to "economic calculation problem" on several layers, then gastronomic liberalism is inevitable. Total obedience is no long-term answer. Money is a particularly divisive ideology. Storming the barricades is no liberal method. As Elinor Ostrom (1990, 14) decided, advocates of both strong government and privatization became "too sweeping in their claims." Reality remained too complex for simple institutional models. Rather, reaffirming the Epicurean "pleasure of the stomach" restores the intricate cooperation, especially through participatory democracy, in which everybody labors at everyday meals and converses, so that knowledge collects up and distributes.

Appetites always look forward to the next meal, which will be irredeemably bodily and natural, will belong to the domestic and market economies, and will also be assuredly political. Given that the appetite's hopes are pressing, politics cannot await the next election and demands continuous conversation, and nudging this way or that. One person might feel they can do nothing, but they do not dine alone. Plucking a peach from the tree can be an individual indulgence, but company adds laughter, education, and news of the local baker, swapped for tips on making stock. The right-wing cry of "personal responsibility" has a basis in liberal reality but applies not merely to navigating the labor market and avoiding sugar, but to every decision of the *volonte générale*, the supreme will of the people.

Among implications for higher-level policy, a liberal government cannot relegate involvement in health and housing to picking up the pieces. Nutrition must be a central concern, likewise, with wide ramifications— from consumer protection to agriculture favoring taste. In a banqueting society, education cannot be allowed to deteriorate into training but must stay more comprehensive, along Enlightenment lines. As Jean-Jacques Rousseau recognized so acutely, republican reliance on the *volonté générale* requires well-educated *individuals*. Conversations are safer kept from the sway of *sociétés particulières*, which were for him purposive organizations like the church and the military, and now notably include profit-pursuant corporations.

Meanwhile, macroeconomics cannot be left aside, and some economists and policy colleagues have begun, at least in New Zealand, to judge government performance by the people's "wealth" interpreted as "well-being." From 2019 the national budget broadened indicators used in "maximizing the benefits" from government expenditures, from just the "imperfect measure of well-being—income" to include, for example, the "four capitals." Government accounts need to monitor the *natural* capital of the "environment needed to support life and human activity"; *human* capital of "people's skills, knowledge and physical and mental health . . . to participate fully in work, study, recreation and in society more broadly"; *social* capital of "norms and values . . . like trust, the rule of law"; and *financial/physical* capital of roads, hospitals, factories, vehicles, and the like (New Zealand Treasury 2018). Introducing these four assets, suggestive of Brillat-Savarin's "four essentials," in 2015, the Organisation for Economic Cooperation and Development (2015, 7) highlighted "key risk factors"—ranging from rising concentrations of greenhouse gases and obesity to recent falls in trust in government and low levels of investment in "economic assets (such as buildings, infrastructure, machinery and equipment)."

In This Together

Unblinking backer of financial dictatorship Ludwig von Mises (e.g., 1966, 166–67, 729) pleaded that "selfish profit-seeking" would guard against the "authoritarian regimentation" of social justice, bureaucratic integration, trade unions, and churches. The government's only job was to protect private wealth. Big money's extolling of liberty has probably helped some liberal advances, such as equality on sexual and perhaps other grounds, while also purchasing considerable freedom to exploit markets, and to put down participatory democracy. One tactic has been to portray the redistributive economy as mere "squabbling politicians." In her study of neoliberal rationality, Wendy Brown (2015, 42) put it this way: "As the province and meaning of liberty and equality are recalibrated from political to economic, political power comes to be figured as their enemy, an interference with both." In a subsequent study, Brown (2019, 8–10, 12) despaired that three decades of "neoliberal assaults on democracy, equality and society" and the "responsibilizing" of individual men had ushered in the "catastrophic" antidemocratic present, although she believed that had been an unintended consequence.

Despite repeated claims to be defending Western values, many on the right have been determinedly anti-Enlightenment, deriding those who are empirical (rely on evidence), civil (respect others), and progressive (retain hope). The secret to neoconservatism was explained from the office of U.S. president George W. Bush in 2004. An unnamed aide (assumed to be Karl Rove) scoffed that his interviewer, Ron Suskind (2004), belonged to the "reality-based community." With Suskind murmuring about "enlightenment principles and empiricism," the man of power went on, "That's not the way the world really works anymore." As the makers of empires, he said, "when we act, we create our own reality. And while you're studying that reality . . . we'll act again, creating other new realities, which you can study too." In other words, the right relied on strong wills, money, and tough ideology, leaving liberals to their sunny discoveries of democracy, the (truly) free market, a vital planet, and philosophizing after dinner.

When former U.S. president Bill Clinton endorsed Barack Obama as presidential candidate, Clinton called the Republican a "winner take all" philosophy, whereas the Democrats stuck with "we're all in it together" (Democratic Convention, September 5, 2012). The fact is that profit seeking can run with white supremacy, with both drug crime and its righteous repression, or with populist autocracy, and its assertion through divisive rhetoric and an adulatory party of the "people's will" over judicial and media independence. President Trump became an exemplar of a money-first, Misesean ridiculer of Enlightenment/liberal commitments to facts, debate, equality, and, indeed, life itself. He made a better banquet buffoon than president.

The political is not just formal and centralized but embraces all manner of community participation. Banquet conversations might be between adjacent diners, across the table, and before long it's a network. That's what is meant by authority bubbling up "from below." Starting with the family, Californian political scientist Janet A. Flammang (2016, 1, 3) asks: "How do we develop a political voice?" The table is where "we learn that people act, not only selfishly, but also for a common good." Mealtime conversations are the "building blocks of democracy." Coffee houses are "public spaces" (Habermas) or "third places" (Oldenburg), where insurrections have been planned, and they can be again. The glances between restaurant tables, chats with strangers at parties, and long-term friendships can add to the communal bonds of civil society.

Perhaps a greater, human economy needs to be conceived, to include the ideas and actions of society more embedded in the natural than even the political, but the political economy is encompassing enough to be going on with. Banquet politics is entangling. Everything is connected. We're in this together. Lose sight of that, demonize the Other, and we're lost, stumbling toward the rulers and the ruled, authoritarianism. The liberal commonwealth should not be slighted as a compulsory and indulgent charity; even calling it a "welfare state" (let alone "nanny state") diminishes it as coordinator of the original "well-fare," that is, the happy and healthy journey.

Wanting to eat and drink happily together might attract accusations of apathy (*a-pathos* is not-suffering), but it is fundamental to economics and politics. Seeking contentment arouses concerns beyond the picket fence, and the picket—requiring all of a healthy body, happy family, hands-on market, responsive commonwealth, and harmony with nature. Appetite was right all along. It's time to regain the power of free and equal banqueters.

The Radical Banquet

We live in market society. More accurately, we live under market capitalism, which is different. And more fully again, this is banquet society presently under far too much corporate control. A political economy relies on market meals, although, strictly, more on contributory ones. Everyone helps and everyone partakes in these supervised potlucks, obedient to a president, who might once have been a monarch but is now (in theory) the people themselves. Market squares are cleaned as stallholders pack; children wind their ways to school; emergency calls are answered; national treasuries run currencies that keep things moving. The usurpers might recast "to redistribute" as merely robbing the rich to pay the poor, but it is assistance and enjoyment across the board.

Food and its substitute communicate powerfully but not as explicitly as actual table talk. In essence, conversation is managerial—not only immediate ("could you pass the salt?"), but discussing meals past and future ("next time, let's try that new baker"). Conversation might have some characteristics of exchange, but talk is not readily commodified, relying instead on the principle "from each according to ability," and engages with every level of economy, ultimately rising "from below," so that banquet commentary passes around and up the line ("surely the liberal view would be . . .").

Given the impracticalities of everyone in the one hall, the banquet is dispersed but still buzzing. Making participatory banquets more visible might remind administrators of their responsibilities: locating the best produce, embellishing with arts and entertainments, ensuring everyone is served, keeping the conversation fruitful, and ensuring sustainable improvement. Public servants might regain confidence as party-givers (just as *apparatchiks* might yet turn into party-makers). Corporations might adjust.

Organizing actual, public banquets is not a new idea. With the storming of the Bastille on July 14, 1789, Marquis Charles de Villette proposed that *liberté, égalité, fraternité* would benefit by replacing Versailles with rich and poor dining together in the streets. From "one end to the other," Paris would be "one immense family, and you would see a million people all seated at the same table; toasts would be drunk to the ringing of church bells and to the sound of a hundred cannon blasts." In the revolutionary optimism of the first anniversary, a Fête de la Fédération required "a meal in every district," although journalist Camille Desmoulins thought he detected a flaw—if all were sitting down, who would serve? Nonetheless, on the previous evening, two thousand spectators watched the members of the National Assembly dine at the Palais-Royal complex. On the day, General Lafayette invited provincial representatives to "endless tables" under the trees of the parc de la Muette. After the official meal for perhaps twenty-two thousand, as many as five thousand of Paris's poor were admitted and partook of leftovers (Spang 2000, 96–102).

For thirty years, radical banquets were staged whenever the populace seemed to need persuading, Brillat-Savarin (1826, §135) decided, but funded insufficiently, so that "the only pleasure is to be found in retrospect." In response, his book's "Bouquet" proposed an annual festival for a new muse called Gasterea. Presiding over the pleasures of taste, she could claim the universe as hers, because "the universe is nothing without life, and everything that lives nourishes itself." After celebrations in her temple, the people would banquet down every street. Brillat-Savarin advocated not only fireworks but also another courtly banquet spin-off, opera.

A national feast's glory, and prime obstacle, being its size, families return home for the U.S. Thanksgiving or entrust it to representatives. President Thomas Jefferson charmed even political opponents around the table, to wide benefit. As late as the 1970s most members of Congress would live with their families in Washington, D.C., and "often socialized with each

FIGURE 14.2 Town and city halls are centered on public banquets. Glasgow City Chambers, Scotland (electric chandelier—"electrolier"—lights installed 1885, photographed 2015. © Colin / Wikimedia Commons / CC BY-SA-4.0.

other regardless of party, and these personal ties curbed members' tendency to demonize each other" (Eilperin 2007, 32).

City and town halls were, traditionally, banqueting rooms, and they might be regained as working parts of the commons. Traditional towns and villages had no problem organizing street parades and festivals. The Iowa State Fair's grilled pork chops on sticks and its soapbox earned a mention in chapter 11. In Australia, and helped by voting being compulsory, "democracy sausages" for a meal or snack becoming fund-raisers at election polling places (often schools and churches), adding to the jollity (Brett 2019). A global version is emerging on New Year's Eve, if only partygoers would dine more explicitly rather than merely carouse to fireworks. When all is said and done, every meal belongs to the banquet.

The Fundamentals of Rights—Charters for Corporations!

The sloganizing of rights (as in the U.S. Declaration of Independence and French national motto) invites the idealization of what are, after all, social constructs. Equality and liberty are not universals, detached from human society, but are grounded in the circulation of sustenance. As chapter 5 showed, Hobbes, Locke, and others developed rights out of nature's law of self-preservation.

These mutually acknowledged rights are the basis for a social contract that cannot directly apply to other species, which remain deeply natural (and the natural world might claim, if so minded, "dominion" over human beings). Not being "reasonable," nature is unlikely to spell that out; nor will it sign any document. Rather than accord rights to other species, society has to deal with its own actions, including through *restraints*. These are not to stop eating but to eat more thoughtfully, more in awe of living nature, which, although animal rights theorists might not like it, can be brutish and short.

Likewise, Enlightenment philosophers did not invite profit-seeking corporations to the banquet. The U.S. Constitution, for example, spoke of "persons," "citizens," and "the people." However, as I showed in chapter 11, high-pressure organizations soon pushed for market and political legitimacy. Rather than gain a specific constitutional place, corporations slotted in as "persons," which error is in desperate need of attention.

Companies remove forests, grab seabeds, buy up water and land, push fossil-powered air conditioners to cool the few and warm the many, and, reducing costs, exploit pickers, textile workers, and meal deliverers. Marketing guns, fast cars, cigarettes, loaded snacks, and plastic packaging, they blame the victims. On one view, corporations can profit only when they serve diners. On another, unable to smell the peaches or mangoes, they pick lower-hanging fruit, innovate first and ask afterward, corrupt conversations, and leave regulators playing catch-up.

Having replaced appetite, stomach, and pleasure with return on investment, accounts department, and annual reports, *Homo economicus* cannot sign a diner's contract. Not "created equal," corporations could never demand the "unalienable" right to pursue happiness. John Locke (*Treatises*, 2.5.25) wrote that "natural reason" tells us that "men, being once born, have a right to their preservation," and so to "meat and drink" and associated requirements, while the same "natural reason" tells us that corporations have no *natural* right to property. Persons have rights to property because, as Locke explained, they swallow exclusive food and gain an associated right to labor for it. Corporations must somehow borrow people and materials. They require separate constitutional, judicial, administrative, and regulatory systems. Corporations pay (and avoid) tax, but why should a corporation contribute as an illegitimate citizen? Benefiting from government activity, businesses must pay, but differently.

On what explicit terms should synthetic players (*sociétés particulières*) participate? One option would be as guests; as such, these strangers would need to abide by house rules. Less sanguinely, corporations might be considered parasites in the original sense of someone who lives off others' tables (Greek *para-* beside, *sitos* food); their continued welcome would require perfect manners. To acknowledge their usefulness, corporations could be reimagined as perfect servants under the control of banqueters. Just as they set up the relationship between people and governments, constitutions need, at the very least, to differentiate unmistakably between the rights of individuals and the *concessions* of corporations. On top of that, to bring corporations back securely into the service of people, democratic governments might return to issuing charters, not putting profit ahead of provisioning.

Through legally enforceable mission statements, the contribution of each corporation would be publicly debated. Charters would set out privileges, responsibilities, ground rules, and expectations. In the way that redistributive institutions are watched through the parliament, courts, press, and popular protest, corporations require monitors. Rather than enshrine commercial secrecy, the glazed exteriors should be opened to view.

A public forum must replace secret lobbying and underhand campaigning. Rule "by the corporation, for the corporation" has to be restrained more than by puny consumer "votes." As U.S. justice William Brennan recognized in 1986, corporate political activity should be regulated so "that organizations that amass great wealth in the economic marketplace not gain unfair advantage in the political marketplace" (FEC v. Mass. Cit. for Life, 479 U.S. 238 [1986]).

Even in advanced capitalist economies, numerous organizations, and not only government-owned corporations and nonprofit cooperatives, already operate in the marketplace with other goals than profit. As yet, a Social Licence to Operate (SLO) is likely little more than a public relations device for a mining company. Corporate-speak has brought in other "stakeholders," such as employees and customers. Likewise, corporations might expand a single "bottom line" into a "triple bottom line," taking into account social and environmental costs and benefits. Some CEOs talk of corporate "purpose" (meaning, other than profit). Such possibilities have begun to be recognized in commercial law. From 2010 some U.S. states adopted legislation not only permitting directors to allow more socially useful and environmentally sustainable goals but to positively require self-nominated "benefit corporations" or "B corporations" to do so. As a basic, corporations might involve greater worker control, along with more permanent employment, rather than the gig, however rational.

The simple suggestion of replacing corporate profit seeking with meal serving is so far-reaching and radical as to seem unlikely, and yet not all economists are macho libertarians. "The correct answer to almost any question in economics is: It depends. Different models, each equally respectable, provide different answers." With that, economist Dani Rodrik (2015, 17, 163–64) pointed to heterodox success in South Korea, Taiwan, and later China. Opening import barriers would have shifted workers into "petty trading," so policy makers subsidized even "inefficient" local manufacturing, instituted currency controls, and actively fostered new industries. They even used varieties of community ownership. Such successes proved standard models not wrong, merely "the wrong models."

Tools are wonderful. The cook's knife turned *Homo faber* (the toolmaker) into *Homo gastronomicus*. Now we turn on the cold-water tap with delight and rely on a motor vehicle only grudgingly. Corporations can be handy, too, but we need to use them, rather than other way around. Victor Frankenstein's monster must be redirected at genuinely economic tasks.

The Global Banquet

The relative virtuality of corporations enabled their freedom of movement, so regions competed to attract them with subsidies, employer-friendly labor laws, government business, and taxation removed to individuals. Corporations pushed brands on nation after nation, relying on cheap commodities here, cheap labor there, and profitable markets everywhere. The *Manifesto* predicted that capital would "nestle everywhere, settle everywhere, establish connexions everywhere." Rationalization eroded old ways of farming and cooking. Yet the same globalization undermined traditional hierarchies. Capitalism to an extent carried, and was carried by, Enlightenment universalism. At least in place of cultural diversity bound to the soil, subcultures flowered.

Laissez-faire or "classical" economists expected that markets would civilize the globe, with mercantilist colonialism replaced by the survival of the financially fittest. English/American activist Thomas Paine already enthused in *Rights of Man* (1791) that commerce could "cordialise mankind, by rendering nations, as well as individuals, useful to each other" (chap. 5). German philosopher Immanuel Kant (1991, 106–11) argued in his essay "Perpetual Peace" (1795) that cultivating a finite globe required landed property and so laws, and then commerce, so that nations "achieved mutual understanding, community of interests and peaceful relations, even with their most distant fellows." Modern neoliberals have believed the Market will bring peace, although without their usual advocacy of market security under, in this case, an international force.

One big thing missing in globalization is much by way of global government. Even that is not exact, because a plethora of institutions make an unacknowledged world government, guarding and improving corporate opportunities. The World Economic Forum brings business and political leaders together with economists at Davos, Switzerland, while technicians attend humdrum, nuts-and-bolts industry committees. The "Washington Consensus" promotes the largely neoliberal policies emanating from the U.S. Treasury, as well as globalizing agencies, including the International Monetary Fund (IMF) and World Trade Organization (WTO). Other transnational managers belong to the G-7 (Group of seven wealthy nations), G-20 (Group of twenty finance ministers and Central Bank governors), OECD, global ratings agencies (Standard and Poor's, Moody's, Fitch), global accountancy firms, regulatory bodies such as the International Telecommunications Union and International Civil Aviation Organization, and numerous industry associations, including the International Federation for Produce Standards that administers PLUs (Price Look Ups—those irritating, coded stickers on fresh fruit and vegetables).

Corporations urge multinational treaties that erode the sovereignty of individual states. Formally established by the Maastricht Treaty of 1993, the European Union extended a corporate market across a shifting list of nations. Governments negotiated the Trans-Pacific Partnership (TPP) for Pacific Rim nations with industry input for seven years in secret. When a thirty-chapter draft was finally released in November 2015, noneconomists saw "free trade" override national environmental, labor, and commercial protections.

A bundle of social justice, environmental, and conflict issues warrants a more determined global response. Perhaps corporations, minimizing (dodging) national taxes, ought to fund new, representative, global institutions. If corporations profit globally, then taxation should occur there, too. If they buy and sell globally, then they need regulating globally. Some monopolies escaping national control—especially in the digital age— might be globalized (if that is the equivalent of "nationalized"). "World government" has been represented as dictatorial, but it could be liberating, viewed in the bottom-up direction, as a grand feast of human enlightenment and hope.

If we share plates then it's usually a meal. What if we share photographs of plates, flashing everywhere? These are in addition to all the recipes books, television shows, and entire channels broadcasting cooking. And they lie on top of a huge trade in foodstuffs. This is one global meal, tying the globe together, and in need of a stronger global polity. Social media used typically to be presented as contributing to individual freedom, although funded by advertising and surveillance, and creating viral influencers and gang warfare. The web is like the roads, people raging at one another, hidden in their metal shells. Moreover, cameras demand eye-catching plates that obscure taste and conviviality.

Perhaps internet communication should be considered less neoliberally and more gastronomically, as helping individuals participate in meals at all levels. Social media could then be conceived less as free expression and as closer to one conversation, each person chatting with their immediate neighbor or the other side of the globe, planning pleasures. Alongside United Nations organizations, the global working-dining-networking community can build on treaties, and regulatory coordination, to enliven the greatest social economy.

Capitalism, Communism, and Complexity

The unitary "the economy" has invited either-or choices: the government either should run the whole thing or nothing. According to Ludwig von Mises (1966, 679) and followers, central planners either ordered every replacement screw or played no part. Lacking "any method of economic calculation," socialism was "not a realizable system," and that left merely capitalism. Another false dichotomy forced by the monolithic "economy" is that private ownership seemed totally desirable or totally undesirable. But whose factory is it?—the workers', the board's, shareholders', the people's, nature's, or God's? A political economy's property law has to adjust to the overlapping claims. It is not good enough to say that all corporations are to be nationalized, or all must submit solely to shareholders, when purpose is the real issue. Corporations no longer need shareholders, but that leaves them in even more need of direction.

Last century's boldest plans were capitalism and communism. They faced off, egged each other on, and slipped into rule by corporations or cadres (and resorted to fascism). Philosophically, both sides forgot what they originally sought, because, as I raised in chapter 4, both trace heritages in large part from Epicurean materialism. So how come liberalism so spectacularly spawned laissez-faire free enterprise and its reaction, class struggle? In brief, in the tussle to control the state, one side vaunted the power of profit-driven "individuals," whereas the others supported ordinary ones, as a "class." Big Business sloganized liberty, and Big People equality.

Radical economist, and former Greek minister of finance, Yanis Varoufakis (2018, xix–xxviii) reread the *Communist Manifesto* of 1848 and expected that Marx and Engels, if they returned, would confess to "insufficient reflexivity," having failed to appreciate that "powerful, prescriptive texts have a tendency to procure disciples, believers—a priesthood." Accordingly, "workers' states would become increasingly totalitarian in their response to capitalist state aggression." Nonetheless, behind its call to class warfare, the *Manifesto* was a "liberal text—a libertarian one, even." For Varoufakis, we are in it together: "If capitalism appears unjust it is because it enslaves everyone, rich and poor, wasting human and natural resources." The *Manifesto* authors were angry that the bourgeoisie had denied others such ideals as "Liberty, happiness, autonomy, individuality, spirituality, self-guided development." The *Manifesto*, Varoufakis concluded, had offered "a touchingly simple answer: authentic human happiness and the genuine freedom that must accompany it."

The gastronomic need for sophisticated decision-making makes a nonsense of both price's total rule, and instant revolution. More realistically, simultaneous reforms require choices between, say, social enterprises, cooperatives, nationalization, green-collar jobs, consumer advice, no logos, urban farms, etc. A new generation of specialists might undertake far-reaching reconsideration in their specialties, whether accountancy, agriculture, catering, philosophy, theology, or economics. The absurdity of simplistic prescriptions applies to the price system even more than to veganism. Given the complexity, calls for "deregulation" might make some sense for genuinely small, household-based businesses, closer to everyday activity, but for anything larger, deregulation is somewhat disingenuous. Corporations run on mainframe loads of files, manuals, specifications, legal drafts, small print, and spin. Faced with complexity, liberals should not let themselves be talked out of regulation. A mass of expertise attends at small benches.

Capitalism, communism, or cataclysm? Conviviality!

Shopping for a Better World?

If revolution is to be achieved at dinner, could that include shopping for a better world? Just as mealtime conversation generates political democracy, so too face-to-face exchanges create markets. Knowing who mills and bakes the grain, people challenge corporate power and its plutocracy. While consumer "votes" might be puny, and maldistributed, they are also numerous, and if everything really did have a price, then shopping could change everything.

In *Foodopoly: The Battle Over the Future of Food and Farming in America*, campaigner Wenonah Hauter (2012, 282, 287) welcomed local and alternative food systems for farmers and eaters to "build community," and for education. Nevertheless, wanting "fundamental structural changes," she urged: "Breaking the foodopoly and fixing the dysfunctional food system require far-reaching legislative and regulatory changes that are part of a larger strategy for restoring our democracy. Food activists must engage with other progressives." More purposive (and less "economic") political organizations might be unavoidable yet undervalue the gastronomic liberalism of "evolution, not revolution"—of numerous small changes "from below."

For Hauter, the "market alone cannot solve the problem," and, certainly, democracy is even more necessary. Yet she worried that the "shopping well" solution was "imbued with the libertarian philosophy: government bad, regulation bad, individual liberty and choice good" (288). In tracking the historical distortion of liberal economics, I have demonstrated that individual responsibility, equality, liberty, property, and contract were cruelly abstracted to suit finance. Gastronomically, people are definitely saved by shopping, and by cooking, and conversing.

The case against shopping solutions was put even more sternly by University of California geographer Julie Guthman (2008, 1175–77). Again, she supported Eric Schlosser's rejection in *Fast Food Nation* (2001) of neo-liberalism's union busting, suppression of real wages, and loosening of food, environmental, occupational health and safety regulations. However, for Guthman, food activism incorporated "neoliberal rationalities," such as "consumer choice, localism, entrepreneurialism and self-improvement," when foodies support nonbinding food labeling that expects the "right" consumer choices; borrow such phrases as "voting with your dollars" and "knowing where your food comes from"; vaunt entrepreneurialism as "green business"; and share a paternalistic belief in education. In a section titled "Foodies on a Mission," Guthman (2011, 158–59) worried that such teaching as Alice Waters's Edible Schoolyard assumed that "food associated with the local, the organic, and the slow is universally good." And that meant would-be educators saw as normal the ideals, aesthetics, and experiences of the "white, educated, urbane and thin."

While admitting to her own foodie tendencies (dining at Chez Panisse and favoring farmers' markets), Guthman (2007, 263–64) objected to "the fantasy that individual, yuppified, organic, slow food consumption choices are the vehicles to move toward a more just and ecological way of producing and consuming food." She wanted the "*structures* of inequality" to be addressed (emphasis added). Roundly dismissing "good food" advocates, including Alice Waters, Michael Pollan, and Marion Nestle, Guthman concluded: "I am fed up with the apolitical conclusions, self-satisfied biographies of food choice, and general disregard for the more complex arguments that scholars of food bring."

Guthman should find rejoinders, point-by-point, in this book. She decried the universalizing of "good food" as some symbol of privilege, as if the need to eat—and to eat well—were not universal. Falling into another trap, calling individual responsibility "neoliberal" was back-to-front, because capitalist purpose abstracted freedom for profit. Moreover, by prioritizing "structures" over their material base, Guthman denied that civilization is made, materially, "one meal at a time." She swallowed neoliberalism herself, disposing of, for example, farmers who love their pigs, as mere "entrepreneurs."

Confessing to white privilege, paternalism-spotter Guthman cared for the "downtrodden." If we believe in some essential humanity, aren't we all "downtrodden," albeit to different degrees? Aren't we all varyingly privileged? Just because some billionaires coldly put others down, aren't they in some way delusional victims? While Guthman demanded government regulations because of them-and-us struggles, surely we want them for the opposite reason: that we are cooperating? A democratic commonwealth is desired as a collaboration of sustenance-needing equals. We're all diminished by injustice, and all galvanized by our collective fate.

Conceding that many foodies were actively worried by inequality, and the problems created by "corporate involvement in food production and consumption," Guthman and a colleague, Alison Hope Alkon, still concluded: "Only by continuing to stand together can we transform our food system into one that nurtures us all" (Alkon and Guthman 2017, 3, 323). What's so powerful about *standing* together? Why not *garden, cook, housekeep, shop*, and *dine* together? While foodie activists are diverse, and some might actually tremble at state involvement and others tangle with New Age "organics," radical liberalism contests corporate freedoms. Actually *sharing* meals will "transform our food system into one that nurtures us all."

Banqueters of the world, to the tables!

EPILOGUE

"Eat, Drink, and Be Merry"

A Taverna on Naxos

On a warm day in the mountains of the Greek island of Naxos, my partner and I alighted at a bus stop on the edge of what was probably the hillside town of Απείρανθος (Apeiranthos). The bus got no closer, because steps in the town's white-paved alleyways preserved them for pedestrians and donkeys. I had not often strolled such ancient-feeling passages, with no street signs, no logos, nothing written. It was almost silent, except for the occasional clatter of hoofs and the rustle of looms, which presumably contributed to a slender cash economy. Even the weaving fell silent in the middle of the day. And so where to eat?

Three or four other young travelers, who had also chanced their luck on the bus up from the tourist port, found a minimal shop on the main road. Forever anticipating the next restaurant, I persevered. No restaurant up or down any alley, until a man popped out of a stone doorway, and put his hand to mouth to illustrate a repeated word that might have been ταβέρνα (taverna).

The two of us followed into an unlit room with no evidence of a meal. My companion preferred to join the others, but I was not giving up. And what a repast! The host led me behind a bulky wooden counter in the gloom—the town presumably had no electricity—to a chair and small table. Out of a wall of rock he pulled a glass and wine. Somewhere else released bread—among the freshest and crustiest I had tasted—along with olives, I seem to recall, and probably olive oil. After my host had extracted something from bins under the counter for a couple of women, I concluded that this was indeed a shop, which remained, in 1978, relatively untouched by branded packages. He asked if I wanted something in words I didn't understand, so he produced it—a fish, beautifully cooked. Was I robbing him of his meal? He was not eating, merely intent on serving me, and I could not elicit his situation. We were in the mountains, so I inquired where fresh fish came from, and he gestured down the valley toward the further coast. There must have been fruit—probably grapes—because it was a full meal. A simple meal, and a miracle.

You might be aware of my dedication to dining, including at some of unquestionably the world's finest restaurants. This was another kind of privilege, and my recall of that simple meal remains strong. Not that the meaning of "simple" is that way itself. For example, I had the owner's complete attention—this was a restaurant for one. The exemplary ingredients

FIGURE E.1 Author's host on the Greek island of Naxos, 1979. Photo by author.

were the product not just of immediate labor but of generations. Many glasses of wine had been lifted in preparation for this one. The ingrained routines had an extraordinary, sun-drenched timelessness. This was a "simple" meal for a frazzled journalist used to newness, neon, and noise. Where I came from, dining had reached an unfortunate point—the pursuit of profit had removed much of the meal to factory farms, had privatized markets with fluoro-drenched aisles, had captured governments, and you could taste it, or not taste it, in the tomatoes.

This report leads to a quandary. Which is preferable, a simple, agrarian life or advanced industrial capitalism with jet travel that took me there? My host's life was arguably "harder" than mine, and many Greek islanders had preferred to migrate to my land, where they found work and women's lib. He lacked such modern compensations as, presumably, a tertiary education. His toilet was the dirt floor in the donkey's indoor stable. But his way of life drew down fewer fossil fuels, threw out fewer pollutants, used little or no plastic, seemed sustainably adjusted to admittedly hard-worn soils, and probably worked shorter, even if sometimes more physically demanding, hours. I had shared school with the children of Greek migrants escaping postwar poverty by working ten hours a day so that their children could become doctors and lawyers, working twelve.

Anthropologist Marshall Sahlins (1974, 3) had only recently argued that "stone age" people were the "original affluent society," and he rejected propaganda about industry liberating people from the gatherer-hunter's "incessant quest for food" and "limited leisure." Even tribes living in what might seem relatively inhospitable climes survived on a few hours' work daily. Speaking generally, agrarian societies, as largely prevailed in the Naxos hinterland into the 1970s, required more labor than Stone Age gathering. And the third, industrial style, pushing peasants into factories, required longer hours again. Artists, writers, and beachcombers tried moving the other way, dropping out to Greek islands.

The corporation carrying me to Naxos was arms manufacturer Boeing, whose weapons disrupted the peace of villagers in the name of globalization. Nor would Monsanto monoculture and Coke necessarily make for a healthier life. In fact, some nutritionists already advocated "Mediterranean" diets, found on Greek islands. Despite living in preindustrial societies,

Epicurus led his school until the age of possibly seventy-two; philosopher Thomas Hobbes, originator of the phrase "nasty, brutish, and short," died at ninety-one; founding economist François Quesnay reached eighty; Thomas Jefferson put Epicurean ideas into wider practice until eighty-three; and Jean-Anthelme Brillat-Savarin published his investigations a few weeks before dying unexpectedly, everyone said, at seventy. Birth used to be more dangerous for both child and mother, but "progress" has been far from flawless.

Foodies respect tradition, inspired by sojourns in Provence, Tuscany, Bali, India, and elsewhere. In Naxos, I respected old village ways. Yet I visited as a liberal, suffering tradition-shredding industrialization. Conservation or development? *Gemeinschaft* or *Gesellschaft*? It comes down to keeping good things and removing bad, requiring judgment. The point of politics is individual "self-preservation," Hobbes and Locke assumed. Gastronomy watches over people's "conservation," as Brillat-Savarin wrote; "sustainability" is another watchword. But working with, and respecting, others means diversity and tolerance, and therefore less patriarchy, autocracy, and Market.

Choosing between my Naxos host's wine, bread, fruit, and fish and my ability to flirt with them is not easy. As between apples and avocados, I hesitate to judge which is "better"; I only know that this is my life, which would be reckless to change too abruptly. This is my socially, culturally, and naturally destructive society, in which the overtourism industry has turned the world into a selfie-stick spectacle, warranting my push toward simplicity in the sense of being more in tune with life's elements. Human beings have shared much without money, and without plastic packaging, gym machinery, and meal replacements. Belonging to a system provides an alibi for questionable actions but also a requirement to do something about waste, chemicalized agribusiness, ridiculous inequality, and the enforced austerity with which econocrats in the financialized North punished the "tradition-bound" Greeks.

I held back from another long-haul flight for thirty years and thus "voted" ineffectively against massive travel industry advertising, and I confess to subsequent dinners in Parma, Paris, Copenhagen, and Vancouver Island to catch up with Sinclair Philip at his Sooke Harbour House, which claimed "luxury with a conscience," with almost everything grown in their gardens or acquired down the road, since 1979. We had other reasons to fly for fourteen hours, nonstop, but it still seemed a long trip to appreciate the fresh and local.

In this book I have expected the reader to cope with many tensions— between actual markets and insubstantial models, between artisans and big business, between freedom and equality, between meals and money. Every time, we do not have to choose either the simple or the sophisticated but learn from both. In final, postprandial philosophizing, I take fright at our society's ever-smudgier horizons and jet home to "eat, drink, and be merry."

Limits to Growth

For several years before the Naxos lunch, I had been my newspaper's young environment reporter, describing black, bubbling, factory-lined waterways, being photographed underwater among "throw-away" cans off an inaccessible Sydney Harbour beach, conducting interviews with Paul Ehrlich about his Zero Population Growth movement, and getting tips from that good Christian and ecologist, Charles Birch.

In mid-1971 Professor Birch flew home to Sydney with a copy of the latest *Playboy* magazine. He belonged to international group Club of Rome that had sponsored computer modeling of the planet's worsening population, resource, and pollution pressures, reported under the magazine's headline, "An End to All This: We Have Handed Our Heirs an Ecological Time Bomb That Birth Control Alone Cannot Defuse" (Koff 1971). The forecast was global collapse before the middle of the twenty-first century. Even coarse modeling, published shortly after in *Limits to Growth* (Meadows et al. 1972), was enough, because relaxing assumptions only delayed catastrophe a few years. The predicament warranted urgent action.

My article on Club of Rome predictions might not have influenced anyone else, but it helps explain my gastronomic commitment. As a newspaper reporter, I did not cope well with the dedication of industry leaders, their lobbyists, and PR operatives to do whatever it took—spin, lie, and even occasionally do the right thing—in pursuit of profit. Anticar

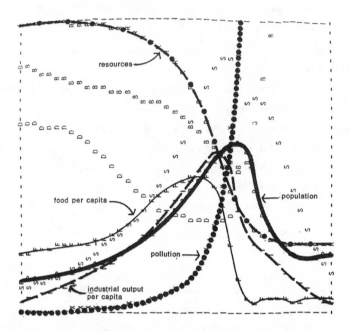

FIGURE E.2 Projected interplay of population, food, resources, industrial output, and pollution between the years 1900 and 2100, published in 1972. Meadows et al., *Limits to Growth*, 1972. Scenario with resources doubled, figure 36, p. 127. Courtesy of Donella Meadows Project at Academy for Systems Change—a project dedicated to Donella Meadows's inspiring vision for systems change.

malcontents wanted to bury the roads in horse manure, they scoffed; reducing aircraft noise would make planes fall out of the sky; consumers *demanded* the convenience of "throw-away" cans. I found that an antilitter campaign, seeking government backing, was set up by packaging interests, intent on shifting the blame to "irresponsible" litterers. Against this onslaught, little seemed possible.

A series of exposés of the city's "Polluters," often multinationals, made an impact, to the *Sydney Morning Herald*'s credit, but the investigation was also dispiriting—depressing, actually. After several months, the gray clouds first parted for a few hours at dinner at friends' in Sydney's Balmain. Watching three others still at table, after some exceptional lamb, was strangely reconnecting. From that moment, meals steadily moved to the center, my mood gradually cheered, and I left daily journalism. During a two-year sojourn in Tuscany, Italy, including that side trip to Greece, I tasted ancient soils and traditions. Comparatively, Australia was a land "without peasants," as I would sum up my country's two centuries of food industrialization (Symons 1982; 2007b). My enthusiasms took me to running eating houses and completing a Ph.D. degree, organizing meal-centered conferences, further books, and research papers.

So here I am, eating, drinking, and being merry. Some health has returned to local waterways. Jets are noticeably quieter (thanks, I understand, to high-bypass turbofan engines). Our society even eats better; well, many people do. Fresh and local have become desirable. The land is overstocked with new generations of winemakers. I can even find proper Jersey milk and cream.

Yet icecaps melt, oceans acidify and plasticize, biodiversity shrinks, soils deplete, cities skyrocket, armaments multiply, and hives collapse. Despite greater environmental awareness, the Club of Rome's *Limits to Growth* predictions have proved too close for comfort (Meadows et al. 1972; Turner 2008). As Thomas Malthus warned in 1798, a "gigantic inevitable famine stalks in the rear, and with one mighty blow levels the population with the food of the world." The logic of *more* prodded activist organization Oxfam to find that the world's eighty-five richest individuals owned as much as the 3.5 billion in the bottom half. An exploding cigar of banknotes scorches the political fabric, carbonizes culture, and vaporizes the thin surface of life.

Numerous heads of state attended the United Nations meeting in 2009 on climate change, the "Copenhagen Summit," which ended in disarray and a weak agreement, viewed by African leaders as a "suicide pact." This was despite, or because of, National Security Agency spies keeping U.S. negotiators abreast of their rivals' positions (Vidal and Goldenberg 2014). After the "Earth summit" in Rio de Janeiro in 2012, British environment writer George Monbiot (2012) reported that those world leaders who bothered to attend "solemnly agreed to keep stoking the destructive fires: 16 times in their text they pledged to pursue 'sustained growth.'" He lamented that governments "concentrated not on defending the living Earth from destruction, but on defending the machine that is destroying it." The Paris summit at the end of 2015 was reliant on corporate sponsorship, so far had economists' assumptions been put into practice.

If not "grab what (and who) you can," what is the right reaction? Should we regenerate a few acres? Join a political party? Expose the lobbyists? Donate to Oxfam? Arm as "survivalists"? Take to the streets? Write poetry? Monbiot (2012) found three reasons for not giving up: first, to draw out the losses as long as possible; second, to preserve what we can in the hope of change; and third, to do things locally. He also promoted "rewilding—the mass restoration of ecosystems." In meditation 10, "The end of the World," Brillat-Savarin worked out how to prepare for catastrophic global warming (caused by a passing comet) but left readers dangling, inviting them to find the solution.

Whatever else, we must accept a degree of hypocrisy. This is a complex world, in which we are necessarily compromised, so that slaveholder Thomas Jefferson set in stone that all are "created equal." In recent times, anticarbon campaigner Bill McKibben jetted the world to lecture on "Global Warming: Do the Math." Genuine liberals accept the trickiness of reality rather than ultrasimplistic economics, or the often hateful glibness of tweets. They reject plutocracy and its preparatory populism.

As a motto, "Eat, drink, and be merry" has been cast as self-indulgent, irresponsible, and defeatist. But that's by opponents of gastronomy. The advice is venerable (thousands of years old), cross-cultural, and frequently repeated. It even crops up in the *Book of Mormon: Another Testament of Jesus Christ* (2 Nephi 28:7–8). Rather than recommend resignation, it is (or, tantalizingly, should have been) a profound answer. Besides being biologically fundamental, the response is intrinsically liberal. It has been the foundation of good economics. English economist Ezra J. Mishan warned about the *Costs of Economic Growth* in 1967. Interviewed a half-century later, he could only see catastrophe, and his "guiding philosophy was simply to resign myself to the inevitable: To 'eat, drink and be merry,' for tomorrow I will cease to be" (2006).

Dining Now, Forever

Observing that the gods kept immortality for themselves, the ale-wife in the Gilgamesh epic advised, possibly as many as four thousand years ago, staying well-fed and making merry (tablet 10X). The same exhortation to enjoy a full belly because we are soon enough dead was used in Egyptian harp songs around 1360 BCE (Pritchard 1969, 467). The saying's wisdom was spelled out in the ancient book of Ecclesiastes (or Quohelet, Koheleth, and other variations), which was an Epicurean text, reproduced in the Hebrew Scriptures and so known to Jews, Christians, and Muslims.

The author of Ecclesiastes had pursued such ambitions as building up wealth and seeking truth, but they did not bring happiness. Why gather silver, gold, slaves, herds, and a harem, only to leave them to a fool?—"vanity of vanities! All is vanity" (1:2). The whims of both natural and temporal authority were to be met with resignation: "all are from the dust, and all turn to dust again" (3:20); although, should a ruler rise against you, show deference (10:4). Despite the failure of reason, the absence of meaning, and the stupidity of power, life made sense. The reiterated recipe became "There is nothing better for mortals than to eat and drink, and find enjoyment in their toil" (2:24). While turning from conspicuous society, seek human companionship. And make merry, "for there is nothing better for people under the sun than to eat, and drink, and enjoy themselves" (8:15).

Nineteenth-century English poet Edward FitzGerald translated, somewhat freely, the four-line poems traditionally credited to Iranian philosopher Omar Khayyám (1048–1131). Pre-Raphaelite artists in England brought out illustrated versions of *Rubáiyát of Omar Khayyám*, which American temperance groups campaigned against as the "Bible for drunkards." Again, the quatrains explored "eat, drink, and be merry" with the repeated idea that everything emerges from, and returns, underfoot, so that the potter shapes clay that might once have been a king or a lover, "fetch the wine." Grand truths have failed: "Religion provides little solace and even less truth. / My rule of life is to drink and be merry." The best-known couplet is from FitzGerald's 1889 version:

> A Book of Verses underneath the Bough,
> A Jug of Wine, a Loaf of Bread—and Thou

In these few words, the poet evokes a rustic hideaway ("the Bough"), bread and wine (the "Loaf" and "Jug"), the pleasure of learning ("Book of

Verses") and company ("Thou"). Providing an overall mood of languor, the recipe extols Brillat-Savarin's four essentials of table-pleasure—adequate setting, food and wine, companionship, and time.

On a basic level, "eat, drink, and be merry" is unexceptionable. We all must eat and drink, typically with sensory reward. Brillat-Savarin (1826, §70) was sure that humans were permitted some pleasure in compensation for all the suffering—from toothache to wars. Philosophers can even play around with such titles as *Eat, Think, and Be Merry* (Allhoff and Monroe 2007). Yet the phrase has aroused antagonism. One objection seems to have been to making merry. This is not helped by "merry" being a British euphemism for tipsy, so that a preferable word might be the New Testament's mealtime "joy" (*chará*), Jefferson's "happiness," or Brillat-Savarin's "table-pleasure." But who could really disapprove of being "joyous, full of laughter or gaiety," as the dictionary defines "merry"? And the real point is that making merry has to be shared with others. Eating and drinking might start out as self-centered, but merrymaking requires company, and with food conspicuously present, this is not the "party, party" depicted in beer and spirits advertising. It's a civilized meal—wine, bread, book, bough, and thou.

The motto's real sin in some eyes would be one of omission. It's *just* eating, drinking, and conviviality. The advice fails to mention gods, virtues, truths, or any number of other higher causes. As the Christian evangelist Paul declared: "If the dead are not raised, 'Let us eat and drink, for tomorrow we die'" (1 Cor. 15:32). John Locke (*Essay*, 2.21.55) accepted that, "with no prospect beyond the grave, the inference is certainly right, 'let us eat and drink,' let us enjoy what we delight in, 'for tomorrow we shall die.'" That is the point: "for tomorrow we die" presses home life's limits, and not just to lifespans but to knowledge. Aspirations to wealth, power, glorious victories, heaven, and total understanding come dangerously close to vanity (they are "meaningless," "futile," or "pointless," as some recent translations of Ecclesiastes prefer). Dictatorships eventually turn to dust. But the cycle of meals, each looking forward to the next, provides contentment, until the end.

The attitude is not oblivious but engaged—paying close attention to material life, without getting overly distracted by dreams, promises, and fantasies, especially of the rich and powerful. Those who care for their meals are not constrained from taking up wider issues. Quite the reverse: eating and drinking require attention to suppliers, artisans, companions, land, and sea. In leading an international study of street-food vendors, and so of lively sociability, food sociologist Krishnendu Ray (2019) overturned the social science preoccupation with "suffering" (along with its analytical aide, criticism), in favor of a more bottom-up, democratizing "epistemology of pleasure and a post-liberal politics of joy."

Eating and drinking in company might seem ineffectual against Midas economics, reshaping the world. Can the hubristic meal-deniers be answered by reading aloud in the shade? Sipping chardonnay? Baking sourdough? Quietly following Slow Food's "universal right to pleasure"? Can great works be achieved without demagogues? Yes, when multitudes of ordinary people, each paying attention to the here-and-now, avoid ideological entrapment and so freely, equally, pursue happiness. They remain natural Epicureans—liberals, if you like.

Roman poet Horace was avowedly Epicurean and expressed the idea as "*carpe diem, quam minimum credula postero*," usually translated as "Seize the day . . ." or "Live for the day, and put little trust in the morrow." As mentioned earlier, Thomas Jefferson noted that motto in a student notebook. When setting out Epicurean doctrines for former secretary William Short (letter, Monticello, October 31, 1819), Jefferson further argued that "true felicity" was "indolence" (a term Locke used in his *Letter Concerning Toleration*), and which, Jefferson explained, negated the Latin *dolere* (pain). He wrote: "The *summum bonum* is to be not pained in body, nor troubled in mind. i.e. In-do-lence of body, tranquillity of mind."

Taken seriously, the "eat, drink, make merry" says that life begins not with obedience, duty, virtue, financial power, or any other of those higher things, but with sensations, pleasures, companions, cooperation, and ordinary inquiry with meals in mind. Governments are not entirely democratic, actual markets are never perfect, and families not always happy, but that does not detract from the principle of individuals participating in economies naturally, spontaneously, and joyfully. The corollary is that individuals cannot be organized into purposive structures, or made the creatures of ideology, without some loss of humanity. Epicurean methods might be slow, but they are sure; any tardiness does not make them wrong, just late.

Envoy

Given the one certainty, death, "all human striving appears vain and futile"; all the "hurrying, pushing, and bustling are nonsensical." Yet we are for the present alive, which means obeying the "cardinal impulse, the *élan vital*"—the innate drive, supported by human reason, "to preserve and to strengthen life." With such parting thoughts, hard-right economist Ludwig von Mises (1966, 881–85) beseeched readers to leave all to the Market. Economic knowledge was the unrivaled foundation on which "all the moral, intellectual, technological, and therapeutical achievements of the last centuries have been built." In the final sentence of *Human Action*, he threatened that if people failed to take best advantage of the "rich treasure" of economics "and disregard its teaching and warnings, they will not annul economics; they will stamp out society and the human race."

Also fleeing in the 1930s from Vienna, where he had been a student a few years after Mises, although moving not to the United States but to Britain, Karl Polanyi also worked on his *Great Transformation* during the Second World War. Similarly talking death, resignation and bodily life, Polanyi (1944, 256–58B) also found that the "market utopia" had been discarded. Whereas Mises longed for its return, Polanyi welcomed its passing as promising "an era of unprecedented freedom." For Polanyi, complex society required "planning, regulation and control," including for greater freedom. He scoffed at the free enterprise "illusion" that contractual relationships alone made people free. The "giant trusts and princely monopolies" might serve "those whose income, leisure and security need no enhancing," but they permitted a "mere pittance of liberty" for those attempting to "gain shelter from the power of the owners of property." Power and planning must be used to create "more abundant freedom for all," his book concluded.

Through much of human history, a succession of self-perpetuating lords have held sway, proclaiming varieties of divine right. Inheriting the

Enlightenment response to landowning autocracy, both Mises and Polanyi began with the metabolic individual benefiting from cooperation, but economists like Mises twisted the liberal framework into capitalist divine right. They ran with the latest claimant, the Market, submitting life to the intrinsically unequal power of money. As Pope Francis warned in *Evangelii Gaudium* (Joy of the Gospel) (2013, 47–48), a "new tyranny, invisible and often virtual" brought "the dictatorship of an impersonal economy lacking in a truly human purpose" (§55–56). This present book has found that, for two centuries, economists reimagined markets for bread, meat, and beer as price systems. They thought of wealth not as well-being but as financial power. They reformulated the natural law of self-preservation as the corporate law of financial gain. Applied politically, mainstream economics backed neoliberalism.

The individual might feel helpless, confronted by the circular logic of ascetic business. Yet our lives have to be lived, articulated, discussed, and optimized, and not left to an almighty "hand." According to liberal theory, which foodies naturally adopt, economies themselves have resilience. While price is but a flickering tally, here and there, actual individuals keep planning and regulating for the common good, all the while supporting the tastes and textures, settings and sociabilities of table-pleasure. Also according to liberal theory, the humble individual is all-important. We have to get back to economic basics, meaning sensible eating, drinking, and making merry.

Great teams can help, so long as government agencies remain truly responsive and corporate purposes remain supportive. Some good people overlook the "live unknown" injunction and struggle publicly for healthy values. Nonetheless, the basic here-and-now answer remains working as equals in free economies—interconnected bodies, families, markets, republics, and ecosystems. Through a delicious revolution of eating, drinking, and companionship, we take back control and restore our homes, all our homes, our civilization, here on earth.

Brillat-Savarin (§60) loved the table's "chit-chat," which wove this meal with the previous, and the next, and between companions at hand and wider contacts, and built up knowledge. Joining together at meals might not make the nightly news, nor go viral, but metabolic change steadily restores people, customs, and nature, and economics. Meals are radical, and their own reward. So enjoy your meals. Love the market. Brave souls can go, hesitantly, into representative politics. Taste nature, and keep it for further generations.

French novelist Voltaire's hero set out brightly in *Candide, ou l'optimisme* (*Candide, or Optimism*) (1759), and after much disillusionment concluded, "but we must cultivate our garden." Apparently not much of a gardener, Brillat-Savarin gave a parting salute that urged gastronomers to "profess, for the good of the science; digest, in your individual interest." Or cook for all our good. At shop, stove, and bench, I have prepared many meals, getting ready with a glass of wine, and Franz Schubert.

ACKNOWLEDGMENTS

The diner's sense of the world comes from meals, and this work comes from more meal companions than I should even start to name. Nonetheless, I must mention Marion Maddox, university professor, baker, beekeeper, who puts up with a partner who loves, to once more quote Brillat-Savarin, "chit-chat." Along with the privilege of establishing a domestic economy together, I have had the honor of her scholarly companionship, including at more restaurant and domestic meals than could ever be enough. Special thanks also to Shirley Maddox and to Anna Bianchi, Dorothy Symons, restaurant partner Jennifer Hillier, John Fitzpatrick, Professor Paul Morris, Professor Ted Schmidt, Professor David E. Sutton, two further impressively helpful, anonymous reviewers, Jennifer Crewe and her team at Columbia University Press, and some inspiring restaurants, including, and adding to those already mentioned in the text, Salama, Tony's Bon Goût, Le Gavroche, Sabatini, Berowra Waters Inn, Claude's, l'Archestrate, Allard, Tullio ai Tre Cristi, that trattoria in Siena, Possum's, Café di Stasio, Silo, Nikau, Ritual, Sixpenny, Waldheim, . . . and there I go again.

This book is dedicated to Marion, Dorothy, and Lawrence Symons Maddox (1999–2009), who together have taught me so much about meals, and thereby everything.

GLOSSARY

List of Ingredients

A gastronomic economics necessarily gathers up a range of terms from political philosophy, history of ideas, social theory, food studies, cultural studies, assorted brands of economics, and elsewhere. A root-and-branch rethink further rearranges the language. Many of my usages might therefore be unfamiliar, unexpected, or disputed; hence this glossary. For example, *liberalism* has had competing claimants (here, closer to the American, leftish sense). The *banquet* deserves greater recognition as the heart of politics. Some older food connotations are restored, to highlight their subsequent shift to suit financial thinking, with *economics* being exemplary. It is also polite to introduce some of the key protagonists, along with their dates and one or two principal works. Keeping entries brief, they are often evocative rather than analytical.

Bold indicates cross-reference.

ANIMAL ECONOMY Eighteenth-century term for human physiology.

APPETITE Satiable desire that leads through **TASTE-PLEASURES** to cooperation on shared **TABLE-PLEASURE**; see also **MEAL**; **PLEASURE OF THE STOMACH**; cf. **GREED**.

ARISTOTLE (385–322 BCE) Ancient Greek philosopher, whose *Politics* distinguished between sustaining **ECONOMICS** and acquisitive **CHREMATISTICS**.

AUSTRIAN SCHOOL Economists, not necessarily Austrian, but identifying with **CARL MENGER**, Eugen Böhm von Bawerk, **LUDWIG VON MISES**, and **FRIEDRICH HAYEK**, who were. Led the reimagining of individuals as profit-seekers.

BANQUET Meal at the heart of a **POLITICAL ECONOMY**, at which a central authority, **PRESIDENT**, or **GOVERNMENT** redistributes pooled contributions, originally foods, later their **CONCOCTION** as taxes. Based at town **HALL**.

BEAUVILLIERS, ANTOINE (1754–1817) Parisian restaurateur who established the classical à la carte style.

BECKER, GARY S. (1930–2014) Chicago economist with misleading titles: *Economic Approach to Human Behavior* (1976); *Treatise on the Family* (1981).

BODY POLITIC POLITICAL ECONOMY, circulating nourishment in the manner of an **ANIMAL ECONOMY**, but through a **BANQUET**, its head preferably being the *VOLONTÉ GÉNÉRALE*.

BRILLAT-SAVARIN, JEAN ANTHELME (1755–1826) French judge who wrote the seminal text of **GASTRONOMY**, *Physiology of Taste*, dated 1826, and which might equally have been entitled *Economics of Taste*; see also **FOUR ESSENTIALS**; **TABLE-PLEASURE**; and much of this book.

CAPITALISM Switching money from a means to an end. Definitely not to be confused with the **MARKET (LOWERCASED)**.

CATALLACTICS The study of **MARKET (CAPITALIZED)** exchange. Name advocated by Richard Whately in 1832, later by **MISES**, **HAYEK**, and insufficient others; see also **CHREMATISTICS**.

CARLYLE, THOMAS (1795–1881) Scottish historian and essayist, dismayed by the "dismal science" of the "cash nexus."

CAVENDISH, MARGARET (1623–1673) English materialist poet, scientist, fiction-writer, and playwright. *Poems and Fancies* (1653).

CHREMATISTICS (ARISTOTLE) Science of financial greed (from ancient Greek chrēma, possession), rather than **ECONOMICS** or household management.

CITY (CAPITALIZED) Center of financial power, often also referred to as the bourgeoisie.

CLASSICAL ECONOMICS SAY, **RICARDO**, **MALTHUS**, and others developing supply-and-demand mathematics of profit, rent, and wages; see also **NEOCLASSICAL ECONOMICS**.

"CLASSICAL" LIBERALISM Nineteenth-century **LAISSEZ-FAIRE** advocacy. Wanting **FREEDOM** without **EQUALITY**; a distortion of **LIBERALISM**, and precursor to **NEOLIBERALISM**.

COMMODIFICATION Money's grab for everything or, more politely, bringing everything on to the market, including labor, pleasure, and the even more seemingly priceless.

COMMUNISM Shared ownership, and distribution "from each according to ability, to each according to need." Characteristic of the **FAMILY**.

CONCOCTION (HOBBES) Sublimation of food into money—that is, conversion into a form more readily circulated in the **BODY POLITIC** for turning back into food, where needed.

CONVIVIALITY Living together, and the translation here of the French national motto's *fraternité*.

COOKING Distributing food and, with it, labor. This makes cooks exemplary sharers, and knives the paradigmatic human tool. Secondarily, transforming raw ingredients through fire, etc.

COOPER, THOMAS (1759-1839) Anglo-American chemist, political economist, and materialist firebrand. *Lectures on the Elements of Political Economy* (1826).

CORPORATION PURPOSIVE ORGANIZATION aimed almost invariably at profit these days, and yet an **INDIVIDUAL**, legally, and according to modern economics. Entirely lacks **APPETITE**.

DAVID, ELIZABETH (1913-1992) After Second World War reopened England and parts beyond to good food. *French Country Cooking* (1951), *Italian Food* (1954), *French Provincial Cooking* (1960).

DELICIOUS REVOLUTION (WATERS) Realization of the ramifications of the **MEAL**, especially socially.

DIDEROT, DENIS (1713-1784) Cofounder of the *ENCYCLOPÉDIE*, and its principal editor and contributor. Left one of the earliest reports of a **RESTAURANT**.

DINER'S KNOT Total interdependence of diners; see also **PARADOX OF THE TABLE**; **SOCIAL CONTRACT**.

DIVISION OF LABOR Flipside of food distribution at a **MEAL**.

DOMESTIC ECONOMY Economy based on communal meals; see also **COMMUNISM**; **FAMILY**; *OIKOS*.

ECONOMIC CALCULATION PROBLEM Austrian chorus, sung by **LUDWIG VON MISES** in 1920, that economies are too complex to manage, leaving government merely protecting **MARKETS (CAPITALIZED)**, which handle all the necessary resource allocation. The world is certainly far too complicated to be run just by money.

ECONOMICS Household management. From the ancient Greek *OIKOS* and *nemō* (manage), and generalized to other households; cf. **CHREMATISTICS**.

ECONOMIST Expert on household management, lately narrowed to the **MARKET**.

ECONOMY Household, centered on a **MEAL**. Organization of (1) mutual and (2) comprehensive life-support. Types include **ANIMAL**, **MARKET (LOWERCASED)**, **POLITICAL**, and **NATURAL ECONOMIES**; cf. **MARKET (CAPITALIZED)**; **PURPOSIVE ORGANIZATION**.

EMPIRICISM Relying for knowledge on the senses and practical experience; cf. **RATIONALITY**.

***ENCYCLOPÉDIE* (1751–1772, 28 VOLS.)** Encapsulation of knowledge during the French **ENLIGHTENMENT** in 74,000 articles by named experts, including **DIDEROT, QUESNAY, ROUSSEAU**.

ENLIGHTENMENT Intellectual movement, centered on late-seventeenth- and eighteenth-century Europe, emphasizing empirical inquiry, convivial discussion, and **LIBERALISM**.

EPICUREANISM (LOWERCASED) Refined **GOURMANDISE**.

EPICUREANISM (CAPITALIZED) Understanding the world through the "pleasure of the stomach." Major influence on the **ENLIGHTENMENT**.

EPICURUS (341–270 BCE) Ancient Greek materialist philosopher who put meals first; see also **EPICUREANISM (CAPITALIZED)**.

EQUALITY Starting assumption of **LIBERALISM**, trivialized by economists as **MARKET (CAPITALIZED)** players are *identical*, profit-seeking "black boxes."

FAMILY DOMESTIC ECONOMY, especially referring to the members.

FINANCIALIZATION Capitalism of capitalism. Prodigious power of financial accumulations, debts, bets, and equity since the 1970s.

FISHER, M. F. K. [MARY FRANCES KENNEDY] (1908–1992) U.S. gastronomy great. Translated and annotated **BRILLAT-SAVARIN**'s *Physiology of Taste* in 1949.

FOODIE A person whose passion is growing, preparing, sharing, tasting, talking about, and learning about food. A natural **EPICUREAN (CAPITALIZED)**, therefore partial to **LIBERALISM**.

FOUR ESSENTIALS (BRILLAT-SAVARIN) Minimum requirements for **TABLE-PLEASURE**, adequacies of setting, food and drink, companionship, and time.

FREE MARKET (LOWERCASED) Individuals exchanging (typically on behalf of domestic households) without interference from **PURPOSIVE ORGANIZATIONS**.

FRIEDMAN, MILTON (1912–2006) Chicago economist and popularizer of **GREED**. *Capitalism and Freedom* (1962).

GASTRONOMICS A **GASTRONOMY** of economies, that is, examining economies particularly through their inner workings, namely, **MEALS**.

GASTRONOMY The diner's sense of the world. Bringing together the ancient Greek *gaster*, stomach, and *nomos*, law. Launched as a science by **BRILLAT-SAVARIN**.

***GEMEINSCHAFT* and *GEMEINSCHAFT* (TÖNNIES)** Contrasting traditional, personal ties (community) and business-like connections (modern society).

GOURMANDISE (BRILLAT-SAVARIN) The intelligent pursuit of **TASTE-PLEASURE**.

GOVERNMENT Central authority (head) in a redistributive or **POLITICAL ECONOMY**; see also **LEVIATHAN; PRESIDENT;** *VOLONTÉ GÉNÉRALE*.

GREAT TRANSFORMATION (POLANYI) The construction of the capitalist "market society" during the "critical eighty years (1834–1914)."

GREED Insatiable desire for **MONEY;** cf. **APPETITE.**

HAYEK, FRIEDRICH (1899–1992) Economist of the **AUSTRIAN SCHOOL.** Developer of **LUDWIG VON MISES**'s **NEOLIBERALISM.** *Individualism and the Economic Order* (1948).

HALL Setting for political **BANQUETS.**

HEDONISM Attending to pleasure and pain, with a preference for pleasure.

HEILBRONER, ROBERT (1919–2005) Seduced generations of students with the mainstream economics of "the avarice of private greed . . . redounding to the welfare of society." *The Worldly Philosophers* (1953).

HOBBES, THOMAS (1588–1679) Great English political philosopher. *Leviathan, or The Matter, Forme and Power of a Common Wealth* (1651); see also **CONCOCTION; LEVIATHAN; LIBERALISM; SOCIAL CONTRACT.**

HOMO ECONOMICUS Rational pursuer of gain. Combines political freedoms of a natural person with **GREED** of a **CORPORATION;** see also **MARKET (CAPITALIZED); RATIONALITY.**

HOSPITALITY An **ECONOMY** meeting basic needs of a nonmember; see also **OPEN DOMESTIC HOUSEHOLD.**

IDEALISM According priority to forms, ideas, signs, **RATIONALITY;** cf. **MATERIALISM;** see also **PLATO.**

INDIVIDUAL A living person, although, for **MAINSTREAM ECONOMICS,** more like a **CORPORATION;** see also *HOMO ECONOMICUS;* **METHODOLOGICAL INDIVIDUALISM.**

INVISIBLE HAND (SMITH) Social pressure. Particularly the **MARKET (CAPITALIZED),** through which **MONEY** organizes society.

JEFFERSON, THOMAS (1743–1826) Slaveholder, principal author of U.S. Declaration of Independence, third U.S. president, and supporter of **EPICUREANISM (CAPITALIZED).**

JEVONS, WILLIAM STANLEY (1835–1882) English economist. Early proponent of **MARGINALISM** in "A General Mathematical Theory of Political Economy" (1862).

KOCH, CHARLES (1935–) U.S. billionaire believer in **LUDWIG VON MISES** and prominent funder of right-wing campaigns and neoliberal **THINK-TANKS.**

LAISSEZ-FAIRE "Let us manage our business." Corporate request to be protected by government; see also **"CLASSICAL" LIBERALISM.**

LEVIATHAN (HOBBES) Redistributive authority, either a monarch, assembly, or the people as a whole; see also **GOVERNMENT; PRESIDENT.**

LIBERAL Befitting a "free person," namely, a full member of the civic, market, domestic, and other economies. Closer here to U.S. than European usage; see also **LIBERALISM**.

LIBERALISM Set of political arguments, often identified with **JOHN LOCKE**, based in **ECONOMICS**. Since natural appetites bring individuals together for self-preservation, they treat one another as equally in need of sufficient **FREEDOM** and **PROPERTY** to maintain life and pursue happiness. Corrupted as **"CLASSICAL" LIBERALISM** and **NEOLIBERALISM**; see also **LIBERAL**.

LOCKE, JOHN (1632–1704) English political philosopher. *Essay Concerning Human Understanding* and *Two Treatises of Government*, both dated 1690; see also **LIBERALISM**.

MCDONALDIZATION (RITZER) Corporate **RATIONALIZATION** of the world to increase "efficiency, calculability, predictability, and control."

MAINSTREAM ECONOMICS Mathematical science of the **MARKET (CAPITALIZED)**, assuming rational maximizers in competition, leading to supply and demand in balance ("equilibrium"). Also called **NEOCLASSICAL ECONOMICS**, although closer to **CHREMATISTICS**; see also **GREED**; *HOMO ECONOMICUS*; **MARGINALISM**.

MALTHUS, ROBERT (1766–1834) English classical political economist debating with **RICARDO**. *Essay on the Principle of Population* (1798) and *Principles of Political Economy* (1820).

MARCET, JANE HALDIMAND (1769–1858) Early popularizer of **CLASSICAL ECONOMICS**. *Conversations on Political Economy* (1816).

MARGINALISM With water more elusive in a desert than beside a stream, the infinitesimal calculus models how much *more* a buyer is prepared to spend for more **UTILITY**; see also **MARGINAL REVOLUTION**.

MARGINAL REVOLUTION **JEVONS** and **MENGER** led the application of mathematical calculus to supply and demand in 1870s; see also **MARGINALISM; NEOCLASSICAL ECONOMICS**.

MARKET (LOWERCASED) Exchange of food, and other goods and services, typically at public stalls; cf. **MARKET (CAPITALIZED)**.

MARKET (CAPITALIZED) Price mechanism. The power structure through which **MONEY** rules; see also **INVISIBLE HAND**.

MARKET ECONOMY System in which individuals exchange rather than pool resources (**DOMESTIC ECONOMY**) or distribute through central organiser (**POLITICAL ECONOMY**).

MARKET SOCIETY (POLANYI) Life under capitalist corporations, following **GREAT TRANSFORMATION**.

MARSHALL, ALFRED (1842-1924) Cambridge economist. Codified **NEOCLASSICAL ECONOMICS** in textbook, *Principles of Economics* (1890).

MARX, KARL (1818-1883) German-English metabolic economist for the working class; early works with Friedrich Engels. *German Ideology* (1846), *The Communist Manifesto* (1848). *Capital: Critique of Political Economy, Volume One* (1867).

MATERIALISM Valuing the empirical, substantial, everyday. Inverted by **IDEALISM**; see also **EPICUREANISM; MARX**.

MEAL Distribution of food and its labor at the heart of any social economy; see also **BANQUET; COOKING; MARKET (LOWERCASED)**.

MENGER, CARL (1840-1921) Founder of **AUSTRIAN SCHOOL** and proponent of **MARGINALISM**. *Principles of Economics* (1871).

MERCANTILISM State-controlled trade, under chartered corporations.

METHODOLOGICAL INDIVIDUALISM Studying economies as if they were the result only of **INDIVIDUAL** actions, denying systemic properties, and disguising corporations. Promoted by **WEBER** and **MISES**; cf. **ORGANICISM**.

MIDAS Mythological Greek king, cursed by his ability to turn everything he touched into gold. His feast was useless.

MILL, JOHN STUART (1806-1873) "Classical" or "liberal" economist. Proponent of utilitarianism. "On the Definition of Political Economy" (1836).

MISES, LUDWIG VON (1881-1973) AUSTRIAN economist, nonfoodie, and godfather of **NEOLIBERALISM**. Advocated scientific capitalism in *Human Action: A Treatise on Economics* (1949); see also **ECONOMIC CALCULATION PROBLEM**.

MONEY THE CONCOCTION of food that facilitates the **POLITICAL** (redistributive) and **MARKET (LOWERCASED)** (exchange) **ECONOMIES**, wealth accumulation, and unequal power.

MONT PELERIN SOCIETY Neoliberal network of economists, right-wing intellectuals, and business leaders. Named after Swiss resort where **HAYEK** organized the first conference in 1947.

NATURAL ECONOMY Term still used in Charles Darwin's day for ecology.

NATURAL LAW The reality of an individual being a member of a **NATURAL ECONOMY**. The natural law of self-preservation is basic to **LIBERALISM**; see also **PLEASURE OF THE STOMACH**.

NEOCLASSICAL ECONOMICS Following the **MARGINAL REVOLUTION** of late nineteenth century; see also **CLASSICAL ECONOMICS; MAINSTREAM ECONOMICS**.

NEOLIBERALISM Political program championing the core assumptions of **MAINSTREAM ECONOMICS**. Associated with economists **MISES, HAYEK,** and **FRIEDMAN**, and instituted by President **RONALD REAGAN**, Prime Minister **MARGARET THATCHER**, and such billionaires as **CHARLES KOCH**; see also **"CLASSICAL" LIBERALISM**.

OIKOS The standard transliteration of the ancient Greek *οἶκος* for "household," giving prefix "œco-"/"eco-."

OIKONOMIA Household management, or **ECONOMICS**.

OPEN DOMESTIC HOUSEHOLD Providing a household speciality to the **MARKET**; see also **HOSPITALITY; RESTAURANT**.

ORGANICISM Attention to systemic, self-adjusting properties. Characteristic of an economy; cf. **METHODOLOGICAL INDIVIDUALISM**.

OSTROM, ELINOR (1933-2012) The first and only woman, until Esther Duflo in 2019, to win a Nobel Prize in economics, "for her analysis of economic governance, especially the commons." *Governing the Commons* (1990).

PALAIS-ROYAL Parisian palace converted into center of consumer society with cafes, restaurants, and theaters especially from 1780s. Le Grand Véfour survives from that era.

PARADOX OF THE TABLE The self-centered quest for the **PLEASURE OF THE STOMACH** creates society's primary bonds; see also **DINER'S KNOT; SIMMEL**.

PHILOSOPHES Public intellectuals in France during the **ENLIGHTENMENT**.

PHYSIOCRATS Name eventually accorded eighteenth-century French *économistes* (Mirabeau, **QUESNAY, TURGOT**). "Physiocracy" is rule by the *phusis* (nature), especially circulation of sustenance

PLATO (C.428 OR C.424-C.348 BCE) Greek philosopher of **IDEALISM**, who upended the world, belittling agriculture, the senses, and **COOKING**. *Timaeus* (c.360 BCE); *Symposium* (c.385-370 BCE).

PLEASURE OF THE STOMACH (EPICURUS) The source of knowledge and the good; see also **APPETITE**.

POLANYI, KARL (1886-1964) Hungarian economic historian of government intervention to create **MARKET SOCIETY**. *The Great Transformation* (1944).

POLITICS Activities within the **POLITICAL ECONOMY**.

POLITICAL ECONOMY BODY POLITIC, such as a city (*polis*) or nation, based on **REDISTRIBUTION** under a **GOVERNMENT**; see also **BANQUET; LEVIATHAN; PRESIDENT**.

POMPADOUR, MADAME DE (1721-1764) Louis XV's mistress; influential supporter of the *ENCYCLOPÉDIE*, physician **QUESNAY**, and the *CITY*.

PRESIDENT Central authority of a **POLITICAL ECONOMY**, taking responsibility for the **BANQUET**; see also **GOVERNMENT**.

PROPERTY Following **LOCKE,** the necessities for self-preservation, especially nourishment and the means for its obtaining.

PURPOSIVE ORGANIZATION Task-directed team. Important types are **GOVERNMENT** agency and business **CORPORATION;** cf. **ECONOMY;** see also *SOCIÉTÉS PARTICULIÈRES.*

QUESNAY, FRANÇOIS (1694–1774) Madame de **POMPADOUR**'s physician, founded modern **ECONOMICS** (later called **PHYSIOCRACY**) on **ANIMAL ECONOMY** (physiology). *Tableau économique* (1758).

RAND, AYN (1905–1982) New York novelist and apostle of "rational self-interest." Her philosophy of "Objectivism" promotes right-wing libertarianism. *The Fountainhead* (1943).

RATIONALIZATION (WEBER) Making activities more calculated, systematic, efficient, goal-oriented—suppressing gastronomic considerations. Suits **PURPOSIVE ORGANIZATIONS** and only indirectly human beings; see also **MCDONALDIZATION.**

RATIONALITY Using logical deduction and calculation, rather than the senses, observation, and experience of **EMPIRICISM. MAINSTREAM** economists further elevate that to the financial; see also **RATIONALIZATION.**

REAGAN, RONALD (1911–2004) U.S. president (1981–1989), keen on applying **MAINSTREAM** assumptions, a.k.a. "Reaganomics."

REDISTRIBUTION Pooling food and other resources under a **GOVERNMENT** for social use; see also **POLITICAL ECONOMY.**

REED, DONNA (1921–1986) Hollywood actor and producer. *The Donna Reed Show* (1958–1966) promoted the family table.

RESTAURANT Originally a restorative broth, provided by a restaurateur, whose trade **ROZE DE CHANTOISEAU** invented in Paris in 1766. Transformed into an **OPEN DOMESTIC HOUSEHOLD** offering individual choice at a high level; see also **BEAUVILLIERS.**

RICARDO, DAVID (1772–1823) English **CLASSICAL** economist with formal studies of rent, profit, and wages. *Principles of Political Economy and Taxation* (1817).

RITZER, GEORGE (1940–) American sociologist studying **RATIONALIZATION** in *McDonaldization of Society* (1993); see also **MCDONALDIZATION.**

ROBBINS, LIONEL (1898–1984) London School of Economics economist allied to the Austrian school. Much-quoted definition of economics in terms of "scarcity." *Essay on the Nature and Significance of Economic Science* (1932).

ROBINSON, JOAN (1903–1983) Cambridge economist more than usually wary of mainstream theory as "theology," "metaphysics," and "ideology." *Economics Is a Serious Subject* (1932); *The Economics of Imperfect Competition* (1933).

ROUSSEAU, JEAN-JACQUES (1712-1778) Except for its androcentrism, his *ENCYCLOPÉDIE* entry on "**ECONOMICS**" remains obligatory. Emphasized the *VOLONTÉ GÉNÉRALE* (general will) and worried about its corruption by *SOCIÉTÉS PARTICULIÈRES*.

ROZE DE CHANTOISEAU, MATHURIN (17??-1806) Publisher of commercial guides and activist *economiste*, who invented the **RESTAURANT** in Paris in 1766.

SAY, JEAN-BAPTISTE (1767-1832) Influential French interpreter of Adam Smith. *Treatise on Political Economy* (1803).

SCHUMPETER, JOSEPH (1882-1950) AUSTRIAN economist early, moving to Harvard University. Fascinated by entrepreneurs and "creative destruction." *History of Economic Analysis* (1954).

SIMMEL, GEORG (1858-1918) German sociologist. "Sociology of the Meal" (1910) explores **PARADOX OF THE TABLE**. "The Metropolis and Mental Life" (1903); *Philosophy of Money* (1907).

SMITH, ADAM (1723-1790) Scottish philosopher, more sensible about "**INVISIBLE HAND**" of the **MARKET (CAPITALIZED)** than many self-proclaimed followers. *The Wealth of Nations* (1776).

SOCIAL CONTRACT Notional rules of engagement for a political community (analogous to marriage contract), expressed constitutionally and in laws.

SOCIÉTÉS PARTICULIÈRES **(ROUSSEAU)** Private, special associations or **PURPOSIVE ORGANIZATIONS** whose interests potentially corrupt the *VOLONTÉ GÉNÉRALE* (general will).

SPECTACLE The world according to marketing. Adapted from Guy Debord's *Society of the Spectacle* (1967).

STEUART, JAMES (1713-1780) Scottish philosopher. Author of first book in English with "political economy" in the title. *Principles of Political Economy* (1767).

TABLE-PLEASURE [*LE PLAISIR DE LA TABLE*] (BRILLAT-SAVARIN) Thoughtful enjoyment of food in society. Has driven economic development; see also **DINER'S KNOT; FOUR ESSENTIALS; TASTE-PLEASURES**.

TASTE-PLEASURES [*LES JOUISSANCES DU GOÛT*] (BRILLAT-SAVARIN) Appetite's reward, served through **TABLE-PLEASURE**; see also **GOURMANDISE**.

THATCHER, MARGARET (1925-2013) British prime minister pushing **NEOLIBERALISM** through the 1980s in a conservative guise; see also **RONALD REAGAN**.

THINK-TANK Advocacy research institute, often neoliberal and clandestinely funded; see also **CHARLES KOCH**.

TÖNNIES, FERDINAND (1855-1936) German sociologist. *GEMEINSCHAFT UND GESELLSCHAFT* (*Community and Association*) (1887).

TURGOT, ANNE-ROBERT-JACQUES (1727-1781) French administrator and *économiste* influencing friend **ADAM SMITH**. *Réflexions sur la formation et la distribution des richesses* (1766).

UTILITY Nonfinancial benefit of an exchange, which Austrian school economists set aside as "subjective." See also **MARGINALISM**.

VALUE Intrinsic worth, or it might depend on usefulness (utility), prestige (signification), or care and attention (labor theory). **NEOCLASSICAL ECONOMICS** opted for **MARKET (CAPITALIZED)** price.

VOLONTÉ GÉNÉRALE (ROUSSEAU) General or collective will of the people as the supreme power in a **BODY POLITIC**, corrupted by *SOCIÉTÉS PARTICULIÈRES* (private associations).

WATERS, ALICE (1944-) Californian restaurateur (Chez Panisse, 1971–) and **DELICIOUS REVOLUTION** activist. Launched Edible Schoolyard project in 1995.

WEALTH Came to be used for money-power, despite original connotations of well-ness, well-being, and wel-fare.

WEBER, MAX (1864-1920) German economic sociologist. *The Protestant Ethic and Spirit of Capitalism* (1904–1905), *Economy and Society* (1925); see also **METHODOLOGICAL INDIVIDUALISM; RATIONALIZATION**.

NOTES

PROLOGUE

1. Four Australian expatriates opened La Cantina di Toia in 1979 for the Tesi family, who were the main landowners in the village of Bacchereto, overlooking Prato in the hills near Carmignano. The restaurant occupied one end of a large farm building, said to have been Leonardo da Vinci's grandmother's.
2. Another examiner, an anthropologist, responded by wondering how he might have felt as a sociologist. I again thank my supervisors, Bryan Turner and Bob Holton, for taking me on, and seeing me through, respectively.
3. My translation of aphorism 2, *Les animaux se repaissent; l'homme mange; l'homme d'esprit seul sait manger.* Others have agreed the animals "feed" and people "eat," but the *homme d'esprit* provides difficulties. U.S. food writer M. F. K. Fisher continued: "only wise men know the art of eating," and others have spoken of "the man of intellect," "the intelligent man," and "the man of the mind." *Homme d'esprit* was a common phrase, suggesting a clever conversationalist.
4. Sociologist Georg Simmel advised that dinner talk should blend the light and heavy; see chapter 8.

3. BRILLAT-SAVARIN'S QUEST FOR TABLE-PLEASURE

1. Differences between the many editions of Jean Anthelme Brillat-Savarin's *Physiologie du gout* (*Physiology of Taste*) make for confusion in citations. The most convenient referencing is section numberings, as rationalized by French publishers from at least 1834 (although

the Monselet edition of 1879 followed the erratic original). While these are more or less adopted by translators, M. F. K. Fisher's numbering depends on an anonymous translation in 1884, published by Nimmo and Bain, remaining identical until §61, when numbers become one lower; after §87, they are equal again; and at §120, up one. Anne Drayton's translation, which appears to follow a French edition of probably 1923, runs one higher than those used here from §120 onward.

4. EPICURUS AND THE PLEASURE OF THE STOMACH

1. E.g., Ray Shelton, "Epicurus and Rand," *Objectivity* 2, no. 3, http://www.objectivity-archive.com/volume2_number3.html; and Jakub Wozinski, "Hayek and Departure from Praxeology," *Libertarian Papers*, October 29, 2010, https://mises.org/library/hayek-and-departure-praxeology.

9. LUDWIG VON MISES, NEOLIBERAL GODFATHER

1. Mont Pelerin Nobel winners include Friedrich Hayek (1974), Milton Friedman (1976), George Stigler (1982), James M. Buchanan (1986), Maurice Allais (1988), Ronald Coase (1991), Gary Becker (1992), and Vernon Smith (2002).
2. Admittedly, Reagan's farewell address on January 11, 1989, included the statement "All great change in America begins at the dinner table."

12. FREE THE MARKET!

1. Visiting Hungary in the late 1970s, I despaired of state-organized food. For a belated lunch on the road to Lake Balaton, however, what looked like a concrete bunker revealed the enthusiastic cooking of a seemingly family-based business.

13. VALUE FAMILIES!

1. My advocacy of domestic economies is not without experience as an (imperfect) housekeeper. For more than two decades, with my wife as breadwinner, I have been a work-at-home father of two children, in large part in charge of shopping, cooking, and laundry.

REFERENCES

References are less necessary in the internet age, in which sources are readily located and standard facts checked, but I have still used them in this book, especially where my research is more original and sources scarcer. For classics with several editions, such as Hobbes's *Leviathan* and Smith's *Wealth of Nations*, my preference is, rather than author-date, short title along with chapter/section number. For a guide to the inconsistent section numberings for Brillat-Savarin's *Physiologie du gout*, see the reference to his 1826 work below and note 1 in chapter 3 of this book.

I take responsibility for many translations from French and German.

Abarca, Meredith E. 2007. "*Charlas Culinarias*: Mexican Women Speak from Their Public Kitchens." *Food and Foodways* 15 (3–4): 183–212.

Abramovici, Jean-Christophe. 2013. "Epicureanism." In *Encyclopedia of the Enlightenment*, ed. Michel Delon, 468–71. New York: Routledge [originally 1997].

Alkon, Alison Hope, and Julie Guthman, eds. 2017. *The New Food Activism: Opposition, Cooperation, and Collective Action*. Oakland: University of California Press.

Allhoff, Fritz, and Dave Monroe, eds. 2007. *Food & Philosophy: Eat, Think, and Be Merry*. Malden, Mass.: Blackwell.

[Aptekar, Sidney] "Thomas Mario." 1961. *The Playboy Gourmet: A Food and Drink Handbook for the Host at Home*. New York: Crown.

Aristotle. 1932. *Politics*. Trans. H. Rackham. Cambridge, Mass.: Harvard University Press (Loeb).

——. 1935. *Athenian Constitution. Eudemian Ethics. Virtues and Vices*. Trans. H. Rackham. Cambridge, Mass.: Harvard University Press (Loeb).

References

Arrow, Kenneth J. 1994. "Methodological Individualism and Social Knowledge." *American Economic Review* 84 (2): 1–9.

Arrow, K. J., and F. H. Hahn. 1971. *General Competitive Analysis.* San Francisco: Holden-Day.

Athenaeus. 1927–1941. *The Deipnosophists.* Trans. Charles Burton Gulick. 7 vols. Cambridge, Mass.: Harvard University Press (Loeb).

Bailey, Cyril. 1926. *Epicurus: The Extant Remains.* Oxford: Clarendon Press.

Banerjee, Abhijit V., and Esther Duflo. 2019. *Good Economics for Hard Times: Better Answers to Our Biggest Problems.* London: Allen Lane

Barr, Anne, and Paul Levy. 1985. *The Official Foodie Handbook.* Adapted for Australia by David Dale. Sydney: Doubleday.

Barthes, Roland. 1975. "Lecture de Brillat-Savarin." In *Physiologie du goût*, by Brillat-Savarin, 7–33. Paris: Hermann.

Battalio, Raymond C., Leonard Green, and John H. Kagel. 1981. "Income-Leisure Trade-offs of Animal Workers." *American Economic Review* 71 (4): 621–32.

BBC News. 2010. "McDonald's 'Wrong' to Fire Worker Over Cheese Slice." January 26. http://news.bbc.co.uk/2/hi/europe/8481827.stm.

Beauvilliers, Antoine. 1814. *L'Art du Cuisinier.* 2 vols. Paris.

Becker, Gary S. 1964. *Human Capital: A Theoretical and Empirical Analysis with Special Reference to Education.* Chicago: University of Chicago Press.

——. 1976. *The Economic Approach to Human Behavior.* Chicago: University of Chicago Press.

——. 1981. *A Treatise on the Family.* Cambridge, Mass.: Harvard University Press.

Belasco, Warren. 1989. *Appetite for Change: How the Counterculture Took on the Food Industry, 1966-1988.* New York: Pantheon.

Bénégui, Laurent. 1991. *Au petit Marguery.* Paris: Bernard Barrault [film adaptation, dir. Laurent Bénégui, 1995, Téléma].

Bentham, Jeremy. 1843. "Anarchical Fallacies: Being an Examination of the Declarations of Rights Issued During the French Revolution." In *Works of Jeremy Bentham*, vol. 2, ed. John Bowring, 489–534. Edinburgh.

[Berchoux] "J. B. . . ." 1804. *La Gastronomie, ou l'homme des champs à table, poëme didactique en IV chant.* 3rd ed. Paris.

Berry, Wendell. 2010. *What Matters: Economics for a Renewed Commonwealth.* Berkeley: Counterpoint.

Beveridge, William. 1921. "Economics as a Liberal Education." *Economica* 1:2–19.

Bittman, Mark. 2014. "Rethinking the Word 'Foodie.'" *New York Times*, June 25.

[Blagdon, Francis William.] 1803. *Paris: As It Was and as It Is, . . . in a Series of Letters, Written by an English Traveller, During the Years 1801–2, to a Friend in London.* Vol. 1. London.

Boissel, Thierry. 1989. *Brillat-Savarin, 1755–1826: Un chevalier candide.* Paris: Presses de la Renaissance.

Boswell, James. 1848. *Boswell's Life of Johnson, in One Volume.* Ed. John Wilson Croker. London: John Murray.

——. 1924. *Boswell's Journal of a Tour to the Hebrides with Samuel Johnson.* Ed. R. W. Chapman. London: Oxford University Press.

Bourne, H. R. Fox. 1876. *Life of John Locke.* Vol. 1. New York.

Bowles, Samuel. 2016. *The Moral Economy: Why Good Incentives Are No Substitute for Good Citizens.* New Haven, Conn.: Yale University Press.

Brett, Judith. 2019. *From Secret Ballot to Democracy Sausage: How Australia Got Compulsory Voting.* Melbourne: Text.

Brillat-Savarin, Jean Anthelme. 1801. *Vues et projets d'économie politique. Par le Cn. Brillat-Savarin, ex-constituant, membre du Tribunal de Cassation, et de plusieurs sociétés savantes . . .* [Prospects and proposals for political economy]. Paris.

——. 1826. *Physiologie du goût, ou Méditations de gastronomie transcendante; ouvrage théorique, historique et à l'ordre du jour, Dédié aux Gastronomes parisiens, par un professeur, membre de plusieurs sociétés litteraires et savantes . . . .* 2 vols. Paris. [*Note*: This book uses *Physiologie*'s § numbers, generally standardized by publishers since at least 1834, but see chapter 3, note 1. Among major translations, M.F.K. Fisher's numbering remains identical until §61, when numbers become one lower; after §87, they are equal again; and at §120, up one. Anne Drayton's run one higher from §120 onward.]

——. 1838. *Physiologie du goût, ou Méditations de gastronomie transcendante; ouvrage théorique, historique et à l'ordre du jour, Dédié au Gastronomes parisiens, par un professeur, Membre de plusieurs sociétés savantes, Dis-moi ce que tu manges, je te dirai qui tu es. Aphor. Du Prof.* Paris [includes introduction signed "M. de V."].

——. 1865. *Handbook of Dining, or Corpulency and Leanness, Scientifically Considered.* Trans. L. F. Simpson. New York.

——. 1948. *The Physiology of Taste: Meditations on Transcendental Gastronomy.* Preface by Charles Monselet. New York: Liveright [originally London, 1884].

——. 1971. *The Physiology of Taste: or Meditations on Transcendental Gastronomy.* Trans. M. F. K. Fisher. New York: Knopf [originally 1949].

Brown, Wendy. 2015. *Undoing the Demos: Neoliberalism's Stealth Revolution.* Brooklyn, N.Y.: Zone.

——. 2019. *In the Ruins of Neoliberalism: The Rise of Antidemocratic Politics in the West.* New York: Columbia University Press.

Buchanan, James M. 1964. "What Should Economists Do?" *Southern Economic Journal* 30 (3): 213–22.

Bureau of Labor Statistics. 2018. "May 2018 National Occupational Employment and Wage Estimates." U.S. Department of Labor. https://www.bls.gov/oes/current/oes_nat.htm, accessed June 14, 2019.

Burgess, John. 2013. "Tipping Exchange in American and Australian Public Bars: Tipping as a Social Fact." Doctoral dissertation, University of Melbourne.

Burke, Edmund. 1800. *Thoughts and Details on Scarcity, Originally Presented to the Right Hon. William Pitt, in the Month of November 1795.* London.

Carlyle, Thomas. 1840. *Chartism.* 2nd ed. London: James Fraser [originally 1839].

——. 1843. *Past and Present.* New York.

——. 1849. "Occasional Discourse on the Negro Question." *Fraser's Magazine for Town and Country*, December: 670–79.

——. 1860. "The Present Time." In *Latter-Day Pamphlets*, ed. Thomas Carlyle, 1–60. Andover [originally 1850].

Carrington, Christopher. 1999. *No Place Like Home: Relationships and Family Life Among Lesbians and Gay Men*. Chicago: University of Chicago Press.

Carsten, Janet. 2004. *After Kinship*. Cambridge: Cambridge University Press.

[Cavendish, Margaret]. 1653. *Poems and Fancies: Written by the Right Honourable, the Lady Margaret, Countess of Newcastle*. London.

Charles, Nickie, and Marion Kerr. 1988. *Women, Food and Families*. Manchester: Manchester University Press.

Chira, Susan. 1982. "Followers of Ayn Rand Provide a Final Tribute." *New York Times*, March 10. http://www.nytimes.com/1982/03/10/nyregion/followers-of-ayn-rand-provide-a-final-tribute.html.

Clay, Diskin. 2009. "The Athenian Garden." In *The Cambridge Companion to Epicureanism*, ed. James Warren, 9–28. Cambridge: Cambridge University Press.

Coleman, James S. 1990. *Foundations of Social Theory*. Cambridge, Mass.: Harvard University Press.

Condillac, M. l'Abbé de [Étienne Bonnot de]. 1776. *Le Commerce et le gouvernement considérés relativement l'un à l'autre*. Amsterdam.

Cook, Ian, et al. 2011. "Geographies of Food: 'Afters.'" *Progress in Human Geography* 35 (1): 104–20.

Cook, Simon J. 2009. *The Intellectual Foundations of Alfred Marshall's Economic Science: A Rounded Globe of Knowledge*. Cambridge: Cambridge University Press.

Coontz, Stephanie. 2000. *The Way We Never Were: American Families and the Nostalgia Trap*. New York: Basic Books [originally 1992].

Cooper, Thomas. 1826. *Lectures on the Elements of Political Economy*. Columbia, S.C.

Cross, Gary S., and Robert N. Proctor. 2014. *Packaged Pleasures: How Technology and Marketing Revolutionized Desire*. Chicago: University of Chicago Press.

Croÿ, Emmanuel Duc de. 1906. *Journal inédit de Duc de Croÿ (1714–1784)*, vol. 1. Paris: Flammarion.

Dalby, Andrew. 2003. *Food in the Ancient World from A to Z*. London: Routledge.

Darwin, Charles. 1859. *On the Origin of Species by Means of Natural Selection.* . . . London.

Davenport, Herbert J. 1913. *The Economics of Enterprise*. New York: Macmillan.

David, Elizabeth. 1987. *Italian Food*. London: Penguin [originally 1954].

Debord, Guy. 1977. *The Society of the Spectacle*. Detroit: Black & Red.

Defoe, Daniel. 1831. *The Life and Adventures of Robinson Crusoe [etc.]*, vol. 1. London [originally 1719].

Derrida, Jacques. 2002. "Hostipitality [sic]." In *Acts of Religion*, ed. Gil Ankdjar, 356–420. London: Routledge.

de Solier, Isabelle. 2013. *Food and the Self: Consumption, Production, and Material Culture*. London: Bloomsbury.

Destutt Tracy, Count [Antoine Destutt de Tracy]. 1817. *A Treatise on Political Economy, . . . Translated [by Thomas Jefferson] from the Uunpublished French Original.* Washington, D.C. [*Traité de la volonté,* fourth volume of *Élémens d'idéologie,* Paris, 1818].

DeWitt, Norman Wentworth. 1954. *Epicurus and His Philosophy.* Minneapolis: University of Minnesota Press.

Diderot, Denis, ed. 1751–1772. *Encyclopédie or Dictionnaire Raisonné des Science, des Arts et des Métiers, par un société de gens de lettres.* 28 vols. Paris [originally coedited with Jean Le Rond d'Alembert].

——. 1875–1877. *Lettres à Sophie Volland.* Text by J. Assézat and M. Tourneux. Garnier.

Du Pont, [Pierre Samuel]. 1768. *Physiocratie, ou Constitution naturelle du gouvernement, Le plus avantageux au genre humain, Recueil publié par Du Pont.* Leiden.

Dworkin, Ronald. 2000. *Sovereign Virtue: The Theory and Practice of Equality.* Cambridge, Mass.: Harvard University Press.

Earle, Joe, Cahal Moran, and Zach Ward-Perkins. 2017. *The Econocracy: The Perils of Leaving Economics to the Experts.* Manchester: Manchester University Press.

Economist. 2013. "The New American Capitalism: Rise of the Distorporation." *Economist,* October 26.

Eilperin, Juliet. 2007. *Fight Club Politics: How Partisanship Is Poisoning the House of Representatives.* Lanham, Md.: Rowman & Littlefield.

Elias, Megan J. 2008. *Stir It Up: Home Economics in American Culture.* Philadelphia: University of Pennsylvania Press.

Ellwanger, George H. 1902. *The Pleasures of the Table: An Account of Gastronomy from Ancient Days to Present Times.* New York: Doubleday Page.

Enders, Giulia. 2015. *Gut: The Inside Story of Our Body's Most Underrated Organ.* Trans. David Shaw. Vancouver: Greystone [originally *Darm mit Charme,* 2014].

Engels, Friedrich. 1948. *The Origin of the Family, Private Property and the State in the Light of the Researches of Lewis H. Morgan.* Moscow: Progress [originally 1884].

Epicurus. See Bailey, Cyril.

Erickson, Karla A. 2009. *The Hungry Cowboy: Service and Community in a Neighborhood Restaurant.* Jackson: University Press of Mississippi.

Ewing, Jack, and Milan Schreuer. 2019. "A Lone Trader Shook the World's Financial System." *New York Times,* May 5. https://www.nytimes.com/2019/05/03/business/central-counterparties-financial-meltdown.html.

Fairchild, Fred Rogers, Edgar Stevenson Furniss, and Norman Sydney Buck. 1926. *Elementary Economics.* 2 vols. New York: Macmillan.

Farrand, Max, ed. 1911. *The Records of the Federal Convention of 1787.* 3 vols. New Haven, Conn.: Yale University Press.

Ferguson, Priscilla Parkhurst. 1998. "A Cultural Field in the Making: Gastronomy in Nineteenth-Century France." *American Journal of Sociology* 104 (3): 597–641.

——. 2003. "Belly Talk: Gastronomie, Gastrolâtrie, and Gourmandise in the 19th Century." *Dix-Neuf: Journal of the Society of Dix-Neuviémistes* 1:2–15.

——. 2004. *Accounting for Taste: The Triumph of French Cuisine.* Chicago: University of Chicago Press.

References

Festugière, A. J. 1955. *Epicurus and His Gods*. Trans. C. W. Chilton. Oxford: Basil Blackwell.

Fisher, M. F. K. 1983. *Two Towns in Provence*. New York: Vintage [includes *A Map of Another Town*, 1964].

——. 1990. *The Art of Eating*. New York: Wiley [compilation of her five first books].

FitzGerald, Edward. 1889. *Rubáiyát of Omar* Khayyám. 5th ed. London.

Flammang, Janet A. 2009. *The Taste for Civilization: Food, Politics, and Civil Society*. Urbana: University of Illinois Press.

——. 2016. *Table Talk: Building Democracy One Meal at a Time*. Urbana: University of Illinois Press.

Fleurichamp, Jules ["Jules Paton"]. 1853–1860. "Brillat-Savarin." In *Dictionnaire de la conversation et de la lecture*, vol. 3, ed. M. W. Duckett, 715–16. Paris.

Folbre, Nancy. 1998. "The 'Sphere of Women' in Early Twentieth-Century Economics." In *Gender and American Social Science: The Formative Years*, ed. Helene Silverberg, 35–60. Princeton, N.J.: Princeton University Press.

——. 2009. *Greed, Lust & Gender: A History of Economic Ideas*. Oxford: Oxford University Press.

Force, Pierre. 2003. *Self-Interest Before Smith: A Genealogy of Economic Science*. Cambridge: Cambridge University Press.

Francis [Pope]. 2013. *Evangelii Gaudium* [Joy of the Gospel]. [Vatican]: Vatican Press.

Frank, Robert H., Thomas Gilovich, and Dennis T. Regan. 1993. "Does Studying Economics Inhibit Cooperation?" *Journal of Economic Perspectives* 7 (2): 159–71.

Franklin, Benjamin. 1978. "Principles of Trade." In *The Papers of Benjamin Franklin*, vol. 21: *January 1, 1774, Through March 22, 1775*, ed. William B. Willcox, 169–77. New Haven, Conn.: Yale University Press [originally coauthored with George Whatley, 1774].

Freeman, Michael. 1977. "Sung." In *Food in Chinese Culture: Anthropological and Historical Perspectives*, ed. K. C. Chang, 141–76. New Haven, Conn.: Yale Unversity Press.

Freud, Sigmund. 1963. *Civilization and Its Discontents*. Trans. Joan Riviere. London: Hogarth Press.

Friedman, Milton, with the assistance of Rose D. Friedman. 1962. *Capitalism and Freedom*. Chicago: University of Chicago Press.

——. 1991. "Say 'No' to Intolerance," edited version of talk to Future of Freedom Conference. *Liberty* 4 (6) (August 1990): 17–18, 20 [video extract available at http://www.youtube.com/watch?v=xtDM7VF3_Rc].

Fultz, Jay. 1998. *In Search of Donna Reed*. Iowa City: University of Iowa Press.

Funck-Brentano, Frantz. 1929. *The Old Regime in France*. Trans. Herbert Wilson. London: Edward Arnold [*L'Ancien Régime*, 1926].

Garval, Michael. 2001. "Grimod de la Reynière's *Almanach des gourmands*: Exploring the Gastronomic New World of Postrevolutionary France." In *French Food on the Table, on the Page, and in French Culture*, ed. Lawrence R. Schehr and Allen S. Weiss, 51–70. New York: Routledge.

Gibson-Graham, J. K. 1995. "Waiting for the Revolution, or How to Smash Capitalism While Working at Home in Your Spare Time." In *Marxism in the Postmodern Age:*

Confronting the New World Order, ed. Antonio Callari et al., 188–95. New York: Guilford [originally 1993].

Gilgamesh Epic. Many online sources, e.g., http://www.ancienttexts.org/library/meso potamian/gilgamesh/tab10.htm.

Gleeson-White, Jane. 2011. *Double Entry: How the Merchants of Venice Shaped the Modern World—and How Their Invention Could Make or Break the Planet*. St. Leonard's, NSW: Allen & Unwin.

Goldenberg, Naomi R. 2015. "The Category of Religion in the Technology of Governance: An Argument for Understanding Religions as Vestigial States." In *Religion as a Category of Governance and Sovereignty*, ed. Trevor Stack, Naomi R. Goldenberg, and Timothy Fitzgerald, 280–92. Leiden: Brill.

Goldstein, Bill. 2002. "Word for Word / 'Greenspan Shrugged'; When Greed Was a Virtue and Regulation the Enemy." *New York Times*, July 21.

Goncourt, Edmond, and Jules de Goncourt. 1888. *Madame de Pompadour*. New ed. Paris.

Gonyea, Don. 2015. "Eat, Speak and Stumble: Candidates Visit the Iowa State Fair." *WUSF News*, August 13. http://wusfnews.wusf.usf.edu/post/eat-speak-and-stumble-candidates -visit-iowa-state-fair#stream/0.

Grimod de la Rèyniere, A.B.L. 1803. *Almanach des Gourmands, Première Année, Quatriène Édition*. Paris.

——. 1810. *Almanach des Gourmands, Première Année, Quatriène Édition*. Paris [originally 1803].

Guthman, Julie. 2007. "Commentary on Teaching Food: Why I Am Fed Up with Michael Pollan et al." *Agriculture & Human Values* 24 (2): 261–64.

——. 2008. "Neoliberalism and the Making of Food Politics in California, Introduction to Special Issue." *Geoforum* 39 (3): 1171–83.

——. 2011. *Weighing in: Obesity, Food Justice and the Limits of Capitalism*. Berkeley: University of California Press.

Guyau, M. [Jean-Marie]. 1878. *La Morale d'Épicure et ses rapports avec les doctrines contemporaines*. Paris.

Hammond, Bray. 1957. *Banks and Politics in America from the Revolution to the Civil War*. Princeton, N.J.: Princeton University Press.

Hammond, N.G.L., and H. H. Scullard, eds. 1970. *The Oxford Classical Dictionary*. 2nd rev. ed. Oxford: Oxford University Press.

Harcourt, Bernard E. 2011. *The Illusion of Free Markets: Punishment and the Myth of Natural Order*. Cambridge, Mass.: Harvard University Press.

Harvey, David. 2005. *A Brief History of Neoliberalism*. Oxford: Oxford University Press.

Hausman, Daniel M. 1992. *The Inexact and Separate Science of Economics*. Cambridge: Cambridge University Press.

Hauter, Wenonah. 2012. *Foodopoly: The Battle Over the Future of Food and Farming in America*. New York: New Press.

Hayek, Friedrich. 1944. *The Road to Serfdom*. Chicago: University of Chicago Press.

——. 1948. *Individualism and Economic Order*. Chicago: University of Chicago Press.

——. 1967. *Studies in Philosophy, Politics and Economics*. London: Routledge & Kegan Paul.

——. 1976. *Law, Legislation and Liberty*, vol. 2: *The Mirage of Social Justice*. Chicago: University of Chicago Press.

——. 1999. "*The Road to Serfdom* in Cartoons." In *The Road to Serfdom with the Intellectuals and Socialism* [condensed ed.], by Friedrich A. Hayek, 71–89. London: Institute of Economic Affairs [originally 1944].

Hazlitt, Henry. 2011. *Business Tides: The* Newsweek *Era of Henry Hazlitt*. Comp. Marc Doolittle. Auburn, Ala.: Ludwig von Mises Institute.

Heal, Felicity. 1990. *Hospitality in Early Modern England*. Oxford: Oxford University Press.

Heilbroner, Robert L. 1980. *The Worldly Philosophers: The Lives, Times, and Ideas of the Great Economic Thinkers*. 5th ed. New York: Touchstone [originally 1953].

——. 1999. *The Worldly Philosophers: The Lives, Times, and Ideas of the Great Economic Thinkers*. Rev. 7th ed. New York: Touchstone

[Herbert, Claude-Jacques]. 1753. *Essai sur la police générale des grains*. London.

——. 1759. *Sur la Liberté du commerce des grains*. Amsterdam.

Hightower, Jim. 1975. *Eat Your Heart Out: Food Profiteering in America*. New York: Crown.

Hill, Lisa. 2013. "The Science of Welfare: Adam Smith's Political Thought." Paper delivered to APSA conference, Perth.

Hobbes, Thomas. 1651. *Leviathan: Or, the Matter, Forme and Power of a Common Wealth Ecclesiasticall and Civil*. London.

——. 1994. *The Elements of Law Natural and Politic: Part I, Human Nature, Part II, De Corpore Politico*. Ed. J.C.A. Gaskin. Oxford: Oxford University Press [written 1640].

Hogan, David Gerard. 1997. *Selling 'Em by the Sack: White Castle and the Creation of American Food*. New York: New York University Press.

Hook, Sidney. 1933. *Towards an Understanding of Karl Marx*. New York: John Day.

Horace. 2004. *Odes and Epodes*. Cambridge, Mass.: Harvard University Press (Loeb).

Hülsmann, Jörg Guido. 2007. *Mises: The Last Knight of Liberalism*. Auburn, Ala.: Ludwig von Mises Institute.

Hume, David. 1751. *An Enquiry Concerning the Principles of Morals*. London.

ISIPE. 2014. "An International Student Call for Pluralism in Economics." Open Letter from International Student Initiative for Pluralism in Economics (ISIPE). http://www.isipe.net/open-letter/.

Jackson, Andrew. 1835. *Annual Messages, Veto Messages, Protest, &c, of Andrew Jackson, President of the United States*. 2nd ed. Baltimore.

Jaucourt, Chevalier L. de. 1765. "Hospitalité." In *Encyclopédie*, vol. 8: *H–Itzehoa*, ed. Diderot, 314–18. Paris.

Jefferson, Thomas. 1787. Letter to William Short, Aix-en-Provence, March 27. http://founders.archives.gov/documents/Jefferson/01-11-02-0242.

——. 1816. Letter to George Logan, Poplar Forest near Lynchburg, November 12. https://founders.archives.gov/documents/Jefferson/03-10-02-0390.

——. 1819. Letter to William Short, Monticello, October 31. https://founders.archives.gov/documents/Jefferson/98-01-02-0850.

Jevons, W. Stanley. 1866. "Brief Account of a General Mathematical Theory of Political Economy." *Journal of the Royal Statistical Society* 29:282–87.

——. 1871. *Theory of Political Economy*. London. https://archive.org/details/theoryof politicaoojevouoft.

——. 1905. *The Principles of Economics: A Fragment of a Treatise on the Industrial Mechanism of Society and Other Papers*. London: Macmillan.

Johnson, Paul. 2010. *Making the Market: Victorian Origins of Corporate Capitalism*. Cambridge: Cambridge University Press.

Johnston, Josée, and Shyon Baumann. 2010. *Foodies: Democracy and Distinction in the Gourmet Foodscape*. New York: Routledge.

Jones, Peter. 2002. "Introduction." In *Introduction to Hospitality Operations: An Indispensable Guide to the Industry*. 2nd ed. London: Cengage Learning.

Kant, Immanuel. 1991. "Perpetual Peace: A Philosophical Sketch." In *Kant: Political Writings*, ed. Hans Reiss, trans. H. B. Nisbet, 93–130. 2nd ed. Cambridge: Cambridge University Press [originally 1795].

Kapczynski, Amy. 2019. "Free Speech, Incorporated." In *Economics After Neoliberalism*, ed. Joshua Cohen, 156–73. *Boston Review Forum* 11 (44.3).

Kaplan, Steven L. 1976. *Bread, Politics and Political Economy in the Reign of Louis XV*, vol. 1. The Hague: Martinus Nijhoff.

Kaufmann, Jean-Claude. 2010. *The Meaning of Cooking*. Trans. David Macey. Cambridge: Polity [originally *Casseroles, amour et crises*, 2005].

Kavanagh, Thomas M. 2016. "Epicureanism Across the French Revolution." In *Lucretius and Modernity: Epicurean Encounters Across Time and Disciplines*, ed. Jacques Lezra and Liza Blake, 89–101. Basingstoke, U.K.: Palgrave Macmillan.

Kenney, E. J. 1984. *The Ploughman's Lunch: Moretum, A Poem Ascribed to Virgil*. Bristol: Bristol Classical Press.

Keynes, John Maynard. 1931. "Economic Possibilities for Our Grandchildren (1930)." In *Essays in Persuasion*, by John Maynard Keynes, 358–72. London: Macmillan.

——. 1936. *The General Theory of Employment, Interest and Money*. London: Macmillan.

Kielburger, Craig, Marc Kielburger, and Holly Branson. 2018. *Weconomy: You Can Find Meaning, Make a Living and Change the World*. Hoboken, N.J.: Wiley.

King, Carol A. 1995. "Viewpoint: What Is Hospitality?" *International Journal of Hospitality Management* 14 (3–4): 219–34.

[Kitchiner, William]. 1821. *The Cook's Oracle: Containing Receipts for Plain Cookery on the Most Economical Plan for Private Families: etc*. 3rd ed. London.

Knight, Frank H. 1933. *The Economic Organization*. Chicago: University of Chicago.

Koch, Charles. 2007. *The Science of Success: How Market-Based Management Built the World's Largest Private Company*. Hoboken, N.J.: Wiley.

Koff, Richard M. 1971. "An End to All This: We Have Handed Our Heirs an Ecological Time Bomb That Birth Control Alone Cannot Defuse." *Playboy*, July: 112, 114, 206–8.

Korsmeyer, Carolyn. 1999. *Making Sense of Taste: Food and Philosophy*. Ithaca, N.Y.: Cornell University Press.

Korten, David C. 1996. *When Corporations Rule the World*. London: Earthscan.

Krugman, Paul. 2014. "How to Get It Wrong." *New York Times*, September 15.

Krugman, Paul, and Robin Wells 2009. *Economics*. 2nd ed. New York: Worth.

[Kuznets, Simon]. 1934. "Uses and Abuses of National Income Measurements." In *National Income, 1929–32: Letter from the Acting Secretary of Commerce, Transmitting in Response to Senate Resolution No. 220 (72D Cong.)*, 5–8. Washington, D.C.: U.S. Congress (January 4).

Kyd, Stewart. 1793. *A Treatise on the Law of Corporations*, vol. 1. London.

Lashley. Conrad. 2000. "Towards a Theoretical Understanding." In *In Search of Hospitality: Theoretical Perspectives and Debates*, ed. Conrad Lashley and Alison J. Morrison, 1–17. Oxford: Elsevier Butterworth-Heinemann.

——. 2008. "Studying Hospitality: Insights from Social Sciences." *Scandinavian Journal of Hospitality and Tourism* 8 (1): 69–84.

Law, John. 2004. *After Method: Mess in Social Science Research*. London: Routledge.

Leonhardt, David. 2018. "Big Business, Squashing Small." *New York Times*, June 18.

Leshem, Dotan. 2016. *The Origins of Neoliberalism: Modeling the Economy from Jesus to Foucault*. New York: Columbia University Press.

Lévi-Strauss, Claude. 1978. *Introduction to a Science of Mythology*, vol 3: *The Origin of Table Manners*. New York: Harper & Row.

Lewis, Paul, and Rob Evans. 2013. *Undercover: The True Story of Britain's Secret Police*. London: Faber & Faber.

Locke, John. 1690. *An Essay Concerning Humane Understanding: In Four Books*. London.

——. 1690. *Two Treatises of Government: In the Former, The False Principles, and Foundation of Sir Robert Filmer, and His Followers, Are Detected and Overthrown. The Latter Is an Essay Concerning the True Original, Extent, and End of Civil Government*. London.

——. 2003. *Two Treatises of Government and A Letter Concerning Toleration*. Ed. Ian Shapiro. New Haven, Conn.: Yale University Press [originally appeared anonymously in December 1689, dated 1690].

Love, John F. 1986. *McDonald's: Behind the Arches*. Toronto: Bantam.

Lucretius. 1951. *On the Nature of the Universe [De Rerum Natura]*. Trans. R. E. Latham. Harmondsworth, U.K.: Penguin.

Luynes, Charles Philippe d'Albert duc de. 1860. *Mémoires du duc de Luynes sur la cour de Louis XV (1735–1758)*, vol. 2. Paris.

Maas, Harro. 1999. "Mechanical Rationality: Jevons and the Making of Economic Man." *Studies in the History and Philosophy of Science, Part A*, 30 (4): 587–619.

MacDonogh, Giles. 1992. *Brillat-Savarin: The Judge and His Stomach*. Chicago: Ivan R. Dee.

Maddox, Marion. 1998. "Religion and the Secular State Revisited." *Australian Religion Studies Review* 11 (2): 98–113.

Malone, Dumas. 1971. *Jefferson and His Time*, vol. 6: *The Sage of Monticello*. Boston: Little, Brown.

Malthus, Thomas. 1798. *An Essay on the Principle of Population, etc.* London.

——. 1820. *Principles of Political Economy, Considered with a View to Their Practical Application*. London.

Marçal, Katrine. 2015. *Who Cooked Adam Smith's Dinner? A Story About Women and Economics*. Trans. Saskia Vogel. London: Portobello [originally *Det enda könet*, 2012].

[Marcet, Jane Haldimand]. 1817. *Conversations on Political Economy: In Which the Elements of That Science Are Familiarly Explained*. By the author of "Conversations on Chemistry." 2nd ed. London [originally 1816].

Marshall, Alfred. 1890. *Principles of Economics*. London.

Marx, Karl. 1973. *Grundrisse: Foundations of the Critique of Political Economy*. Trans. Martin Nicolaus. London: Penguin in association with New Left Review.

——. 1975. "Difference Between the Democritean and Epicurean Philosophy of Nature." In *Collected Works*, vol. 1, by Karl Marx and Friedrich Engels, 25–107. London: Lawrence & Wishart [completed 1841].

——. 1976. *Capital: A Critique of Political Economy, Volume One*. Intro. by Ernest Mandel, trans. Ben Fowkes. London: Pelican [originally 1867].

——. 1977. *Economic and Philosophic Manuscripts of 1844*. Moscow: Progress.

Marx, Karl, and Friedrich Engels. 1952. *Manifesto of the Communist Party*. Moscow: Progress [*Manifest der Kommunistischen Partei*], London, 1848; standard English trans. by Samuel Moore, 1888 [see also Varoufakis, 2018].

——. 1976. *The German Ideology*. Moscow: Progress [originally 1845].

Matthews, Glenna. 1987. *"Just a Housewife": The Rise and Fall of Domesticity in America*. Oxford: Oxford University Press.

Mayer, Jane. 2016. *Dark Money: The Hidden History of the Billionaires Behind the Rise of the Radical Right*. New York: Doubleday.

McCloskey, Deirdre N. 1983. "The Rhetoric of Economics." *Journal of Economic Literature* 21:481–517.

——. 2006. *The Bourgeois Virtues: Ethics for an Age of Commerce*. Chicago: University of Chicago Press.

Meadows, Donella H., Dennis L. Meadows, Jørgen Randers, and William W. Behrens III. 1972. *The Limits to Growth: A Report for the Club of Rome's Project on the Predicament of Mankind*. New York: Universe.

Menger, Carl. 2007. *Principles of Economics*. Trans. James Dingwall and Bert F. Hoselitz, intro. by F. A. Hayek. Auburn, Ala. Ludwig von Mises Institute [originally *Grundsätze der Volkswirtschaftslehre*, 1871].

Mennell, Stephen. 1985. *All Manners of Food: Eating and Taste in England and France from the Middle Ages to the Present*. Oxford: Basil Blackwell.

——. 2003. "Eating in the Public Sphere in the Nineteenth and Twentieth Centuries." In *Eating Out in Europe*, ed. Marc Jacobs and Peter Scholliers, 245–60. Oxford: Berg.

Menuret de Chambaud, Jean-Joseph. 1765. "Œconomie animale." In *Encyclopédie*, vol. 11: *N–Parkinsone*, ed. Diderot, 360–66. Paris.

Mill, John Stuart. 1836. "On the Definition of Political Economy, and on the Method of Investigation Proper to It." *London and Westminster Review*, October: 1–29.

——. 1848. *Principles of Political Economy: With Some of Their Applications to Social Philosophy*. London.

[Mirabeau, Victor Riquetti de]. 1763. *Philosophie Rurale, ou Économie générale et politique de l'agriculture, Réduite à l'ordre immutable de Loix physique & morales, qui assurent la prospérité des Empire*, vol. 1. Amsterdam.

Mises, Ludwig von. 1935. "Economic Calculation in the Socialist Commonwealth." In *Collectivist Economic Planning: Critical Studies on the Possibilities of Socialism*, ed. Friedrich Hayek, 87–130. London: Routledge [essay originally 1920].

——. 1940. *Nationalökonomie: Theorie des Handelns und Wirtschaftens*. Geneva: Union.

——. 1966. *Human Action: A Treatise on Economics*. 3rd rev. ed. Chicago: Regnery [originally 1949, elaboration of Mises, 1940].

——. 1976. *Epistemological Problems of Economics*. Trans. George Reisman. 2nd ed. New York: New York University Press [originally 1933].

——. 1981. *Socialism: An Economic and Sociological Analysis*. Trans. J. Kahane. Indianapolis: Liberty Classics [original German ed., 1922; 2nd rev. ed. 1932, Jonathan Cape, 1936].

——. 1985. *Liberalism: In the Classical Tradition*. Trans. Ralph Raico. Irvington-on-Hudson, N.Y.: Foundation for Economic Education and San Francisco: Cobden Press [originally 1927, 1st English ed., *The Free and Prosperous Commonwealth: An Exposition of the Ideas of Classical Liberalism*, 1962].

Mises, Margit von. 1976. *My Years with Ludwig von Mises*. New Rochelle, N.Y.: Arlington House.

Mishan, Ezra J. 1967. *The Costs of Economic Growth*. New York: Praeger.

——. 2006. "Derek Turner Interview and 'Preface.'" *Social Contract Journal* 17 (1): 25–33.

Mitford, Nancy. 1968. *Madame de Pompadour*. London: Hamish Hamilton [1954].

Monbiot, George. 2012. "We Have All Conspired to Trash the Planet." *Guardian Weekly*, July 6, 20.

——. 2016. "Neoliberalism: The Ideology at the Root of All Our Problems." *Guardian*, April 16. http://gu.com/p/4tbfb/sbl.

Murcott, Anne. 1982. "On the Social Significance of the 'Cooked Dinner' in South Wales." *Social Science Information* 21 (4–5): 677–95.

——. 1997. "Family Meals: A Thing of the Past?" In *Food, Health and Identity*, ed. Pat Caplan, 32–49. London: Routledge.

Murdock, George Peter. 1949. *Social Structure*. New York: Macmillan.

Nestle, Marion. 2016. "Food Industry Funding of Nutrition Research: The Relevance of History for Current Debates." *JAMA Internal Medicine*. http://archinte.jamanetwork.com/article.aspx?articleid=2548251.

New Zealand Treasury. 2018. *The Treasury Approach to the Living Standards Framework*. Wellington: New Zealand Treasury.

O'Neill, John. 1999. "Have You Had Your Theory Today?" In *Resisting McDonaldisation*, ed. Barry Smart, 41–56. London: Sage.

Organisation for Economic Cooperation and Development (OECD). 2015. *How's Life? 2015: Measuring Well-being*. Paris: OECD.

Ostrom, Elinor. 1990. *Governing the Commons: The Evolution of Institutions for Collective Action*. Cambridge: Cambridge University Press.

Ostry, Jonathan D., Prakash Loungani, and Davide Furceri. 2016. "Neoliberalism: Oversold?" *Finance & Development* 53 (2): 38–41.

Paine, Thomas. 1791. *Rights of Man: Being an Answer to Mr Burke's Attack on the French Revolution*. London.

Pantaleoni, Maffeo. 1898. *Pure Economics*. Trans. T. Boston Bruce. London [originally *Principii di Economia Pura*, 1889].

Pergament, Danielle. 2007. "In Palermo, Life Vibrates in a Fading Market." *New York Times*, May 20. http://www.nytimes.com/2007/05/20/travel/20journeys.html.

Piketty, Thomas. 2014. *Capital in the Twenty-First Century*. Trans. Arthur Goldhammer. Cambridge, Mass.: Harvard University Press [originally 2013].

Polanyi, Karl. 1944. *The Great Transformation: The Political and Economic Origins of Our Time*. New York: Rinehart.

——. 1957. "The Economy as Instituted Process." In *Trade and Market in the Early Empires: Economies in History and Theory*, ed. Karl Polanyi, Conrad M. Arensberg, and Harry W. Pearson 243–70. Glencoe, Ill.: Free Press.

——. 1977. *The Livelihood of Man*. Ed. Harry W. Pearson. New York: Academic Press.

Pollan, Michael. 2009. *Food Rules: An Eater's Manual*. New York: Penguin.

——. 2013. *Cooked: A Natural History of Transformation*. New York: Penguin.

Portinari, Folco. 1989. "The Slow Food Manifesto," endorsed by Slow Food delegates, December 10. Paris. http://www.slowfood.com/about_us/eng/manifesto.lasso.

Powell, Lewis F. 1971. "Confidential Memorandum: Attack on the American Free Enterprise System." Typescript to Eugene B. Sydnor, August 23. http://law.wlu.edu/deptimages/Powell%20Archives/PowellMemorandumTypescript.pdf.

Pritchard, James B., ed. 1969. *Ancient Near Eastern Texts Relating to the Old Testament*. 3rd ed. Princeton, N.J.: Princeton University Press.

Quesnay, François. 1736. *Essai phisique sur l'oeconomie animale*. Paris.

——. 1747. *Essai physique sur l'oeconomie animale*, vol. 3. 2nd ed. Paris: chez Guillaume Cavelier.

——. 1756. "*Fermiers.*" In *Encyclopédie*, vol. 6: *Er–Fne*, ed. Diderot, 528–40. Paris.

——. 1757. "*Grains.*" In *Encyclopédie*, vol. 7: *Foang–Gytheum*, ed. Diderot, 812–31. Paris.

——. 1765. "Observations sur le Droit naturel des hommes réunis en société." *Journal de l'agriculture, du commerce & des finances*, vol. 2, part 1 (September): 4–35.

——. 1888. *Oeuvres Économiques et philosophiques de F. Quesnay, fondateur du système physiocratique . . . une introduction et des notes par Auguste Oncken*. Frankfurt [includes "Analyse du Tableau Économique," 305–29].

Quiggin, John. 2010. *Zombie Economics: How Dead Ideas Still Walk Among Us*. Princeton, N.J.: Princeton University Press.

Ray, Krishnendu. 2019. "ASFS Presidential Address 2018: Towards an Epistemology of Pleasure and a Post-Liberal Politics of Joy." *Food, Culture & Society* 22 (1): 3–8.

Raymond, Daniel. 1820. *Thoughts on Political Economy: In Two Parts*. Baltimore.

Ricardo, David. 1817. *On the Principles of Political Economy and Taxation*. London.

References

Richerand, A[nthelme]. 1801. *Nouveaux élémens de physiologie*. Paris.

——. 1803. *The Elements of Physiology: Containing an Explanation of the Functions of the Human Body; in which the modern improvements in chemistry, galvanism, and other sciences, are applied to explain the actions of the animal economy*. Trans. Robert Kerrison. London [translation of 1801].

Rist, J. M. 1972. *Epicurus: An Introduction*. Cambridge: Cambridge University Press.

Ritzer, George. 1993. *The McDonaldization of Society: An Investigation Into the Changing Character of Contemporary Social Life*. Thousand Oaks, Calif.: Pine Forge.

Robbins, Lionel. 1932. *An Essay on the Nature & Significance of Economic Science*. London: Macmillan.

——. 1935. *An Essay on the Nature and Significance of Economic Science*. 2nd, exp. ed. London: Macmillan.

Robinson, E.A.G. 1941. *Monopoly*. Cambridge: Cambridge University Press

Robinson, Joan. 1932. *Economics Is a Serious Subject: The Apologia of an Economist to the Mathematician, the Scientist and the Plain Man*. Cambridge: Heffer.

——. 1933. *The Economics of Imperfect Competition*. London: Macmillan.

——. 1962. *Economic Philosophy: An Essay on the Progress of Economic Thought*. Chicago: Aldine.

——. 1978. *Contributions to Modern Economics*. Oxford: Blackwell.

Rodrik, Dani. 2015. *Economics Rules: The Rights and Wrongs of the Dismal Science*. New York: Norton.

Romer, Paul. 2015. "Mathiness in the Theory of Economic Growth." *American Economic Review: Papers & Proceedings* 105 (5): 89–93.

——. 2016. "The Trouble with Macroeconomics." Stern School of Business, New York University. https://paulromer.net/wp-content/uploads/2016/09/WP-Trouble.pdf.

Rousiers, Paul de. 1892. *American Life*. Trans. A. J. Herbertson. Paris.

Rousseau, Jean-Jacques 1754. *Discours sur l'origine et les fondements de l'inégalité parmi les hommes* [Discourse on the origin and basis of inequality among human beings]. Amsterdam.

——. 1755. "Économie ou œconomie: Morale et politique." In *Encyclopédie*, vol. 5: *Do–Esymnete*, ed. Diderot, 337–49. Paris.

——. 1973. *The Social Contract and Discourses*. Trans. G.D.H. Cole, rev. J. H. Brumfitt and John C. Hall. London: J. M. Dent [originally 1762].

Sahlins, Marshall. 1974. *Stone Age Economics*. London: Tavistock.

Samuelson, Paul A., and William D. Nordhaus. 1998. *Economics*. 16th ed. Boston: Irwin/McGraw Hill.

Sawer, Marian. 2003. *The Ethical State? Social Liberalism in Australia*. Melbourne: Melbourne University Publishing.

Say, Jean-Baptiste. 1821. *A Treatise on Political Economy: Or the Production, Distribution, and Consumption of Wealth*. Trans. from 4th French ed. by C. R. Prinsep, intro. trans. Clement C. Biddle. Boston [originally 1803].

Schlosser, Eric. 2001. *Fast Food Nation: The Dark Side of the All-American Meal*. New York: Houghton Mifflin.

Schor, Juliet B. 2010. *Plenitude: The New Economics of True Wealth*. New York: Penguin.

Schumpeter, Joseph A. 1954. *History of Economic Analysis*. Ed. from manuscript by Elizabeth Boody Schumpeter. New York: Oxford University Press.

——. 1976. *Capitalism, Socialism and Democracy*. London: George Allen & Unwin [originally 1943].

——. 1980. *Methodological Individualism*. Preface by F. A. Hayek. Brussels: L'Institut Européen [extract from *Wesen und Hauptinhalt der theoretischen Nationalökonomie*, originally 1908].

Sen, Amartya. 1981. *Poverty and Famines: An Essay on Entitlement and Deprivation*. Oxford: Clarendon Press.

Shepherd, Gordon M. 2012. *Neurogastronomy: How the Brain Creates Flavor and Why It Matters*. New York: Columbia University Press.

Sheraton, Mimi, and Nelli Sheffer. 1997. *Food Markets of the World*. New York: Abrams.

Sidgwick, Henry. 1907. *The Methods of Ethics*. 7th ed. London: Macmillan [originally 1874].

Simmel, Georg. 1959. "The Handle." In *Georg Simmel, 1858–1918: A Collection of Essays, with Translations and a Bibliography*, ed. Kurt H. Wolff, 267–75. Columbus: Ohio State University Press.

——. 1971. "The Metropolis and Mental Life." In *On Individuality and Social Forms*, ed. Donald N. Levine, 324–39. Chicago: University of Chicago Press.

——. 1978. *The Philosophy of Money*. Trans. Tom Bottomore and David Frisby. Boston: Routledge & Kegan Paul [originally *Philosophie des Geldes*, Berlin 1907].

——. 1994. "The Sociology of the Meal." Trans. Michael Symons. *Food & Foodways* 5 (4): 345–50 [originally "Soziologie der Mahlzeit" in "Der Zeitgeist," supplement to *Berliner Tageblatt*, October 19, 1910].

Sismondi, Jean Charles de. 1803. *De la richesse commerciale, ou Principes d'économie politique*. Geneva.

——. 1819. *Nouveaux principes d'économie politique, ou de la richesse dans ses rapports avec la population [Par J.-C.-L. Simonde de Sismondi]*. Paris.

Slattery, Paul. 2002. "Finding the Hospitality Industry." *Journal of Hospitality, Leisure, Sport, and Tourism Education* 1 (1): 19–28.

Smith, Adam. 1761. *The Theory of Moral Sentiments*. 2nd ed. London [originally 1759].

——. 1776. *An Inquiry Into the Nature and Causes of the Wealth of Nations*. 2 vols. London.

——. 1890. *An Inquiry Into the Nature and Causes of the Wealth of Nations*. London [originally 1776].

Smollett, T. [Tobias George]. 1825. *The Expedition of Humphry Clinker*. London [originally 1771].

Sommer, Jeff. 2014. "Jeers and Cheers Over Tax Inversions." *New York Times*, September 14.

Spang, Rebecca L. 2000. *The Invention of the Restaurant: Paris and Modern Gastronomic Culture*. Cambridge, Mass.: Harvard University Press.

Spengler, Oswald. 1991. *The Decline of the West*. Trans. Charles Francis Atkinson. Abridged ed. Oxford: Oxford University Press.

Steuart, Sir James. 1767. *An Inquiry Into the Principles of Political Œconomy: Being an Essay on the Science of Domestic Policy in Free Nations. In Which Are Particularly Considered*

Population, Agriculture, Trade, Industry, Money, Coin, Interest, Circulation, Banks, Exchange, Public Credit, and Taxes. 2 vols. London.

Stiglitz, Joseph E. 2013. "Inequality Is a Choice," Great Divide blog. *New York Times*, October 13. http://opinionator.blogs.nytimes.com/2013/10/13/inequality-is-a-choice/.

Stillingfleet, Benjamin. 1775. ed., *Miscellaneous Tracts Relating to Natural History, Husbandry, and Physick.* 3rd ed. London [translations of Linnaean school, including Isaac J. Biberg, "The Oeconomy of Nature," 37–129].

Storace, Patricia. 2006. "A Country Made for Living." *Condé Nast Traveler*, September. http://www.cntraveler.com/features/2006/09/A-Country-Made-For-Living.

Suskind, Ron. 2004. "Faith, Certainty and the Presidency of George W. Bush." *New York Times Magazine*, October 17. http://www.nytimes.com/2004/10/17/magazine /17BUSH.html?_r=0.

Sutton, David. 2007. "Tipping: An Anthropological Meditation." In *The Restaurants Book: Ethnographies of Where We Eat*, ed. David Beriss and David Sutton, 191–204. Oxford: Berg.

Swift, Jonathan. 1812. "Thoughts on Various Subjects, Moral and Diverting." In *The Works of the Rev. Jonathan Swift, D.D*, vol. 14, ed. Thomas Sheridan, 165–83. New York.

Switzer, John B. 2007. "Hospitality." In *Encyclopedia of Love in World Religions*, ed. Yudit Kornberg Greenberg, 313–16. Santa Barbara, Calif.: ABC-CLIO.

Symons, Michael. 1982. *One Continuous Picnic: A History of Eating in Australia*. Adelaide: Duck Press.

——. 1992. "Eating Into Thinking: Explorations in the Sociology of Cuisine." Ph.D. dissertation, Flinders University of South Australia.

——. 1993. *The Shared Table: Ideas for Australian Cuisine*. Canberra: AGPS.

——. 1994a. "Simmel's Gastronomic Sociology: An Overlooked Essay." *Food & Foodways* 5 (4): 333–51 [includes as appendix Georg Simmel, "The Sociology of the Meal"].

——. 1994b. "Olive Oil and Air-Conditioned Culture." *Westerly* 39 (4): 27–36.

——. 1995. "Simmel and Gastronomic Depth." *Simmel Newsletter* 5 (2): 23–34.

——. 1998. *The Pudding That Took a Thousand Cooks: The Story of Cooking in Civilisation and Daily Life*. Ringwood, Victoria: Viking [repub. as Symons, 2000].

——. 2000. *A History of Cooks and Cooking*. Urbana: University of Illinois Press [new ed. of Symons, 1998].

——. 2006. "Grandmas to Gourmets: The Revolution of 1963." *Food, Culture, and Society* 9 (2): 179–200.

——. 2007a. "Epicurus—the Foodies' Philosopher." In *Food & Philosophy: Eat, Think, and Be Merry*, ed. Fritz Allhoff and Dave Monroe, 13–30. Malden, Mass.: Blackwell.

——. 2007b. *One Continuous Picnic: A Gastronomic History of Australia*. Clayton, Victoria: Melbourne University Press [2nd ed. of Symons, 1982].

——. 2009. "From Modernity to Postmodernity: As Revealed in the Titles of New Zealand Recipe Books." *Food & Foodways* 17 (4): 215–41.

——. 2013. "The Rise of Restaurants and the Fate of Hospitality." *International Journal of Contemporary Hospitality Management* 25 (2): 247–63.

Telfer, Elizabeth. 1996. *Food for Thought: Philosophy and Food*. London: Routledge.

Teulon, Fabrice. 1998. "Gastronomy, *Gourmandise* and Political Economy in Brillat-Savarin's *Physiology of Taste*." *European Studies Journal* 15 (1): 41–53.

Thatcher, Margaret. 1987. "Interview for *Woman's Own* ('No Such Thing as Society')." Margaret Thatcher Foundation, September 23. http://www.margaretthatcher.org/speeches/displaydocument.asp?docid=106689.

Tönnies, Ferdinand. 1974. *Community and Association (Gemeinschaft und Gesellschaft)*. Trans. Charles P. Loomis. London: Routledge & Kegan Paul [originally 1887].

Trump, Donald J., and Robert T. Kiyosaki. 2011. *The Midas Touch: Why Some Entrepreneurs Get Rich and Why Most Don't*. Scottsdale, Ariz.: Plata.

[Turgot, Anne Robert Jacques]. 1766. *Réflexions sur la formation et la distribution des richesses*. N.p.

——. 1795. *Reflections on the Formation and Distribution of Wealth*. London [trans. of Turgot 1766].

——. 1844. "Éloge de Gournay: Lettre de Turgot a Marmontel. A Paris, ce 22 juillet 1759." In *Œuvres de Turgot, nouvelle edition, avec les notes de Dupont de Nemour*, vol. 1, 262–91. Paris.

Turner, Graham. 2008. "A Comparison of the Limits to Growth with Thirty Years of Reality." *Socio-Economics and the Environment in Discussion: CSIRO Working Papers Series 2008–09*. Canberra: CSIRO Sustainable Ecosystems.

U.S. Department of Agriculture. 2016. *2016 National Farmers Market Directory*. Washington, D.C.: U.S. Department of Agriculture, Agricultural Marketing Service. http://farmersmarkets.usda.gov.

Varoufakis, Yanis. 2018. "Introduction." In *The Communist Manifesto*, by Karl Marx and Friedrich Engels, vii–xxix. London: Vintage.

Vidal, John. 1997. *McLibel*. London: Macmillan.

Vidal, John, and Suzanne Goldenberg. 2014. "Snowden Revelations of NSA Spying on Copenhagen Climate Talks Spark Anger." *Guardian*, January 31. http://www.theguardian.com/environment/2014/jan/30/snowden-nsa-spying-copenhagen-climate-talks.

Walker, Thomas. 1928. *The Art of Dining*. London: Cayme [extracts from Walker's short-lived weekly *The Original*, 1835].

Waring, Marilyn. 1988. *If Women Counted*. Intro. by Gloria Steinem. San Francisco: Harper & Row.

Warner, Richard, ed. 1791. *Antiquitates Culinariae: Or Curious Tracts Relating to the Culinary Affairs of the Old English*. London [reprinted by Prospect Books, London, n.d.].

Waters, Alice, with others. 2007. *The Art of Simple Food: Notes, Lessons, and Recipes from a Delicious Revolution*. New York: Clarkson Potter.

——. 2009. "Alice Waters Applies a 'Delicious Revolution' to School Food." Center for Ecoliteracy. http://www.ecoliteracy.org/essays/delicious-revolution.

Weber, Max. 1968. *Economy and Society: An Outline of Interpretive Sociology*. 2 vols. Ed. Guenther Roth and Claus Wittich. Berkeley: University of California Press [originally *Wirtschaft und Gesellschaft: Grundriß de verstehenden Soziologie*, 1922].

References

——. 1976. *The Protestant Ethic and the Spirit of Capitalism*. Trans. Talcott Parsons and intro. by Anthony Giddens. London: George Allen & Unwin [originally *Die protestantische Ethik und der Geist des Kapitalismus*, 1905].

Whately, Richard. 1832. *Introductory Lectures on Political Economy: Delivered in Easter Term, MDCCCXXXI*. 2nd ed. London.

Willyard, Cassandra. 2011. "Microbiome: Gut Reaction." *Nature* 479 (November 24): S5–S7.

Wilson, Catherine. 2009. "Epicureanism in Early Modern Philosophy." In *The Cambridge Companion to Epicureanism*, ed. James Warren, 266–86. Cambridge: Cambridge University Press.

——. 2015. *Epicureanism: A Very Short Introduction*. Oxford: Oxford University Press.

Wolin, Sheldon S. 1961. *Politics and Vision: Continuity and Innovation in Western Political Thought*. Boston: Little, Brown.

Wolpert, Daniel. 2011. "The Real Reason for Brains." Talk at TEDGlobal. https://www.ted.com/talks/daniel_wolpert_the_real_reason_for_brains?language=en.

Woods, Vicki, Jonathan Meades, Patrick O'Connor, and Ann Barr. 1982. "Cuisine Poseur." *Harper's & Queen*, August: 66–70, 140 [ringleader Paul Levy could not then be named as author].

Wrangham, Richard W. 2009. *Catching Fire: How Cooking Made Us Human*. New York: Basic.

Xenophon. 2013. *Memorabilia. Oeconomicus. Symposium. Apology*. Trans. E. C. Marchant and O. J. Todd. Cambridge, Mass.: Harvard University Press (Loeb).

Zeldin, Theodore. 1994. *An Intimate History of Humanity*. London: Minerva.

INDEX

Index

Index

ARTS AND TRADITIONS OF THE TABLE
PERSPECTIVES ON CULINARY HISTORY

Albert Sonnenfeld, Series Editor